# PATHWAYS TO GROWTH:

## COMPARING EAST ASIA
## AND LATIN AMERICA

Nancy Birdsall and Frederick Jaspersen
Editors

**Published by the Inter-American Development Bank**
**Distributed by The Johns Hopkins University Press**

Washington, D.C.
1997

Produced by the IDB Publications Section
Distributed by The Johns Hopkins University Press
2715 North Charles Street
Baltimore, Maryland 21218-4319

The views and opinions expressed in this publication are those
of the authors and do not necessarily reflect the official position
of the Inter-American Development Bank.

**Cataloging-in-Publication data provided by the**
**Inter-American Development Bank**
**Felipe Herrera Library**

Conference Development Experience of the Latin American and East Asian
Countries (1994: Santiago, Chile)

    Pathways to growth: comparing East Asia and Latin America/
    Nancy Birdsall and Frederick Jaspersen, editors.
     p. cm.
    Includes bibliographical references ( p.)
    ISBN: 1-886938-13-X
    1. Economic development—Congresses. 2. Latin America—Economic policy—
Congresses. 3. East Asia—Economic policy—Congresses. 4. Saving and investment— Congresses. 5. Capital market—Congresses. I. Birdsall, Nancy.
II. Jaspersen, Frederick Z. III. Inter-American Development Bank. IV. Title.
338.9 P38—dc20                    97-712220

# Table of Contents

# Acknowledgments

The genesis of this book was an IDB-sponsored conference, "Development Experience of the Latin American and East Asian Countries," held in Santiago, Chile in June 1994. The conference was attended by policymakers, scholars and community leaders from Latin America, North America and East Asia. The Japan Special Fund and the Economic Commission for Latin America and the Caribbean provided financial and logistical support.

The papers presented in this volume draw on the conference discussions. Valuable contributions and comments came from many participants, including government officials from Latin American and Caribbean countries and staff of the World Bank, ECLAC, and IDB. Particular thanks are due to the IDB's Development Policy Research Division staff, who helped organize the conference, including Pilar Bilecky, Justino de la Cruz, Antoni Estevadeoral, and Alberto Melo; and to Paul Ernst Kohling, the IDB's Resident Representative in Chile at that time. Deborah Davis prepared the manuscript for publication and Luisa Choy-Luy contributed skilled secretarial support. Carlos Lozada provided able research assistance. Julie Clugage and Eva Greene edited the final text.

# Foreword

Each region has a unique social, cultural, and political heritage, which influences its institutions, political processes, economic structures, social challenges, and responses to new events, be they favorable or adverse. Latin America and the Caribbean and East Asia are no exception: within these regions, development will always be based upon each nation's unique history. Nevertheless, the design of public policies and the response of economic agents to policy changes are also key factors that shape a country's development. In debates over development policy, therefore, it is the responsibility of scholars and policymakers to examine the evidence of policies that have achieved particular development objectives, why they have worked, and what initial conditions are required for success in the context of changing social, political, and economic conditions.

Since its inception, the Inter-American Development Bank has contributed to effective development policies and supported efforts by individual countries to adapt such policies to their particular circumstances. The Bank has also actively shared the development experience of Latin America and the Caribbean with the international development community and encouraged efforts by the region's scholars and policymakers to examine the experience of other countries. In this spirit the Bank sponsored a conference in 1994 to compare the development experience of Latin America and the Caribbean with that of East Asia. The conference, held in Chile, was attended by a diverse group of scholars and policymakers from both regions, as well as from North America and Europe.

The papers in this book, motivated by discussion at the conference, explore the policy choices that have enabled countries in East Asia to achieve rapid and equitable economic growth. While they offer diverse interpretations of this experience and of the policy lessons for Latin America and the Caribbean, most of the authors attribute the East Asian success to macroeconomic stability, increased savings and investment, high levels and quality of investment in human resources, efficient allocation of resources, flexibility in adapting to changing economic circumstances, rapid modernization of the state and consistent efforts to share the benefits of economic growth with all segments of the population. In opening the conference, former Chilean President Patricio Aylwin argued that, while countries attempting to accelerate growth must rely on markets for critical allocation choices, experience shows that rapid economic growth is sustainable only if accompanied by the deliberate action of an efficient state. Governments must ensure that markets operate optimally; in case of market failure, they must undertake corrective action, especially including investment in human resources to ensure equality of opportunity. A number of authors here support this conclusion.

While much can be learned from the experience of East Asia, Latin America's policy design and pattern of development will continue to be unique. Similarities may appear among regions and countries in the broad policy framework for successful development, but the design of individual development policies and their implementation will necessarily differ. In all cases, however, commitment to growth with equity will remain an essential ingredient of success.

Enrique V. Iglesias, President
Inter-American Development Bank

# List of Acronyms

| | |
|---|---|
| **AFPs** | Pension funds (Chile) |
| **ASEXMA** | Manufactured Goods Export Association (Chile) |
| **BIS** | Bank for International Settlements |
| **CONOSUR** | The southern tip of South America (Argentina, Chile, and Uruguay) |
| **CORFO** | Chilean National Development Agency |
| **CPF** | Central Provident Fund (Singapore) |
| **CPI** | Consumer price index |
| **DFI, FDI** | Direct foreign investment |
| **ECTA** | Entrepreneurial Councils for Technology Administration (Chile) |
| **EGT** | Endogenous growth theory |
| **FONDECYT** | National Fund for Scientific and Technological Development (Chile) |
| **FONDEF** | Fund to Promote Scientific and Technical Development (Chile) |
| **FONSIP** | Fund for Research Projects of Public Interest (Chile) |
| **FONTEC** | National Fund for Technical and Production Development (Chile) |
| **GDP** | Gross domestic product |
| **GNP** | Gross national product |
| **HPAEs** | High-performing Asian economies |
| **IDB** | Inter-American Development Bank |
| **IFC** | International Finance Corporation |
| **IMF** | International Monetary Fund |
| **IPR** | Intellectual property rights |
| **ISI** | Import-substituting industrialization |
| **ITRI** | Industrial Technology Research Institute (Taiwan, China) |
| **KIST** | Korean Institute of Science and Technology |
| **LDC** | Less-developed country |
| **MNC** | Multinational corporation |
| **MPM** | Metal products, electronics, and machinery |
| **NAFTA** | North American Free Trade Agreement |
| **NICs** | Newly industrialized countries |
| **NIS** | National innovative system (Chile) |
| **OECD** | Organisation for Economic Cooperation and Development |
| **R&D** | Research and development |
| **RCA** | Revealed comparative advantage |
| **S&L** | Savings and loan |
| **SMEs** | Small and medium-scale enterprises |
| **TFP** | Total factor productivity |
| **TIs** | Technological institutes |

# CHAPTER 1

# Lessons from East Asia's Success

*Nancy Birdsall and Frederick Jaspersen*

The remarkable economic achievements of a group of East Asian countries over the past 25 years have profoundly influenced our thinking about development policy. Since World War II, these countries have grown faster, over a longer period, than any other group—more than three times faster, on average, than the Latin American and Caribbean countries during the past quarter century. Their growth has been especially notable in terms of penetration of world markets, made possible by sophisticated manufactured exports and competitive production of intermediate inputs. Rapidly rising real wages have accompanied this growth in productivity, as have substantial and rising investments in human resources and a more egalitarian distribution of income. Poverty has decreased sharply in the East Asian countries, while indicators of health, education, and other measures of well-being have soared. Per capita income has, in fact, risen so fast that some of these economies are no longer classified as "developing."

The diverging experiences of Latin America and East Asia are especially interesting, considering that after World War II most countries in both regions had similar economic structures and were at the same stage of transition—from predominantly rural, agrarian-based economies to more urban economies based on industrialization. During much of this period they also shared the same development objectives of growth and social progress. Although political systems differed within and across regions, with few exceptions most countries in both regions were "mixed economies," in which a combination of market forces and some state intervention and management were seen as critical to development.

There were also important differences. Compared to Korea and the island economies of Hong Kong and Singapore, Latin America was and remains much richer in natural resources, and its prewar growth was based largely on exploitation and export of agricultural and mineral commodities. Compared to those countries and to Malaysia and Thailand, Latin America began the postwar period with lower levels of education (relative to in-

come) and higher levels of income inequality. Latin America was and remains less densely populated, on average, than most of the East Asian
countries, with resultant higher unit costs of public infrastructure and services—but the region had more population *growth* than East Asia, due to
later and slower fertility declines.

## Sources of Growth

In Chapter 2, John Page examines evidence on the sources of high growth in
East Asia. He concludes that, for all eight of the economies examined,
higher levels of investment in physical and human capital explain much of
the higher growth as compared to Latin America. In five of the eight—Japan, Hong Kong, Thailand, Taiwan, China, and Korea—higher rates of total
factor productivity growth were also important. He examines three policies
that led to success in East Asia: good macroeconomic management, savings
enhancement, and trade and industrial policies that encouraged manufactured exports. The first two were central in bringing about rapid accumulation of physical and human capital, while the third lies at the heart of the
controversy about the strategic role of government in pushing productivity
growth.

  In her comment on Page's paper, Barbara Stallings asks why Latin
American countries have been less successful in accelerating growth, expanding exports, accumulating human capital, and maintaining fiscal discipline, despite the consensus among Latin American researchers and
policymakers that strong performance is critical in these areas. Stallings
suggests three possibilities: (i) that more time is needed for the policy reforms introduced in Latin America in the 1990s to produce results; (ii) that
Latin America is lacking strong state involvement in key economic functions and protection of domestic markets; and (iii) that constraints resulting
from the lost decade of the 1980s (reduced public investment, weakening of
private firms, and increased inequality) have slowed development.

## The Role of Policy

Analysis of the sources of growth suggests that policy is a major factor in
explaining differences in economic performance. Thus, the remaining
papers in this volume focus on six critical areas: macroeconomics, human
resources, savings, the financial sector, trade and institutions. In each area,
differences between East Asia and Latin America in initial conditions,
policy and performance are set out. The primary purpose is to explore how

policy differences in these areas, sometimes the result of prior conditions and performance, have resulted in long-run divergences in the growth paths of the two regions.

A central message of this volume is that key development policies have been fundamental to East Asia's success, and that—despite the regional differences in culture, history, and political institutions—this experience carries important lessons for Latin America and the rest of the world. We return below to this central message—that there is potential to replicate East Asia's success in Latin America.

## Macroeconomic Stability

There is overwhelming empirical evidence that macroeconomic stability is fundamental to growth. Countries that have maintained macroeconomic equilibrium have outperformed those that have not. The credibility of government policy plays an important role in ensuring this macroeconomic equilibrium, and credibility rests upon policy continuity over time, particularly in fiscal policy.

Without fiscal balance, private investment is crowded out, inflationary pressure increases, capital market development slows, debt problems tend to worsen, and a country's external position deteriorates. Avoiding an overvalued real exchange rate through appropriate fiscal and monetary policies is essential for preserving international competitiveness and growth. In recent years Latin America has made great progress in reducing fiscal deficits and achieving price stability. Deeper reforms would allow further reductions in real interest rates and enhance the region's growth potential.

In Chapter 3, Fred Jaspersen notes that the East Asian countries' experience illustrates the important interaction between macroeconomic policy and the beneficial impact of other pro-growth policies. Maintaining macroeconomic balance in these countries was easier mainly because financing constraints were less binding, and not so much due to lower fiscal deficits. Due to rapid growth, the East Asian countries were able to maintain greater price stability while financing their deficits, since higher growth increased the demand for financial assets. In the area of trade policy a strategy of import-substituting industrialization was common to both the Latin American and East Asian regions early in the period. However, in most of Latin America it was not complemented with adequate export incentives, was less performance oriented, and was continued for a longer period. Because producers faced a more rigorous market test in East Asia, they became more competitive internationally. As a consequence, East Asia was able to export its way out of the adverse external shocks of the 1970s and early 1980s, whereas many of the countries in Latin America initially borrowed but then were forced to cut investment and growth to adjust.

In his comment on Chapter 3, Humberto Petrei notes that a number of countries in Latin America, including Argentina, have adopted policies in recent years similar to those that have served the East Asian countries so well. These include greater reliance on prices to allocate resources, adoption of fiscal and monetary policies designed to achieve macroeconomic stability, and deregulation and trade liberalization to reduce producer costs and increase international competitiveness. Just as in Asia, these policies have brought positive results: a sharp reduction of inflation; increased savings, investment, and labor force participation; adoption of new technology; and a return to economic growth.

## Human Resources

Along with macroeconomic policy, human resource policy also influences differences in country performance. Again, the evidence and conclusions are powerful. Productivity, distribution, and growth are directly determined by a country's stock of human capital and the pace at which it accumulates. High levels of schooling and good health and nutrition, when controlling for a country's initial level of development, are good predictors of subsequent performance. Progress in education and health plays a key role in development, which confirms its overwhelming importance in public policy. Returns on investment in women's education and health are especially high in countries where the gender gap is great, because of the favorable impact on infant mortality, fertility, and the subsequent pace of human capital accumulation. Educational attainment is an important determinant of equality, and there is growing evidence that countries with the least inequality grow fastest. In Latin America there are critical gaps in human resource policy, and important productivity-related and distributional reasons for public support of human resource investments.

In Chapter 4, Nancy Birdsall, David Ross, and Richard Sabot focus on low rates of human capital accumulation as a key factor in the lower growth and higher levels of inequality in Latin America. They present empirical evidence of two vicious cycles that were, until recently, fed by poor policies in Latin America. First, an inward-looking, capital-intensive development strategy reduced both the demand for education and its returns. Then the lower quantity and quality of schooling made available by the public sector further reduced the supply of human capital, which contributed to lower economic growth. This lower growth contributed to weaker feedback effects on household behavior and to less demand for and lower investment in education. In the second cycle, weaker educational performance in Latin America contributed to the region's high income inequality compared to East Asia, where the abundance of educated workers eroded the scarcity rents they would have commanded. High income inequality, in turn, reduced household and public investments in education. The authors present results of cross-country growth regressions which suggest that lower income inequality is a stimulus to growth.

In her comment on Chapter 4, Nora Lustig points to the substantial body of analytical work that supports the authors' conclusion that income inequality has a negative impact on growth. She notes that the "new political economy" finds income inequality to be a possible factor that slows growth, by raising the demand for fiscal redistribution through distortionary taxation and by reducing political stability. She warns, however, that additional unexplained regional characteristics may help to account for Latin America's poor performance.

### Savings Rates

In Chapters 2 and 3, high rates of savings and physical investment are seen as key to East Asia's rapid growth. In Chapter 4, high rates of human capital investment are emphasized. These high investment or accumulation rates were financed largely by domestic savings rather than through borrowing abroad. Not only public but private savings rates in East Asia have been higher than in other regions. What accounts for East Asia's high savings rates?

A set of papers in this volume approaches this issue from different perspectives. One conclusion is clear: though culture may matter, growth probably matters more, and government policy and institutions are also relevant. In East Asia, relatively stable deposit interest rates and a strong, government-supported banking system helped to mobilize resources and facilitate their efficient transformation into investment. In a few countries of Latin America, increasingly developed capital markets, deepened by fully funded private pension systems, are helping to mobilize private savings. But most countries in Latin America still rely on foreign savings—and pay the price of vulnerability to the volatility of these flows.

In Chapter 5, Sebastian Edwards assesses the causes of low saving rates in Latin America (savings-to-GDP ratios are lower today than before the debt crisis, despite financial sector and fiscal reforms), as well as the prospects for increasing savings. Using cross-country regressions to assess the determinants of savings, Edwards concludes that although public savings are associated with some decline in private savings, the decline is by no means proportional. Thus the surest way to increase national savings is to increase public savings—by cutting expenditures, by creating new institutions such as privately run social security capitalization systems, and through increased depth of the financial system.

In Chapter 6, Michael Gavin, Ricardo Hausmann, and Ernesto Talvi argue that national savings rates are fundamentally an outcome of economic growth, and that increasing savings should not be, in itself, an immediate policy target. They present evidence that Latin America's saving rates are not structurally different from those in East Asia. Low savings in Latin America are principally the result of low and volatile economic growth compared to that of East Asia. Moreover, trade and financial liberalization may actually have triggered a transitory decline in private savings in Latin America in recent years by reducing prices and permitting borrowing to finance consumption. Consequently, during this transition period, current account deficits are likely to be high. The authors emphasize that complementary fiscal and financial policies, including close supervision of banks to discourage credit booms, need to be implemented to reduce vulnerability to external shocks.

Andrés Solimano comments on the two papers concerning savings rates. He urges caution in interpreting Edwards' results. Determining causality, he says, is itself a problem; although savings contribute to growth, they are also probably the outcome of growth. Solimano agrees that increasing public savings is an important way to increase overall savings and growth, but emphasizes a lesson from the 1980s: fiscal adjustment that cuts the expenditures required to maintain strong economic and social infrastructure can be detrimental to growth. A virtuous cycle between private savings and growth, he says, is more likely to come from a shock due to positive terms of trade or to another cause, rather than through fiscal austerity. In his comment on the Gavin-Hausmann-Talvi paper, Solimano observes that causality among savings, investment, and growth is not yet sufficiently established to rely on the "passive savings" view, either. A lag occurs between policy reform and economic growth, he notes, which can delay a growth-induced rise in savings. Policies to promote savings, such as a consumption tax or a tax on distributed rather than retained earnings, can raise private savings sooner and thereby reduce vulnerability to external shocks.

Paulo Vieira da Cunha also comments on the Gavin-Hausmann-Talvi paper. Comparing the East Asian experience to that of the Soviet economy after 1960, where high rates of savings and investment were dissipated by economy-wide distortions that lowered the returns to capital, he emphasizes the overriding importance of the efficiency with which savings are transformed into investment. He also notes that all instances of sustained high growth have been accompanied by rapid development of financial markets; growth may be low in Latin America, he says, because financial systems have generally been weak. Due to measurement problems and the difficulties in disaggregating the causes and effects of savings and growth, Vieira da Cunha agrees that policymakers should not emphasize savings as an immediate policy target, but instead should focus on macroeconomic stability and the development of human resources.

## Financial Markets

In Chapter 7, Paul Boeker examines the experience with financial sector development in East Asia, Latin America in general, and Chile since 1983. He concludes that macroeconomic stability is the precondition for development of the financial sector, and that mobilizing financial savings in Latin America will require strong, prudential regulation and supervision of banks, including independent appraisal of asset quality. In addition, Boeker argues that pension reform is the most important single step for the development of Latin American capital markets. He emphasizes that Chile's success with pension reform, a source of high private savings, required that government to establish a bond market by issuing debentures over a range of maturities, which provided low-risk benchmarks for pricing private issues. The creation of strong private pension funds also required adequate supervision and the ability of fund managers to seek a diversified, safe portfolio that included international bonds and equities.

Eleanor Howard's comment on Boeker's paper focuses on the favorable experience of Chile in comparison with the East Asian countries. She attributes Chile's success to a number of factors, including: (i) limitation of the government's direct role in financial markets; (ii) creation of independent, professionally managed regulatory institutions; and (iii) periodic updating of the regulatory framework in response to the maturation of financial markets. Howard also elaborates on Boeker's point that the lending practices of development banks in Latin America retarded development of the bond market and diverted resources from investments with high rates of return. She notes that in Chile this behavior gave rise to a major overhaul of CORFO, the country's development bank, from a retail bank into a second-tier term lending institution. Since that time, Chile has seen an explosive growth of its corporate bond market, and CORFO has played a key role in fostering the development of leasing companies, which have been an important source of financing for entrepreneurial activity.

## Trade, Exports and Technology Transfer

Policies to promote rapid export growth, a hallmark of East Asia's experience, also seem to be central to success. Both microeconomic studies and those based on aggregate data suggest that the rapid growth of exports, and supporting policies, play a fundamental role in productivity growth. Trade liberalization, which gives exporters access to least-cost inputs worldwide, also improves the allocation of resources in the local economy through increased domestic competition. Even more important, it gives exporters access to the advanced technology embodied in imported inputs, and facilitates reduction of the technology gap between newly industrializing countries and more advanced economies. Maintaining appropriate incentives for exports is an essential part of fostering their rapid growth, and here macroeconomic policy is crucial. Demand management must validate a real exchange rate favorable for exports over time; strong government savings is an essential part of this, especially where capital inflows are important, as in a number of Latin American countries.

In Chapter 8, Howard Pack develops the view that international trade (and especially exports) is a major source of growth because it helps newly industrializing countries to close the technology gap. In turning to export markets and to the world for technology, the East Asian countries not only became aware of new products and production methods, but were provided with considerable amounts of product information and technology by importers. Pack presents evidence that by dampening fluctuations in output, exports encourage investment, and by absorbing underemployed labor, they help accelerate total factor productivity growth and improve the distribution of income. The rapid growth of East Asia's exports was achieved by a combination of supportive public policy, including macroeconomic stability and a nonvolatile real exchange rate, and rapid acquisition of technology. Latin American countries, he argues, could reap the same benefits from a rapid growth of exports.

Eduardo Bitran and Pablo Serra's comment extends Howard Pack's paper by exploring technology policy in Latin America, specifically Chile. Bitran and Serra argue that Chile and other Latin American countries will have to make a considerable effort to acquire new technology in order to sustain adequate rates of economic growth. Rejecting direct subsidies to firms for research and development (R&D), they are skeptical of the effectiveness of state-sponsored technology institutes like those in Chile and other Latin American countries. Instead, they advocate subsidizing technology supply (an approach that was used successfully in East Asia) and an institutional framework that facilitates R&D collaboration among firms through private councils that would directly contract R&D. Such councils could be financed jointly by the government and firms in a specific sector.

## Institutions

A sixth lesson of the East Asian experience is that strong public institutions are needed to foster growth-enhancing synergy between government and the private sector. This requires building a technically competent, reliable civil service that can formulate policy and implement it with integrity. Recruitment and promotion must be merit-based; compensation, broadly measured, must be competitive with the private sector. Creating an independent monetary authority capable of resisting political pressure and electoral expediency can help achieve stability. Budgetary institutions and processes must be designed to achieve improved allocation of resources within hard budget constraints. An efficient, transparent judicial system is essential to protect property rights and to ensure noncorrupt conflict resolution. Social service delivery systems should be driven by demand rather than supply.

In the past decade Latin America struggled to overcome one of its most serious structural weaknesses—a bloated government bureaucracy and out-of-control public finances. It was largely successful in the latter. But deficit reduction was achieved largely by cutting investment. And most countries that went beyond this, by restructuring the public sector through privatization, have yet to take the final, most difficult step: to build strong public institutions capable of supporting an effective development policy.

In Chapter 9, Guy Pfeffermann argues that an important result of strong institutions in East Asia is the exceptional credibility of public policy—i.e., the degree to which economic agents believe the policy environment will not take a sudden change for the worse. This credibility, he says, helps to explain why the share of private investment in GDP is almost twice as high in East Asia as in Latin America. While substantial downsizing of the public sector has taken place in Latin America, Pfefferman notes that small government is not necessarily effective government. Adequate regulation and supervision of banking, of securities markets, and of the "natural monopolies" that are created when infrastructure is privatized are especially important. Even if one agrees that "skillful industrial policies" can accelerate growth, the highly politicized environment in which public sector institutions operate in Latin America makes it hard to implement such policies successfully. Pfefferman believes that open, market-driven systems, with their built-in discipline, offer the best hope.

John Shilling, in his comment, calls attention to the quality of public institutions as a central factor in the development process and notes that this is an argument in favor of public sector reform. While the public sector should not become involved in activities that the private sector can perform more efficiently, government has a vital role to play in defining and enforcing the rules of the game so that markets work. Shilling also observes that East Asia has some remaining needs, in particular a comprehensive commercial code and stronger legal institutions.

In Chapter 10, Vinod Thomas and Jisoon Lee explore the process of economic reform. Comparing Latin America and East Asia, they conclude that rapid and comprehensive reform results in higher returns, because different elements of the reform package create self-reinforcing externalities. However, a gradual approach is often necessary due to sociopolitical considerations. Since reforms take time to bear fruit, it is essential to mobilize long-term support. The experiences of the two regions demonstrate the importance of credibility: where reforms were delayed or inconclusive, costs were high and corrective action later proved difficult.

Mary Shirley's comment on the Thomas-Lee paper explores the difficulties of formulating general conclusions about reform. Current analyses of institutional economics emphasize that organizational structures, rules, and laws are path dependent, evolving out of a country's history and circumstances. If reformers try to replace weak institutions with good institutions without considering what preconditions may be necessary for success of the new institutions, they are likely to fail. Creating reformed institutions that fail because conditions were not yet right, Shirley notes, may be worse than not undertaking reforms at all. It is also important to consider existing incentives; if incentives are contrary to proposed reforms, the newly created institutions may be doomed from the start.

## Replicability

Over the last four decades, East Asia and Latin America have pursued very different economic policies, with different degrees of effectiveness. East

Asia placed emphasis much earlier on manufactured exports and lower direct and indirect taxation of agriculture, while Latin America had a longer period of import substitution, greater reliance on external financing, and an earlier opening of financial markets. East Asia was more effective in maintaining macroeconomic balance, relying much more on domestic savings to finance investment. Throughout these decades, public sector management was more effective in East Asia; in addition to generating the policy credibility that supported high levels of private investment, effective public sector management resulted in faster expansion of roads, electricity, and other public infrastructure services, and of education and health services.

While policies may have made the difference, the question remains, can they be replicated in Latin America despite cultural and institutional differences? The answer appears to be that they can. A case in point is Chile, which has been able to establish a rate of growth comparable to those achieved by countries in East Asia by adopting and sustaining a number of the same kinds of economic policies and structural reforms, appropriately adapted to local circumstances and Chile's comparative advantage. More recently there has been considerable progress in this same direction throughout Latin America. Fiscal reforms, macroeconomic balance and trade liberalization in support of exports stand out as major achievements. With differing degrees of success, efforts are being made to carry out broader reforms—strengthening institutions in health and education, privatizing state enterprises, overhauling bankrupt social security systems, accelerating development of capital markets—in virtually every country in the region. As these reforms are deepened and the synergy between them takes hold, the underlying forces of growth will be cemented, raising growth rates and making growth more sustainable. Moreover, these reforms will bring groups once left out of the growth process in Latin America into more productive activities, so income distribution will also improve. In short, a growing number of countries will increasingly replicate the successful East Asian experience.

While the experience of East Asia has much to offer policymakers in Latin America, there are important differences in terms of policy options. Economic policymakers in Latin America are less likely to be insulated from political pressure, so their policies and institutions must be designed differently to be effective. Vulnerability to political pressure also means that management of destabilizing external shocks, transmitted through volatile international commodity markets and international capital flows, is more difficult in Latin America. Latin America's comparative advantage in natural resources makes it more vulnerable to commodity price fluctuations. Its greater ethnic and racial heterogeneity and historically unequal distribution of assets and income make it more difficult to build strong public management and to deliver broad-based, high quality public services. Moreover, Latin America's historic legacy of high rates of inflation has an impact on the use of policy instruments such as the exchange rate, where there is a tradeoff between its being employed as a nominal anchor to curb inflation or as an instrument for overcoming imbalances between production of traded and nontraded goods. The increasing willingness of Latin American policymakers to consider the value of experiences outside the region means that policy will become increasingly pragmatic and eclectic. The broad approach to development, however, will remain uniquely Latin American.

# CHAPTER 2

# The East Asian Miracle and the Latin American Consensus: Can the Twain Ever Meet?

*John Page*

Despite East Asia's remarkable record of economic growth—from 1965 to 1990 its 23 economies grew more than three times faster than the economies of Latin America and the Caribbean—most Latin American economists drew few development policy lessons from East Asia until the debt crisis of the 1980s (Edwards 1995). But the contrast between Asia's success in the 1980s and 1990s and Latin America's relative economic stagnation was too great to ignore. Edwards, among others, argues that policy lessons drawn from the successful East Asian economies are among the factors that led to a new "Latin American consensus" on economic policy. The elements of this new consensus—stable and effective macroeconomic management, opening the external sector to international competition, reducing and focusing the role of the state in the economy, and developing policies to reduce poverty—have much in common with the policy fundamentals pursued by eight high-performing Asian economies (HPAEs)—Japan, the four Tigers (Hong Kong, the Republic of Korea, Singapore, and Taiwan, China), and three in Southeast Asia (Indonesia, Malaysia, and Thailand).[1]

These eight East Asian superstars have a wide range of policy frameworks—from Hong Kong's nearly complete laissez-faire system to the highly selective and interventionist policy regimes of Japan and Korea. The coexistence of rapid growth and selective industrial policies in Japan, Korea, Taiwan, China, and Singapore has led some analysts to assert that the elements of the Latin American consensus are insufficient to promote the same kind of growth. They argue that the unusual success of Japan, Korea, and Taiwan, China in catching up technologically to the advanced economies and achieving high rates of total factor productivity (TFP) growth was

---

[1] These eight HPAEs are the subject of the World Bank (1993a) study, *The East Asian Miracle: Economic Growth and Public Policy.* This essay draws extensively on that study and on Page (1994).

due to activist government policies designed to alter industrial structure and promote technological learning, sometimes at the expense of static allocative efficiency. While acknowledging the importance of international competition, they note that incentives deriving from quantitative restrictions on imports, tariffs, and subsidies were not neutral among sectors (or firms) during the rapid growth periods of these economies (Amsden 1989, Wade 1990, Singh 1992, Shiratori 1993). If these authors are correct, strategies for technological learning should be an additional element of development policy in Latin America.

More recently, a number of American economists have argued that factor accumulation is the dominant, if not unique, source of high growth rates among the HPAEs (Young 1995; Krugman 1994). They attribute Asia's success to policies that increased physical and human capital per worker, and dismiss as irrelevant or harmful those policies designed to promote technological learning. Moreover, the HPAEs may have compelled their societies to save and invest too much, thus setting the stage for an inevitable—and possibly abrupt—growth slowdown (Krugman 1994). If so, there may be few lessons for Latin America, beyond the application of sound macroeconomic management.

This paper looks at the characteristics and sources of growth in the eight high-performing East Asian economies and in Latin America. The eight Asian superstars are distinct from Latin America not only because of their rapid growth, it argues, but also because their growth has been sustained and widely shared. Evidence on the relative roles of accumulation and productivity change is then presented, which shows that both have been significant sources of the difference in growth rates between Latin America and Asia. Next, three aspects of East Asia's development policy are examined in detail: macroeconomic management, policies to promote savings, and industrial and trade policies. The first two are key elements of the HPAEs' success in achieving high levels of physical capital formation, while the third is the focus of controversy concerning their productivity performance. In conclusion, we outline some priorities for development policy in Latin America.

## The Nature of the Miracle—Rapid Growth with Equity

The HPAEs are a highly diverse group of economies that differ in natural resources, population, culture, and economic policy. Three characteristics set them apart from other developing economies, however. First, their *rapid growth* has been unusual. Figure 2.1 shows the relationship between

**Figure 2.1  GDP Growth Rate and GDP per Capita**

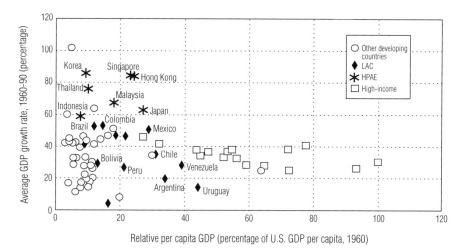

Sources: Summers and Heston (1991), and World Bank data.

relative income level in 1960 and per capita income growth between 1960 and 1990 for a sample of 119 countries—the "convergence picture" first presented in Romer (1986). Per capita income growth is essentially independent of the level of relative income in 1960, and, as Romer and others have found, developing countries on average are not catching up to the advanced economies.[2]

The eight high-performing Asian economies, however, are all "converging" on the high-income countries. While Malaysia, Indonesia, and Thailand are closer to their predicted values, the remaining five economies (Taiwan, Korea, Japan, Singapore, and Hong Kong) are significantly above their predicted GDP per capita growth rates on the basis of relative income. On the other hand, the major Latin American economies—except Brazil, Mexico, and Colombia—are generally failing to converge. Per capita in-

---

[2] A regression of per capita income growth (in constant 1980 international prices) on 1960 income per capita, including nonlinear terms up to the second power, has no explanatory value. The fit of the regression is poor and the significance of individual coefficients low. Dollar (1991) finds a similar pattern using a sample of 114 countries and the absolute level of per capita income in 1960. He finds a clearer pattern in which the lowest deciles have the lowest per capita income growth rates, the middle income deciles have the highest, and the high income countries are in between. However, he also reports low significance of his regression results.

come growth over the period has lagged behind that of both the East Asian superstars and the high-income economies.

Second, the HPAEs are an exception to recent work on *growth rate persistence*, which suggests that growth rates for individual economies are highly unstable over time (Easterly, Kremer, Pritchett, and Summers 1993). The four Tigers plus Japan consistently rank with the handful of rapid-growth economies. Indeed, Easterly et al. conclude that "the widespread perception of strong country effects in growth is strongly influenced by the 'Gang of Four' [the Tigers]."

Finally, the HPAEs combine rapid, sustained growth with *highly equal income distribution*. Figure 2.2 illustrates the positive association between growth and low inequality in the HPAEs, and the contrast with other economies. Forty economies are ranked by the ratio of the income share of the richest fifth of the population to the income share of the poorest fifth, and by per capita real GDP growth, during 1965–1989.[3] The northwest corner of the figure identifies economies with high growth (GDP per capita greater than 4.0 percent) and low relative inequality (the ratio of the income share of the top quintile to that of the bottom quintile is less than 10). Of the nine high-growth, iow-inequality economies, seven are HPAEs; only Malaysia, which has an index of inequality above 15, is excluded. Among the major Latin American economies, on the other hand, only Chile, Bolivia, and Venezuela have indices of inequality lower than Malaysia's.

### Sources of the Miracle: Accumulation and Productivity Change

Differences in growth between East Asia and Latin America can be empirically explained by differences in factor accumulation and productivity growth. These sources of growth provide important clues to the policy origins of East Asia's success and Latin America's relative failure.

### *East Asia's Record of Accumulation*

Figure 2.3 shows the relationship between income level in 1960 and the average investment rate for 1960-85. The estimated nonlinear regression relating initial income level to investment is also shown. Substantially more

---

[3] Because the timing and frequency of observations on income distribution vary among countries in the sample, the ratio of the top to bottom quintile is taken at the date closest to the midpoint.

**Figure 2.2   Income Inequality and Growth of GDP, 1965-89**

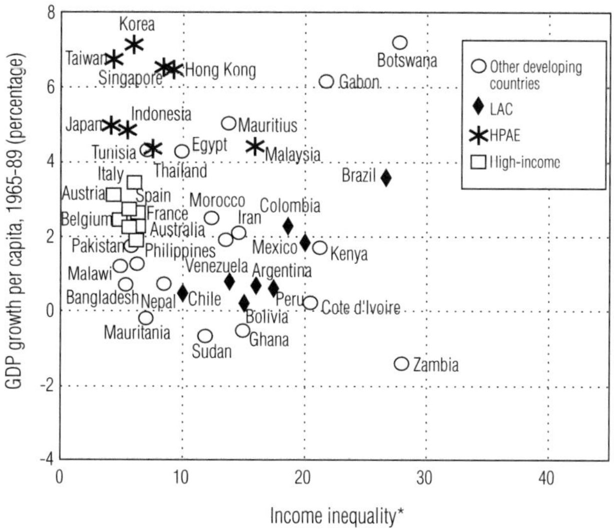

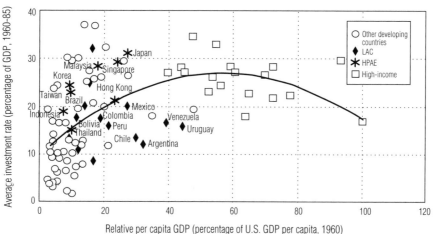

*Note:* Income inequality is measured by the ratio of the income shares of the
richest 20 percent and the poorest 20 percent of the population in each country.
*Sources:* Summers and Heston (1991) and World Bank data.

**Figure 2.3   Average Investment Rate as a Percentage of GDP, and GDP per Capita**

*Note:* Regression equation: I6085 = 10.125 + 59.120 RGDP60 - 51.881 RGDP60.   N=119; adj R =0.295$^2$
                           (1.383)  (10.344)          (12.593)
*Sources:* Summers and Heston (1991) and World Bank data.

regularity appears in the relationship between investment share and relative income than in the relationship between growth and relative income.[4] The investment rate for all countries increases with income up to about 70 percent of U.S. GDP in 1960, and then declines.

The HPAEs conform much more strongly to the cross-country pattern of investment rates than to the pattern of growth rates. Thailand and Hong Kong lie close to their predicted values on the basis of the cross-country regression. Japan, Korea, and Malaysia are the outliers among HPAEs, but they are not extreme in the distribution. Thus high investment rates are part of the Asian success story, but they cannot fully explain the extent to which the growth of per capita income in the HPAEs diverges from the typical pattern. All of the major Latin American economies, in contrast, are at or below their predicted values. What is particularly striking is the extent to which the relatively more advanced Latin American economies in 1960— Argentina, Chile, Uruguay, and Venezuela—have lagged behind investment rates not only in East Asia, but also in the high-income economies. Clearly the growth crisis in Latin America over the past thirty years is in part related to an investment crisis.

Figures 2.4A and 2.4B summarize how two measures of human capital vary with initial income. Figure 2.4A plots the primary school enrollment rate in 1960 against relative per capita income, while Figure 2.4B presents the scatter of Barro and Lee's (1993) average measure of educational attainment over the period 1960–85 against initial income. Both scatters confirm that the HPAEs were relatively well-endowed with human capital. The Asian economies again conform more closely to the cross-country pattern based on relative income than is the case for income growth.

Latin America and East Asia are more similar in terms of human capital than they are for any other source of growth. Both primary enrollment rates and education stocks in Latin America generally conform to predicted values on the basis of relative incomes. In 1960, primary enrollment rates in the major Latin American economies were approximately equal, on average, to those of the eight East Asian superstars and showed similar variations across countries. Average education stocks for the period 1960–85 for Argentina and Chile were higher than for any East Asian economy except Japan. Mexico, Bolivia, and Brazil had average educational endowments similar to those of Thailand, Malaysia, and Singapore.

---

[4] The fit of the regression is markedly better, as is the variance of the estimated coefficients.

### Figure 2.4A  Initial Income Level and Primary Enrollment Rate, 1960

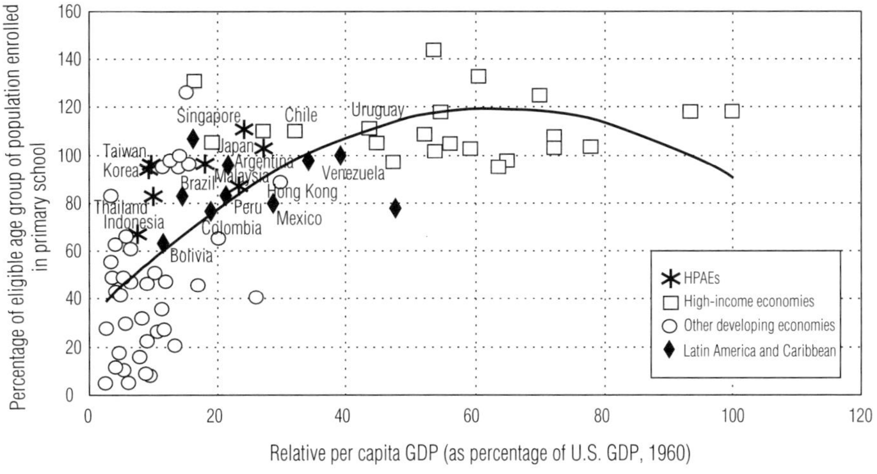

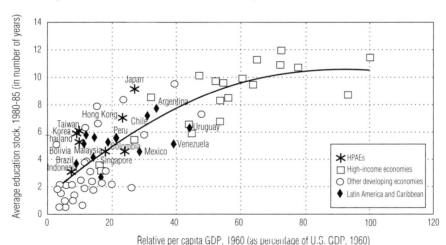

*Sources:* Summers and Heston (1991) and World Bank data.

### Figure 2.4B  Initial Income Level and Average Education Stock, 1960-85

*Sources:* Summers and Heston (1991) and Barro and Lee (1992).

*Productivity Change*

Table 2.1 presents estimates of total factor productivity derived by subtracting from output growth the portions of growth due to capital accumulation,
to human capital accumulation, and to labor force growth. Because income
share data are not available for most countries in our sample, output elas-
ticities were estimated directly using a simple cross-economy production
function. Annual log output growth was regressed on log capital growth,
log human capital growth, and log labor growth between 1960 and 1990,
specifying the production function to be Cobb-Douglas with constant returns to scale. Economy-specific dummy variables were used to estimate
individual rates of TFP change for each of the sample's economies. Net investment is derived from constant price capital stock data (Nehru and
Dhareshwar 1993). Measures of human capital are incorporated in the
specification using Barro and Lee's (1993) measure of educational attainment. Table 2.1 reports the production function parameters and the estimated TFP growth rates.

    The low elasticity of output with respect to capital from the cross-
country sample is striking but not altogether surprising. There is a subset of
13 developing economies that have positive net investment in physical and
human capital per worker, but negative growth in output per worker. The
marginal product of both physical and human capital was negative in these
economies, an indication of severe allocative inefficiency. This is reflected
empirically in an elasticity of output of both physical and human capital in
the production function (which is lower for the whole sample than for only
those economies with nonnegative growth of output per worker).[5]

---

[5] The production function can be estimated based only on high-income economy input-output
relationships. This reflects the assumption that allocative efficiency in the high income economies is greater than in the whole sample, and hence, that TFP growth rates estimated on the
basis of the production function parameters will contain less "noise" due to allocation mistakes. These results and the estimated TFP growth rates derived from standard growth accounting methods are displayed in Table 2.1. The elasticity of output with respect to capital in
the high-income economy production function rises to more conventional levels. TFP estimates, particularly for those economies with rapidly growing capital stocks, are correspond-
ingly reduced.
    When we compare our estimates of TFP growth with two other independently derived
estimates for a large sample of countries (Elias 1991; Fischer 1993), the pattern of productivity
growth rates in Figure 2.5 is remarkably robust to the specification of the growth accounting
equation and to the capital stock series used. The IMF's 1993 *World Economic Outlook,* contrasting Asia with other developing economies, reaches similar conclusions, with respect to both
the estimated magnitudes of TFP change and the relative contribution of TFP change to output
growth. Thomas and Wang (1993) and Edwards (1992) also reach broadly similar results concerning the pattern of productivity change in the HPAEs compared to other economies.

**Table 2.1  Elasticity of Output for Full Sample and High-Income Economies**

|  | Observations | Capital SK | (t-stat) | Labor SL | (t-stat) | Human Capital SH | (t-stat) |
|---|---|---|---|---|---|---|---|
| Full sample | 2,093 | 0.178 | 10.895 | 0.669 | 6.411 | 0.154 | 1.49 |
| High-income economies | 460 | 0.399 | 10.237 | 0.332 | 1.679 | 0.269 | 1.476 |

**Resulting Total Factor Productivity Growth Estimates, 1960–89**

| Economy | TFP Growth (full sample parameter estimates) | TFP Growth (high-income only, parameter estimates) |
|---|---|---|
| Hong Kong | 3.6470 | 2.4113 |
| Indonesia | 1.2543 | -0.7953 |
| Japan | 3.4776 | 1.4274 |
| Korea, Republic of | 3.1021 | 0.2355 |
| Malaysia | 1.0755 | -1.3369 |
| Singapore | 1.1911 | -3.0112 |
| Taiwan, China | 3.7604 | 1.2829 |
| Thailand | 2.4960 | 0.5466 |
| Latin America | 0.1274 | -0.9819 |

*Source:* World Bank data.

## The Sources of Growth

The contrast in the sources of growth between Latin America and the HPAEs is apparent in Figure 2.5. The diagram shows the relative contribution to output growth of factor accumulation (share-weighted total input growth) and TFP growth. TFP estimates are based on the parameters derived from the full 85-country sample. Three broad patterns appear:

(i) The range of TFP growth rates for high-income countries is quite compact, especially in comparison with the low and middle-income countries.

(ii) Nearly one third (32 percent) of the low and middle-income countries in the sample had negative rates of TFP growth for the period 1960–89, regardless of the parameter estimates used.

(iii) The low and middle-income countries exhibit very little productivity-based catch-up.

These results are not promising for the developing world. Despite the potential for developing countries to achieve rapid growth through adopting known "best-practice" technologies, very few countries appear to have

**Figure 2.5  Total Factor Productivity Growth and Part Due to Growth of Factor Inputs, 1960-89**

*(Percent per year)*

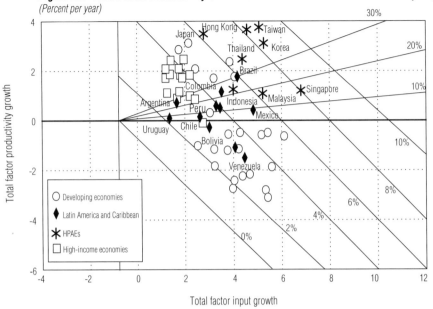

Total factor input growth

*Note:* Total factor productivity growth is calculated using full sample parameter estimates. Diagonal lines give all possible combinations of factor input growth and TFP growth for a given output growth rate.

*Source:* World Bank staff estimates.

realized these potential gains.[6] Catch-up, when it occurs, is due primarily to higher rates of factor accumulation. With the exception of Brazil and Colombia, TFP growth rates for the Latin American economies lag behind those of the advanced economies.

Five of the East Asian eight—Japan, Hong Kong, Thailand, Taiwan, and Korea—outperform all of the Latin American economies in terms of both output growth and productivity change. The three investment-driven economies of the East Asian group—Indonesia, Malaysia, and Singapore—have rates of TFP change similar to the performance of Latin American countries, but higher rates of total factor input growth, and hence output growth. A comparison among Japan, Malaysia, and Brazil, the best-performing Latin American economy, illustrates the differences in sources of essentially similar economic performance. All three economies grew at ap-

---

[6] For a concise review of the arguments for technologically based catch-up, see Pack (1993).

proximately six percent a year in real terms between 1960 and 1990. Japan did so with total factor input growth of about three percent a year, with the remaining output growth due to productivity change; Brazil's total input growth rate was about four percent, while Malaysia's was more than five percent. The contrasting sources of growth of Hong Kong, Korea, and Singapore, all of which shared essentially the same rate of growth, are a good illustration of the same phenomenon among the HPAEs.

The East Asian success story is primarily due to factor accumulation. Depending on the parameter estimates used, between 60 and 120 percent of their output growth derives from accumulation of physical and human capital and labor force growth. Nevertheless, the subset of productivity-driven HPAEs is unusual among developing economies because of the relatively important role of TFP in their growth. They are also among the very few developing countries keeping pace with or catching up to the moving target of international best practice. Latin America, in contrast, is a story of low rates of physical capital accumulation reinforced by similarly undistinguished rates of productivity change. Argentina, Bolivia, Chile, and Venezuela all had TFP growth rates that were nearly zero or negative. Mexico's and Peru's TFP growth rates were less than one percent.

## Three Policies That Led to Success

Despite policies ranging from market-oriented to state-led, which varied across economies and over time, a number of common threads bind the HPAEs. Macroeconomic management was unusually good and macroeconomic performance unusually stable, thus providing the essential framework for private investment. Policies to increase the integrity of the banking system, and to make it more accessible to nontraditional savers, increased the levels of financial savings. All of the HPAEs promoted exports—especially manufactured exports—and in many of these economies the government also intervened, systematically and through multiple channels, to foster the development of specific industries. This section reviews the HPAEs' performance in macroeconomic management, in policies to promote savings, and in industrial and trade policies.

### Macroeconomic Management

In contrast to Latin America, the HPAEs have been remarkably successful in creating and sustaining macroeconomic stability. This was reflected in their successful management of three macroeconomic variables: budget

**Table 2.2  Consolidated Public Sector Deficits**

| Economy/Region | Average public deficit, percentage of GDP, 1980–88 | Rank among 40 developing countries (1= highest deficit) |
|---|---|---|
| *HPAEs* | | |
| Korea, Republic of | 1.89 | 34 |
| Malaysia | 10.80 | 6 |
| Thailand | 5.80 | 23 |
| | | |
| *Average, 40 developing countries* | 6.39 | |
| *Average, OECD economies* | 2.82 | |
| | | |
| **Latin American economies** | | |
| Argentina | 9.62 | 10 |
| Brazil | 4.02 | 29 |
| Mexico | 6.73 | 18 |

*Source:* Easterly, Rodríguez, and Schmidt-Hebbel (1994).

deficits, external debt, and exchange rates. It is no coincidence that the HPAEs have experienced exceptionally high growth by world standards, and, over the long run, all have managed their macro economies with unusual success. Cross-economy econometric studies generally find that the opposite results—higher inflation, larger budget deficits, and distorted foreign exchange markets—reduce growth (Fischer 1993; Rodrik 1994).

*Budget Deficits and Inflation*

International experience suggests that the macroeconomic consequences of public sector deficits depend upon how the deficits are financed. Although their budget deficits are not dramatically smaller than those of other developing economies, the HPAEs have been better at keeping deficits small enough to finance them without destabilizing the macroeconomy.[7] The financing limits have also been higher due to more rapid HPAE growth.

---

[7] The analysis in this section draws on W. Easterly and K. Schmidt-Hebbel, "The Macroeconomics of Public Sector Deficits: A Synthesis," in Easterly, Rodríguez, and Schmidt-Hebbel (1994). The data on consolidated public deficits, as well as the rest of the data in this section except where otherwise indicated, are from the same source. Consolidated public deficits, though less widely available than central government deficits, are a much more reliable indicator of fiscal management, since they include operating deficits of public enterprises.

Table 2.2 shows consolidated public sector deficits for the 1980s for three East Asian countries (for which good data are available) compared to a sample of OECD and three major Latin American economies. As a percentage of GDP, Korea's budget deficits were below even the OECD average. Malaysia and Thailand present a more complicated picture. Thailand's budget deficits were about average for developing economies in the 1980s, while deficits in Malaysia were substantially larger than average. Both ran larger budget deficits than such troubled Latin American economies as Brazil, Argentina, and Mexico.

Unlike other economies that encountered difficulties, however, Malaysia and Thailand successfully financed their deficits. This was possible for the following reasons:

• First, there was *feedback from high growth.* Because rapid growth increased the demand for financial assets, Malaysia and Thailand were able to absorb higher levels of monetary financing without a rapid rise in inflation. Moreover, rapid growth in GDP raised the level of sustainable domestic and external borrowing.

• Second, there was *feedback from high financial savings.* Savings rates were high in Malaysia and Thailand, and much of this saving went into the domestic financial system (rather than into real assets or capital flight, as in Latin America). This further increased the demand for money and other domestic financial assets, making increased domestic financing of the deficit possible without resorting to inflationary financing. In Malaysia, the state-run Central Provident Fund mobilized domestic saving for the government's use in noninflationary financing of the deficit.

• Third, there were *low initial debt ratios.* In Thailand, the initial level of external debt to GDP was very low, so that external financing was available when needed.

All of the HPAEs except Indonesia and Korea have been long-period low-inflation economies, while Indonesia and Korea fall into the moderately low-inflation category. Moderate inflation was a result of fiscal prudence.[8] By holding public deficits within the bounds of prudent financing, the HPAEs have avoided the inflation-inducing bursts of money creation

---

[8] Recent research suggests that inflation below 20 percent, a level not breached by any of the HPAEs during their rapid growth periods, can be maintained for long periods without generating macroeconomic instability (Dornbusch and Fischer 1993).

**Figure 2.6  Revenues from Money Creation as a Percentage of GDP**
*(Percent)*

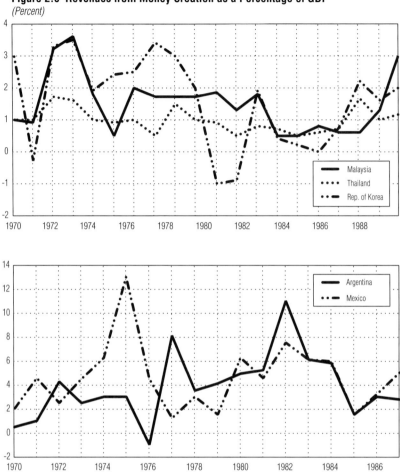

*Note:* These revenues are defined as ratio of nominal change in high-powered money to nominal GDP.
*Source:* World Bank data.

that afflict other developing economies. Figure 2.6 shows money creation as a ratio to GDP in Korea, Malaysia, and Thailand and in Argentina and Mexico. The contrast is striking: while money creation has been relatively constant among the Asian economies, both Argentina and Mexico experienced two episodes of rapid money creation when fiscal balances deteriorated or external financing dried up. Because their deficits were within financeable limits, East Asian governments never had to rely heavily on the inflation tax, as shown in Table 2.3. In general, HPAE governments have

**Table 2.3  Inflation Rates**
*(Percent)*

| Economy/Region | Change in CPI, 1961–91 |
|---|---|
| *HPAEs* | 7.5 |
| Hong Kong | 8.8 |
| Indonesia | 12.4 |
| Korea, Republic of | 12.2 |
| Malaysia | 3.4 |
| Singapore | 3.6 |
| Taiwan, China | 6.2 |
| Thailand | 5.6 |
| *All low and middle-income economies* | 61.8 |
| *Latin America and the Caribbean* | 192.1 |

*Notes:* Averages for HPAEs are unweighted. Hong Kong's average is for 1972–91, and Indonesia's for 1969–91.
*Sources:* World Bank data; World Bank (1992); Taiwan (1992).

been strong enough to alter public spending and foreign borrowing as needed.

The ways that inflation and budget deficits reduce growth are key to understanding the differences between Latin America and the HPAEs. Fischer (1993) concludes that high inflation and high budget deficits reduce both the rate of capital accumulation and the rate of productivity change. Uncertainty, arising primarily from the variability of inflation and the inconsistency of relative price signals, reduces both private investment and the efficiency of resource allocation. One result of low-to-moderate inflation, particularly welcome to business, is a stable real interest rate. Figure 2.7 shows real interest rates in Korea, Malaysia, and Thailand and a sample of Latin American countries. As with money creation, the contrast is remarkable. In the East Asian cases, low inflation and flexible financial policies have kept real interest rates within a narrow range.

Private and public investment as a share of GDP is shown in Figure 2.8, for a sample of 47 low and middle-income economies (LMIEs, including seven major Latin American economies and five of the developing country HPAEs) for which consistent data are available.[9] The HPAEs are remarkable for their high share of private investment. Private investment is about seven to ten percentage points higher in the HPAEs than in other middle-income economies. It averaged nearly 22 percent between 1975 and

---

[9] The data are drawn from Pfeffermann and Madarassy (1992).

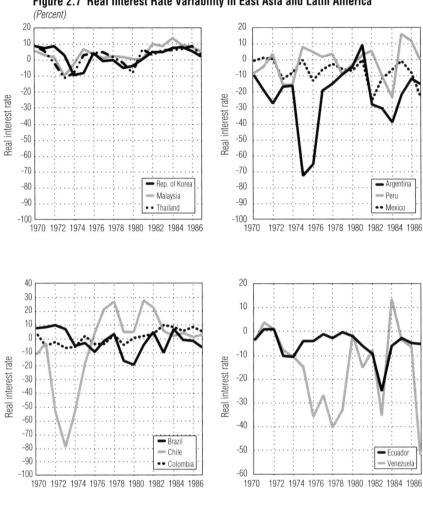

**Figure 2.7  Real Interest Rate Variability in East Asia and Latin America**
*(Percent)*

*Source:* World Bank data.

1984. Private investment in the HPAEs contracted sharply between 1984 and 1986, reflecting the global recession, but recovered by 1988.[10] In contrast, private investment in other low and middle-income countries has remained relatively stable at less than 10 percent of GDP.

---

[10] This basic pattern is observed in four individual economies—Korea, Thailand, Singapore, and Malaysia. The pattern for Indonesia differs; real private investment declined continuously during the 1980s from a peak of 20 percent of GDP to a low of 13 percent in 1989.

**Figure 2.8  Public and Private Investment**
*(Percent of GDP)*

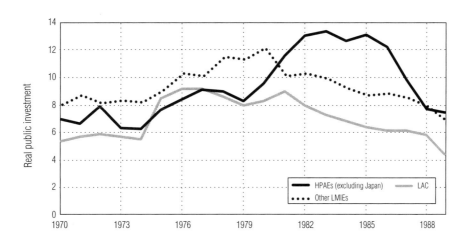

Source: World Bank data.

## Exchange Rate Management

The evolution of exchange rate regimes in the HPAEs has been broadly similar. Most moved from long-term fixed rate regimes to fixed-but-adjustable rate regimes, with occasional steep devaluations, to managed floating rate regimes. Under the managed floating regimes that began in the early 1980s, policymakers no longer set rates but attempted to influence them at the margin, generally to move parallel to the U.S. dollar. Due to the combi-

**Figure 2.9  Examples of Real Exchange Rate Variability**

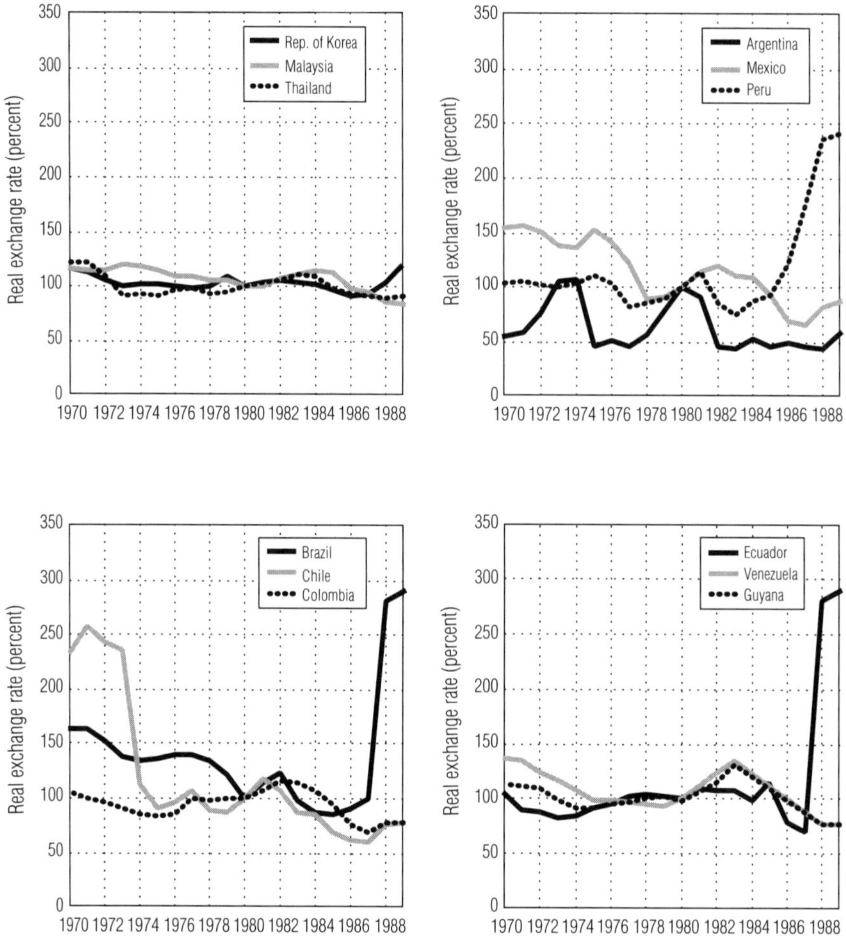

Note: Index of real exchange rate: 1980=100; real depreciation is down.
Source: World Bank data.

nation of moderate inflation and active exchange rate management, the
HPAEs avoided the severe exchange rate appreciation that beset Latin
America, and achieved unusual real exchange rate stability. The HPAEs'
success in maintaining stable real exchange rates is apparent in Figure 2.9,
which contrasts real exchange rates since 1970 in Korea, Malaysia, and
Thailand with nine Latin American economies.

Several HPAE governments used exchange rate policies to offset the adverse impact of trade liberalization on producers of import substitutes. A few went beyond this objective, however, and used deliberately undervalued exchange rates to assist exporters. In these instances, exchange rate policy and the fiscal and monetary tools to carry it out became a part of an overall strategy to push exports. Taiwan, China is the most notable example of this, but Korea and Indonesia also deliberately undervalued their currencies to boost exports. We briefly discuss all three below.

• The very large current account surpluses that Taiwan, China ran in the 1980s, especially from 1984 to 1987 (when the surpluses averaged 16 percent of GDP, with an extraordinary peak of 20 percent in 1986), resulted from government efforts to manage the exchange rate. What would have happened if the New Taiwan dollar had been allowed to appreciate more rapidly? Exports would have become less competitive, reduced export growth would probably have had a deflationary effect, and this in turn could have reduced savings. Alternatively—and more realistically—the potential deflationary effect would have been offset by increased public expenditure, leading to a budget deficit.
• Korea used exchange rate protection from 1986 to 1989 when it ran a current account surplus (which peaked at 8 percent of GDP in 1988). A desire to protect export industries was certainly a factor in Korean exchange rate policy, but the main concern was to reduce the debt ratio and build up reserves to avoid repeating the close brush with a foreign debt crisis that occurred in 1984–85.
• The Indonesian devaluation of 1978 can be classified as anticipatory exchange rate protection. There was no immediate balance of payments problem, since the adverse effects of a real appreciation on exports other than oil had been offset by the rise in the quantity and value of oil and natural gas exports. Rather, the aim of devaluation was to reverse the effects of the real appreciation that occurred from 1970 to 1978. By 1982, when the balance of payments had sharply deteriorated, the wisdom of the 1978 devaluation was clear.

*Response to Macroeconomic Shocks*

One important element of the HPAEs' success in maintaining macroeconomic stability has been their prompt and effective response to macroeconomic shocks. Two characteristics of the HPAEs enabled them to respond so well. First, by limiting transfers to public enterprises and tightly supervising banks, governments reduced the spillover from the real sector into the financial sector that in other economies exacerbated fiscal woes. Second, flexible labor and capital markets enabled the real sector to react quickly to government initiatives, setting off new growth cycles that eased the recessionary impact of stabilization measures.

Effective responses to macroeconomic shocks may also have contributed to the HPAEs' long-run growth. Relatively cautious fiscal and foreign borrowing policies meant that serious debt crises were avoided. This reduced the stop-go pattern of crisis and response, which characterized many Latin American economies in the 1980s. Avoiding crises and the need for rescheduling meant that creditworthiness was maintained, making it easier to borrow in the short term and to avoid very deep cuts, especially in investment.

In the 1970s overall levels of public investment did not differ markedly between the HPAEs and other developing economies; over the decade public investment rates in all economies rose from about 7 to 10 percent (Figure 2.8). During the 1980s, public investment was higher in the HPAEs than in other developing economies, but had declined to more typical levels by the end of the decade. The HPAEs as a group responded to the economic contraction of the 1980s by increasing public investment above historically maintained levels. In contrast, sudden reductions in aggregate demand and in investment, compelled by debt crises, were major causes of the sharply declining growth rates in many heavily indebted Latin American economies.

Better responses to macroeconomic shocks may also have resulted in better measured productivity growth. A recent examination of the sources of TFP change in developing countries concludes that productivity levels in Latin America increased relative to international best practice until 1973 and declined from 1973 onwards, primarily because these economies could not adapt to external shocks. The decline was large enough in Latin America to offset gains due to technical progress (Friedberg, Khamis, and Page 1993). The HPAEs, in contrast, are the only regional grouping of developing economies that show steady improvement in productivity levels relative to international best practice. While macroeconomic contractions are clearly visible in the HPAEs' pattern productivity level change over time, the difference is that the HPAEs return more rapidly to prior productivity levels following the period of adjustment.

## Asian Societies Worked to Raise Domestic Savings

As with the case of macroeconomic management, some of the major explanations for East Asia's high savings rates are themselves outcomes of the HPAEs' rapid growth and structural transformation. Government policy also encouraged (and sometimes compelled) increased savings through a variety of means. One fundamental policy improvement that supported high savings rates in the HPAEs was macroeconomic stability. In addition, the HPAEs have used a variety of institutional measures to boost savings rates.

### Growth and Demographics—the Effect on Savings

Studies of the income-savings relationship in a broad cross-section of economies indicate that while income and savings growth are highly correlated, incomes often rise before savings rates increase: this suggests that growth drives savings, rather than the other way around. Recent econometric studies support the idea that rapid income growth raises savings rates as households acquire resources faster than they adjust consumption (Carroll, Weil, and Summers 1993). Income growth has been a remarkably good predictor of increased savings rates in Japan, Korea, Indonesia, Thailand, and Taiwan, China, but not vice versa (World Bank 1993a). Results are mixed for Hong Kong and Malaysia and causation might run either way. In Singapore income changes were not a significant factor in the spectacular rise in savings rates in the 1970s and 1980s, consistent with the view that demographic factors and the policies of the Central Provident Fund, a forced savings program, determined the rise (Monetary Authority of Singapore 1991).

Another means by which rapid growth may have contributed to rising savings was through change in the size and age composition of households. As birth rates fell, the dependency ratio—the ratio of non-working-age people to working-age people—decreased.[11] For the HPAEs other than Japan, there is evidence that household savings are related to demographic change. The Singapore study showed that most of the increased savings rate from 1970 to 1989 was attributable to declining dependency ratios

---

[11] Theories of savings based on the life cycle predict that societies with a high proportion of prime-age workers will save more than those with higher proportions of young or old people (Ando and Modigliani 1963; Modigliani 1970). Of course, in the long run, the benefit of falling birth rates will be reversed as the population ages and the old-age dependency ratio rises, an effect seen in studies of OECD economies and Japan (see Blumenthal 1970, Horioka 1990).

(Monetary Authority of Singapore 1991). In Taiwan, China, where house-hold savings rates are generally very high, households headed by prime-age workers tend to save more, possibly reflecting in part preparation for old age. But savings in older households are also remarkably high and stable, contrary to the view that rising dependency ratios should result in lower household savings (Deaton and Paxson 1992). Demographic factors may also interact with corporate behavior to increase savings. In Japan the tradition of employees working beyond retirement age at reduced wages appears to contribute significantly to higher savings rates (Horioka 1990).

*Stable Macroeconomy and Public Saving*

In addition to benefiting from higher growth and demographic shifts con-ducive to savings, East Asian governments selected, often through trial and error, policies that encourage saving. Foremost among these was the effort to control inflation, and the resultant maintenance of positive real interest rates on saving. Because high inflation rates tend to be volatile, real interest rates are often negative and unpredictable in countries with high inflation, discouraging domestic financial savings. Moreover, unanticipated high in-flation erodes the real value of financial assets, and hence, increases the risk associated with holding them. On the other hand, low to moderate infla-tion, particularly at stable rates, encourages financial saving. Several stud-ies have documented the positive association between real interest rates and the growth of savings deposits and broad money aggregates (Fry 1988; Lanyi and Saracoglu 1983; Gelb 1989). This is especially evident for changes from highly negative to positive real rates of interest. For example, when Taiwan, China raised real interest rates on bank deposits from a negative 300 percent in 1949 to about 8.5 percent in 1953, the ratio of time and sav-ings deposits to money stock rose from 2 percent to 34 percent in three years. Korea and Indonesia achieved similarly dramatic increases in finan-cial savings after stabilizing inflation and shifting from negative to positive real interest rates (as have Mexico, Chile, and Argentina more recently).

One way that any government can directly address the concern that aggregate savings are too low is to generate public sector saving through a combination of tax and expenditure policies. Rational, forward-looking pri-vate savers should theoretically increase consumption (and reduce savings) to match any increase in public saving (because their future obligations are reduced). But if households are faced with liquidity constraints and cannot act upon expectations, total savings may rise (Summers 1985). Empirical

**Table 2.4  Public and Private Savings of HPAEs and Selected Latin American Economies**

*(Percent of GDP)*

| Economy/year | Public Savings | Private Savings |
|---|---|---|
| **HPAES** | | |
| Indonesia | | |
| 1981–88 | 7.7 | 14.0 |
| Japan | | |
| 1945–54 | 5.3 | 12.0 |
| 1955–70 | 6.2 | 17.2 |
| 1971–80 | 4.6 | 20.1 |
| 1981–88 | 5.1 | 15.8 |
| Malaysia | | |
| 1961–80 | 3.2 | 18.7 |
| 1981–90 | 10.3 | 19.1 |
| Singapore | | |
| 1974–80 | 5.5 | 22.6 |
| 1981–90 | 18.5 | 24.0 |
| Thailand | | |
| 1980–85 | 14.3 | 4.7 |
| 1986–87 | 8.6 | 14.6 |
| | | |
| ***Latin American economies*** | | |
| Argentina | | |
| 1980–85 | 1.9 | 11.0 |
| 1986–87 | 4.2 | 1.2 |
| Brazil | | |
| 1980–85 | 5.1 | 10.5 |
| 1986–87 | 6.9 | 12.5 |
| Chile | | |
| 1980–84 | 3.9 | 2.3 |
| 1985–87 | 7.9 | 0.6 |
| Colombia | | |
| 1980–84 | 2.6 | 13.6 |
| 1985–87 | 7.2 | 14.0 |
| Costa Rica | | |
| 1980–87 | 7.3 | 7.7 |
| Mexico | | |
| 1980–87 | 4.3 | 17.5 |
| Venezuela | | |
| 1980–87 | 16.0 | 5.6 |

*Sources:* Corbo and Schmidt-Hebbel (1991); Monetary Authority of Singapore (various years); Yan (1991); World Bank (1989b); Japanese Economic Planning Agency (various years).

studies show that government saving does not fully crowd out private saving and that the method of raising public saving matters. On average, increasing public saving through reduced expenditure is more effective than
raising taxation. For example, Corbo and Schmidt-Hebbel (1991) show for a
sample of 13 developing economies that a transitory increase of a dollar in
public saving, made through a cut in expenditures, reduces private saving
by only 16 to 50 cents. If the dollar increase in public saving is achieved
through a current period tax increase, private saving declines by 48 to 65
cents.

Through a combination of tax policy and expenditure restraint, most
HPAEs have maintained high public saving compared with other low and
middle-income economies (Table 2.4). For example, Singapore's public
saving rose from 5.5 percent of GDP in 1974–80 to 18.5 percent of GDP in
1981–90, and private saving rose from 22.6 percent to 24 percent. Malaysia's
public saving increased from an average 3.2 percent of GDP in 1961–80 to
10.3 percent in 1981–1990, while its private saving increased slightly.

While in some Latin American economies (e.g., Venezuela), public
saving is relatively high and accounts for a major part of national savings,
generally public saving is substantially lower than in the HPAEs and has
declined. Both public and private saving declined in the early 1980s in Argentina, Brazil, Chile, and Colombia. For example, Brazil's public saving
dropped from 8.3 percent of GDP in 1980 to 3.2 percent for the period 1983–
1985. Mexico's public saving was a low 2 percent of GDP in 1981–1986, in
contrast to an average of about 5 percent of GDP over the preceding decade.
However, since the mid-1980s, public saving in Brazil, Argentina, Costa
Rica (since 1983), Mexico (in 1987), Colombia, and Chile has increased in
response to fiscal adjustments, causing national savings to rise (Edwards
1995).

*Promoting Confidence in Financial Institutions*

East Asian governments have attached great importance to maintaining
savers' confidence in financial institutions.[12] Their policies have often gone
beyond prudential regulations to include protecting banks from competition (and encouraging oligopolies) in order to increase the financial

---

[12] In Japan, through managing competition, industrial policy may have also assisted in the
stability of financial institutions. Japan's recession cartels, for example, may have avoided
large and systematic bankruptcies, which surely helped the solvency of financial institutions.

strength of banking institutions. Sometimes this has been done at the expense of long-run efficiency. In addition, when necessary, all HPAE governments have bailed out troubled financial institutions through financial and management assistance or mergers with stronger banks.

This is not to say that the HPAEs have not experienced banking crises. Indeed, some financial instability is probably unavoidable in economies expanding as rapidly as those in East Asia. Nonetheless, the crises that did occur (for example, in the wake of the 1980s real estate speculation boom in Japan, Korea, Hong Kong, Thailand, and Malaysia) were minor in comparison with the protracted and disruptive banking crises in Chile, Bolivia, Argentina, and Mexico during the same period.

Central banks and departments of finance in the HPAEs appear to have been more successful in supervising commercial banks, which have reported a relatively low proportion of nonperforming loans in their portfolios. There are some major exceptions: Korea in the early 1980s, Indonesia in the late 1980s, and Malaysia's Bank Bumiputra in the 1970s. Generally, however, nonperforming loans have been less of a problem in the HPAEs than in many developing economies. For example, one study of 12 Latin American economies found that nonperforming loans accounted for nearly 14 percent of total loans in 1987, while the proportion of bad loans surpassed 20 percent in Uruguay, Honduras, Venezuela, and Argentina.

The more effective prudential regulation of East Asian banks is also apparent in the ease with which most of them adopted the international capital adequacy requirements set by the Bank for International Settlements (BIS) to ensure that banks do not take on inappropriate levels of risk. Japan, Hong Kong, and Singapore began to strengthen prudential regulation in the 1970s, and Malaysia, Thailand, and Taiwan, China followed suit in the 1980s. All HPAEs have since adopted the BIS capital adequacy requirements. Indonesia, the last to do so, has had some difficulty achieving BIS capital requirement levels because it introduced proper prudential regulations rather late.[13] By contrast, a 1990 World Bank study of banking systems in Latin America found that only Ecuador adhered to BIS standards, while Colombia was in the process of adopting the standards. Moreover, some Latin American governments still have not established minimum capital requirements for new banks.

---

[13] The danger of easing interest rates and entry controls for banks without simultaneously strengthening prudential regulations and capital adequacy requirements has been evident in Indonesia, where low capital requirements for entry and poor enforcement of prudential regulations has led to mounting concern about insolvent banks.

In spite of generally good prudential regulation, there have been financial crises in East Asia brought about by a mix of macroeconomic shocks, occasional insufficient regulation, and speculative lending. However, rapid and effective response has enabled governments to maintain confidence by acting as implicit insurer, without excessive fiscal cost. Rapid growth and spiraling real estate prices have often tempted financial institutions into property and stock speculation. This has happened repeatedly in Hong Kong (in 1965, 1982, and 1986), and has also been a problem in Thailand, Malaysia, and, most recently, Japan. By the late 1980s, financial institutions in each of these economies were facing difficulties, as nonperforming loans rose due to the economic downturn. Korea encountered similar difficulties but for somewhat different reasons, including the heavy indebtedness of firms that had been beneficiaries of government-directed credit.

When financial distress has occurred, HPAE governments have come to the rescue. While only Korea and Taiwan, China have established explicit deposit insurance (both in the early 1980s), they and other HPAEs have for decades implicitly insured deposits by stepping in whenever necessary to prevent bank failures. In some cases, especially in Japan, stronger banks were pressed to take over banks in financial trouble. When mergers have been impractical, East Asian governments have served as lender of last resort.

*Creating Postal Savings Institutions*

Japan, Korea, Singapore, Malaysia, and Taiwan, China have established government-run postal savings systems to attract small savers. Postal savings institutions offer low-income households greater security and lower transaction costs than private banks, and provide two important elements that encourage savings—security and an orientation toward small savers.

Japan established the region's first postal savings program in 1875, drawing on British experience, with the explicit goal of fostering saving by rural dwellers and people with low to moderate incomes in the cities and towns. Until then, such people were effectively excluded from the financial system, which lacked rural networks and discouraged small depositors by requiring high minimum balances or paying very low interest rates on small deposits. The Japanese government heavily promoted postal savings among low-income households and made the interest income of postal savings deposits below a certain amount tax free.

Similar institutions with the same goal of mobilizing saving were later established in Korea, Singapore, Malaysia, and Taiwan, China. Like Japan, both Korea and Taiwan, China have granted tax-exempt status to the interest income from long-term postal savings. In Taiwan, China, postal savings offices account for about a third of all financial institution offices, and the postal savings service has longer business hours than other financial institutions. In Malaysia and Singapore, where postal savings have also accounted for a large proportion of domestic deposits, the governments separated management of the savings system from the post office in the early 1970s, when the proportion of postal savings in total savings declined, evidently because postal employees were not enthusiastic promoters of savings. Even so, the savings system continued to utilize the post offices as a deposit-taking branch network.

Postal savings systems can be an effective way of mobilizing household saving, provided that governments take care that the costs of administering the systems do not outstrip the benefits. In Japan, the postal savings system piggy-backed on the mail-delivery infrastructure, thus minimizing overhead and fixed costs. In the early years, the system often operated out of the houses of wealthy landowners that were already serving as postal branches. As postal savings expanded and the administrative burden rose, postal officials demanded wage increases. Overall, however, costs of accepting deposits through the postal system have been lower than those of the private banks (Mukai 1963).

*Forced Savings*

In addition to the measures described above, some HPAEs have tried to compel savings through mandatory pension schemes, restrictions on consumption and borrowing for consumption, and other measures that constitute more active interventions in markets. The efficacy of such measures, even in East Asia, is open to question because restrictions on consumer choices, including the basic consumption-savings decision, have welfare costs. Moreover, similar efforts in other economies have been spectacular failures. Examples include the widespread deprivation and massive waste associated with forced savings in the now-defunct command economies.

Three economies in East Asia—Japan, Singapore, and Malaysia, have well-developed mandatory pension plans. The impact of these plans on aggregate savings depends on the degree to which they substitute for voluntary savings. Evidence on the impact of pension funds in Japan and Singapore, the only two economies where the issue has been studied, is inconclusive. One study of savings in Japan found that pension funds had no significant impact on total savings, while another found a small negative effect (Dekle 1988; Noguchi 1985). This suggests that the Japanese pension fund might have squeezed out a portion of voluntary savings. On the other hand, Singapore's Central Provident Fund (CPF) boosted aggregate savings by about 4 percent of GDP during the 1970s and 1980s (Monetary Authority of Singapore 1991).

The lack of consumer credit to purchase housing, consumer durables, and other consumer items may have induced increased household saving in some East Asian economies. Specifically, bank regulators in Japan, Korea, and Taiwan, China restricted credit available for the purchase of consumer durables. Maki (1993) offers evidence that the rapid increase in savings in Japan after World War II was driven by the need to acquire consumer durables, and he shows that the same pattern existed in Korea and Taiwan, China. As household incomes and the demand for consumer durables increased, savings as a proportion of income rose rapidly. Once the excess demand for consumer durables was met, savings rates stabilized and even declined.

### Industrial Policy and Export Promotion

Proponents of both trade neutrality and intervention cite the high-performing East Asian economies in support of their views. Balassa (1991), Krueger (1993), Hughes (1992) and others argue that openness to international trade, based on largely neutral incentives, was the critical factor in East Asia's rapid growth. On the other hand, advocates of interventions, while acknowledging the importance of trade, note that incentives deriving from quantitative restrictions on imports, tariffs and subsidies were not neutral among sectors (or firms) during the HPAEs' periods of rapid growth. They argue that the HPAE governments successfully intervened to change comparative advantage (Amsden 1989; Wade 1990; Singh 1992).

Industrial policy interventions, which often use trade policy instruments, are motivated by the belief that shifting industrial structures toward newer, more modern sectors increases opportunities for capturing the dynamic scale economies that result from learning. Industrial policies, as distinct from trade policies, are here defined as government efforts to alter industrial structure to promote productivity-based growth. Such growth may derive from learning, technological innovation, or catch-up to international best practice. All of the HPAEs except Hong Kong have employed industrial policies as defined above. Japan and Korea had the most systematic set of policies to alter industrial structure. Taiwan's efforts were less systematic but were nonetheless widespread. Industrial policy in Singapore was more functionally directed at the rapid upgrading of technology by direct foreign investors, regardless of type of output. Malaysia, Indonesia, and Thailand have all used industrial policies but much less systematically than the HPAEs in Northeast Asia.

Industrial targeting could have resulted in extensive rent-seeking and great inefficiency, but apparently it did not. The success or failure of selective interventions therefore are among the most controversial aspects of the East Asian success story. Some of the reasons why selective interventions do not appear to have had the disastrous results of those pursued in other developing economies are straightforward. Labor market policies in the HPAEs tended to emphasize flexibility and competitive determination of wages (Fields 1992), and directed credit programs were undertaken within a framework of generally low subsidies to borrowers and careful monitoring (Vittas and Cho 1993). As a consequence, the relative prices of labor and capital in the HPAEs were closer to their scarcity values than in other developing economies (World Bank 1993a).

Nevertheless, especially in the cases of Japan, Korea, and Taiwan, China, governments made systematic efforts to alter industrial structure for the purpose of accelerating productivity change. How these policies influenced the growth of the HPAEs remains a topic of heated debate.[14] This section proposes two policy lessons: first, that promotion of manufactured exports was a significant source of measured TFP change, and second, that industrial policies mattered relatively little in the overall record of East Asia's extraordinary growth. The conclusion is that export—not industrial—promotion was at the heart of the HPAEs' productivity performance.

*Export Growth and Productivity Change*

Although all HPAEs except Hong Kong passed through an import substitution phase, with high and variable protection of domestic import substitutes, these periods ended earlier than in other economies. Hong Kong, Malaysia, and Singapore adopted trade regimes that were close to free trade; Japan, Korea, and Taiwan, China adopted mixed regimes that were largely free for export industries. Indonesia and Thailand began to reduce protection in the 1980s. Exchange rate policies were liberalized, and currencies were frequently devalued to support export growth.

Export push strategies were implemented in three very different ways

---

[14] See, for example, the collection of essays in *World Development* (1994) and Rodrik (1994), which critically review World Bank (1993a).

in the HPAEs. In Hong Kong and Singapore, with free trade regimes linking their domestic prices to international prices, the export push was an outcome of the very limited size of the domestic market coupled with neutral incentives between producing for the domestic or international market. Both economies made export credit available, although they did not subsidize it, and Singapore focused its efforts on attracting foreign investment in exporting firms. In Japan, Korea, and Taiwan, China, incentives, on average, were essentially neutral between import substitutes and exports, but within the traded goods sector, export incentives coexisted with substantial protection of the domestic market. Export incentives, moreover, were not neutral among industries or firms. There were efforts in Japan, Korea, Singapore, and Taiwan, China to promote specific exporting industries. Protection was combined with either compulsion or strong incentives to export. In Korea, firm-specific export targets were established; in Japan and Taiwan, China, access to subsidized export credit and undervaluation of the currency acted as an offset to the protection of the local market. What was important in all cases was that governments were credibly committed to the promotion of manufactured exports. They adopted an export push strategy.[15]

The HPAEs' export performance was reflected in their steadily rising share of world exports. As a group, the HPAEs increased their share in world exports from 7.9 percent in 1965 to 13.1 percent in 1980 and to 18.2 percent in 1990. Manufactured exports have provided most of this growth. One obvious effect of rapid export growth has been a marked increase in the openness of these economies as measured by the share of exports plus imports in GDP.

Recent theoretical and empirical studies of growth have emphasized the potential benefits of technological learning and productivity change derived from exposure to the world economy. Most explanations of the link between TFP growth and exports emphasize such static factors as improved resource allocation among sectors (presumably arising from reductions in anti-export bias), economies of scale, and improved capacity utilization. These factors may account for a high level of productivity being achieved after a short period of export orientation, but not for continuing

[15] Colin Bradford was the first to introduce the concept of export push into the analysis of East Asia's rapid growth. He has defined it as effective exchange rates (EER) for exportable goods exceeding those for importable goods (Bradford 1994). We use the term somewhat more broadly to indicate a credible commitment to a policy regime that will ultimately yield effective exchange rates for exportable goods equal to or greater than the EER for importables.

**Table 2.5  Determinants of Total Factor Productivity Growth, 1960–89**
*(Dependent variable = rate of TFP growth)*

| Number of Observations | 56 | 62 | 47 | 47 | 64 | 49 | 49 |
|---|---|---|---|---|---|---|---|
| Intercept | -83.1863** | -0.3584 | -64.9123** | -71.1186** | -0.1315 | -72.0692** | -70.8604** |
|  | (15.6575) | (0.2614) | (14.0585) | (14.8657) | (0.3244) | (15.6104) | (15.4608) |
| GDP relative to U.S., 1960 | -4.5638* | -3.3864** | -4.8047* | -5.5757** | -1.4501 | -2.3509 | -2.1562 |
|  | (2.1994) | (1.0189) | (1.9771) | (2.0637) | (1.1912) | (2.3225) | (2.3008) |
| Educational attainment, 1960 | 0.3083** | 0.2158** | 0.1471 | 0.0680 | 0.2269* | 0.1574 | 0.0738 |
|  | (0.0951) | (0.0808) | (0.0874) | (0.1082) | (0.0990) | (0.1064) | (0.1207) |
| Dollar index | 0.8328** |  | 0.6493** | 0.7154** |  | 0.7225** | 0.7134** |
|  | (0.1579) |  | (0.1417) | (0.1508) |  | (0.1574) | (0.1558) |
| Average manufactured exports/total exports, 1960-85 |  | 0.0345** | 0.0314** | 0.0159 |  |  |  |
|  |  | (0.0058) | (0.0066) | (0.0142) |  |  |  |
| Interaction term: Education attainment 1960 times manufactured exports/total exports, 1960-85 |  |  |  | 0.0032 |  |  |  |
|  |  |  |  | (0.0026) |  |  |  |
| Average manufactured exports/GDP, 1965-85 |  |  |  | 0.0828** | 0.0625* | -0.0686 |  |
|  |  |  |  | (0.0279) | (0.0269) | (0.0966) |  |
| Interaction term: Education attainment 1960 times manufactured exports/GDP, 1965-85 |  |  |  |  |  | 0.0284 |  |
|  |  |  |  |  |  | (0.0201) |  |
| Adjusted R2 | 0.4854 | 0.4665 | 0.6333 | 0.6376 | 0.1950 | 0.4507 | 0.4628 |

\* Statistically significant at the 0.05 level.
\*\* Statistically significant at the 0.01 level.
*Note:* Coefficient is top number. Standard error is bottom number in parentheses.
*Source:* World Bank staff estimates.

high TFP growth rates. The relationship between exports and productivity growth may arise from export's role in helping economies adopt and master international best practice. Because exporting firms have greater access to best practice technology, in imperfect world technology markets there are both benefits to the enterprise and spillovers to the rest of the economy that are not reflected in market transactions (Pack and Page 1993; Bradford 1994). These information-related externalities can be an important source of rapid TFP growth.

Trade and educational strategies, moreover, may have worked together. High levels of cognitive skills in the labor force permit better firm-level adoption, adaptation, and mastery of technology (Birdsall and Sabot 1994). The HPAEs, with their highly skilled domestic engineers and workers, were able to make productive use of foreign knowledge and imported capital. Thus, exports and human capital formation may have interacted to provide a particularly rapid phase of productivity-based catch-up.

To test the hypothesis that export orientation played a significant role in the HPAEs' TFP growth, we attempt to explain variations across economies in TFP growth rates in terms of relative income, educational attainment (as measured by the average stock of education per person), a measure of trade orientation, and measures of manufactured export performance (Table 2.5).

The relative level of GDP in 1960 is included in the explanatory regression to test for the presence of conditional, productivity-based catch-up. The interpretation of the variable is not straightforward, however, since it also captures the resource allocation gains arising from structural transformation at low levels of income. Because these potential gains decline with increases in per capita income, the relative income variable also captures the effect of structural change on the TFP estimates (Pack 1993).

Numerous efforts have been made to test the relationship between outward orientation and productivity growth.[16] Dollar (1990) uses the international comparisons of price levels compiled for 121 market countries by Summers and Heston (1988) to develop an index of outward orientation for 95 developing countries. We employ Dollar's index in our basic specification and find a significant and positive relationship between outward orientation and TFP growth. However, the interpretation of this variable is also not straightforward. Rodrik (1994) has discussed the problems of constructing and interpreting the index and prefers to regard it as an index of exchange rate mismanagement. To the extent that this latter interpretation is correct, our results differ from those of Fischer (1993), in that we find a significant positive relationship between appropriate exchange rate policy and productivity growth.

Manufactured export performance is strongly correlated (at the one percent level) with increased rates of TFP growth. We use two measures of export orientation that have somewhat different interpretations. The first is the share of manufactured exports in total exports. This is a crude measure of the probability that the marginal export will be a manufactured good.

---

[16] See, for example, Thomas and Wang (1993) and Nishimizu and Page (1991).

The second is the more conventional share of manufactured exports in GDP, which measures manufactured export concentration for the economy. Both the share of manufactured exports in total exports and the share of manufactured exports in GDP are significantly and positively correlated with TFP growth, controlling for relative income and educational attainment.[17]

When the manufactured export variables are introduced together with the Dollar index both are significant, although the coefficient on the share of manufactured exports in total output is less precisely estimated. Our interpretation of these results is that controlling for overall outward orientation (or appropriate exchange rate policy), high manufactured export orientation increases TFP growth. A high concentration of manufactured exports relative to total exports, rather than the relative size of the manufactured export sector, is more closely associated with productivity growth in a cross-economy framework. This is consistent with the hypothesis that export-based learning is more closely related to manufactured export orientation than to manufactured export volume.

The education stock variable is included as a crude test of educationally based externalities. We find, consistent with this hypothesis, that the education stock variable is positively and significantly associated with TFP growth when either the Dollar index of outward orientation or the index of manufactured export orientation is used independently in the regressions. When both indices of outward orientation are introduced jointly, however, the magnitude of the coefficient on educational attainment declines, as does its significance (to the .10 level). This suggests an interaction between trade orientation and educational attainment.

We also find some evidence of a positive interaction between the stock of education and the share of manufactured exports in both total exports and national income. The coefficient of the interaction term between these two variables is positive but not significant at conventional levels, and the export share variable becomes insignificant. However, when we take the

---

[17] The evidence from our cross-economy estimates is supported by a number of recent microeconomic studies that attempt to test the link between exports and productivity growth. Pack and Page (1993) present evidence from Korea and Taiwan, China, that at the sectoral level, rapid export growth is correlated with the pattern of productivity change; exporting sectors have higher sectoral rates of TFP growth. Wei (1993) uses city-level data from Taiwan, China and finds a statistically significant relationship between export growth and productivity growth. Aw and Hwang (1993), using firm-level microeconomic data from Taiwan, China, find a statistically significant relationship between productivity level differences among manufacturing firms and export orientation.

variables together, to explain the variation in TFP growth rates, their contribution is statistically positive. We conclude that export performance and education interact positively; that is, higher levels of education raise the contribution of manufactured export concentration to TFP growth.[18]

## Industrial Policy and Productivity Change

HPAE industrial growth patterns differ from the patterns in most other low and middle-income economies in the relative size and growth rates of two important industrial subsectors: metal products, electronics, and machinery (MPM); and textiles and garments. Among the HPAEs, MPM has grown unusually fast. The sector's share of value-added in manufacturing doubled in Singapore and Japan, nearly tripled in Korea and Indonesia, and quadrupled in Malaysia. More surprising than the growth in MPM, a sector which provides vital inputs to numerous other manufacturing subsectors, was the continued importance of textiles and garments even as the rapidly developing Asian economies shifted from labor-intensive to capital-intensive production.

Detailed sectoral growth rates of TFP are available only for Japan, Korea, and Taiwan, China. For advocates of industrial policy, there is both good news and bad news in the productivity performance of East Asian industry. The good news is that, on average, rates of productivity change in industry in Japan (before 1973), Korea, and Taiwan, China, were high by international standards (Page 1990).[19] With sufficiently long time-series data, we can now conclude that in these economies, TFP growth has accounted for a substantial fraction of the growth of constant price value added in manufacturing. Given the length of time of the observations, it seems unlikely that the measured growth rates of TFP could be attributable to cyclical phenomena or to the growing capacity utilization of initial large investments.

---

[18] We ran two joint F-tests on the regressions including the interactive term. The F-tests were both consistent with a high degree of multicollinearity between the interaction term and the export term. The F-test rejects the null hypothesis that, taken jointly, the coefficients on the three variables (education, manufactured exports/total exports, and the interactive term) are not significantly different from zero (taken together, the three are significantly different from zero at the .01 level). Likewise, the F-test rejects the hypothesis that, taken jointly, the interactive term and the export variable are not significantly different from zero (taken together, the two are significantly different from zero at the .01 level). Where a high degree of multicollinearity appears between the variables, the coefficients on the interaction term and the export variable, despite being separately insignificant, should still be treated as best point estimates.

[19] Young (1995) disputes even this assertion, although his sample of LDC comparators is small.

The bad news is that, in general, productivity change has not been higher in promoted sectors. Japan may be an exception. Between 1960 and 1979, chemicals and the metalworking machinery complex had unusually good TFP performance (Jorgenson, Kuroda, and Nishimizu 1987). Japan's industrial structure differs from international norms in these sectors and exhibits quite high values of the share of value-added in total manufacturing. Observers usually point to these industries as having benefitted from significant government efforts to stimulate productivity growth.

A number of calculations of TFP have been carried out for Korea for different periods (Dollar and Sokoloff 1990; Lim 1991). From these studies several broadly consistent patterns can be identified. What is most striking are the high values of TFP change in most sectors by international standards (Nishimizu and Page 1991). Although the Korean government selectively promoted chemicals and iron and steel (included in the basic metals sector), the large growth in the share of iron and steel was accompanied by quite low TFP performance between 1966 and 1985; textiles and clothing, on the other hand, had very high rates of TFP growth. The promoted chemical sector, whose relative size was decreasing during this period, was characterized by considerably higher than average TFP growth.

Although the government in Taiwan, China, did not attempt to influence sectoral evolution as strongly as did the government of Korea, it did devote substantial effort to encouraging specific sectors, particularly those viewed as either capital- or technology-intensive. However, there has been no relationship between capital intensity and productivity change at the sectoral level. In fact, the highest sectoral rates of TFP change have been recorded in textiles and apparel.

## Toward a Consensus—Policies and Institutions for Rapid Growth

For the three public policy areas reviewed in this paper, there is little divergence between the Latin American consensus and the origins of the East Asian miracle. In large measure the HPAEs achieved high growth by getting the basics right. Private domestic investment, combined with rapidly growing human capital, were the principal engines of growth. In this sense there is nothing miraculous about the HPAEs' superior record of growth, it has been due largely to superior accumulation. But effective allocation rules and superior productivity performance played important roles as well. Macroeconomic stability and the capacity to respond effectively to macroeconomic shocks helped to accelerate growth through all three mechanisms—increasing accumulation, improving resource allocation, and increasing productivity growth. Moderate and predictable inflation, combined with institutional innovations in the financial sector, helped to boost East Asia's domestic savings rates.

The weight of evidence indicates that the promotion of specific individual industries made relatively little difference to the HPAEs' success. Overall, the evidence is weak that industrial policy systematically promoted sectors with high productivity change. Japan provides some support for the assertion that TFP growth was higher in selected sectors, while in Korea and Taiwan, China, activities not promoted (for example, textiles) had equally impressive TFP performance. Rather, export push strategies have been the most generally successful selective approach used by the HPAEs and hold the greatest promise for Latin America.

Export orientation, rather than industrial policy, was mainly responsible for improving productivity growth in Japan and Korea. These economies, although selectively promoting capital- and knowledge-intensive industries, still aimed at creating profitable, internationally competitive firms. The yardstick used to evaluate industrial policy success—mainly export performance—provided a market test of the success or failure of the policy instruments chosen. The strategy of picking winners may have succeeded because Japan and Korea set export targets for promoted industries and used export performance to assess the success of policies, rather than because of success in selecting industrial subsectors. The more recent export push efforts of the Southeast Asian newly industrialized economies (NIEs) have relied less on highly specific incentives and more on gradual reductions in import protection, coupled with institutional support of exporters and a duty-free regime for inputs into exports. These GATT-friendly export promotion strategies offer substantial scope for adoption by Latin American economies.

But economists and policymakers in Latin America still may have missed an important lesson of East Asia in their quest to establish growth policy. The success of the East Asian economies stems only partly from the policies they have adopted; they also created the institutional mechanisms necessary to facilitate and support the implementation of these policies. All of the HPAEs established secure institutional environments for private investment that led to very high levels of private sector–led growth. HPAE civil services range from the highly meritocratic and insulated bureaucracies of Japan, Korea, Singapore, and Taiwan, China to the less effective and less insulated public administrations of Indonesia and Thailand. Nevertheless, each of these economies has a core of technocratic managers. In Indonesia and Thailand, their scope is limited to managing the macroeconomy. In the other HPAEs, competent civil services administer a much wider range of policy instruments.

How did these economies create a reputable bureaucracy? First, pay mattered. The salaries of bureaucrats (except in Singapore) did not match salaries for equivalent positions in the private sector, but they were sufficiently high to attract and retain good economic managers. Second, in the HPAEs with high-quality bureaucracies, rules and procedures governing public sector employment were institutionalized and insulated from political intervention. In particular, recruitment and promotion were merit-based. Third, public employment was accorded high status. These factors improved the quality of the bureaucracy, discouraged corruption, and created an *esprit de corps* among civil servants that helped insulate the bureaucracy from political pressures (World Bank 1993a).

Each of the HPAE governments created institutions to improve communication with the private sector (Campos and Root 1995). Formal deliberation councils established in five of the economies—Hong Kong, Japan, Korea, Malaysia, and Singapore—included government officials, journalists, labor representatives, and academics. The economic and political benefits of these councils, and of the less formal mechanisms in the other HPAEs, are impossible to measure systematically, but they probably improved coordination among firms and the flow of information between businesses and government. Politically, they helped establish a shared commitment to growth and reduced rent seeking. Information sharing made it harder for firms to curry special favors from the government and for government officials to grant special concessions. Thus the deliberation councils helped check opportunistic behavior.

The deliberation councils in Japan, Korea, and Singapore also performed an important monitoring function, assessing performance at the industry or economy level. Consultative mechanisms in Indonesia and Thailand were less formal, and their role in facilitating business-government communication was much more limited. Malaysia's experiment with deliberation councils is quite recent, but appears to hold some promise in the area of macroeconomic management.

Few Latin American economies have applied these lessons of institutional development (Naím 1995). Without increased attention to the implementation of development policy, Latin American governments may risk a consensus without commitment, and the economic performances of East Asia and Latin America may continue to diverge.

---

*John Page is Chief Economist, Middle East and North Africa Region, the World Bank.*

# Commentary

*Barbara Stallings*

The World Bank's study of the East Asian miracle is one of the most important discussions of development in the past decade, for four main reasons. First, it provides massive amounts of data on the economic development experience of East and Southeast Asia. Second, it presents a number of important debates about development policies and strategies. Third, the analysis of the Asian cases appears to have brought some modest change in the World Bank's position with respect to appropriate policies. Fourth, the study shows that the Japanese government has adopted a more aggressive stance in putting forward an alternative development model based on the Asian experience.

However, the East Asian miracle is not the last word on events in Asia. To the contrary, publication of the World Bank study catalyzed a new round of debate among Asians and Asian specialists, about how to interpret the development experience of that region.[1]

Since the main purpose of this comment is to discuss some possible lessons for Latin America based on the Asian experience, I will begin by looking at some lessons enjoying a widespread consensus in Latin America, which are similar to policies advocated in the World Bank study. Then, to understand why these lessons have generally not been implemented, I return to the debates on how to interpret the Asian experience.

Virtually all policymakers and economists in Latin America agree that the following four lessons can be adapted from East and Southeast Asia, but certain caveats must be added.[2]

(1) *Latin America should increase its exports,* both in absolute terms and as a percentage of GDP. However, it is not sufficient just to increase the volume of exports of traditional primary products. The well-known problems

---

[1] See, for example, Amsden (1994) and Fishlow et al. (1994). On the Japanese side, several studies have been completed or are underway with respect to the East Asian miracle. See Japanese Economic Planning Agency (1994).

[2] Part of the reason for the agreement is that these lessons have been advocated independently of the Asian experience. Nonetheless, the evidence of their positive impact in Asia has strengthened the position of their advocates in Latin America.

with such items (e.g., price volatility, low income elasticity) led in East Asia to an emphasis on diversifying toward non-traditional exports, new agricultural products, and manufactures and services. In addition, the domestic market must be considered: as the Asian experience demonstrates, efficient import substitution is a necessary component of a well-rounded development strategy.

(2) *Latin America should expend more resources on human capital,* especially education and health. However, neither expenditure nor quantitative targets are sufficient to measure these aspects of development. Indeed, on quantitative indicators, Latin America compares quite favorably with other developing regions. In the 1990s, the key is to measure qualitative advances, both in overall terms and across income groups, in order to eliminate disparities. Training programs for workers will be crucial in this context.

(3) *Latin America should increase its savings rate* in order to finance higher investment in both physical and human capital. The crucial point here is that ways must be found to raise domestic savings, both public and private, to avoid excessive reliance on foreign savings. Nonetheless, foreign savings will continue to play an important role in the region for a long time to come. It is therefore necessary to encourage the types of foreign capital that will augment investment, rather than encourage consumption or speculation.

(4) *Latin America must pursue fiscal discipline,* as an important contribution to macroeconomic stability and as an aid to domestic savings. The question is how to bring about fiscal discipline. Whether the emphasis is on spending cuts or on revenue enhancement, discipline is crucial to ensure that fiscal policies are sustainable and consistent with other goals. Cutting government expenditures on education and infrastructure investment will undermine development in the long run, as will tax increases so large as to dissuade the private sector from investing. Government must seek a delicate balance.

What's puzzling about Latin America is that, despite a high degree of consensus on these four goals, the record of accomplishment has been poor in the decade since market-oriented development became the norm in the region. With respect to the first three goals, little has been achieved. On the fourth, more has been done, but often in a perverse way. After reviewing the evidence briefly, I consider why there is such a large gap between rhetoric and action.

Figures on Latin America's exports in the recent period are disappointing, especially in terms of value. The average increase in export value between 1985 and 1992 was only 3.6 percent, compared to a 16.2 percent rise in Asia during the same years. Volume increases showed a different pattern. That is, the increase in volume of Latin American exports averaged 4.6 percent, higher than the rise in value when prices were falling. In Asia, by contrast, volume increased more slowly than value. This different pattern was due to the composition of exports. In 1992, 82 percent of Asian exports were manufactured goods, whose price trends were more favorable, while only 48 percent of Latin American exports consisted of manufactures. Unfortunately, there has been little change in the composition of exports in Latin America, and export-led growth has yet to emerge in the region.[3]

Investment in human capital is a second area of consensus among Latin American policymakers. An examination of available data for the period between 1980/81 and 1992/93, however, indicates that public expenditure on education and health as a share of GDP generally declined. For the ten countries for which data are available, the drop was from 5.8 percent to 5.0 percent; only Brazil and Uruguay saw increases. In constant dollars per capita, the decline was from $118 to $100[4] (Cominetti and di Gropello 1995). What the data do not show is that Latin America puts a large part of its education budget into university education rather than primary or secondary education or job training. So the human capital emphasis is also missing from the development effort.

With respect to savings rates in Latin America, there are arguments over the figures, but it appears that gross domestic savings stagnated during the 1980s and actually fell during the 1990s, as foreign capital began to return to the region. Domestic savings are now only 18 percent of GDP, compared to 32 percent in East and Southeast Asia. Rather than complementing domestic savings, foreign savings seem to have acted as a substitute, thus increasing the region's reliance on foreign resources. Investment also fell between 1980 and 1992. Gross domestic investment as a share of GDP was less than 20 percent in Latin America in 1992, compared to 33 percent in East and Southeast Asia.[5]

Of the four goals mentioned above, Latin America has made significant progress only in the area of fiscal discipline. Especially with respect to

---

[3] See ECLAC (1994), pp. 33 and 39.
[4] Cominetti and di Gropello (1995).
[5] Data are from *World Tables 1994*.

central government accounts, most countries (except in Central America) have much smaller deficits than in the early 1980s. Nonetheless, the deficit reduction that has been achieved remains fragile. Some of it has been based on one-time revenue from privatizations. In addition, cuts in expenditure on infrastructure and social areas will eventually have to be restored. Likewise, cuts in salaries for the bureaucracy will not help to build the kind of expertise that is universally acknowledged to have been so important in Asia.

Why is it that Latin American countries have not learned these obvious lessons from the experience of other regions? Three possible answers are worth considering. One answer, which is consistent with the World Bank's interpretation of the East Asian miracle, is that more time is needed for the new Latin American policies to produce results. In many countries, the reforms have only been in place for a few years. Chile, which began the reform process in the mid 1970s, arguably has the best record in the region on exports and savings. It has also done well on fiscal policy and is now making a special effort in the social arena. The need for more time is probably valid, although it is difficult to draw conclusions from a single case with some very special conditions.

A second answer, more in the spirit of those who believe the World Bank has misinterpreted the Asian experience, is that the new Latin American policies are lacking in precisely those elements that were crucial to the Asian success. Although the World Bank report questions whether other countries are capable of replicating the successful performance of the Asian economies, the report's critics argue that the withdrawal of the state from important economic functions, and the sudden and drastic opening of the Latin American economies to international competition, are not likely to foster rapid export growth and high savings or more investment in human capital. Even in the World Bank's analysis, government policies such as selective export subsidies, forced savings, and expenditures for schooling and health contributed to the success of the Asian economies. The real issue, therefore, is whether other governments are capable of replicating the successful performance of the Asian governments.

A third answer, which is not inconsistent with the previous two, focuses on the recent history of Latin America, e g , both the 1980s crisis and the reform process itself. Ironically, the "lost decade" of the 1980s was both the impetus to look for a new approach to development (and to begin to study the Asian experience) and the source of problems that have made it difficult to emulate the Asians.

A first problem arising from that period has to do with the capacity to respond to the incentives provided by the new economic policies to produce growth and exports. Here we need to look at the micro level, at firms, as well as at policies. It is often forgotten that the Asian countries also went through the import-substitution industrialization (ISI) process; the ISI firms then served as the basis for export-oriented industrialization. In the Latin American case, much of the potentially viable industry was drastically weakened by the debt crisis and by a rapid trade liberalization process that was much faster than Asia's. Although a small group of firms (often in alliance with foreign capital) has clearly become more internationally competitive, most firms are currently not able to respond positively to incentives.

A second problem focuses on the role of foreign capital, which is necessary both as a complement to domestic savings and as an actor in the production process. It is well known that during the 1980s, Latin America became an exporter of capital from the point of view of net transfers. This process clearly had a negative impact on the ability to invest and grow. In the early 1990s, foreign capital suddenly returned to the region, marking a new phase in the boom-bust cycle that has been typical of Latin America, in contrast with the more stable Asian pattern. In addition, the type of foreign capital arriving in Latin America had a different profile than that in Southeast Asia. (The newly industrialized countries, or NICs, in East Asia relied on their own capital to a significant extent, and they have recently become important investors in Southeast Asia.) That is, the Japanese and NIC investments have basically gone to establish factories to produce exports, while capital flows to Latin America have mainly been portfolio investments. The latter can flee rapidly, do not necessarily support investment, and tend to stimulate an appreciation of the currency that undermines export capacity (Calvo, Leiderman, and Reinhart 1994).

A third problem for Latin America arising out of the 1980s is an increase in the already high levels of inequality in both income and assets, at a time when evidence increasingly indicates a positive relationship between growth and equity. For example, the East Asian miracle report emphasizes that region's concept of shared growth and a virtuous cycle of equity and investment in human capital. Indeed, one observer goes so far as to say that the levels of equity and education in the early 1960s account for the high growth rates in Asia (Rodrik 1994). Without going this far, it seems reasonable to assume that greater inequality will make reforms more difficult in political as well as economic terms.

The issue of equity is closely tied to the fourth development coming out of the 1980s: the political model under which Asian and Latin American reforms have taken place. The earliest and most difficult phases of all the Asian experiences took place under authoritarian governments. The same has been true of Chile, which makes Latin Americans wary of holding it up as a model. After the experiences of the 1980s, Latin Americans have embraced democracy, as well as a greater reliance on the market. This simultaneity puts much greater emphasis on creating consensus with respect to economic policies. Thus, equity has an important role to play in narrowing the gap between winners and losers.

To summarize, there are a number of lessons from the Asian experience that most Latin Americans would accept. The question is why these lessons have not been implemented already and how to increase the chances that they will be carried out in the future. In thinking about these issues, it is crucial to focus on the particular Latin American context in the 1990s. Whatever may have worked for the East Asian NICs in the 1960s and 1970s, the world is different in the 1990s, and Latin American governments and the private sector are also operating in a different modality. Indeed, more relevant than the experience of the East Asian NICs (especially Korea and Taiwan, China) is that of the so-called second-tier NICs in Southeast Asia (Thailand, Malaysia, Indonesia, and even the Philippines). Their factor endowments and the (later) timing of the development surge in these countries are more similar to today's Latin America. Their less interventionist and more open approaches to development, with respect to both trade and foreign investment, also bear a greater resemblance to current Latin American thinking.

What seems most relevant from the Southeast Asian experience is a heavy emphasis on meso-level activities. That is, the state should continue to play an important role in development, by providing various kinds of necessary infrastructure in conjunction with the private sector. This includes physical infrastructure, such as improved communications and transportation systems. But it also includes development of a domestic capital market, assistance in gaining access to technology and adapting it to local circumstances, and help in breaking into export markets.

In terms of people and institutions, the Asian experience suggests establishing training programs for workers, improving primary and secondary education, and implementing significant programs for reducing poverty. Also, the means must be found to coordinate the activities and interests of workers, employers, and government. To be effective, a unified framework is needed to integrate policies on trade, industry, technology, worker training, and entrepreneurial development.

Without these kinds of activities, which benefit all sectors of the economy, it seems unlikely that Latin Americans can ever aspire to the achievements of their Asian counterparts. In carrying out such activities, greater knowledge of and closer contact with Asian countries could be very useful. The East Asian miracle has provided a valuable starting point, but Latin America must now move beyond it.

---

*Barbara Stallings is Officer in Charge, Economic Development Division, ECLAC, Santiago, Chile.*

# CHAPTER 3

# Growth of the Latin American and East Asian Economies

*Frederick Jaspersen**

East Asia and Latin America experienced markedly different patterns of growth during the three decades ending in 1990. This paper provides an overview of Latin America's development strategy during that period, and then identifies some of the important differences in approach taken by countries in the region compared with those in East Asia.

Countries in both regions pursued import-substituting industrialization strategies of development from the early post World War II period until the 1960s, when the East Asian countries shifted to an export-oriented approach. The paper highlights the different adjustment responses to the external shocks of the 1970s and early 1980s that help to explain the divergent growth paths of the two regions. A cross-sectional analysis is presented that identifies the key sources of growth of the two regions. The paper highlights the importance of high levels of investment in both human and physical capital and the mix of policies used to achieve this. In conclusion, it traces the interactions among demographic events, human capital accumulation, and income equality, which have contributed to the greater shared growth that occurred in East Asia.

The divergent growth paths of the two regions are especially instructive, because most countries in both regions pursued import-substituting industrialization in the postwar period. The anti-export bias of the Latin American trade regimes was reinforced by policies aimed at sustaining growth while protecting domestic industry. This frequently resulted in overvalued real exchange rates. As a consequence, from the early postwar years until the beginning of the 1960s, Latin America's exports stagnated. The combination of expansionary demand management and increasingly restrictive trade policies resulted in periodic outbreaks of inflation and recurring balance-of-payments crises. The result was a stop-go pattern of growth.

---

* This paper was prepared with the assistance of the staff of the IDB's Policy Research Division.

Latin American countries responded to the crisis by adopting a secondary import substitution strategy, while the East Asian countries responded by adopting an export-oriented strategy. East Asia's transition to an outward-oriented development strategy in the 1960s was preceded by control of inflation. This commitment to low inflation enabled East Asian countries to maintain their international competitiveness without the considerably skewed changes in the real exchange rate that occurred in Latin America.

The economic performances of Latin America and East Asia diverged sharply following the oil shocks of the 1970s and early 1980s. To replace the real resource loss, reestablish internal and external balance, and sustain rapid growth, the East Asian oil-importing countries implemented policies that expanded output of tradable goods more rapidly than domestic demand. Thus, these countries adjusted by exporting more. Latin American countries, in contrast, relied much more heavily on external borrowing at variable interest rates.

Despite the deterioration in the terms of trade, the real value of wages was generally maintained throughout this period by indexing wages to inflation. While East Asian countries maintained their outward-oriented policies, most countries in Latin America placed a renewed emphasis on import-substituting industrialization by tightening import restrictions and raising tariffs.

Several characteristics of the East Asian countries made it possible for them to successfully pursue an export-led growth strategy in the 1970s and 1980s. They were for the most part successful in controlling fiscal deficits and monetary expansion, holding inflation to low levels, avoiding excessive external and domestic indebtedness, and maintaining an economic environment conducive to high rates of savings and investment. They kept their economies open to foreign technology and put in effect an incentive system that concentrated the export drive on technology-intensive products. Flexible labor and capital markets enabled the real sector to react quickly to government initiatives, setting off new growth cycles that eased the recessionary impact of stabilization measures. Finally, by limiting distortions and tightly supervising the financial system, governments reduced the spillover from the real sector into the financial sector.

Throughout the past three decades, factor accumulation in Latin America and East Asia differed considerably. Labor participation rates have been stable and relatively low in Latin America. By contrast, participation rates, as well as their change over time, have been much higher in East Asia. Intersectoral transfers from agriculture to industry have also been much higher in the East Asian economies, and physical capital has accumulated much more rapidly, facilitated by rising domestic savings rates. The contribution of human capital has also differed markedly in the two regions. At the beginning of the period, East Asian countries were relatively well endowed with human capital, while Latin America generally was less well endowed, controlling for level of development. Differences in human capital accumulation are generally linked to changes in productivity; the most important factor differentiating East Asia from Latin America was its differentially higher growth of total factor productivity. Most analysts have attributed high productivity growth to the rapid growth and change in the structure of manufactured exports, which has enabled these economies to improve their technical efficiency.

The divergence in growth performance between East Asia and Latin America is traditionally attributed to human capital and demographic forces. New research in endogenous growth, however, suggests that if human-to-physical capital ratios are initially high, a country's subsequent economic performance will feature high rates of physical capital investment and income growth. The cross-sectional analysis presented in this chapter indicates that the initial level of schooling is significant and positively correlated with growth. Thus the link between demographic changes and accumulation of human capital appears to have played an important role in explaining the divergence in growth of the two regions.

An additional factor reinforcing this link is shared growth. Asian countries are more egalitarian in terms of income distribution, and the more egalitarian among them have grown faster. Even before their rapid development, the East Asian countries had roughly half the inequality of those in Latin America, and this more equal distribution of income in East Asia appears to have been translated into policy actions that gave rise to shared growth that favored mass education. This may have contributed strongly to a virtuous cycle in East Asia, where rapid expansion of education and reductions in inequality reinforced each other. In Latin America this dynamic was either absent or operated at a lower level.

Over the past 35 years, eight countries in East Asia increased their income per capita by nearly 6 per cent annually. Enormous growth-enhancing structural changes occurred in their economies during that period. Many of their industries now rank among the world's most technologically advanced manufacturing giants, and a number have set the standard for international best practice. Moreover, the benefits of this growth have been broadly shared by the population, not just by a narrow elite.

During the same period, Latin America's experience was mixed.

Rapid expansion of world trade in the 1960s benefited the Latin American economies. A few countries such as Brazil and Colombia, where reforms reduced the anti-export bias of their import-substitution regimes, were successful in expanding their exports. These countries raised their world market share and experienced rapid economic growth.

In the 1970s, Latin America achieved strong growth with relatively high levels of investment, financed in part by substantial external borrowing. The sustainability of this growth depended heavily on negative real international interest rates, on favorable terms of trade, and on rapid growth of export markets. Weakened by currency overvaluation, large fiscal deficits, inefficient public enterprises, and high levels of protection, the international competitiveness of the Latin American countries was compromised. Negative external shocks, combined with the deep structural weaknesses of these economies at the beginning of the 1980s, produced a sharp decline in investment and growth. By the end of the decade, per capita output in Latin America was at the same level as in 1980. Annual economic growth for the entire 25-year period averaged 1.2 percent, compared to 5.6 percent in East Asia. Even during the 1960–80 period of relatively strong growth in Latin America, growth of per capita output was about half that of East Asia.

## Diverging Development Strategies

The contrast in economic performance between Latin America and East Asia is stark. Throughout the past three decades East Asia has consistently grown more rapidly, and the divergence in growth has increased over time. During the decade preceding the first oil shock, real GDP in Asia expanded by 8.2 percent a year, compared to 5.0 percent in Latin America (see Table 3.1, following this chapter). Growth continued to be more rapid in Asia during the 1970s despite Latin America's increasingly heavy and unsustainable reliance on external savings to boost its investment. Divergence in growth was greatest in the 1980s period of adjustment. While East Asia adjusted to external shocks by rapidly increasing its exports, by high rates of output expansion, and by stable domestic prices, most Latin American countries experienced a vicious cycle of balance-of-payments crises, accelerated and persistent inflation, and declining per capita output.

The divergent growth paths of the two regions are especially instructive because import-substituting industrialization was pursued by most of their countries in the initial stages of postwar development. Both regions had an initial commodity export phase going back to the late nineteenth century, when output typically consisted of primary products and semi-processed raw materials. Latin American countries maintained relatively open trade regimes during this period. Macroeconomic adjustment was, for the most part, achieved through change in the level of domestic economic activity, since most countries were on the gold standard up to the early 1930s. With the collapse of international commodity and capital markets and sharply increased protection in the industrial countries in the early 1930s, most Latin American countries attempted to delink from the world economy by imposing discriminatory trade restrictions and exchange controls, and by implementing counter-cyclical fiscal and monetary policies (Diaz-Alejandro 1983).

This shift in policy heralded the beginning of half a century of uninterrupted import-substituting industrialization (ISI), a strategy of circumstance rather than deliberate policy design. In its initial phase, this strategy aimed at producing locally most of the basic consumer goods that were being imported, including processed food products, clothing, textiles, and footwear. Production of import substitutes was encouraged through government allocation of bank credit, foreign exchange, and essential inputs at subsidized prices. At the same time, the production of traditional exports was discouraged by domestic pricing policies, overvalued exchange rates, export taxes, and the exclusion of foreign competition.

What began as a policy response to the collapse of the world economy in the early 1930s was reinforced by the disruption of trade in manufactures during World War II. Following the war and throughout the 1950s, trade policy focused exclusively on protecting emerging manufacturing sectors and creating new second-stage import substitution industries. Protection was provided through a complex system of multiple exchange rates, high and widely differentiated tariffs, and nontariff barriers (Table 3.2). Because of delayed adjustment and erratic fiscal and monetary policies, real exchange rates fluctuated widely. While the initial consequence of protection was rapid expansion of manufacturing for the domestic market, growth slowed as the easiest opportunities for import substitution were exhausted.

An important result of ISI was slower export growth. The trade regime's anti-export bias was reinforced by policies to sustain growth while protecting domestic industry, which frequently resulted in overvalued real exchange rates. As a consequence, from the early postwar years until the early 1960s, exports from Latin America stagnated.

Import substitution policies shifted relative prices between agriculture and industry, promoting industrial growth at the expense of agriculture. As the resources taxed away from primary exports failed to increase, the budget came under pressure from subsidies for industrial investment and from growing direct government involvement in import-substituting industries such as steel, petroleum, and chemicals that produced for the local market (Corbo 1986). The combination of expansionary demand management and increasingly restrictive trade policies resulted in periodic outbreaks of inflation and recurring balance-of-payments crises. The result was a stop-go pattern of growth. What began as a policy response to transitory external shocks was coopted by new industrialist and labor groups, which successfully lobbied for protections that became enshrined in the prevailing development ideology.

Most countries in Latin America and East Asia were pursuing import-substituting industrialization policies during this period. But East Asian countries were using tariffs and nontariff barriers as major protective devices, and they simultaneously introduced powerful export incentives in the early 1960s to offset the bias of the import regime. Policymakers in Latin America, however, were slower to recognize the shortcomings of the ISI development strategy and the transitional nature of these policies. Over time, a system more conducive to industrial efficiency and export expansion was needed.

In the late 1960s, a few Latin American countries, especially Chile, Brazil, and Colombia, introduced some measures aimed at reducing the anti-export bias. Chile, followed by Brazil and Colombia, introduced crawling-peg exchange rates, which accommodated high rates of inflation while avoiding overvaluation of the real exchange rate. To promote nontraditional exports, fiscal and other incentives were put in place. Where these and other reforms went farthest, gains in efficiency and growth were greatest. This was especially true in Brazil, where economic growth was sustained at close to 10 percent a year from 1968 to 1977.

Comparison of the incentive systems in Latin America and East Asia indicate that export incentives were much more effective in East Asia. Even in Brazil, despite the successful export promotion program of the 1960s, there was still a strong anti-export bias in the trade regime. The limited evidence available supports the conclusion that the incentive system remained heavily biased against exports. Balassa (1991) provides some data on effective protection rates, which at the end of the 1960s reached 47 percent in Argentina, compared with 5 in Taiwan and 10 in Korea. For manufacturing, the corresponding figures were 97, 19, and 1 percent.

Divergence in development strategy stemmed from the ways countries in both regions responded to the problems of continuing ISI. The virtuous cycle experienced by the East Asian countries, while helped by the favorable global environment in the 1960s, was also partly due to the authorities' success in controlling the rapid inflation that raged in the early postwar years.

The East Asian countries began to emphasize the exports of manufactured goods at a time of extraordinary dynamism in the world economy. World industrial production in the 1960s was growing at 5.6 percent, and world trade at 7.3 percent. During this period of relative stability in the international economy, the industrialized countries were experiencing low inflation and high employment. The rapid growth of the East Asian countries' export earnings in the 1960s enabled them to remove the dual constraints of foreign exchange shortages and low domestic savings, making it possible for imports and investment to increase rapidly. Exploitation of their dynamic comparative advantage enabled them to raise productivity and overall economic efficiency. Rapid productivity growth restrained the rise of unit labor costs. This, combined with the stable import prices then prevailing, facilitated the maintenance of domestic price stability. These developments were helped by the rising savings rates that resulted in part from the accelerating growth of per capita income, and by the stronger domestic financial markets facilitated by stable domestic prices.

In many Latin American countries, by contrast, failure to expand exports and the lagging response of domestic investment and imports to cyclical changes in primary exports caused periodic balance-of-payments difficulties and macroeconomic imbalance. Under this pattern of development, the growth of labor productivity and per capita income remained modest, limiting the growth of real wages. This, in turn, restricted the authorities' policy options for controlling inflation. In a number of countries, the authorities relied on indexation schemes to ease the distortions caused by inflation, perpetuating the vicious cycle (Lin 1988).

Why did Latin American countries respond to a crisis in primary ISI by adopting a secondary ISI strategy, while the East Asian countries responded by adopting an export-oriented strategy? Several authors have argued that lack of social consensus was an important factor. This, in turn, depended largely on differences in natural resources, market size, population pressures, and historic circumstance. East Asia had no choice but to pursue an export strategy, while some Latin American countries had larger potential markets. In Latin America, vested industrial and labor interests associated with import substitution were strongly entrenched by the 1950s. In East Asian countries, neither the landed class nor organized labor constituted powerful political groups; the former had lost power through land reforms instituted early in the postwar years, whereas the latter had never become important, partly because of the Confucian ethic (Table 3.3). This situation allowed a group of technocrats to push through policy reforms in favor of new industrial export activity at a crucial moment in the industrialization process.

Japan, for example, undertook a variety of institutional reforms in order to diffuse social tensions in rural areas, develop more cooperative labor management relations, institute fiscal discipline, and improve financial intermediation between savings and investment. Taiwan and Korea also, in addition to land reforms in the early 1950s, carried out intensive reform of trade policy to shift the overall thrust of incentives in favor of export activity. In Latin America, however, both the rural landed class and urban organized labor had considerable but opposing influence with the import-substituting sectors (Sachs 1986). Under these circumstances, political conflicts were frequent.

In addition to the shift of policy incentives in favor of export activity, the growth of manufacturing exports was supported by stability of the real exchange rate. In East Asia, the transition to an outward-oriented development strategy in the 1960s was preceded by control of inflation in the early 1950s. During the 1960s inflation in East Asia was below 5 percent, compared to 21 percent in Latin America (Table 3.4). This commitment to low inflation enabled East Asian countries to maintain their international competitiveness without having to rely excessively on indexing and nominal devaluations. By contrast, Latin American countries required periodic devaluations to maintain their international competitiveness. Frequently, such devaluations were implemented with a lag, resulting in considerably skewed changes in the real exchange rate.

Both stabilization efforts and trade policy reforms in Latin America were inadequate, in part because the rich natural resource endowment and the cyclical expansion of primary exports sometimes permitted the removal of foreign exchange constraints, enabling authorities to continue inward-oriented industrialization. In countries such as Chile and Argentina, inflationary pressure remained strong and the incentive systems remained biased against exports. Despite the favorable environment of the 1960s, these countries failed to establish a sustainable pattern of economic growth. Chile did not significantly strengthen its export incentives, while its fiscal deficit remained large during the second half of the 1960s. Because of social and political pressures, Argentina was unable to keep a consistent set of policies in place long enough to have an impact on economic performance (Corbo 1986). After failing to establish a sustainable pattern of economic growth over a long period, despite a rich resource base, Chile and Argentina eventually implemented more comprehensive liberalization and stabilization measures during the 1970s and beyond.

In contrast, Brazil was successful in accelerating growth of its exports and of real output for a decade, beginning in the mid 1960s. The improvement in Brazil's economic performance followed major policy reforms in the mid 1960s, including a significant strengthening of export incentives, a sharp reduction in fiscal deficits, and the institution of a variety of indexation schemes, which initially helped reduce the frequency of wage adjustments while protecting the domestic financial system. Inflation was reduced, savings and investment rose, and growth of exports and output accelerated.

### Response to External Shocks

Divergence in the economic performance of Latin America and East Asia increased sharply following the oil shocks of the 1970s and early 1980s. In the Latin American countries, growth of output fell from 4.9 percent a year in the 1970s to 2 percent in the 1980s. Growth of the East Asian countries also declined but by much less: from 7.8 percent in the 1970s to 6.6 percent in the 1980s. Why were the East Asian countries more successful in sustaining rapid growth? Was it because Latin American countries were affected more severely by the external shocks of the 1970s?

The sharp increase in oil prices in 1973–74 and in 1979–80, and the emergence of a new and massive supply of international credit at negative real rates of interest, had far-reaching consequences. The increased availability of credit at low interest rates was initially favorable for countries in both regions. Although it is difficult to measure the magnitude of these external shocks and their impact on economies with different degrees of openness and structures of production, available evidence indicates that on average, the magnitude and direction of the shocks were roughly equivalent for the two regions. The terms of trade shock had differential effects, however.

As oil importers, Korea and Thailand in Asia, as well as Brazil, Chile, Colombia, and Costa Rica in Latin America faced sharp declines in their terms of trade during the oil price increases of 1973–74 and 1979–80 (Table 3.5). Indonesia, Malaysia, Mexico, Venezuela and to some extent Argentina, as exporters of oil, benefited from the oil price increase.

Columns 1 and 4 in Table 3.5 report results from a recent study on the size of external shocks as a share of GDP (Little, et al. 1993) for two periods, the mid 1970s and the early 1980s. The study found that the 1974–75 shocks for Korea and Thailand were smaller than those faced by Chile and Costa Rica, about the same as for Brazil, and greater than those experienced by Argentina, Colombia, and Mexico. For the 1979–81 period, the shock due to deterioration in the terms of trade and rising interest rates was about 6 per cent of GDP for Korea and Thailand. This was less than for Chile, somewhat more than for Brazil, and much more than for Argentina. Argentina, Mexico, and Venezuela had positive (or slightly negative) net shocks, while Korea and Thailand had very large negative shocks relative to GDP. If the relative impacts of the shocks were similar, why were the two regions affected so differently?

The net impact of these shocks on most countries in the two regions was to diminish the real resources at their command. They could have adjusted to this decline through direct income effects (reduced income and absorption) and indirect monetary effects (loss of international reserves, contraction of the monetary base, and decline in aggregate demand). Almost all the countries attempted to offset these contractionary forces by replacing the real resource loss, so that essential intermediate and capital goods imports could be maintained at levels required to sustain rapid economic growth. But this was done by different means in Latin America and East Asia.

To replace the real resource loss, reestablish internal and external balance, and sustain rapid growth, the East Asian countries implemented classic absorption reduction, switching, and incentive policies, which were successful in expanding output of tradable goods more rapidly than domestic demand. So they adjusted by exporting more (Table 3.6). Latin American countries also expanded their exports, but at a slower pace, and relied much more heavily on external borrowing at variable interest rates. Despite deterioration in the terms of trade, real wages were generally maintained throughout this period by indexing wages to inflation. While East Asian countries maintained their outward-oriented policies, most countries in Latin America renewed their emphasis on ISI by tightening import restrictions and raising tariffs.

Both East Asia and Latin America were successful in sustaining relatively rapid growth throughout this period. But whereas East Asia added to the strength of its economic base, making it possible to achieve strong economic growth in the 1980s, the Latin American countries increased their vulnerability to external shocks. When new interest rate and terms of trade shocks occurred in the early 1980s, their sharply increased debt burden and the deteriorating world markets for their exports led to a sudden shift in creditors' perceptions. No longer able to finance macroeconomic imbalance with external borrowing, the national authorities were compelled to undertake the long-delayed stabilization and adjustment efforts. Delay in adjustment resulted in a "lost decade" of growth.

By contrast, adjustment in the East Asian countries was generally completed by the late 1970s. They were well prepared to absorb the impact of the second oil shock and regain export and economic growth in the early 1980s as the world economy recovered. Even Korea, which overexpanded from 1979 to 1980, quickly undertook stabilization and adjustment policies, regained internal and external balance, and resumed strong growth in 1982–83.

Several characteristics of the East Asian countries made it possible for them to successfully pursue an export-led growth strategy in the 1970s and 1980s. As analyzed in detail in *The East Asian Miracle,* macroeconomic policy was insulated from domestic politics and was designed more to maintain price and real exchange rate stability (World Bank 1993a). For the most part they were able to control fiscal deficits and monetary expansion, hold inflation to low levels, avoid excessive external and domestic indebtedness, and maintain an economic environment conducive to high rates of savings and investment. Keeping their economies open to foreign technology, they established an incentive system that had the result of concentrating the export drive on technology-intensive products (Tables 3.7 and 3.8). Flexible labor and capital markets enabled the real sector to react quickly to government initiatives, setting off new growth cycles that eased the recessionary impact of stabilization measures. Finally, by limiting distortions and tightly supervising the financial system, the government reduced spillover from the real sector into the financial sector.

Differences in macroeconomic policy also help to explain the less successful performance of the Latin American countries. Inflation was much higher in Latin America, averaging 75 percent annually in the three decades ending in 1990, compared to 18 percent for all developing countries and 8 percent in East Asia. Latin American countries were burdened by the distortionary effects of high and variable rates of inflation, by wide swings in relative prices between tradables and nontradables, and by the disincentive effects on exports, savings, and investment. East Asian countries never became dependent on the inflation tax because fiscal deficits were generally held within financeable limits. Seigniorage (government revenue from the manufacture of money) from 1975 to 1985 was much higher in Latin America than in East Asia, as Table 3.9 shows.

The experience of the East Asian countries illustrates the important interaction between macroeconomic policy and the beneficial impact of other pro-growth policies. By maintaining relative price stability, they were able to sustain an environment conducive to high rates of savings, investment, and growth. Budget deficits in East Asia were not smaller than in Latin America, but financing constraints were less binding (see Tables 3.10 and 3.11). Because growth was higher, the East Asian countries were able to finance larger fiscal deficits while avoiding price instability, since higher growth increases the demand for financial assets.

## Accounting for Growth in the Two Regions

Previous sections focused on the differences in development strategy and macroeconomic policy to help explain the diverging economic performance of the two regions. This section identifies the sources of growth that have resulted from those policies, as well as the factors that explain the growth disparity between the two regions.

Both neoclassical theories and the new endogenous growth theories predict that higher levels of accumulation of physical and human capital are key sources to per capita income growth, although they differ on whether economies will converge over time. In both approaches, factor accumulation does not explain all economic growth. For neoclassical theorists the increase in productivity that cannot be accounted for by accumulation of factor inputs is the change in total factor productivity (TFP), also referred to as technical progress or the Solow Residual. The new endogenous growth theories explain this residual by the interaction between "ideas" and accumulation, which results in increasing returns to scale of physical and human capital (Romer 1986).

Throughout the past three decades, factor accumulation in Latin America has differed widely from that of East Asia. Demographic developments in the two regions, analyzed in the next section, have led to substantial differences in aggregate labor participation rates. Total labor force participation rates have been stable and relatively low in Latin America. By contrast, participation rates, as well as their change over the period, have been much higher in East Asia (Table 3.12).

Intersectoral transfers from agriculture to industry have also been unusually high in the East Asian economies. Industrial employment has grown four times more rapidly in East Asia than in Latin America (Table 3.13). The rapid increase of the share of industrial output, and in particular of manufacturing output, in total output has been unusually rapid compared to other developing economies, especially those in Latin America (Table 3.14).

Physical capital accumulation has also been much faster in East Asia. Except for Japan and Hong Kong, investment-to-GDP ratios have risen rapidly over time (Table 3.15). In recent years, the average investment share of GDP in Latin America has been half that in East Asia. Higher investment rates in East Asia have been accompanied by high and rising domestic savings rates, averaging about 50 percent higher than in Latin America (Table 3.16). For most Latin American countries, the domestic savings ratio has been relatively stable throughout the period.

Investment rates in Korea increased from 5 percent in the early 1950s to 15 percent in the mid 1960s, to 30 percent in 1985, and to almost 40 percent in 1991. This extraordinary accumulation has been replicated almost exactly in the other three Southeast Asian NICs. It can be explained by differences in the growth and composition of public investment in infrastructure, financial sector policies, the macroeconomic environment, and other policies (see World Bank 1993a). Growth of investment by the private sector also accounts for a substantial portion of these high rates.

The pace of human capital accumulation has also differed markedly in the two regions. While primary school enrollment rates are now about the same in the two regions, they have risen more rapidly in East Asia. There is an even larger difference in secondary school enrollment. By 1990, East Asia had an average 64 percent enrollment rate in secondary education, compared to 53 percent in Latin America (Table 3.17).

Figure 3.1 plots secondary enrollment rates in 1965 against per capita income. At the beginning of the period, East Asian countries were relatively well endowed with human capital compared to the rest of the world and Latin America generally was less well endowed, controlling for level of development. Differences in human capital accumulation are linked in complex ways with demographic events, income inequality, and public investment efforts in primary and secondary schooling. The next section of this paper analyzes the interactions among demographic transition, income inequality, and human capital accumulation.

Following similar studies of productivity growth, columns (1) and (2) in Table 3.18 report the results of a cross-country growth regression where the dependent variable is the average rate of real per capita income growth, using Summers-Heston data from 1960–85 for a sample of 113 countries. This specification includes as explanatory variables the following: the average share of investment in GDP over the period 1960–85, measures of human capital based on schooling enrollment rates in 1960, and the rate of growth of the economically active population. The regression also includes a shift variable constructed with the GDP level in 1960, which captures the

**Figure 3.1  Secondary Enrollment Rates, 1965**
*(Percentage of age group)*

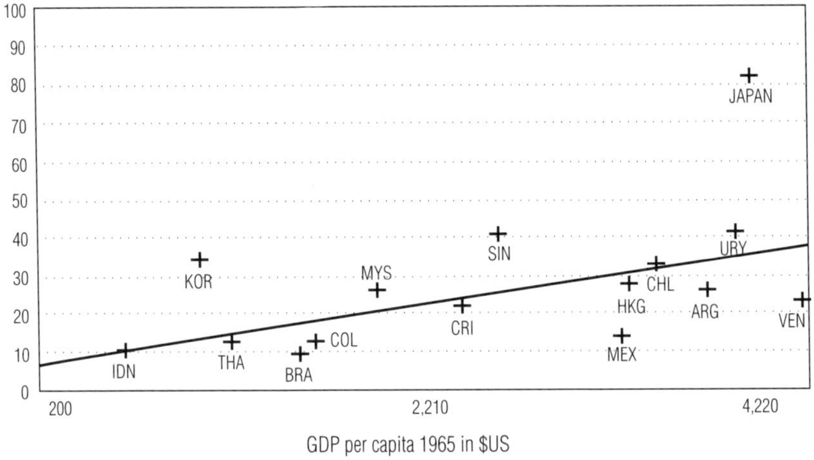

GDP per capita 1965 in $US

*Source:* World Bank data.

observed more rapid growth experienced by the poorest countries (a catch-ing up effect). The estimated equation compares well with alternative speci-fications used in cross-country growth studies (Barro 1991). The overall fit is good and the coefficients of the variables are correctly signed and significant.

Residuals of a regression like this can be interpreted as growth of TFP. To account for the different growth performance of the two regions, dummy variables for Latin America and East Asia have been included in the regressions. The Latin American dummy is negative and significant, whereas for East Asia it is positive and significant. The component of TFP growth, independent of the convergence term, seems to be driving much of the exceptional growth of the East Asian economies, and also the lower growth of Latin America.

This is illustrated graphically in Figure 3.2. The figure plots the com-ponents of 1960–85 GDP per capita growth and of the investment/GDP ra-tio, which are orthogonal to 1960–85 labor force growth, to the primary school enrollment rate in 1960, and to the 1960 initial GDP per capita level. It provides a partial scatter of growth on investment, controlling for labor, human capital and the component of TFP change related to the catching up

**Figure 3.2 GDP Growth and Average Investment, 1960-85**

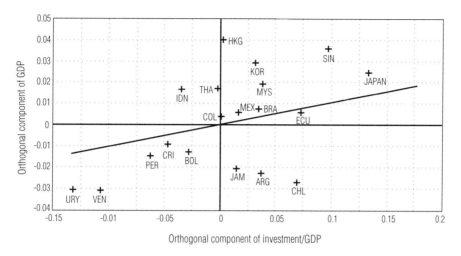

*Note:* The X and Y components are orthogonal to real GDP per capita in 1960, growth rate of population 1960-85 and primary school enrollment in 1960.
*Source:* World Bank data.

effect. All East Asian economies are positive outliers, indicating their common trait as productivity-driven economies compared to the Latin American sample, with the exception of Colombia, Mexico, and Brazil, which lie close to the predicted relationship between investment and productivity growth. Most analysts have attributed this high productivity growth to the rapid growth and change in the structure of manufactured exports (Table 3.8), which has enabled these economies to improve their technical efficiency (Pack and Page 1994).

Some authors have argued that the difference in productivity performance between the two regions can be attributed to differences in the role of government and to political instability. In column (3) of Table 3.18, the specification is expanded to include two additional variables that capture the size of nonproductive government expenditure and a measure of political disruption based on the number of revolutions and coups per year (following the Barro 1991 specification). The regression results confirm that East Asia is still a positive outlier, while Latin America appears as a negative outlier and more significant than in the previous specification.

## Demographic Forces, Human Capital, and Shared Growth

A number of factors help to explain the divergent growth of Latin America and East Asia. Among the HPAEs, substantial investment in infrastructure supportive of private investment was further facilitated by a high rate of savings and effective means of allocating savings to productive investment. Their other advantages included: efficient use of advanced technology imported from industrial countries; a stable political climate; availability of better educated and trained human resources; and an export-oriented strategy. These factors, in turn, are linked in complex ways with demographic developments.

Traditional approaches have attributed a good share of the differences in growth performance between East Asia and Latin America to human capital and demographic forces (Denison and Chung 1976). On different theoretical grounds, the new endogenous growth literature implies that if human-to-physical capital ratios are initially high, a country's subsequent economic performance will feature high rates of physical capital investment and income growth. In the previous section it was shown that growth is significant and positively correlated with initial (1960) schooling levels. This relationship is especially strong for East Asian countries (Korea and Japan) where growth from 1960 to 1985 was raised by as much as 1.5 percent a year due to above average initial levels of schooling (Barro 1991). How were the high returns to initial human capital endowments related to and reinforced by demographic events?

Population growth rates are subject to changes in fertility, mortality, and migration patterns. These factors in turn play a vital role in the multidimensional process of demographic transition and therefore in the accumulation of human capital, a key factor of production. In the process of slowing population growth, the labor force continues to grow for a number of years after fertility declines, thereby increasing the percentage of the population engaged in productive activities. As fertility declines, more economic resources can be allocated to those in the labor force in order to equip them with better physical capital. In addition, increased availability of resources facilitates improvements not only in the coverage of the education system, but also in its quality.

The high-performing countries of East Asia (Japan, Korea, Singapore, Hong Kong, and Taiwan) are now at the latter stage of the demographic transition which produced these economic advantages. To show the diversities of the demographic transition, a rough index has been computed using a formula proposed by Cho and Togashi (1984) that takes into account fertility, mortality, and urbanization rates. Table 3.19 indicates that Japan, Hong Kong, and Singapore completed their demographic transition by 1985–90, with Korea being very close to completion. The process in Hong Kong and Singapore during 1960–75 was especially rapid. The three other Asian countries shown in Table 3.20 are still at an early stage in their transition, but the pace at which current levels have been achieved is impressive. By 1985–90 most countries in Latin America had reached only an intermediate stage (0.80), and the pace of their transition has been much slower.

A second element of the demographic transition relates to the intertemporal changes in the relationship between demographic factors and human resource development. As a result of both pronounced fertility declines and remarkable mortality improvements in East Asia, the age composition of these countries has been changing rapidly since the 1960s. Conventional wisdom holds that the decline in the dependency rate in East Asia, compared to that in Latin America, stimulated a greater accumulation and capital deepening through increases in the saving rate. In addition, one can also expect human capital responses, such as increased investments in schooling. Low dependency rates among the young imply sparsely populated cohorts among those of schooling age, placing weak demands on the schooling sector. School systems are likely to respond either by admitting some students who otherwise might not have attended, or by raising school quality. Low dependency rates among the young may also make it easier for parents to send their children to school. On the other hand, falling dependency rates among the young are likely to coincide with rising dependency rates among the old. This may serve to deflect public resources from educating the young to supporting the old, especially among the advanced countries in East Asia that have moved into more mature demographic stages.

This link between demographic changes and accumulation of human capital appears to have played an important role in explaining the divergence in growth of the two regions. An additional factor has reinforced this link: the phenomenon of shared growth. Traditionally, economists have supported a growth and equality tradeoff, which assumes that redistribution from the poor to the rich increases the supply of private savings and thus raises the rate of capital accumulation. The current competing view holds that this Kuznets-Kaldor tradition overlooked a vast range of policy options that would enhance growth by raising the value of the assets of the less well-off (i.e., investment in public health, mass education, and rural infrastructure). The now well-documented East Asian shared growth experience, and recent studies for Latin America (Morley 1995a-b) not only reject this tradeoff, but support the view that equality fosters growth (Williamson 1993; Birdsall and Sabot 1993).

Tables 3.20 and 3.21 show unambiguously that Asian countries are more egalitarian, and that the more egalitarian among them have grown faster. The East Asian countries had roughly half the inequality of those in Latin America. The initial inequality in Latin American agrarian economies, characterized by large-scale commercial farms *(latifundios)* in which land ownership was highly concentrated, may have created an inegalitarian policy regime throughout post-World War II Latin America. By contrast, East Asian agricultural technology, based on rice, encouraged small-scale family farms, and labor-intensive and less concentrated land holdings. Thus, there was a more egalitarian starting point that fostered creation of an egalitarian policy regime (Williamson 1993).

Japan, Korea, and Taiwan, China introduced land reform in the late 1940s and early 1950s. Not only was land redistributed, thereby raising the incomes of the poorest, but taxpayers (largely the middle class) did not have to pay much since the value of government bonds used to compensate landowners was eroded by rapid inflation (Sachs 1985). At the same time, the destruction of wealth by war and inflation had redistributive effects. First, it equalized incomes, since the rich held most of the physical and financial assets. Second, it may have contributed to the impressive saving rates characteristic of postwar East Asia.

These initial conditions translated later into policy actions that gave rise to shared growth favoring mass education in East Asia. Over time, this may have contributed strongly to a virtuous cycle in East Asia where rapid expansion of education and reductions in inequality reinforced each other (Birdsall and Sabot 1993). In Latin America, however, this dynamic operated at a much lower level. A more egalitarian society would have fostered more rapid human capital accumulation, since the poor would have had wider access to education.

*Frederick Jaspersen is Lead Economist in the Economics Department, International Finance Corporation.*

## Table 3.1  Growth Performance
*(Annual percentage growth averaged over the periods)*

| | Real GDP Growth Rates | | | | Real Per Capita Growth | |
|---|---|---|---|---|---|---|
| | 1960-70 | 1970-80 | 1980-91 | 1980-85 | 1965-90 | 1980-90 |
| **Latin America** | | | | | | |
| Argentina | 4.2 | 2.2 | -0.4 | -1.4 | -0.3 | -1.5 |
| Brazil | 5.4 | 8.4 | 2.5 | 1.3 | 3.3 | 0.5 |
| Chile | 4.5 | 2.8 | 3.6 | -1.1 | 0.4 | 1.6 |
| Colombia | 5.1 | 5.9 | 3.7 | 1.9 | 2.3 | 1.2 |
| Mexico | 7.2 | 5.2 | 1.2 | 0.8 | 2.8 | -0.5 |
| Uruguay | 1.2 | 3.5 | 0.6 | -3.9 | 0.8 | -0.4 |
| Venezuela | 6.0 | 5.0 | 1.5 | -1.6 | -1.0 | -1.3 |
| Costa Rica | 6.5 | 5.8 | 3.1 | 0.5 | 1.4 | 0.7 |
| *Average* | 5.0 | 4.9 | 2.0 | -0.4 | 1.2 | 0.0 |
| **East Asia** | | | | | | |
| Japan | 10.9 | 5.0 | 4.2 | 3.8 | 4.1 | 3.6 |
| Korea | 8.6 | 9.5 | 9.6 | 7.9 | 7.1 | 8.7 |
| Singapore | 8.8 | 8.5 | 6.6 | 6.5 | 6.5 | 5.3 |
| Hong Kong | 10.0 | 9.3 | 6.9 | 5.9 | 6.2 | 5.6 |
| Taiwan | | | | | 6.8 | |
| Indonesia | 3.9 | 7.6 | 5.6 | 3.5 | 4.5 | 3.9 |
| Malaysia | 6.5 | 7.8 | 5.7 | 5.5 | 4.8 | 2.9 |
| Thailand | 8.4 | 7.2 | 7.9 | 5.1 | 4.4 | 5.9 |
| *Average* | 8.2 | 7.8 | 6.6 | 5.5 | 5.6 | 5.4 |

*Source:* World Bank data.

## Table 3.2  Effective Rates of Protection, Late 1960s and Late 1970s
*(Percent)*

| | Japan | Malaysia | | Indonesia | Argentina | | Brazil | Chile | |
|---|---|---|---|---|---|---|---|---|---|
| Sectors | L60s | L60s | L70s | L70s | L60s | L70s | L60s | L60s | L70s |
| Textiles | 31 | | 58 | 232 | 498 | 83 | 379 | 492 | 14 |
| Apparel | 33 | 400 | 45 | | | 75 | | | 14 |
| Wood products | 26 | 33 | 38 | -1 | 320 | | 45 | -4 | 15 |
| Paper and printing | 18 | 140 | 66 | 87 | 601 | 118 | 118 | 95 | 17 |
| Chemicals | 18 | 230 | 32 | 28 | 294 | 60 | 59 | 64 | 13 |
| Rubber | 22 | 60 | 129 | | 213 | 122 | 136 | 304 | 15 |
| Iron and steel | 30 | 84 | 63 | 18 | | 42 | | | |
| Metal manufacturing | 20 | 40 | 26 | | 347 | 64 | 58 | 92 | 15 |
| Nonelectrical machinery | 15 | 1600 | 89 | | | 62 | 41 | 76 | 13 |
| Electrical machinery | 17 | 130 | 4 | | 393 | 73 | 215 | 449 | 13 |
| Transportation | 32 | 185 | 59 | | | 408 | 151 | 271 | |
| Nonmetallic minerals | 16 | | | 64 | 20 | 86 | 1 | | |
| Metallic minerals | 34 | | | | | | 35 | | |

*Sources:* For Asia, World Bank (1993); for Latin America, Papageorgiou et al (1991).

**Table 3.3  Labor Union Strength Indicators, 1983**
*(Percent of unionization)*

| | |
|---|---|
| *Latin America* | |
| Argentina | 16.6 |
| Brazil | 48.6 |
| Chile | 28.5 |
| Mexico | 23.6 |
| Colombia | 24.0 |
| *Average* | 28.3 |
| | |
| *East Asia* | |
| Korea | 7.0 |
| Taiwan | 17.3 |
| Thailand | 1.1 |
| Malaysia | 8.7 |
| Indonesia | 4.8 |
| *Average* | 7.8 |

*Source:* Banuri and Amadeo (1991).

**Table 3.4  Inflation, 1960-91**
*(Average annual percent growth of Consumer Price Index)*

| | 1960-70 | 1970-80 | 1980-91 | 1960-91 |
|---|---|---|---|---|
| **Latin America** | | | | |
| Argentina | 21.7 | 130.8 | 416.9 | 197.1 |
| Brazil | 46.1 | 36.7 | 327.6 | 143.0 |
| Chile | 33.2 | 185.6 | 20.5 | 77.9 |
| Colombia | 11.9 | 22.0 | 25.0 | 19.8 |
| Mexico | 3.6 | 19.3 | 66.5 | 31.0 |
| Uruguay | 51.1 | 62.3 | 64.4 | 59.4 |
| Venezuela | 1.3 | 12.1 | 21.2 | 11.8 |
| Costa Rica | 1.9 | 15.2 | 22.9 | 13.6 |
| **East Asia** | | | | |
| Japan | 4.9 | 7.5 | 1.5 | 4.5 |
| Korea | 17.4 | 19.8 | 5.6 | 14.0 |
| Singapore | 1.1 | 5.1 | 1.9 | 2.7 |
| Hong Kong | 2.4 | 8.2 | 7.5 | 6.1 |
| Malaysia | -0.3 | 7.5 | 1.7 | 2.9 |
| Thailand | 1.8 | 9.9 | 3.7 | 5.1 |
| Indonesia | 20.5 | 8.5 | 9.6 | |

*Source:* World Bank, *World Tables, 1982, 1987,* and *1993.*

**Table 3.5 Impact of External Shocks**

| | Mid 1970s | | | Early 1980s | |
|---|---|---|---|---|---|
| Author: | Little | Helleiner | Helleiner | Little | Sachs |
| Period: | 1974-75 | 1975-78 | 1979-81 | 1979-81 | 1979-83 |
| Measure: Terms of trade effects | Terms of trade effects + export effects+ interest rate effects | | | Terms of trade effects + interest rate effects | |
| **Latin America** | | | | | |
| Argentina | -1.2 | -2.2 | -0.9 | -1.8 | 1.6 |
| Brazil | -3.1 | -1.6 | -3.8 | -5.2 | -5.0 |
| Chile | -17.5 | -19.4 | -1.8 | -9.2 | -6.2 |
| Mexico | -1.5 | 1.0 | -1.0 | -0.3 | 1.2 |
| Venezuela | | | | | 16.2 |
| Colombia | -0.2 | 1.6 | -2.8 | -4.3 | -2.8 |
| Costa Rica | -6.1 | | | 3.7 | |
| **East Asia** | | | | | |
| Korea | -3.2 | -5.2 | -9.0 | -6.3 | -3.8 |
| Indonesia | 14.0 | 14.0 | 7.8 | 10.7 | 6.2 |
| Malaysia | | 8.3 | -1.3 | | 4.8 |
| Thailand | -3.8 | -1.9 | -3.4 | -6.1 | -3.3 |

*Sources:* Little, et al. (1993), Helleiner (1986), Sachs (1985).

**Table 3.6 Export Growth**
*(Average annual growth rate)*

| | 1960-70 | 1970-80 | 1980-91 | 1960-91 |
|---|---|---|---|---|
| **Latin America** | | | | |
| Argentina | 3.8 | 8.3 | 2.1 | 4.6 |
| Brazil | 5.3 | 8.8 | 4.3 | 6.1 |
| Chile | 0.7 | 9.5 | 5.2 | 5.1 |
| Colombia | 2.6 | 2.2 | 12.0 | 5.8 |
| Mexico | 3.4 | 8.6 | 3.5 | 5.1 |
| Uruguay | 2.8 | 5.9 | 3.1 | 3.9 |
| Venezuela | 1.1 | 7.2 | 0.1 | -1.9 |
| Costa Rica | 9.6 | 4.5 | 4.6 | 6.2 |
| *Average* | 3.7 | 5.1 | 4.4 | 4.4 |
| **East Asia** | | | | |
| Japan | | | 3.9 | |
| Korea | 34.7 | 20.2 | 12.2 | 22.0 |
| Singapore | 4.2 | | 8.9 | |
| Hong Kong | 12.7 | 9.4 | 4.4 | 8.7 |
| Indonesia | 3.5 | 4.4 | 4.5 | 4.1 |
| Malaysia | 6.1 | 3.8 | 10.9 | 7.1 |
| Thailand | 6.2 | 2.6 | 14.4 | 7.9 |
| *Average* | 11.2 | 8.1 | 8.5 | 9.2 |

*Source:* World Bank, *World Tables 1993.*

**Table 3.7  Technology-Intensive Products**

*(Average annual growth rate)*

|  | Exports | Imports |
| --- | --- | --- |
| *Latin America* | | |
| Argentina | 10.4 | 7.4 |
| Brazil | 23.7 | 5.6 |
| Chile | n.a. | 10.0 |
| Colombia | 12.1 | 10.5 |
| Mexico | 20.3 | 10.2 |
| Uruguay | 19.1 | 10.5 |
| *Average* | 17.1 | 9.0 |
| *East Asia* | | |
| Korea | 36.4 | 20.7 |
| Singapore | 25.1 | 18.7 |
| Hong Kong | 20.4 | 19.9 |
| Philippines | 36.4 | 7.9 |
| Indonesia | 20.8 | 18.0 |
| Malaysia | 33.2 | 14.8 |
| Thailand | 44.2 | 17.8 |
| *Average* | 27.0 | 17.6 |

*Note:* Technology-intensive products include Standard International Trade Classification (SITC) codes 51, 54, 58, 71, 72, 73 and 86.
*Source:* Betz 1993.

## Table 3.8  Structure of Merchandise Exports

*(Percent of total exports)*

|  | Fuels, Min. and Metals | | Other Prim. Commodities | | Mach. and Transp. Equip. | | Other | | Textiles and Clothing | |
|---|---|---|---|---|---|---|---|---|---|---|
|  | 1970 | 1991 | 1970 | 1991 | 1970 | 1991 | 1970 | 1991 | 1970 | 1991 |
| *Latin America* | | | | | | | | | | |
| Argentina | 1 | 8 | 85 | 64 | 4 | 7 | 10 | 21 | 1 | 2 |
| Brazil | 11 | 16 | 75 | 64 | 4 | 18 | 11 | 38 | 1 | 4 |
| Chile | 88 | 50 | 7 | 35 | 1 | 1 | 4 | 14 | 0 | 1 |
| Colombia | 11 | 29 | 81 | 38 | 1 | 3 | 7 | 31 | 2 | 11 |
| Mexico | 19 | 41 | 49 | 14 | 11 | 24 | 22 | 20 | 3 | 2 |
| Costa Rica | 0 | 2 | 80 | 72 | 3 | 3 | 17 | 23 | 4 | 5 |
| Uruguay | 16 | 1 | 1 | 79 | 59 | 1 | 2 | 20 | 38 | 14 |
| Venezuela | 97 | 86 | 2 | 2 | 0 | 1 | 1 | 11 | 0 | 1 |
| *Average* | 29 | 29 | 57 | 39 | 3 | 7 | 12 | 25 | 3 | 5 |
| *East Asia* | | | | | | | | | | |
| Hong Kong | 1 | 2 | 3 | 3 | 12 | 24 | 84 | 72 | 44 | 40 |
| Korea | 7 | 3 | 17 | 4 | 7 | 38 | 69 | 55 | 36 | 21 |
| Japan | 2 | 1 | 5 | 1 | 41 | 66 | 53 | 31 | 11 | 2 |
| Singapore | 25 | 18 | 45 | 8 | 11 | 48 | 20 | 26 | 5 | 5 |
| Indonesia | 44 | 43 | 54 | 16 | 0 | 2 | 1 | 39 | 0 | 14 |
| Malaysia | 30 | 17 | 63 | 22 | 2 | 38 | 6 | 23 | 1 | 6 |
| Thailand | 15 | 2 | 77 | 32 | 0 | 22 | 8 | 45 | 1 | 17 |
| *Average* | 18 | 12 | 38 | 12 | 10 | 34 | 34 | 42 | 14 | 15 |

*Source:* World Bank, *World Development Report 1993.*

## Table 3.9  Seigniorage 1975–85

| | As % of Nonseigniorage Government Revenue | As % of GDP |
|---|---|---|
| *Latin America* | | |
| Argentina | | 10.8 |
| Brazil | 18.36 | 4.13 |
| Chile | 7.48 | 2.39 |
| Colombia | | 2.7 |
| Mexico | 18.70 | 2.71 |
| Venezuela | 10.76 | 3.05 |
| *Average* | 13.83 | 4.30 |
| | | |
| *East Asia* | | |
| Korea | 10.70 | 1.84 |
| Indonesia | | 1.3 |
| Malaysia | | 1.6 |
| Thailand | 7.06 | 0.94 |
| *Average* | 8.88 | 1.42 |

*Note:* These figures represent averages of annual data for the period, where available.
Source: Sachs and Larraín (1993).

## Table 3.10  Public Surplus/Deficit, 1974-89
*(Percentage of GDP)*

| | 1974-77 | 1977-81 | 1982-84 | 1985-89 |
|---|---|---|---|---|
| *Latin America* | | | | |
| Argentina | | | -8.42 | -4.11 |
| Brazil | | -1.91 | -3.85 | -12.98 |
| Chile | -1.23 | 3.18 | -2.19 | -0.77 |
| Colombia | 0.03 | -1.22 | -4.41 | -1.70 |
| Mexico | -3.89 | -3.76 | -9.86 | -11.30 |
| Uruguay | -2.99 | -0.61 | -6.32 | -1.41 |
| Venezuela | -0.21 | -0.72 | -0.58 | -2.40 |
| Costa Rica | -2.35 | -5.51 | -1.21 | -2.16 |
| *Average* | -1.77 | -1.51 | -4.60 | -4.60 |
| | | | | |
| *East Asia* | | | | |
| Japan | -4.94 | -7.09 | -6.31 | -3.94 |
| Korea | -1.81 | -2.14 | -1.75 | 0.20 |
| Singapore | 0.92 | 1.49 | 3.09 | 1.96 |
| Indonesia | -2.80 | -2.41 | -0.98 | -2.11 |
| Malaysia | -6.74 | -7.52 | -10.78 | -4.95 |
| Thailand | -2.10 | -3.88 | -4.66 | -2.86 |
| *Average* | -2.91 | -3.59 | -3.57 | -1.95 |

*Source:* World Bank, *World Tables 1993.*

**Table 3.11  Public Surplus/Deficit, 1974-89**
*(Percentage of gross domestic investment)*

|  | 1974-77 | 1977-81 | 1982-84 | 1985-89 |
|---|---|---|---|---|
| *Latin America* | | | | |
| Argentina | | | -55.20 | -41.33 |
| Brazil | | | -22.56 | -62.33 |
| Chile | -5.27 | 15.93 | -19.08 | -5.57 |
| Colombia | 0.45 | -6.13 | -22.30 | -8.76 |
| Mexico | -17.93 | -14.60 | -45.76 | -57.63 |
| Uruguay | -16.30 | -2.81 | -40.71 | -11.59 |
| Venezuela | 0.95 | -1.85 | -1.76 | -7.53 |
| Costa Rica | -9.97 | -21.44 | -5.04 | -8.33 |
| *Average* | -8.01 | -5.15 | -26.55 | -25.38 |
| *East Asia* | | | | |
| Japan | -15.26 | -22.38 | -22.03 | -13.80 |
| Korea | -6.49 | -6.80 | -6.04 | 0.65 |
| Singapore | 2.26 | 3.39 | 6.41 | 5.23 |
| Indonesia | -12.09 | -9.38 | -3.36 | -7.10 |
| Malaysia | -26.06 | -23.98 | -29.41 | -19.73 |
| Thailand | -8.26 | -14.40 | -19.19 | -12.50 |
| *Average* | -10.98 | -12.26 | -12.27 | -7.88 |

*Source:* World Bank, *World Tables 1993.*

**Table 3.12  Labor Force Participation Rate**
*(Percent)*

|  | 1965 | 1990 |
|---|---|---|
| *Latin America* | | |
| Argentina | 39 | 35 |
| Brazil | 32 | 37 |
| Chile | 32 | 37 |
| Colombia | 30 | 33 |
| Mexico | 29 | 34 |
| Uruguay | 40 | 39 |
| Venezuela | 30 | 35 |
| Costa Rica | 30 | 35 |
| *Average* | 33 | 35 |
| *East Asia* | | |
| Japan | 50 | 50 |
| Korea | 34 | 42 |
| Singapore | 32 | 48 |
| Hong Kong | 38 | 49 |
| Thailand | 50 | 53 |
| Malaysia | 34 | 41 |
| Indonesia | 38 | 39 |
| *Average* | 39 | 46 |

*Source for 3.12-3.16:* World Bank, *World Development Reports.*

**Table 3.13  Structural Changes in Labor, 1960–80**
*(In percent)*

|  | Agriculture | | | Industry | | | Services | | |
|---|---|---|---|---|---|---|---|---|---|
|  | 1960 | 1980 | % change | 1960 | 1980 | % change | 1960 | 1980 | % change |
| **Latin America** | | | | | | | | | |
| Argentina | 20 | 13.0 | -35.0 | 36 | 33.8 | -6.1 | 44 | 53.1 | 20.7 |
| Brazil | 52 | 31.2 | -40.0 | 15 | 26.6 | 77.3 | 33 | 42.2 | 27.9 |
| Chile | 30 | 16.5 | -45.0 | 20 | 25.1 | 25.5 | 50 | 58.4 | 16.8 |
| Colombia | 51 | 34.2 | -32.9 | 19 | 23.5 | 23.7 | 30 | 42.3 | 41.0 |
| Mexico | 55 | 36.5 | -33.6 | 20 | 29.0 | 45.0 | 25 | 34.5 | 38.0 |
| Uruguay | 21 | 15.7 | -25.2 | 29 | 29.1 | 0.3 | 50 | 55.1 | 10.2 |
| Venezuela | 35 | 16.0 | -54.3 | 22 | 28.4 | 29.1 | 43 | 55.5 | 29.1 |
| Costa Rica | 51 | 30.8 | -39.6 | 19 | 23.1 | 21.6 | 30 | 46.1 | 53.7 |
| *Average* | | | -38.21 | | | 27.05 | | | 29.66 |
| **East Asia** | | | | | | | | | |
| Japan | 33 | 11.2 | -66.1 | 30 | 34.3 | 14.3 | 37 | 54.6 | 47.6 |
| Korea | 66 | 36.4 | -44.8 | 9 | 26.8 | 197.8 | 25 | 36.8 | 47.2 |
| Singapore | 8 | 1.6 | -80.0 | 23 | 37.7 | 63.9 | 69 | 60.7 | -12.0 |
| Indonesia | 75 | 57.2 | -23.7 | 8 | 13.1 | 63.8 | 17 | 29.7 | 74.7 |
| Malaysia | 63 | 41.6 | -34.0 | 12 | 19.1 | 59.2 | 25 | 39.3 | 57.2 |
| Thailand | 84 | 70.9 | -15.6 | 4 | 10.3 | 157.5 | 12 | 18.9 | 57.5 |

**Table 3.14  Structural Changes in Output, 1960–91**
*(Percentage share of GDP)*

|  | Agriculture | | | Industry | | | Manufacturing | | | Services | | |
|---|---|---|---|---|---|---|---|---|---|---|---|---|
|  | 1960 | 1991 | % change | 1960 | 1991 | % change | 1960 | 1991 | % change | 1960 | 1991 | % change |
| **Latin America** | | | | | | | | | | | | |
| Argentina | 16 | 15 | -6.3 | 38 | 40 | 5.3 | 32 | | | 46 | 46 | 0.0 |
| Brazil | 16 | 10 | -37.5 | 35 | 39 | 11.4 | 26 | 26 | 0.0 | 49 | 51 | 4.1 |
| Chile | 10 | | | 51 | | | 29 | | | 39 | | |
| Colombia | 34 | 17 | -50.0 | 26 | 35 | 34.6 | 17 | 20 | 17.6 | 50 | 48 | -4.0 |
| Mexico | 16 | 9 | -43.8 | 29 | 30 | 3.4 | 19 | 22 | 15.8 | 55 | 61 | 10.9 |
| Uruguay | 19 | 10 | -47.4 | 28 | 32 | 14.3 | 21 | 25 | 19.0 | 53 | 58 | 9.4 |
| Venezuela | 6 | 5 | -16.7 | 22 | 47 | 113.6 | | 17 | | 72 | 48 | -33.3 |
| Costa Rica | 26 | 18 | -30.8 | 20 | 25 | 25.0 | 14 | 19 | 35.7 | 54 | 56 | 3.7 |
| *Average* | | | -33.2 | | | 29.7 | | | 17.6 | | | -1.3 |
| **East Asia** | | | | | | | | | | | | |
| Japan | 13 | 3 | -76.9 | 45 | 42 | -6.7 | 34 | 25 | -26.5 | 42 | 56 | 33.3 |
| Korea | 37 | 8 | -78.4 | 20 | 45 | 125.0 | 14 | 28 | 100.0 | 43 | 47 | 9.3 |
| Singapore | 4 | 0 | -100.0 | 18 | 38 | 111.1 | 12 | 29 | 141.7 | 78 | 62 | -20.5 |
| Hong Kong | 4 | 0 | -100.0 | 39 | 25 | -35.9 | 26 | 17 | -34.6 | 57 | 75 | 31.6 |
| Malaysia | 37 | | | 18 | | | 9 | | | 45 | | |
| Indonesia | 54 | 19 | -64.8 | 14 | 4 | 192.9 | 8 | 21 | 162.5 | 32 | 39 | 21.9 |
| *Average* | | | -84.0 | | | 77.3 | | | 68.6 | | | 15.1 |

Table 3.15  Investment Performance

| | Gross Domestic Investment (% of GDP) | | | Average Annual Growth Rates (%) | |
|---|---|---|---|---|---|
| | 1965 | 1985 | 1991 | 1970-80 | 1980-91 |
| **Latin America** | | | | | |
| Argentina | 19.0 | 9.0 | 12.0 | 3.1 | -6.9 |
| Brazil | 25.0 | 16.0 | 20.0 | 8.9 | -0.1 |
| Chile | 15.0 | 14.0 | 19.0 | 1.0 | 5.1 |
| Colombia | 16.0 | 18.0 | 15.0 | 5.0 | -0.2 |
| Mexico | 22.0 | 21.0 | 23.0 | 8.3 | -1.9 |
| Uruguay | 11.0 | 8.0 | 13.0 | | -5.9 |
| Venezuela | 24.0 | 15.0 | 19.0 | 7.1 | -3.9 |
| Costa Rica | 20.0 | 23.0 | 23.0 | 9.2 | 4.4 |
| *Average* | 19.0 | 15.5 | 18.0 | 6.1 | -1.2 |
| **East Asia** | | | | | |
| Japan | 32.0 | 28.0 | 32.0 | 2.5 | 6.0 |
| Korea | 15.0 | 30.0 | 39.0 | 14.2 | 13.0 |
| Singapore | 22.0 | 43.0 | | 7.8 | 4.3 |
| Hong Kong | 23.0 | 26.0 | 29.0 | 12.1 | 4.4 |
| Thailand | 20.0 | 23.0 | 39.0 | 7.2 | 9.8 |
| Malaysia | 20.0 | 28.0 | 36.0 | 10.8 | 4.4 |
| Indonesia | 8.0 | 30.0 | 35.0 | 14.1 | 6.9 |
| *Average* | 20.0 | 29.7 | 35.0 | 9.8 | 7.0 |

Table 3.16  Saving Behavior
*(Gross domestic saving as percentage of GDP)*

| | 1965 | 1985 | 1991 |
|---|---|---|---|
| **Latin America** | | | |
| Argentina | 23.0 | 16.0 | 15.0 |
| Brazil | 27.0 | 22.0 | 30.0 |
| Chile | 16.0 | 16.0 | 24.0 |
| Colombia | 17.0 | 17.0 | 23.0 |
| Mexico | 21.0 | 26.0 | 20.0 |
| Uruguay | 18.0 | 12.0 | 17.0 |
| Venezuela | 34.0 | 24.0 | 23.0 |
| Costa Rica | 9.0 | 22.0 | 22.0 |
| *Average* | 20.6 | 19.4 | 21.8 |
| **East Asia** | | | |
| Japan | 33.0 | 32.0 | 34.0 |
| Korea | 7.0 | 31.0 | 36.0 |
| Singapore | 10.0 | 42.0 | 47.0 |
| Hong Kong | 29.0 | 27.0 | 32.0 |
| Indonesia | 8.0 | 32.0 | 13.0 |
| Malaysia | 24.0 | 33.0 | 30.0 |
| Thailand | 21.0 | 21.0 | 32.0 |
| *Average* | 18.9 | 31.1 | 32.0 |

**Table 3.17  Educational Effort, 1965 and 1990**
*(Enrollment ratios)*

|  | Primary | | Secondary | | Tertiary | |
|---|---|---|---|---|---|---|
|  | 1965 | 1990 | 1965 | 1990 | 1965 | 1990 |
| **Latin America** | | | | | | |
| Argentina | 101 | 111 | 28 | | 14 | |
| Brazil | 108 | 108 | 16 | 39 | 2 | 12 |
| Chile | 124 | 98 | 34 | 74 | 6 | 19 |
| Mexico | 92 | 112 | 17 | 53 | 4 | 14 |
| Colombia | 84 | 110 | 17 | 52 | 3 | 14 |
| Uruguay | 106 | 106 | 44 | 77 | 8 | 50 |
| Venezuela | 94 | 92 | 27 | 35 | 7 | 29 |
| Costa Rica | 106 | 102 | 24 | 42 | 6 | 26 |
| *Average* | 102 | 105 | 26 | 53 | 6 | 23 |
| **East Asia** | | | | | | |
| Japan | 100 | 101 | 82 | 96 | 13 | 31 |
| Korea | 101 | 108 | 35 | 87 | 6 | 39 |
| Singapore | 105 | 110 | 45 | 69 | 10 | 8 |
| Hong Kong | 103 | 106 | 29 | | 5 | |
| Thailand | 78 | 85 | 14 | 32 | 2 | 16 |
| Malaysia | 90 | 93 | 28 | 56 | 2 | 7 |
| Indonesia | 72 | 117 | 12 | 45 | 1 | |
| *Average* | 93 | 103 | 35 | 64 | 6 | 20 |

*Source:* World Bank, *World Development Report 1993.*

## Table 3.18  Growth Regressions, 1960–85

### Dep. Var:  Rate of Growth of Real GDP per capita, 1960–85

| Regression | (1) | (2) | (3) |
|---|---|---|---|
| Observations | 114.00 | 113.00 | 98.00 |
| Adj. $R^2$ | 0.42 | 0.53 | 0.61 |
| Intercept | -0.01 | 0.006 | 0.02 |
|  | (0.98) | (0.93) | (2.69) |
| Real GDP p.c. in 1960 | -0.00 | -0.002 | -0.004 |
|  | (4.00) | (2.74) | (6.04) |
| Avg. Investment/GDP, 1960-85 | 0.11 | 0.09 | 0.07 |
|  | (4.59) | (3.00) | (2.28) |
| Primary enrollment, 1960 | 0.03 | 0.02 | 0.02 |
|  | (4.06) | (4.01) | (2.63) |
| Growth of population, 1960-85 | -0.13 | -0.10 | -0.29 |
|  | (0.66) | (0.56) | (2.05) |
| East Asia dummy |  | 0.03 | 0.02 |
|  |  | (5.96) | (5.50) |
| Latin America dummy |  | -0.01 | -0.01 |
|  |  | (1.86) | (2.39) |
| Government expenditure/GDP |  |  | -0.09 |
| (net of defense and education) |  |  | (3.06) |
| Number of revolutions and |  |  | -0.02 |
| coups per year (1960-85) |  |  | (3.79) |

Note: T statistics in parentheses are calculated using White's standard errors.

### Table 3.19  Indices of Demographic Transition

|  | 1960-65 | 1965-70 | 1970-75 | 1975-80 | 1980-85 | 1985-90 |
|---|---|---|---|---|---|---|
| **Latin America** | | | | | | |
| Argentina | 0.79 | 0.80 | 0.81 | 0.82 | 0.84 | 0.87 |
| Brazil | 0.41 | 0.50 | 0.58 | 0.65 | 0.70 | 0.77 |
| Chile | 0.54 | 0.64 | 0.73 | 0.82 | 0.87 | 0.89 |
| Mexico | 0.40 | 0.44 | 0.50 | 0.62 | 0.71 | 0.77 |
| Colombia | 0.39 | 0.47 | 0.59 | 0.67 | 0.75 | 0.81 |
| Uruguay | 0.84 | 0.85 | 0.85 | 0.86 | 0.90 | 0.92 |
| Venezuela | 0.48 | 0.56 | 0.65 | 0.72 | 0.78 | 0.81 |
| Costa Rica | 0.40 | 0.52 | 0.64 | 0.71 | 0.77 | 0.80 |
| *Average* | 0.53 | 0.60 | 0.67 | 0.73 | 0.79 | 0.83 |
| **East Asia** | | | | | | |
| Japan | 0.89 | 0.92 | 0.94 | 0.99 | 1.00 | 1.02 |
| S. Korea | 0.43 | 0.54 | 0.62 | 0.77 | 0.84 | 0.90 |
| Taiwan | | | | | | |
| Singapore | 0.71 | 0.84 | 0.92 | 0.99 | 1.01 | 1.02 |
| Hong Kong | 0.68 | 0.80 | 0.90 | 0.96 | 1.02 | 1.03 |
| Thailand | 0.31 | 0.36 | 0.47 | 0.55 | 0.62 | 0.72 |
| Malaysia | 0.33 | 0.43 | 0.52 | 0.63 | 0.68 | 0.73 |
| Indonesia | 0.29 | 0.30 | 0.36 | 0.42 | 0.50 | 0.60 |
| *Average* | 0.52 | 0.60 | 0.68 | 0.76 | 0.81 | 0.86 |

Source: United Nations, *World Population Prospects*, 1992.
Note: The index of the percentage of the demographic transition completed was constructed using the following formula: Index=.4[(7.5-TFR)/5.3]+.4[1-(75-e)/43]+.2[u], where TFR=Total Fertility Rate per woman; e=life expectancy at birth; u=proportion of urban population.

**Table 3.20  Income Distribution (Late 1970s) and GNP Per Capita, 1960–81**

|  | Income share of | | Ratio Top to Bottom | GNP p.c. growth per annum, 1960–81 |
|---|---|---|---|---|
|  | Bottom 20% | Top 20% |  |  |
| **Latin America** |  |  |  |  |
| Argentina (1970) | 4.4 | 50.3 | 11.4 | 1.9 |
| Brazil (1972) | 2.0 | 66.6 | 33.3 | 5.1 |
| Mexico (1977) | 2.9 | 57.7 | 19.9 | 3.8 |
| Venezuela (1970) | 3.0 | 54.0 | 18.0 | 2.4 |
| Costa Rica (1971) | 3.3 | 54.8 | 16.6 | 3.0 |
| Peru (1972) | 1.9 | 61.0 | 32.11 | 1.0 |
| Panama (1973) |  |  |  | 3.1 |
| *Average* | 3.1 | 56.7 | 19.8 | 2.9 |
| **East Asia** |  |  |  |  |
| Japan (1979) | 8.7 | 37.5 | 4.3 | 6.3 |
| Korea (1976) | 5.7 | 45.3 | 8.0 | 6.9 |
| Taiwan (1976) | 9.5 | 35.0 | 3.7 | 6.6 |
| Hong Kong (1980) | 5.4 | 47.0 | 8.7 | 6.9 |
| Thailand (1975-6) | 5.6 | 49.8 | 8.9 | 4.6 |
| Malaysia (1973) | 3.5 | 56.1 | 16.0 | 4.3 |
| Indonesia (1976) | 6.6 | 49.4 | 7.5 | 4.1 |
| *Average* | 6.4 | 45.7 | 8.1 | 5.7 |

*Source:* Williamson (1993).

**Table 3.21  Income Distribution**
*(Gini coefficient)*

|  | 1960s | 1970s | 1980s |
|---|---|---|---|
| **Latin America** |  |  |  |
| Brazil | 0.53 | 0.60 | 0.57 |
| Chile | 0.46 | 0.46 |  |
| Mexico | 0.55 | 0.50 |  |
| Colombia |  | 0.57 |  |
| Costa Rica | 0.50 | 0.49 | 0.42 |
| *Average* | 0.51 | 0.52 | 0.50 |
| **East Asia** |  |  |  |
| Korea | 0.34 | 0.39 | 0.36 |
| Taiwan | 0.31 | 0.28 | 0.27 |
| Singapore |  | 0.37 | 0.42 |
| Hong Kong | 0.49 | 0.43 | 0.45 |
| Thailand | 0.41 | 0.45 | 0.47 |
| Malaysia | 0.42 | 0.53 | 0.48 |
| Indonesia | 0.33 | 0.32 | 0.31 |
| *Average* | 0.38 | 0.40 | 0.39 |

*Source:* Fields and Jakubson (1993).

# Commentary

*Humberto Petrei*

This paper is an excellent summary of various experiences, still unfolding today, that have provided fruitful lessons for development. The paper compares several rapidly developing Asian countries with several of the better-developed countries in Latin America to determine the reasons for the different growth patterns of the two regions. By examining each region's foreign trade policies, industrial policies, savings and investment patterns, labor markets, and public sector management, the paper gives the reader a clear understanding of the different paths each has taken towards growth.

Including Japan among the Asian countries, however, appears to hinder the comparison in some ways. It would seem preferable to compare countries at stages of development not quite so far apart. Nevertheless, since data are provided on a country basis, the reader can focus on those countries of greatest interest.

The first part of this comment summarizes my views on the question of how the Asian experience has been or can be useful in designing Argentina's economic policy. The second consists of comments and some additional quantitative information on the countries included in Mr. Jaspersen's study.

## Lessons for Argentina

Many of the policies adopted by Argentina in recent years are similar to policies implemented by the East Asian countries.

*Market deregulation.* Argentina's economy has been opened up, markets have been deregulated, and labor conditions are being made more flexible. The gradual opening of the economy, initiated several years ago, took on new momentum in 1991, and today the average tariff is less than 10 percent, with most quantitative restrictions eliminated. The economy has also been opened up to foreign investment and capital transactions. Price controls, which had been in place for several decades, were lifted beginning in 1990, and a number of regulated markets were liberalized in 1991.

*Macroeconomic equilibrium.* Macroeconomic equilibrium has done more to lay the groundwork for sustained development in Argentina than any other policy. It has improved the investment climate, promoted greater savings, and provided an adequate horizon for business planning. Stability also has improved income distribution and thus the likelihood that the benefits of growth will be shared more equitably.

*Absorbing adjustments and people participation.* Latin America in general, and Argentina in particular, have entered a stage of strengthening democracy, with economic growth benefiting most segments of society. Average wages were 11 percent higher in real terms at the end of 1994 than in 1990, while programs involving occupational training have enhanced social services, and higher pension payments have helped to achieve this shared growth. As the population has shared in the benefits of growth, it has accepted the efforts toward economic adjustment, which in turn have helped to lay a solid foundation for sustaining that growth. For example, the process of opening up the economy, lifting controls, and reforming the state has meant displacing a significant number of workers, with state reform having shifted about 400,000 persons to the private sector. This was done in an orderly fashion, with adequate compensation, and without any kind of social tension or disturbance.

*Convertibility and the exchange rate.* Argentina's experience in adopting the convertibility plan will serve as an important lesson for other countries. The country has for some time posted an external current account deficit, and although many are calling for devaluation as the best way to restore balance, that would mean abandoning the stabilization effort. Three bouts of hyperinflation within a short period of time have affected the population deeply, and any sign that the convertibility principle is about to be abandoned would unleash stubborn inflationary expectations.

One alternative for restoring balance would be to promote primarily an efficient export sector, although this might not be the best route. A better option might be to work toward improving general competitiveness—for example, by generating investment in the so-called nontradeable sectors. This would result in lower costs, which would soon be reflected in the internal costs of export goods.

*Results.* The experiences of the East Asian countries have influenced the design of Argentina's recent economic policy. Even though there has been no attempt to apply these lessons directly, the economic theories used in East Asia that were tried out in Argentina have brought similar results. Argentina's once high inflation is now comparable to the inflation rate of the more advanced countries; investment, savings, and employment have risen; new technologies are being adopted at a much faster pace; and the gross domestic product has grown six to seven percent for four consecutive years.

## The Comparative Study

This section comments on the ways in which trends in public spending, industrial policy, labor supply, and political conditions account for the different growth patterns in the East Asian and Latin American countries.

*Investment, savings, and trends in public spending.* One reason for the differences between the two regions is public spending policy. In Latin America there are two central issues involving public spending: the low productivity of public investment, and the composition of spending. Regarding low productivity, weaknesses in public sector institutions in Latin America have often led to investment projects that are either unprofitable or so poorly implemented that cost overruns have absorbed the projected returns. As for the composition of public spending, a large proportion of public spending has been earmarked for social security. This expenditure, although acceptable from the standpoint of redistribution, was taken on at a very early stage in these countries' economic development, and therefore has had adverse effects on employment incentives and expansion of the labor force.

Another difference between the two regions is the rate of savings. Large amounts of foreign investment flowed into the East Asian countries at the beginning of their rapid development phase, but in Latin America much of the capital has come from foreign borrowing. To compensate for this, some Latin American countries have adopted a strategy of first promoting foreign investment and then increasing savings. Such a strategy, although risky, seems feasible.

*Industrial policy.* Although the import substitution approach arose in Latin America in response to external shocks, there was an ideological element underlying the design of such policies. In addition to the reasons the author gives for Latin America's anti-export bias, another is the notion of achieving a surplus in the primary production sector and transferring it to other, presumably cash-poor sectors. In this, resource-rich Latin America has had opportunities not available to the East Asian countries. (The idea of transferring surpluses from one sector to another has historically been applied by other countries, including Japan.) The East Asian countries managed to offset the anti-export bias imposed by initial protection by using subsidies or high exchange rates, but they probably had no other choice.

On the other hand, whether high exchange rates were an essential factor in all cases is unclear. Some Asian countries, such as Korea, sustained high rates of growth for many years in combination with an overvalued exchange rate. And, despite running higher trade deficits than those posted recently by Argentina and Mexico, they were still able to grow.

On the subject of industrial policy, the debate over whether to favor certain sectors has not taken place in Latin America because of the urgency of adjustment and the enormous pressures imposed by circumstances. Some East Asian countries have favored certain sectors to a very moderate degree. Is such a strategy transferable to Latin America? Perhaps, but the history of failed intervention in Latin America has created an adverse political climate for such an approach. Nevertheless, the political climate is improving to the point where such an approach might now be discussed. Consensus-building will, of course, be essential if a policy favoring certain sectors is adopted.

In my view, however, the urgent need for development leaves little room for such a discussion at this time. A less risky strategy would be to focus on correcting market shortcomings and hastening adjustment, and here something can be done. When an imbalance occurs in a market, the best policy is to help the market make the necessary adjustment: i.e., to move the variables in the direction the market indicates. If some sectors have greater potential than others, the market could be helped to concentrate on those sectors first, without the need to use funds directly in the form of subsidies or special treatment.

*Supply of labor.* This section of the paper poses interesting questions and encourages further research. The interrelationship between demographic transition and savings may be a valid working hypothesis, but it seems less convincing than other hypotheses. When the degree of urbanization is introduced, the index assigns special features to the Asian countries. A more traditional analysis based on the proportion of age groups would probably contribute to a better understanding of the author's message. In any case, even on the basis of the information given, other conclusions can be drawn.

*Political considerations.* The countries of East Asia have been able to separate macroeconomic policy from domestic politics. This is a very important lesson, and one that Latin America has assimilated only gradually. Strengthening democracy throughout the region has laid the groundwork for a consensus on public policy, and today those political parties whose platforms include defending stability prevail over those with unsound distributional programs. Greater political participation will help Latin America achieve development, coupled with better income distribution, by ensuring that public spending decisions are made by the majority.

---

*Humberto Petrei is Executive Director for Argentina and Haiti at the Inter-American Development Bank.*

CHAPTER

**4**

# Education, Growth and Inequality

*Nancy Birdsall, David Ross, and Richard Sabot*

The difference between East Asia and Latin America in two key dimensions of economic performance is striking: in recent decades Latin American countries experienced slow or negative growth and high inequality, while East Asian countries achieved both extremely rapid growth and low inequality. Figure 4.1 relates GDP growth and income inequality, as measured by the average ratio of the income shares of the top and bottom quintiles, for a number of Latin American countries, concentrated in the southeast corner, and for East Asian countries, which stand alone in the northwest corner.[1]

In this paper we focus on human capital accumulation and its utilization in the labor market as factors contributing to this marked interregional difference in economic performance. We assess the extent to which differences in one measure of the supply of human capital, that is the quantity and quality of schooling, explain both East Asia's higher rates of growth and lower levels of inequality. But the supply of human capital is not the whole story. We provide evidence that the growth payoff of human capital accumulation has been greater in East Asia than elsewhere because its development strategy demanded more labor and skills. Moreover, in addition to increasing growth directly via increased labor productivity, educational expansion may have enhanced growth indirectly by reducing inequality.

---

[1] This essay elaborates upon two earlier essays by Birdsall, Ross and Sabot (1995a and 1995b). The rapid growth in the East Asian region has been unparalleled. Eight "high-performing Asian economies" have not only outperformed the industrial economies since 1960, but also have grown at rates higher than the currently high income countries experienced during their earlier periods of most rapid growth. Since 1960, the gap in per capita income between a substantial majority of developing countries and the industrialized nations has been increasing. In contrast, the East Asian economies have been "catching up," or converging. The decline in poverty and income inequality in East Asia has been equally remarkable. The percentage of people below the poverty line has fallen far more rapidly in East Asia than in other regions (see World Bank 1990). While declines in inequality are more difficult to document, measures such as the Gini coefficient show improvements in the distribution of income in each of the HPAEs between 1965 and 1990 (see World Bank 1993a).

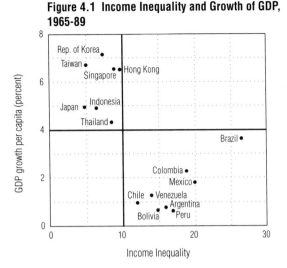

**Figure 4.1  Income Inequality and Growth of GDP, 1965-89**

*Note:* For additional data, see Figure 2.2.
*Source:* Based on World Bank (1993a).

We provide evidence of a negative relationship between inequality and growth and some explanations for this relationship. Finally, we consider why the performance of East Asia in education has been superior to the performance of Latin America. We assess the contribution to the differential in performance of such factors as the allocation of public expenditure across education levels, the feedback of economic growth on education expenditures, the feedback of reductions in fertility on educational spending per eligible child, and the feedback of low inequality on rates of investment in human capital among the poor.

## Interregional Differences in Educational Performance

Figure 4.2 presents a stylized summary of the results of regressing secondary school enrollment rates on per capita national income for more than 90 developing countries for the years 1965 and 1987.[2] Countries in East Asia, with the exception of Thailand, had significantly higher secondary enroll-

---

[2] The analysis we describe was conducted by J. Behrman and R. Schneider and presented in two papers, Behrman and Schneider (1994) and Behrman and Schneider (1996). The regressions control for average per capita income in the relevant year.

**Figure 4.2  Cross-Economy Regression for Secondary Enrollment Rates, 1965 and 1987**

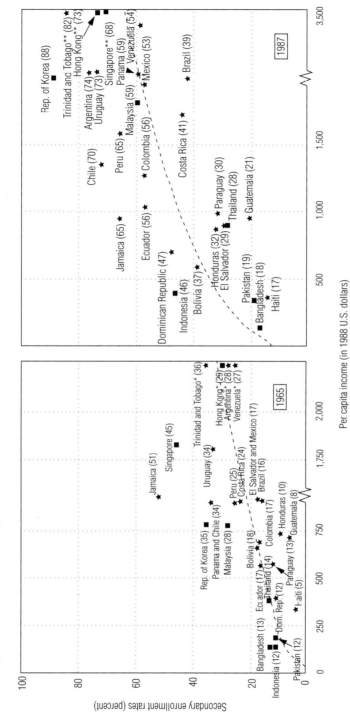

Secondary enrollment rates (percent)

Per capita income (in 1988 U.S. dollars)

*Note:* Figures in parentheses are enrollment rates.
*Per capita income exceeds $2,250.
**Per capita income exceeds $3,500.

*Sources:* Singapore and Hong Kong from World Bank (1994b); all others from Behrman and Schneider (1994) and Behrman (1996).
Per capita income calculated using *World Development Report* (1989 and 1990) and *Statistical Abstract of the United States 1990*.

ment rates than predicted by cross-country comparisons. The performance of Latin American countries is not nearly as strong as that of East Asia and is mixed relative to international norms.[3] Where enrollment rates are low, children of the poor are the least likely to be enrolled. Thus a corollary of Latin America's lower enrollment rates is higher inequality of access by socioeconomic background.[4]

Moreover, in contrast to East Asia where increases in quantity are associated with improvements in the quality of education, expansion of enrollments in many Latin American countries is associated with an erosion of quality, particularly for the poor. In human capital models, inputs matter only to the extent that they affect outputs: it is the output of schooling (cognitive and other skills), not inputs such as years of schooling, that is presumed to affect subsequent productivity. Children with the same number of years of schooling, even if their levels of ability and family backgrounds are similar, may have different levels of cognitive skills. Therefore, a quantitative measure such as years of schooling is not a sufficient indicator of human capital accumulation.

There are four symptoms of the school quality problem in Latin America. First, the expansion of enrollments was not backed by sufficient resources to maintain per-pupil expenditures on such important inputs as books, equipment, and teachers. Average expenditure per primary school child in Latin America fell from an estimated $164 in 1980 to $118 in 1989. Over the same period, per-pupil expenditures increased in East Asia.[5] Declining per-pupil expenditures in Latin America resulted in declining school quality. Given that educational expansion drew in children from relatively poor households, with poorly educated parents whose input to the educational process was necessarily limited, cognitive outputs per year of schooling almost certainly declined in many Latin American countries.

Second, repetition rates are high. Twenty-nine percent of all students in the first six years of primary school fail each year. Forty-two percent of all first graders repeat. In 1989 less than half of all primary students finished six years of school in six years. The aggregate cost of repetition to Latin

---

[3] At the primary and tertiary levels, enrollment rates in Latin American countries compare favorably to other countries at similar levels of income. At the secondary level a number of Latin American countries, most notably Brazil and Guatemala, had enrollment rates well below rates predicted by international experience for countries at their level of income. See Behrman and Schneider (1996).

[4] While inequality of access by socioeconomic background is higher in Latin America than in East Asia, inequality of access by gender is nearly as low in the former as in the latter.

[5] Wolff et al. (1993). For data on Asia, see World Bank (1993a).

American school systems is an estimated $2.5 billion a year.[6] Not all of this is wasted; children do learn more during the year that they repeat. However, one study of rural Brazil suggests that this money would be better spent on improvements in quality, a byproduct of which would be lower repetition rates. Indeed, the study suggests that a dollar invested in quality improvement would save more than a dollar in expenditures associated with repetition.[7]

Third, dropout rates are high, thus completion rates are low and may be declining.[8] In Brazil, the expansion of primary school coverage was associated with a dramatic decline in completion rates, due to the system's inability to offer adequate quality schooling to a larger and more diverse pool of students. By contrast, in East Asia, where quantity and quality were improved simultaneously, completion rates remained high. In the 1950s, Brazil's primary completion rate was higher than Korea's—60 percent compared with 36 percent. Over the next three decades, however, Brazil's primary completion rate dropped, while in Korea more than 90 percent of those enrolled completed primary education.[9]

A fourth symptom of poor school quality is test scores. While studies of cognitive achievement across countries are often as crude as they are scarce, international comparisons of scores on tests that attempt to measure the output of schooling confirm that education systems are performing poorly in Latin America. For example, in one study of reading skills, Venezuelan nine-year-olds ranked last among countries including Hong Kong, Singapore, and Indonesia.[10] In a 1992 assessment of math and science skills, 13-year-old students from China, Israel, Jordan, Korea, and Taiwan all out-

---

[6] Schiefelbein (1995), p. 13.

[7] See Hanushek and Gomes-Neto (1994). The conclusion that investments in school quality more than pay for themselves through improvements in internal efficiency of the school system would be reinforced by taking account of the post-schooling productivity gains that would result from having workers with higher cognitive skills.

[8] As school quality increases so do the productivity-enhancing cognitive skills acquired in school and, hence, the probability of gaining access to higher level educational opportunities rationed by meritocratic criteria and the expected returns to a given number of years of schooling. Higher probabilities of promotion and higher expected returns are an inducement to remain in school.

[9] Birdsall, Bruns and Sabot (1996). Comparisons over time of dropout rates in Brazil are difficult, because the definition of primary school changed from four to eight grades in the 1960s. There is evidence that completion rates through eighth grade dropped in the 1980s. The divergent trends in dropout rates could also be due to Korea's growth path being steeper and more labor and skill-demanding than Brazil's, which resulted in higher rates of return to a given quantity and quality of schooling in Korea than in Brazil.

[10] Schiefelbein (1995), p. 8.

performed Brazilian 13-year-olds. Only one country, Mozambique, had student performance weaker than that of the Brazilian students.[11] In another 1992 assessment of math and science skills, the performance of 13-year-olds in Argentina, Colombia, the Dominican Republic, and Venezuela, except those attending elite private schools, was significantly weaker than that of students in countries such as Thailand.[12]

The next two sections focus on the effects of education on aggregate growth and on income inequality. We first show how poor educational performance (which limited the supply of human capital) in combination with inward-looking, capital-intensive development strategies (which limited the demand for human capital) contributed to slow economic growth in Latin America compared to East Asia. Then we show how poor educational performance contributed to high income inequality, again comparing the two regions.

**Education and Growth**

For decades cross-country comparisons have been a prominent part of research regarding the transformation of low into high-income countries.[13] The accumulation of human capital has consistently emerged as an essential feature of economic growth and development. However, the direction of causality implied by the positive correlation between educational attainment and per capita output in a cross section of countries is unclear: it could simply indicate that education is a luxury consumer good for which demand increases as incomes rise. This concern has been eased by Barro-style growth regressions,[14] in which the characteristics of economies decades ago are used as predictors of subsequent rates of economic growth. In the burgeoning literature on the determinants of growth rates across countries, the importance of education is a robust factor, proving relatively insensitive to changes in either specification or sample composition.[15]

---

[11] Wolff et al. (1993), p. 7.
[12] Schiefelbein (1995), p. 10.
[13] Clark (1940) and Kuznets (1966) were pioneers in this effort. More recently Chenery and Syrquin (1975) provided a comprehensive description of the structural changes that accompany the growth of developing countries and analyzed their relations.
[14] See Barro (1991). He estimates equations to explain variation among 98 countries in the growth rate of real per capita income over the period 1960–85. Among the explanatory variables, he includes the level of per capita GDP at the start of the period and education enrollment rates in 1960, a crude proxy for the initial stock of human capital.
[15] See, for example, Levine and Renelt (1991).

**Figure 4.3 Simulated Average Economy Per Capita GDP Growth Paths, Varying 1960 Primary and Secondary Enrollment Rates**

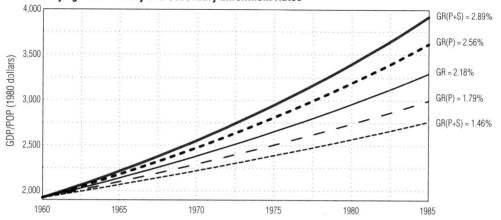

Note: GR represents growth path for average economy. GR(P) represents economy one-half standard deviation above or below primary enrollment rates. GR(P+S) represents economy one-half standard deviation above or below primary and secondary enrollment rates.

This is what human capital theory, the theory of investment in people, would predict: education augments cognitive and other skills, which in turn augment the productivity of labor.[16] Endogenous growth theory also predicts that a larger stock of human capital facilitates technological progress, or, for a country not on the technological frontier, relatively rapid acquisition of technological capability.[17] Moreover, rates of return to human capital may actually be increasing over some range, due to spillover benefits (i.e., the positive impact on the productivity of an entire group of workers resulting from the education of one of their co-workers).[18]

We use a modified version of the Barro regression to conduct counterfactual simulations, as a basis for assessing the contribution of investment in human capital to economic growth. Figure 4.3 (based on Appendix Table 4.A, column 1) shows the growth path of per capita GDP over the quarter century from 1960–1985 for a country characterized by the average value of each variable in the Barro sample. It also shows the changes in growth and per capita GDP for that country, assuming it had achieved a

---

[16] See Becker (1964) and Schultz (1961).
[17] See, for example, Nelson and Phelps (1966) and Romer (1990).
[18] See Lucas (1988) and Becker, Murphy, and Tamura (1990).

1960 primary, or both a 1960 primary and secondary, enrollment rate one-half standard deviation above (or below) the mean. There is a 0.7 percent gap in growth rates between the simulation which varies primary enroll-ments (GR(P)), and a 1.4 percent gap in growth rates between the simula-tions which vary both primary and secondary enrollments (GR(P+S)). Illus-trating the power of compounding, the cumulative effect of these differences in growth rates on 1985 per capita GDP is large: 20 percent and nearly 40 percent, respectively. Korea provides an example: had Korea's en-rollment rates been as low as Brazil's were in 1960, its average annual growth rate would have been 5.6 percent rather than 6.1 percent, resulting in a 1985 per capita GDP 11.1 percent less than that actually attained.

Substituting gender-specific primary school enrollment rates into the original Barro model,[19] our results (Appendix Table 4.A, column 2) indicate no significant difference between the coefficient values for males and fe-males.[20] This suggests that increasing primary school enrollments for girls is just as effective in stimulating growth as increasing primary enrollments for boys.[21] Microeconomic evidence summarized by Summers (1992), con-sistent with the conclusion emerging from cross-country data, indicates that the private rates of return to education among wage-earners are roughly the same for women as for men.[22]

Of course, the rate of participation in the wage labor market is much lower for women than for men. However, besides increasing the productiv-ity of wage labor, educating girls also leads to changes in intrahousehold behavior which yield nonwage social benefits. An important example is the lower fertility rates of more educated women.[23] In East Asia the fertility rate

---

[19] The estimated equation differs from Barro's by dropping the revolution and assassination variables and adding nine additional observations. All other coefficients are qualitatively un-changed.

[20] The relevant test statistic is $F_{1,101} = 0.001$.

[21] There is substantial multicollinearity affecting the estimators of the primary school enroll-ment coefficients in this equation. Taken individually, we are unable to distinguish the coeffi-cients on the enrollment variables from zero. However, a joint F-test ($F_{2,101} = 8.16$) rejects the null hypothesis that both primary school enrollment coefficients are zero. Barro (1993) has con-ducted a similar exercise. His results show that the impact on growth of educating girls is smaller.

[22] See also Behrman (1991) and Schultz (1991) for detailed reviews of the evidence from devel-oping countries. See Birdsall, Ross, and Sabot (1992) and Sathar (1988) for evidence from rural Pakistan.

[23] In addition to having fewer children, educated mothers are also more efficient users of health services for themselves and their children. They send children to school who are already better prepared to benefit from society's schooling investment, and they are more likely to send their own daughters to school. See Summers (1992).

for women with more than seven years of schooling was 54 percent of the rate for uneducated women in the 1970s. The rapid increases in education of girls in post-war East Asia contributed to the early fertility decline starting in the mid 1960s, which in turn resulted in much slower growth of the school-age population in the 1970s. As shown below, the decline in the size of the school-aged cohorts in the 1970s contributed to a relatively rapid growth of public expenditures on basic education per eligible child, permitting East Asia both to increase the quantity and to improve the quality of schooling.

While fertility rates in Latin America have declined, the decline did not begin until the 1970s; and fertility remains high compared to East Asia, particularly in the poorer countries. In Bolivia, Guatemala, Honduras, and Nicaragua, the total fertility rate exceeds five children per mother, compared to less than two children per mother in Korea. This high fertility has placed added stress on already strained resources for education.

### Development Strategy and the Impact of Education on Growth

In short, both the micro and cross-country evidence indicate that the difference between East Asia and Latin America in rates of growth has been due in part to interregional differences in educational performance. However, the supply of human capital is not the whole story behind education's contribution to growth. The demand for human capital is also important. The import-substituting, capital-intensive strategies adopted by most countries in Latin America did not generate a strong demand for labor. In contrast, an export-oriented strategy set East Asia on a labor-demanding growth path. Table 4.1 provides some indicators of the growth of labor demand in East Asia compared to developing countries in other regions, including Latin America. In the manufacturing sector, real earnings, wage employment, and the real wage bill increased at much faster rates in East Asia. Moreover, the growth of the real wage bill relative to GNP growth is also higher for East Asia, suggesting that East Asia's aggregate growth has not only been faster, but also more labor-demanding.

Differences among countries in the demand for skills have been neglected in the cross-country assessments of education's contribution to growth. The resulting omitted variable bias may explain the substantial overprediction, in typical cross-country growth regressions, of growth rates for some countries with higher-than-predicted rates of enrollment in primary and secondary schools in the 1960s. Weak demand for educated labor may explain why countries such as Peru and Argentina, which like East

**Table 4.1  Average Annual Increases in Manufacturing Sector Wage Bill, 1970-90**
*(Percent)*

| Country | Real Earnings of Labor | Wage Employment | Real Wage Bill |
|---|---|---|---|
| Korea | 8.7 | 18.67 | 28.99 |
| Singapore | 4.0 | 11.37[1] | 15.82 |
| Indonesia | 5.2 | 14.35[2] | 20.30 |
| Mauritius | 0.8 | 60.00 | 61.28 |
| India | 1.9 | 1.77[1] | 3.70 |
| Kenya | -2.0 | 7.74 | 5.59 |
| Venezuela | -0.2 | 4.27[3] | 4.06 |
| Bolivia | -3.2 | -0.50[4] | -3.68 |
| Zambia | 0.0 | 1.39[1] | 1.39 |

*Notes:* 1) 1970-89; 2) 1974-89; 3) 1970-84; 4) 1975-89.
*Source:* Calculated from World Bank, *World Development Report* (1993) and ILO *Yearbook of Labor Statistics* (various issues).

Asia had high human capital endowments in 1960 (greater than predicted for their initial levels of income), nevertheless have tended to underperform with respect to growth.

Figure 4.4 illustrates the link between the demand for skill and education's contribution to growth. S and D are, respectively, the skill supply and demand functions of the typical Latin American country; S' and D' are the skill supply and demand functions of the typical East Asian country. S' is shifted to the right due, for example, to greater public commitment to basic education.[24] D' is shifted upward to indicate that, at any given rate of return to skill, skilled workers are in greater demand in East Asia than in the typical Latin American country.[25] As drawn, high levels of demand for skill in East Asia have offset the tendency for educational expansion to induce diminishing returns to investment in human capital; the return (r') in

[24] The supply function for East Asia is more elastic because less absolute poverty means that fewer families are liquidity constrained and more families near the bottom of the income distribution can respond to increases in the returns to human capital investments.

[25] Labor demand in East Asia has become increasingly skill intensive, largely in response to the increased abundance of educated labor and consequent declines in its relative price, and to changes in comparative advantage. East Asian exporters shifted into more technologically sophisticated, and more capital and skill intensive, goods as rapidly rising wages of unskilled labor eroded international competitiveness in labor-intensive manufactured goods. As a share of wage employment, white collar and technical employment increased steadily during the 1970s and the 1980s, for example in Korea from 29 percent in 1980 to 36 percent in 1990, and in Taiwan from 32 to 40 percent over the same period (see Birdsall and Sabot, 1994).

**Figure 4.4  Demand Shifts and Returns to Human Capital**

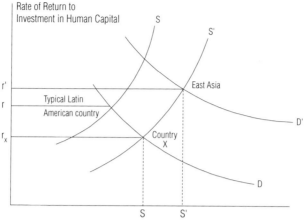

Quantity of Investment in Human Capital

East Asia is as high as in Latin America (r), even though skilled labor is more abundant. In country X, while enrollment rates are higher than in the typical Latin American country, the returns to education are lower ($r_x$). This is because country X has the human capital supply function of East Asia but the skill demand function of the typical Latin American country.

Empirical analysis supports our view that greater demand for skilled labor enhances the impact of a given educational endowment on growth. In our analysis (Appendix Table 4.A, column 3), we use the degree to which an economy is oriented toward manufactured exports as a proxy for the demand side of the skills market.[26] Our hypothesis is that, in a standard growth function, the effect of educational endowments in 1960 is enhanced the greater is an economy's orientation toward manufactured exports; the more oriented is the economy toward manufactured exports, the greater the demand for skilled labor. Though our results are not strong, they support our hypothesis: the contribution of education to economic growth tends to be greater in countries in which manufactured exports as a proportion of GDP are higher.[27] In East Asia, the stimulus that human capital has given to

_____

[26] In doing so we build on evidence that increases in the share of manufactured exports in output are associated not only with increases in the share of physical capital investment in GDP and the rate of economic growth, hence in the derived demand for labor and skill, but also with greater labor and skill intensity of production for a given rate of output growth.
[27] For a full discussion of our conclusion that the export and export-education variables are jointly significant determinants of growth, see Birdsall, Ross and Sabot (1995).

economic growth appears to have been augmented by the economies' export orientation and the resulting labor and skill-demanding growth paths they followed. Latin American countries, following a more inward-looking, capital-intensive growth path, failed to benefit from this positive interaction between human capital and the demand for skilled labor.

## Education and Inequality

In high-income countries, inequality of pay accounts for two-thirds of total income inequality. In low-income countries, as the share of wage employment in total employment increases, so does the share of the inequality of pay in total income inequality.[28] As the number of educated workers increases, the scarcity rents which they earn are eroded. The resulting compression of the educational structure of wages may, in turn, reduce the inequality of pay. By reducing the inequality of pay, educational expansion may reduce total income inequality.

In its effect on the inequality of pay, the compression effect of educational expansion may, however, be counteracted by a composition effect. This composition effect, analogous to the well-known Kuznets effect, can result in increased income inequality as the more-educated segment of the labor force moves into higher-paying jobs. Whether the compression effect or the composition effect dominates determines whether educational expansion decreases or increases the inequality of pay. Empirical work shows that the compression effect has tended to dominate: in a cross-section of more than 80 countries, a strong, statistically significant, negative correlation emerges between basic education enrollment rates and the level of income inequality, as measured by the Gini coefficient.[29]

A comparison of microeconomic data for Brazil and Korea[30] confirms the negative correlation between education and inequality, and suggests that differences in educational attainment contribute to the marked difference in inequality between East Asian and Latin American countries. Brazil and Korea have similar levels of per capita income. However, as noted above, in Korea the share of income going to the top 20 percent of income earners is roughly eight times the share earned by the bottom 20 percent (1976), while in Brazil that ratio is 26 (1983).

---

[28] See Knight and Sabot (1983) and (1991).
[29] See Birdsall and Sabot (1994). The causality could run from low inequality to high enrollment rates.
[30] See Park, Ross, and Sabot (1996).

**Table 4.2  Educational Composition of Male Wage Labor Force**
*(Percent)*

| | Brazil | | | Korea | |
|---|---|---|---|---|---|
| | 1976 | 1985 | | 1976 | 1986 |
| Uneducated | 25.6 | 20.5 | | | |
| Primary (Lower) | 45.5 | 40.8 | Elementary and Below | 19.6 | 7.5 |
| Primary (Upper) | 17.8 | 21.6 | Middle | 30.5 | 25.4 |
| Secondary | 6.7 | 11.1 | High School | 32.2 | 43.5 |
| | | | Junior College | 2.6 | 4.8 |
| University | 4.4 | 6.0 | University | 15.1 | 18.8 |

*Source:* Park, Ross, and Sabot (1996).

Table 4.2 shows that, in Korea, the educational composition of the labor force changed markedly from 1976 to 1985: the proportion of high school and post-secondary graduates in the wage labor force sharply increased and the proportion of workers with elementary school or less declined to only 8 percent.[31] Consistent with the competitive market prediction that the returns to a factor decrease as its relative supply increases, the wage premium earned by educated workers in Korea declined. Table 4.3 indicates that, standardizing for other predictors, in 1976 Korean workers with high school education earned 47 percent more than primary school graduates; by 1986 that premium had declined to 30 percent. Similarly, the premium earned by workers with higher education declined from 97 to 66 percent.[32]

Figure 4.5 summarizes our assessment of how educational expansion affected the inequality of pay in the two countries over the decade between the mid 1970s and the mid 1980s. The figure shows that, by itself, the effect of the compression of the educational structure of wages (WS) would have been to reduce the inequality of pay in Korea. By itself, the change in the educational composition of the wage labor force (CP) would have increased the inequality of pay. The compression effect, however, dominated the composition effect. The net effect (CB) of educational expansion was to reduce the log variance of wages substantially (by 22 percent).

[31] Korea and Brazil have both achieved universal primary education. There has, however, been a large and widening gap between Brazil and Korea in secondary and tertiary enrollment rates.
[32] See Birdsall and Sabot (1994).

**Figure 4.5  Educational Expansion and Inequality**

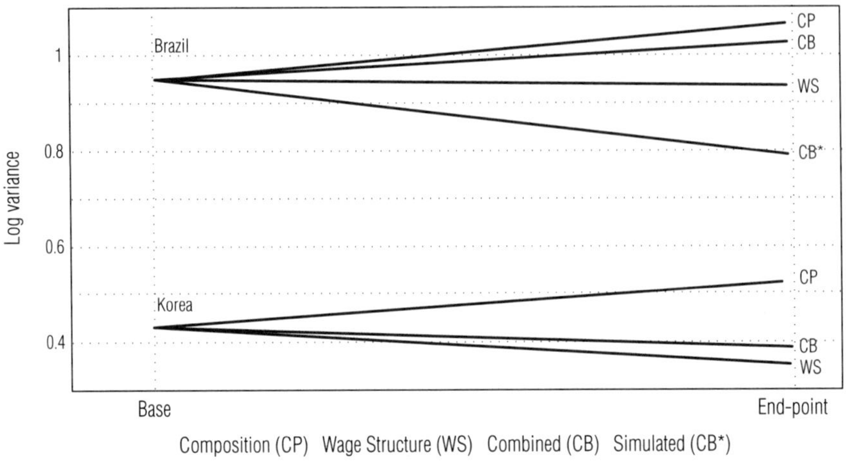

Composition (CP)  Wage Structure (WS)  Combined (CB)  Simulated (CB*)

In Brazil the proportion of workers with secondary or higher education increased as rapidly as in Korea, but from a smaller base. Hence, the absolute increment to the labor force of relatively well-educated workers was so small that even a slight increase in the demand for educated workers could offset any wage compression effect. Table 4.3 shows that the educational structure of wages barely changed in Brazil. For example, the wage premium earned by workers leaving a university was 159 percent in 1976 and 151 percent in 1985.

Brazil did not benefit from a wage structure effect (WS) on inequality, and the impact on pay inequality of changes in the educational composition of the labor force was substantial (Figure 4.5). By itself, the composition effect (CP) would have increased the log variance of wages by 8.1 percent. The net effect of educational expansion in Brazil over the decade (CB) was to increase the log variance of wages by roughly 4 percent, in marked contrast to the 22 percent decline that resulted from educational expansion in Korea.

What would the inequality of pay in Brazil have been had educational policy resulted in educational attainment comparable to that in Korea in the mid 1980s? Simulations (see CB* in Figure 4.5) indicate that Brazil would have had a log variance of wages in the mid 1980s some 17 percent lower than the actual log variance. This 17 percent reduction represents over one-quarter of the gap between Brazil and Korea in the log variance of wages.

**Table 4.3  Male Wage Structure**

|  | Brazil | | Korea | |
|---|---|---|---|---|
|  | 1976 | 1985 | 1976 | 1986 |
| Premium to primary schooling | 0.488 (55.68) | 0.449 (67.23) | 0.176 (19.66) | 0.092 (7.54) |
| Premium to secondary schooling | 0.958 (85.70) | 0.886 (110.53) | 0.473 (48.19) | 0.296 (23.40) |
| Premium to tertiary schooling | 1.593 (100.22) | 1.508 (127.40) | 0.969 (71.48) | 0.655 (42.06) |
| Experience | 0.045 (64.97) | 0.048 (83.91) | 0.067 (61.90) | 0.078 (69.61) |
| Experience$^2$ | -0.0006 (61.41) | -0.0007 (79.27) | -0.001 (39.13) | -0.001 (50.27) |
| Constant | 1.149 | 7.043 | 10.231 | 11.779 |
| $R^2$ | 0.546 | 0.562 | 0.532 | 0.449 |
| N | 85,106 | 118,000 | 23,838 | 24,486 |
| Mean log of wages | 1.864 | 8.095 | 11.363 | 12.895 |

*Note:* Dummy variables were included to control for region, occupation, industry, and head of household (Brazil only); t-statistics appear in parentheses.
*Source:* Park, Ross and Sabot (1996).

## Why Might Low Inequality Stimulate Growth?

Conventional wisdom holds that a tradeoff exists between augmenting growth and reducing inequality. The two most common explanations given for the view that an unequal distribution of income is necessary for, or the likely consequence of, rapid economic growth are: first, following Kaldor (1978), since a high level of savings is a prerequisite for rapid growth, income must be concentrated in the hands of the rich, whose marginal propensity to save is relatively high;[33] second, following Kuznets (1955), as labor shifts from a low-productivity sector to a high-productivity sector, aggregate inequality must initially increase substantially and only later decrease.

---

[33] Kaldor (1978) assumed that a high proportion of profits and a low proportion of wages are saved.

Robinson (1976) observed that this perceived tradeoff had "acquired the force of economic law." Due in part to the recent experience of East Asia, few economists today would make such an extreme statement.[34] As Figure 4.1 shows, the countries of East Asia have experienced rapid growth over three decades, with relatively low (and probably decreasing) levels of income inequality.[35]

High accumulation of human capital and its efficient utilization in the labor market were clearly key to East Asia's escape from the expected growth-equality tradeoff. But is it possible that lower income inequality enhanced growth in East Asia, above and beyond the effects on growth of equity-enhancing human capital development? We think so, and the critical mechanisms hold lessons for Latin America. Consider four possible mechanisms.

First, low and declining inequality is likely to encourage higher levels of savings and investment by the poor. Liquidity constraints due to imperfect capital markets can keep the poor from investing, especially in education, health, nutrition and other forms of human capital, even when expected returns are high. We show below how lower inequality in East Asia may have increased investment by easing such constraints. Lower income inequality implies higher absolute incomes for the poor. Education, nutritious food, and preventive and curative health care are superior goods and services. Therefore, the impact of reducing inequality on consumption by the poor of these goods and services is likely to be larger than the impact on their incomes. A second example is the impact of reduced inequality on labor productivity. Among the poor, the productivity of labor is adversely affected by inadequate nutrition and ill health.[36] By improving the health

---

[34] Indeed, twenty years ago, prior to fulfillment of East Asia's remarkable potential, Ahluwalia (1974) concluded on the basis of the cross-country data then available that "there is no strong pattern relating changes in the distribution of income to the rate of growth of GNP... This suggests that there is little firm empirical basis for the view that higher rates of growth inevitably generate greater inequality." Anand and Kanbur (1993) cite studies that provide empirical evidence of an inverted U-shape relationship between inequality and per capita income. Though most were conducted in the 1970s, these studies demonstrate the sensitivity of the estimated relationship to changes in functional form and choice of observations. See Alesina and Perotti (1993), Alesina and Rodrik (1994), Fields (1992), and Persson and Tabellini (1994) for arguments on why high inequality might constrain growth and for supporting evidence.

[35] Although controversial, the evidence suggests that, unlike many other developing countries during this period, income distribution in East Asian countries either improved or, at the very least, did not worsen. See Findlay and Wellisz (1993); Kuo, Ranis, and Fei (1981); Leipziger et al. (1992), and World Bank (1993a). In some East Asian countries and for some years within this period, there is evidence of worsening inequality (see, for example, Bruton 1992).

[36] See Birdsall (1992).

and nutrition of the poor, greater equality will increase productivity and thus stimulate growth.

We are suggesting that the higher the absolute income of the poor, the greater will be their opportunity for investment in human capital (in other words, the smaller will be the negative impact on their investment rate of the capital market imperfection that prohibits borrowing to finance investment in human capital). This implies that where income inequality is low, the positive association between income and saving rates may not be as strong as Kaldor presumed, or as national income data indicate. Data linking income and savings reflect primarily savings channeled through financial intermediaries, not the household savings in the form of increased investments in human capital that result from eased liquidity constraints.[37]

Second, lower inequality can stimulate growth by increasing political and macroeconomic stability.[38] When the incomes of the elite rapidly increase while the incomes of the non-elite stagnate, the risk is that a large proportion of the population will become politically alienated. On the other hand, declining inequality implies that non-elites are sharing in the benefits of economic growth. This reduces the risk of their political alienation, legitimizes government in popular opinion, and helps build broad-based political support. A more stable political environment is conducive to economic growth because investment is likely to be higher where the risks of political upheaval and property expropriation are reduced.

The likelihood that policies will swing between the extreme of serving the elite's narrowly defined and myopic interests and those of an equally myopic populist extreme is lower when a government has broad-based political support. Such policy swings, much more common in Latin America and Africa than in East Asia, increase economic uncertainty and thereby reduce investment. Policies at each extreme also tend to divert scarce resources from high-return investments to consumption, which suggests another link between the distribution of income and macroeconomic stability.[39]

---

[37] An eased liquidity constraint would similarly affect the investments of the poor, for example in agriculture or small enterprises, although this effect is more likely to be reflected in measured investment rates.

[38] Alesina and Rodrik (1994); Persson and Tabellini (1994). See also World Bank (1993a), p. 105. By macroeconomic stability we mean that inflationary spending is kept under control, internal and external debt remain manageable, and the macroeconomic crises that result from unanticipated shocks are quickly resolved. Macroeconomic stability is an important dimension of an environment conducive to growth. Low inequality may have contributed to the success of East Asian governments in establishing such an environment.

[39] Sachs (1990) discusses the causes and consequences of recurrent populist policies in several countries in Latin America, and the deleterious effects on poorer income groups.

High inequality creates pressure for public spending on favored groups. A relatively generous and earmarked allocation of limited fiscal resources for tertiary education, common in Latin America, is an example of a fiscal policy from which the children of the elite benefit disproportionately, and a policy which contributes little to growth. Since private returns to, and the resulting demand for, tertiary education are high, the private sector would undoubtedly provide this schooling for the children of high-income families in the absence of government provision.[40] The government thus enables the elite to increase their consumption by providing at subsidized rates a service they would finance themselves.

At the other extreme is the provision by the government of make-work jobs in the public sector, in an attempt to satisfy the excess demand for high-wage employment in unequal societies. Because in these circumstances wages in the public sector are generally higher than the marginal product of labor, which may be zero or even negative, this excess employment is heavily subsidized and diverts scarce savings from high-return investments to consumption.[41]

High inequality can also contribute to macroeconomic instability by creating pressure for exchange rate overvaluation. An overvalued exchange rate reduces the price of imports, which the urban elite has a high propensity to consume, at the expense of agriculture (where the poor are often concentrated) and other export-oriented sectors. In many economies this means a worsening of the distribution of income. In addition, overvaluation is likely to exacerbate external imbalance, a common cause of macroeconomic instability. East Asian countries have maintained relatively stable exchange rates over the last two to three decades.[42] Stable exchange rates eased the task of containing inflation and limiting internal and external debt to manageable proportions.

The ability to respond quickly to unanticipated shocks is another link between the distribution of income and macroeconomic stability. To re-

---

[40] Despite lower public spending on universities in Korea, tertiary enrollment rates, at 37 percent, are higher than in Venezuela, at 26 percent (see UNESCO, 1994). See Birdsall and James (1993) for a discussion of this issue.

[41] See Gelb, Knight, and Sabot (1991). High inequality can also result in excessive regulatory institutions that are intended to benefit the poor, but which often have the effect of reducing output and employment.

[42] See World Bank (1993a), Chapter 3. Why did East Asian governments avoid overvaluation while governments elsewhere were so much more prone to the problem? Sachs (1985) suggests that the greater political power of rural areas, which have a stake in a low exchange rate, is a factor. He notes that the proportion of the population living in urban areas in 1980 was markedly higher in Latin America, 72 percent, than in East Asia, 31.5 percent.

spond quickly, a government must have the political legitimacy that derives from substantial popular support, and, closely related, it must have enough power to act independently and not need approval for each major initiative. As noted, reducing inequality is one means of increasing the government's legitimacy in the eyes of the population, since reducing inequality implies that the poor are sharing in the fruits of economic growth.

Those in the bottom half of the income distribution are more likely to be willing to share the burden of adjustment to a negative shock if the short-run consequence is a decline in the growth rate rather than in their absolute income level.[43] If the poor are willing to share the burden of adjustment, the government will be better able to limit domestic absorption by reducing consumption while protecting investment. If the incomes of the poor are not rising or are rising very slowly, an absolute reduction of wages or subsidies as a means of reducing domestic absorption, even if to promote long-term growth, is more likely to provoke a strong negative reaction and could lead to political and economic disruption.

Third, low inequality can stimulate growth directly by increasing the x-efficiency of the poor.[44] Inequality is often associated with reduced opportunities for the poor, which in many societies are the result of long-standing economic and political discrimination against marginalized ethnic and racial groups. If children from low-income households learn from experience that no academic achievement will compensate for the low quality of the schools they attend, they are unlikely to make an extra effort. Similarly, extra effort is unlikely to be forthcoming from low-income workers or farmers who, because of policy biases, face economic incentives that do not reward them. Although difficult to quantify, high productivity or x-efficiency associated with low income inequality may, nevertheless, be important.[45] The work ethic for which East Asian children and labor are well known may be less an exogenous cultural trait than an endogenous response to incentives that reward effort.

---

[43] Mazumdar (1993) notes that, as part of Korea's adjustment to the first oil shock, "the unit cost of labor was reduced by a massive 25 percent," largely accounted for by currency devaluation. He goes on to observe that "even this amount of decline of the real share of labor did not imply a fall in the real wage. Rather the wage increase in 1975 was held down to 1.4 percent, compared with the annual wage increase in excess of 10 percent in 1966–73."
[44] X-efficiency is a measure of workers' productivity holding constant all other inputs to the production process, including the workers' skills. See Leibenstein (1966).
[45] Timmer (1993) argues that the observed link between agricultural growth and increases in national total factor productivity results in part from the rural poor's increased work effort and investments, in response to improved incentives for the agricultural sector.

Land reform is the most straightforward example of an agricultural policy, implemented in Korea and Taiwan, that both reduces inequality and increases productivity. Labor intensity and yield tend to increase as farm size decreases: value added per hectare on small farms (three hectares or less) tends to be three to five times greater than the average for large farms (500 hectares or more).[46] This implies that the reduction in the inequality of land holding and in the average farm size that resulted from the land reforms in Korea and Taiwan also increased agricultural output and labor demand. In Indonesia, Thailand, and Korea, both the average size of farms and the Gini coefficient of farm size distribution are much smaller than in Brazil, Mexico, Argentina, and most other countries in Latin America.[47]

Finally, low income inequality can stimulate growth directly by reducing the risk of costly rent-seeking in the labor market and by increasing the domestic multiplier effect of a given increase in incomes.[48] As a result of policies that contribute to, rather than sap, the dynamism of the agricultural sector, societies with low income inequality will generally have a smaller gap between rural and urban income, and a relatively better-off rural population.[49] Hence, the pressure referred to above, to generate make-work jobs in the high-wage urban public sector, is reduced, as are the negative consequences for growth of an expanding "job sink." The small rural-urban income gap also implies a relatively weak Kuznets effect; that is, the intersectoral transfer of labor due to the rapid growth of the manufacturing-export sector does not tend to induce greater income inequality.

Higher income in the rural and agricultural sectors also means higher demand for the agricultural inputs and consumer goods that can then stimulate the growth of nonagricultural output and employment. For example in Taiwan, agriculture, not manufacturing for export, was clearly the leading sector in the 1950s and early 1960s, and roughly 60 percent of the increment to aggregate demand was domestic. More generally, among Asian countries there is a strong positive correlation between the rate of growth of the agricultural sector and that of the nonagricultural sector.[50] The relationship suggests that the multiplier effects of agricultural growth on manufacturing, construction and services are large: a 1 percent increase

[46] See Squire (1981) and Berry and Cline (1979).
[47] Squire (1981), p. 156.
[48] See Mellor (1993).
[49] A larger share of public investment was allocated to rural areas in East Asia than in other low and middle-income economies. Equally important, levels of direct and indirect taxation of agriculture were lower in East Asia than in other regions. See World Bank (1993a), pp. 32-37.
[50] See Mellor (1993).

in agricultural growth is associated with a 1.5 percent increase in the growth rate of the nonagricultural sector.[51]

Because the relatively simple manufactured inputs and consumer goods demanded by rural residents are generally more efficiently produced with labor-intensive techniques, the employment effects of increases in rural demand are amplified.[52] In contrast, when the incomes of the urban elite increase, the tradables on which they spend their increased income tend to be capital-intensive goods. It is not necessary to be a structuralist to acknowledge the importance of these demand and multiplier effects. Even in fully open economies, the multiplier effects of external demand, especially at early stages of development, may not be as great as the effects of local demand. Moreover, vibrant local markets and competition may be critical to producers developing the expertise and efficiency required to enter external markets.[53] Strong domestic demand gave East Asia's early manufacturers a competitive advantage in international markets by giving them the opportunity to test market labor-intensive goods and achieve economies of scale.

Note that none of these mechanisms relies on redistributive transfers to reduce income inequality. Direct transfers to the poor are unlikely to be good for growth. Transfers often result in the diversion of scarce savings from investment to the subsidization of consumption. They also tend to distort incentives and reduce allocative efficiency. In contrast, education and the mechanisms described above contribute to and are associated with increased productivity and earning capacity of the poor. This suggests another contrast between East Asia and Latin America: an implicit emphasis on opportunities for the poor in East Asia, versus an emphasis on redistributive transfers in Latin America.

---

[51] The relationship also implies that the faster agriculture grows, the faster its share of total output declines. Again with the exception of the East Asian city states, those Asian countries with the fastest rates of growth of agricultural output over the last 30 years have tended to experience the biggest declines in the share of agricultural output in GNP. See World Bank (1993a).

[52] See Ranis and Stewart (1987), and Bell, Hazell, and Slade (1982). A detailed study of these backward and forward linkages in the Muda River region of Malaysia provides microeconomic confirmation of the magnitude of the intersectoral multiplier suggested by the cross-country relationship.

[53] Porter (1990).

*Econometric Results*

In this section we report the results of an econometric analysis of the relationship between income distribution and economic growth in a cross-section of countries, and, as an illustration of the magnitude of the relationship, use those results to quantify the effect on Brazil's economic growth of
its high level of income inequality. Again, we build on the results reported
by Barro (1991). His key finding is that the growth rate is positively related
to the initial stock of human capital and negatively related to initial per
capita GDP. In other words, for a given quantity of initial human capital, a
poor country tends to grow faster than a rich country, so that incomes converge over the period among countries with similar levels of education.[54]

We used Barro-style growth rate functions to assess the impact of the
distribution of income on subsequent economic growth. Clarke (1992)
found a negative relationship between income inequality and average annual growth in per capita GDP for 1970–1988.[55] This relationship is robust to
choice of five inequality measures and alternative specifications of the explanatory variables.[56] We modified the Clarke exercise because: (a) we
wanted estimates for 1960–1985 for comparability with Barro and our other
results; and (b) in Clarke's data set, inequality observations for some countries are as recent as 1980. Current inequality, arguably, is determined simultaneously with growth. We assembled country observations from a variety of sources on the ratio of the income shares of the top 20 percent and
the bottom 40 percent in the postwar period. We chose the earliest available
observation and dropped observations where the measure postdated 1970.
This procedure yielded a data set with 74 observations.

The addition of the inequality measure to the basic Barro growth rate
function reported in Table 4.4, equation 1 does not much change the parameter estimates. The education variables remain significantly positive. The
inequality variable is negative and significant (at the 10 percent level).

How much of a constraint on growth is high inequality? For our
sample of low and middle-income countries, the average annual growth in
per capita GDP between 1960 and 1985 was 1.8 percent. One standard de-

---

[54] All else equal, had per capita real GDP been $1,000 higher in a given country in 1960, growth
over the following 25 years would have been 0.75 percentage points lower per year on average.
Had primary or secondary school enrollment rates been 10 percentage points higher in 1960,
growth would have been, respectively, 0.25 or 0.30 percentage points higher per year on average. See Barro (1991).
[55] See also Alesina and Rodrik (1994) and Persson and Tabellini (1994).
[56] Clarke (1992) does not explore the sensitivity of his results to outliers or alternative samples.

**Table 4.4  Determinants of GDP Growth, 1960–85**

| Variable | Basic Regression (1) | Excludes Education Variables (2) | Excludes the Eight HPAEs (3) |
|---|---|---|---|
| 1960 Real per capita GDP (in thousands of 1980 US$) | -0.0075 (-4.730) | -0.0020 (-1.801) | -0.0061 (-3.547) |
| 1960 Primary enrollment rate | 0.0243 (3.024) | | 0.0199 (2.493) |
| 1960 Secondary enrollment rate | 0.0366 (2.427) | | 0.0361 (2.189) |
| Ratio of real govt. consumption (excluding defense and education) to real GDP, averaged over 1960–85 | -0.1229 (-4.380) | -0.1495 (-4.760) | -0.0969 (-3.162) |
| Number of revolutions and coups (per year, 1960–85) | -0.0176 (-1.867) | -0.0268 (-2.493) | -0.0177 (-1.906) |
| Number of assassinations (per million population per year, 1960–85) | -0.0055 (-1.526) | -0.0067 (-1.626) | -0.0033 (-0.920) |
| Absolute value of the deviation of the PPP Value for the investment deflator (US=1) from the sample mean (1960) | -0.0086 (-1.093) | -0.0176 (-2.012) | -0.0063 (-0.810) |
| National household income distribution (top 20% to bottom 40%) | -0.0013 (-1.897) | -0.0018 (-2.406) | -0.0007 (-1.047) |
| Intercept | 0.0418 (4.185) | 0.0706 (7.871) | 0.0330 (3.108) |
| $R^2$ | 0.5389 | 0.3574 | 0.4542 |
| Number of observations | 74 | 74 | 66 |

*Note:* T-statistics appear in parentheses.

viation increase in primary and secondary education enrollment rates raises the predicted growth rate by 0.62 and 0.34 percentage points, respectively. A one standard deviation decrease in the level of income inequality raises the predicted growth rate by 0.32 percentage points. Although the impact on growth of a change in inequality is smaller than similar changes in enrollment rates, the effect of reducing inequality is still substantial. For example, ceteris paribus, after 25 years, per capita GDP would be 8.2 percent higher in a country with low inequality than in a country with inequality one standard deviation higher.

*Some Simulations*

How big was the effect of high inequality on growth in Latin America? In an attempt to answer this question, we conducted some simulations that assess how much more slowly Korea would have grown if it had had Brazil's high levels of inequality. As mentioned earlier, in 1960 the ratio of the income share of the top 20 percent to the bottom 20 percent was roughly 8 in Korea and 26 in Brazil. Korea grew at an average rate of 5.95 percent between 1960 and 1985. Consider two alternative simulations: in the first, we assume Korea would have grown at 5.95 percent except for the impact of changes in inequality; in the second, we assume Korea would have grown at 5.95 percent except for the impact of changes in 1960 primary and secondary enrollment rates. Using equation 1 from Table 4.4, we alternatively set the inequality and enrollment rate variables to the average for all countries in our sample, to the average for all low and middle-income countries, and to the level for Brazil. We obtain the following predicted growth rates for Korea:

| Country Standard | Inequality | Enrollments |
|---|---|---|
| Average | 5.76 | 5.68 |
| Low/middle income | 5.67 | 4.77 |
| Brazil | 5.29 | 5.39 |

The most striking simulations are the ones in which Brazilian values are substituted for Korean values. If, in 1960, Korea had had Brazil's level of inequality, Korea's predicted growth rate over the following 25 years would have been reduced by 0.66 percentage points each year, implying that, after 25 years, per capita GDP in Korea would have been 15 percent lower. In 1960 the percentage gap in enrollment rates between Korea and Brazil was smaller than the gap in inequality; as a consequence, the impact on Korea's predicted growth of substituting Brazilian enrollment rates is smaller than the impact of substituting Brazilian inequality. Moreover, as we see below, low enrollment rates in Brazil were in part due to the constraint on the demand for schooling imposed by high inequality. If Korea had had Brazil's inequality, Korea's enrollment rates would have been lower, suggesting a still larger gross constraint of high inequality on economic growth. This evidence, crude though the data and methods may be, lends support to the hypothesis that high inequality in Latin America constrained growth and that the impact was large.

## Accounting for the Interregional Gap in Educational Performance

A combination of lower supply of, and demand for, educated workers contributed to the slower growth in Latin America than in East Asia. Why has the performance of systems of basic education been so much weaker in Latin America than in East Asia?

### The Feedback from Growth to Human Capital Accumulation

In East Asia there was a positive feedback from rapid growth and altered household behavior to human capital accumulation. In Latin America this feedback was much weaker. Figure 4.4 illustrates one of the feedback mechanisms. In the absence of the intensification of demand for skilled labor, expansion of the educational system leads to lower returns to education. Investment in human capital by households has been greater in East Asia than in Latin America in part because the demand for educated workers has been greater, and consequently the returns to investment in schooling have been higher.[57] Stronger demand for educated workers elicits a greater supply.

The other feedback mechanism is equally simple: rapid economic growth in East Asia increased the numerator, while declining fertility reduced the denominator, of the ratio of public expenditures on basic education per school age child. Neither in 1960 nor in 1989 was public expenditure on education as a percentage of GNP much higher in East Asia than in Latin America. In 1960 the share was 2.2 percent for all developing countries, 2.3 percent for Latin America, and 2.5 percent for East Asia. Over the three decades, all regions markedly increased the share of national output they invested in formal education, to 3.6 for all developing countries, 3.4 percent in Latin America, and 3.7 in East Asia.[58]

---

[57] In Figure 4.4, S'-S is the difference between the typical East Asian country and country X in the level of investment in human capital induced by the greater demand for educated labor.
[58] See Birdsall and Sabot (1994) for data sources. Government expenditure on education, expressed as a percentage of GNP, was used as an explanatory variable in a cross-country regression in which expected years of schooling of the school age cohort (essentially an aggregate of enrollment rates) was the independent variable. For a sample of 15 Asian and Latin American countries, the expenditure variable was insignificant (see Tan and Mingat 1992).

**Table 4.5  Public Expenditure on Basic Education per Eligible Child and Some Determinants**

| Country | 1970 | 1975 | 1985 | 1989 | % Change, 1970–89 |
|---|---|---|---|---|---|
| **Korea** | | | | | |
| Expenditure on basic education per eligible child | 95.3 | 81.6 | 357.1 | 433.4 | 354.7 |
| Public expenditure as % of GNP | 3.1 | 1.9 | 3.8 | 2.7 | -12.9 |
| Index for absolute expenditure on basic education | 100 | 91 | 388 | 444 | |
| Number of children eligible for basic education (000) | 10,074 | 10,754 | 10,420 | 9,848 | -2.2 |
| **Mexico** | | | | | |
| Expenditure on basic education per eligible child | 68.4 | 124.9 | 113.5 | 111.9 | 63.6 |
| Public expenditure as % of GNP | 1.6 | 2.6 | 2.0 | 2.0 | 25.0 |
| Index for absolute expenditure on basic education | 100 | 222 | 255 | 259 | |
| Number of children eligible for basic education (000) | 16,168 | 19,726 | 24,912 | 25,649 | 58.6 |
| **Kenya** | | | | | |
| Expenditure on basic education per eligible child | 38.6 | | 46.6 | 53.4 | 38.3 |
| Public expenditure as % of GNP | 4.0 | | 4.9 | 4.9 | 22.5 |
| Index for absolute expenditure on basic education | 100 | | 220 | 286 | |
| Number of children eligible for basic education (000) | 3,814 | 4,591 | 6,973 | 7,900 | 107.1 |
| **Pakistan** | | | | | |
| Expenditure on basic education per eligible child | 7.9 | 9.4 | 13.4 | | |
| Public expenditure as % of GNP | 1.1 | 1.6 | 1.6 | | |
| Index for absolute expenditure on basic education | 100 | 150 | 277 | | |
| Number of children eligible for basic education (000) | 20,983 | 26,563 | 34,414 | 42,249 | 101.4 |

*Notes:* a) Absolute expenditures on basic education in real 1987 US dollars used to calculate indices for absolute expenditures on education.
b) Number eligible for basic education calculated using enrollment rates and number of students in the first and second levels.
*Sources:* UNESCO *Statistical Yearbook* (various years); *World Tables* (various years) for real gross national income figures.

It was not, in short, extraordinary government commitment that produced East Asia's extraordinary performance with respect to the provision of education.[59] By the same token, poor educational performance in Latin America cannot be blamed solely on a lack of commitment to education by governments. Aggregate output must grow if the constant share of GDP that goes to education is to grow in absolute terms. From 1965 to 1980, GDP growth averaged 7.4 percent in Malaysia and only 3.4 percent in Argentina. This implies that over the decade from 1965 to 1975, given a constant share of GDP allocated to education, the resources available to the education sector in Malaysia more than doubled, while in Argentina they increased by less than 50 percent.

Table 4.5 indicates that, in 1970, public expenditure on basic education per eligible child was not much higher in Korea ($95 in 1987 dollars) than in Mexico ($68).[60] However, between 1970 and 1989, the figure more than quadrupled in Korea, to $433, whereas in Mexico it did not even double. As a consequence, in 1989 Mexican public expenditure on basic education per eligible child was only 26 percent of Korean expenditure. What accounts for this divergence? Again, it was not government commitment, since public expenditure as a percentage of GNP over this period was actually declining in Korea and rising in Mexico. The absolute level of expenditure on basic education rose much more rapidly in Korea because GNP was growing so much faster than in Mexico and because, while in Mexico the number of children eligible for basic education increased by nearly 60 percent, in Korea the school age cohort was actually 2 percent smaller in 1989 than in 1970.[61]

Of course, rapid growth also raises the demand for labor, hence wages—including the wages of teachers. Because the pay of teachers accounts for a large proportion of recurrent expenditure on education in low-income countries, the tendency for rising costs to diminish the educational benefits of rapid growth would be strong if it were not for an important mitigating factor: rapid accumulation of human capital in one period in-

---

[59] Nor were initial conditions or the colonial legacy decisive in explaining why enrollment rates have been so much higher in East Asia than elsewhere. While Korea had much higher enrollment rates in 1950 than did most other developing countries, the roughly 50 and 70 percentage point increases since then in, respectively, primary and secondary enrollment rates account for much of the current gap between Korea and other middle-income countries. Similar claims can be made for other East Asian countries.

[60] Indeed, in 1975, expenditures per eligible child were higher in Mexico than in Korea.

[61] The difference in fertility rates, of which these diverging trends are a reflection, is in part due to differences in educational attainment, particularly the educational attainment of women.

**Table 4.6  Absolute Income Share of Lowest Quintile**

| Country | GNP per capita (US $) | Population (millions) | Total GNP (US $ millions) | Income share (%) | Absolute income (US $ millions) of bottom 20% of households | Per capita income (US $) |
|---|---|---|---|---|---|---|
| Indonesia, 1976 | 240 | 135.2 | 32,448 | 6.6 | 2,141 | 79 |
| Kenya, 1976 | 240 | 13.8 | 3,312 | 2.6 | 86 | 31 |
| Malaysia, 1987 | 1,810 | 16.5 | 29,865 | 4.6 | 1,374 | 416 |
| Brazil, 1983 | 1,880 | 129.7 | 243,836 | 2.4 | 5,852 | 226 |
| Malaysia, 1987 | 1,810 | 16.5 | 29,865 | 4.6 | 1,374 | 416 |
| Costa Rica, 1986 | 1,480 | 2.6 | 3,848 | 3.3 | 127 | 254 |
| Korea, 1976 | 670 | 36 | 24,120 | 5.7 | 1,375 | 191 |
| Botswana, 1986 | 840 | 1.1 | 924 | 2.5 | 23 | 115 |
| Indonesia, 1987 | 450 | 171.4 | 77,130 | 8.8 | 6,787 | 251 |
| Philippines, 1985 | 580 | 54.7 | 31,726 | 5.5 | 1,745 | 160 |

*Source:* World Bank, *World Development Report*, various years.

creases the potential supply of teachers in the next, thereby reducing the relative earnings premium they command. While growth induces increases in average wages, the wages of more educated workers, including teachers, tend to rise at a slower rate.

## Inequality and the Demand for Schooling

Below-average levels of educational attainment in Latin America have contributed to above-average levels of income inequality. There has also been a feedback effect, closing a vicious cycle, from high inequality to low enrollment rates: high income inequality limits household demand for education and probably decreases public supply.

As discussed above, budgetary constraints and capital market imperfections mean that poor households often do not make human capital investments in their children, even when the returns are high. The pressing need to use income simply to subsist crowds out high return investments and constrains the demand for education. Table 4.6 pairs East Asian countries with countries with very similar levels of average per capita income but considerably higher levels of income inequality, hence considerably lower absolute incomes of the poor. For example, while per capita income in Brazil (in 1983) slightly exceeded per capita income in Malaysia (in 1987), the bottom quintile received 4.6 percent of total income in Malaysia but only 2.4 percent of total income in Brazil. Thus, the per capita income of the bottom quintile in Brazil was only 54 percent of the per capita income of those at the bottom of the income distribution in Malaysia. Given an income elasticity of demand for secondary education of 0.50 (a conservative figure), if the distribution of income were as equal in Brazil as in Malaysia, secondary enrollments among poor Brazilian children would be more than 40 percent higher. There is some evidence that, among the poor, the income elasticity of demand for basic schooling exceeds 1.0, in which case secondary enrollments among poor Brazilian children would be more than 80 percent higher.

In his analysis of the determinants of differences among countries in secondary enrollment rates, Williamson (1993) added a variable measuring inequality in the distribution of income.[62] The income distribution variable

---

[62] Williamson (1993) builds on the analysis of Schultz (1988). The income distribution variable used was the ratio of the share of total income of the bottom 40 percent to the share of total income of the top 20 percent. Among the other variables in the regression were GNP per capita, a measure of teacher cost relative to GNP, and the share of the population that is of school age.

had the predicted effect: more egalitarian societies had higher secondary school enrollment rates.[63] Williamson (1993) then used the estimated equation to decompose the difference in enrollment rates between Brazil and Korea. Table 4.7 summarizes his results. The decomposition indicates that none of the 27 percentage point difference can be explained by GNP per adult. Nor do less costly teachers contribute to the explanation, since teacher pay in relation to GNP per capita was also lower in Brazil. The larger size of the school age cohort in Brazil explains a small proportion of the gap. But nearly all of that portion of the gap that can be explained is due to the greater income inequality in Brazil than in Korea.[64] If income were distributed as equally in Brazil as in Korea, the model predicts that Korea's secondary enrollment rate would be only 6 percentage points higher, instead of 27 percentage points higher. The cross-country evidence is consistent with the microevidence: the impact of differences in income inequality on enrollment rates can be large.

*Allocation of Public Expenditure Between Education Levels*

High income inequality may have an influence on the supply side as well as the demand side of the market for education. For the government to provide subsidized basic educational opportunities to a large segment of the school age population when the distribution of income is highly unequal, the tax burden on the rich must be heavy. High income families are likely to resist such measures and attempt to channel subsidies to higher education, where their children will be the beneficiaries. If incomes are more equally distributed, as is the case in East Asia, the incidence of taxes to finance mass education need not be as concentrated, and thus resistance by high income families is likely to be weaker.

While public expenditure on education as a share of GNP is not significantly lower in Latin America than in East Asia, the share of public expenditure allocated to basic education has been consistently lower, which helps explain why opportunities for basic education are less abundant and

---

[63] In the equation in which expenditure per eligible child was the dependent variable, the income distribution variable was statistically significant; in the enrollment rate equation, the t-statistic on the distribution variable was somewhat lower than conventionally accepted for significance (see Williamson 1993).

[64] Williamson (1993) attributes the unexplained portion of the enrollment rate gap, the residual, to a cultural bias against education in Brazil. Alternatively, it could be due to lower quality schooling in Brazil, hence lower expected returns and lower demand. Of course, any meaning attributed to the residual is speculative.

**Table 4.7  Why Commitments to Secondary Education Were So Different in South Korea and Brazil in the Early 1970s: A Decomposition Analysis**

| Variable | South Korea | Brazil | Difference ($\Delta$) | $\beta_{xj}\Delta x_j$ |
|---|---|---|---|---|
| Enrollment ratio | 0.620 | 0.349 | +0.271 | |
| **Regression Results: Dependent Variable $X_j$** | | | | |
| Log GNP per adult | 6.800 | 6.904 | -0.104 | -0.033 |
| Log relative price teachers | 0.360 | -0.538 | +0.898 | -0.410 |
| Urban ratio | 0.494 | 0.582 | -0.088 | -0.030 |
| School age population ratio | 0.149 | 0.159 | -0.010 | +0.019 |
| Bottom 40%/Top 20% | 0.373 | 0.105 | +0.268 | +0.213 |
| "Culture" = Residual | | | | +0.512 |

Source: Williamson, Jeffrey (1993).

of poorer quality in Latin America. The lower share of public resources allocated to basic education in Latin America may be a function of high inequality in the distribution of income.

Korea and Venezuela are extreme examples. While in 1985 Venezuela allocated 43 percent of its public education budget to higher education, Korea allocated only 10 percent of its budget to post-secondary schooling.[65] Public expenditure on education as a percentage of GNP was actually higher in Venezuela (4.3) than in Korea (3.0). However, after subtracting the share going to higher education, public expenditure available for basic education as a percentage of GNP was considerably higher in Korea (2.5) than in Venezuela (1.3).

By giving priority to expanding the quantity and improving the quality at the base of the educational pyramid, East Asian governments have stimulated the demand for higher education, while relying to a large extent on the private sector to satisfy that demand. In both East Asia and Latin America, the probability of going to university is markedly higher for secondary school graduates from high-income families than for those from low-income families. Typically, government subsidies of university education are not related to need, implying that they disproportionately benefit families with relatively high incomes who could afford to pay fees closer to the actual cost of schooling.

At the same time, in many countries, Brazil being a notable example, low public funding of secondary education results in poorly qualified chil-

---

[65] See Birdsall and Sabot (1994).

dren from low-income backgrounds being forced into the private sector or entirely out of the education system. Because of the higher concentration on basic education in East Asia, public funds are more likely to benefit children of low-income families who otherwise might have difficulty remaining in school. In sum, in East Asia large numbers of poor children benefit from public expenditures, whereas in Latin America small numbers of children from relatively high-income families are the beneficiaries.[66]

## Administrative Inefficiency

Expenditures on basic education per child are higher in East Asia than in Latin America. In addition, administrative inefficiency tends to be greater in Latin America. Brazil provides a notable example of gross inefficiencies in resource use undermining school quality. One problem is overstaffing. In many of the states in Brazil, the recruitment of education staff has histori-cally been driven by patronage rather than efficiency. The ratio of nonteach-ing to teaching staff varies substantially across different state systems, and high ratios (a 2:1 ratio of nonteachers to teachers is not uncommon) are cor-related with low completion and high repetition rates.[67]

## Conclusion

Human capital accumulation has been an important dimension of develop-ment strategy in East Asia and a contributing factor to the difference in eco-nomic performance between East Asia and Latin America. Over the last three and a half decades, East Asian nations have succeeded both in mark-edly increasing the quantity of basic education and improving school qual-ity. In Latin America, on the other hand, there has been a tradeoff: as enroll-ments have increased (at a slower rate than in East Asia), the quality of schooling has eroded. Assessments based on both microeconomic data and cross-country comparisons indicate that this difference in educational per-formance helps explain why East Asia has grown so much faster than Latin America. The labor force in East Asia is better endowed with productivity-enhancing cognitive skills than is the labor force in Latin America, and the former is better able to acquire technological capability. In East Asia, the growth payoff to investments in education has been enhanced by the ex-

---

[66] The public cost of providing a student with instruction is roughly 50 times larger at the uni-versity than at the primary level. See Schultz (1988).

[67] Plank et al. (1996).

port-oriented, labor and skill-demanding growth strategy that has sustained returns to human capital even while educational systems have been expanding rapidly. Rapidly rising levels of education among women have resulted in changes in household behavior ( e.g., marked declines in fertility) that have also stimulated growth. In contrast, development strategy in Latin America has been less export-oriented and less labor and skill-demanding. As a consequence, the growth payoff to investments in education has been lower. The slower spread of education, including for women, has constrained fertility decline and limited the possibilities for other growth-augmenting changes in household behavior.

Superior educational performance in East Asia also contributes to the explanation of its lower income inequality. Increases in the relative abundance of educated workers eroded the scarcity rents they could command in the labor market. Thus, while the absolute wages of educated workers grew, the gap in wages between the more and less educated narrowed, contributing to substantial declines in the inequality of pay. Moreover, cross-country growth regressions suggest that lower income inequality was itself a stimulus to growth in East Asia, while in Latin America high inequality was a constraint on growth.

East Asia's superior educational performance was not due to the allocation of a larger share of GNP to public expenditures on education. Rather it appears to have been due primarily to three factors: the positive feedback from more rapid growth to larger expenditures on education; the allocation of substantially larger shares of public expenditure to basic education; and the markedly slower growth rates of the school age population. Lower income inequality and lower absolute levels of poverty also probably made it easier for poor households to finance schooling.

The contrasting experiences of Latin America and East Asia suggest that, contrary to conventional wisdom, inequalities in the distribution of both education and income may have a significant and negative impact on the rate of economic growth. The unequal distribution of education in Latin America, in terms of both quantity and quality, constrained economic growth in the region by resulting in foregone opportunities to increase labor productivity and change household behavior. At the same time, the relatively small size of the educated labor force and the resulting high scarcity rents commanded by educated workers contributed to high inequality in the distribution of income. Closing a vicious cycle, slower growth and high income inequality, in turn, further limited the supply of, and demand for, education. This contrasts with the experience of East Asia where the poor had relatively equal access to quality basic education, leading to a virtuous cycle of high educational performance that stimulated growth and reduced inequality.

Education policy alone, however, does not explain the tremendous differences in equity and growth across the two regions. We have suggested that macroeconomic and sectoral policies in Latin America, which favored capital-intensive production and were biased against the agricultural sector, almost certainly exacerbated the inequality problem and may, in fact, have hindered growth as well. The East Asian development strategy, in contrast, promoted a dynamic agricultural sector and a labor-demanding, export-oriented growth path.

We have also suggested that low inequality may not only contribute to growth indirectly, by increasing investment in education, but may have a direct positive effect on the growth rate—by increasing investment in dimensions of human capital other than education, by increasing political and macroeconomic stability, by increasing the x-efficiency of the economy (e.g. via greater work effort of the poor), and by decreasing intersectoral income gaps and increasing the domestic multiplier effects of a given increase in income. In East Asia, these mechanisms reflected an implicit emphasis on opportunities, not transfers, for the poor. We present empirical results that support a positive relationship between low inequality and growth.

The experience of East Asia and Latin America is sufficient to reject the conventional wisdom of a necessary link between high income inequality and rapid growth. While our analysis has not been sufficient to confirm the opposite, we hope others now seriously consider the hypothesis that high inequality, and policies that ignore or even exacerbate inequality, constrain growth in the long run. Contrary to the conventional wisdom, the evidence suggests that the association of slow growth and high inequality in Latin America is in part due to the fact that high inequality may be, in and of itself, a constraint to growth. Conversely, East Asia's low level of inequality may have been a significant stimulus to economic growth. The challenge in Latin America, then, is to find ways to reduce inequality, not by transfers, but by eliminating consumption subsidies for the rich and increasing the productivity of the poor. Investment in education is a key to sustained growth, not only because it contributes directly through productivity effects, but because it also reduces income inequality.

---

*Nancy Birdsall is Executive Vice President of the Inter-American Development Bank, David Ross is Professor of Economics at Bryn Mawr College, and Richard Sabot is Professor of Economics at Williams College.*

## Appendix Table 4.A  Growth Regressions

| Dependent variable | (1)<br>Basic<br>Regression | (2)<br>Gender-Specific<br>Enrollment | (3)<br>Manufactured<br>Exports |
|---|---|---|---|
| Number of observations | 98 | 108 | 100 |
| Constant | 0.0302 | 0.0137 | 0.0202 |
| Per capita GDP, 1960<br>(thousands of 1980 dollars) | -0.0075<br>(-6.25) | -0.0056<br>(-4.000) | -0.0069<br>(-5.135) |
| Secondary school<br>enrollment rate, 1960 | 0.0305<br>(3.861) | 0.0357<br>(2.705) | 0.0262<br>(1.723) |
| Primary school<br>enrollment rate, 1960 | 0.0250<br>(4.464) | | 0.0271<br>(4.532) |
| Female primary school<br>enrollment rate, 1960 | | 0.0138<br>(1.340) | |
| Male primary school<br>enrollment rate, 1960 | | 0.0131<br>(1.159) | |
| Ratio of manufactured<br>exports to GDP, 1965 | | | 0.0007<br>(1.539) |
| Secondary school<br>enrollment-export<br>interaction, 1960[a] | | | 0.0005<br>(0.324) |
| Government consumption<br>share of GDP, 1970-85[b] | -0.1190<br>(-4.250) | -0.0604<br>(-2.406) | -0.0566<br>(-2.419) |
| Average annual number<br>of revolutions, 1960-85 | -0.0195<br>(-3.095) | | -0.0168<br>(-1.987) |
| Average annual number<br>of assassinations, 1960-85 | -0.0333<br>(-2.148) | | -0.0024<br>(-0.738) |
| Absolute deviation in<br>investment deflator, 1960[c] | -0.0143<br>(-2.698) | -0.0075<br>(-1.630) | -0.0139<br>(-2.136) |
| $R^2$ | 0.56 | 0.41 | 0.57 |

Note: The first column presents Barro's (1991) results. The other columns present results from Birdsall, Ross and Sabot (1995a, 1995b). T-statistics in parentheses.
a. Ratio of manufactured exports to GDP multiplied by 1960 secondary school enrollment rate.
b. Average annual ratio of real government consumption (exclusive of defense and education) to real GDP.
c. Magnitude of the deviation of the purchasing power parity value for the investment deflator (U.S. = 1.0) from the sample mean.

# Commentary

*Nora Lustig*

Nancy Birdsall, David Ross, and Richard Sabot's paper is a welcome contribution to the growing empirical literature relating growth performance to inequality and income distribution. From the point of view of economic theory, a causal mechanism between income distribution and growth exists only if the economies are off their long-run equilibrium (in the Solow-type models) or because there are multiple long-run equilibria (in the endogenous growth models). Before the recent developments of endogenous growth theory (in particular, the "new political economy" school), the standard result prevalent in economic theory was that income distribution has no effect on steady-state growth. In the Solow model, for example, growth in per capita income is determined solely by the rate of growth of technical progress. All individual incomes grow at this rate, so the distribution of income remains constant. That is, the distribution of income is independent from the steady rate of growth. In the non-neoclassical Kaldor model of growth as well, the distribution of income does not affect steady-state growth.[1]

In the Solow-type growth models, the distribution of income, like other behavioral parameters, may determine the cross-country differences in the level of GDP per capita but not its rate of growth. The distribution of income may influence the rate of growth only when the economy is off the steady state. Subject to the same shock, two economies with different distribution of income may take a different amount of time to return to steady-state growth even if the latter is the same for both. In the endogenous growth models, because of externalities and/or overall increasing returns, the exogenous technical progress term in the Solow model becomes endogenous: i.e., a function of the behavioral or structural parameters of the economy. One of the latter can be the distribution of income. The distribu-

---

[1] The steady-state growth rate is also determined in the Kaldor model by the rate of population growth plus the rate of technical progress. The difference in the Solow and the Kaldor models is the mechanism of adjustment that sets the rate of capital accumulation equal to the exogenously given rate of population growth and the rate of technical progress. In Kaldor's model, the rate of capital accumulation adjusts through changes in income distribution among two classes (workers and capitalists) with different propensities to save. That is, in Kaldor's model, growth does affect the income distribution, but not the other way around.

tion of income has a causal effect on growth only if the model has multiple equilibria so that initial conditions matter.

Initially the endogenous growth literature did not examine the distribution of income as one of the relevant variables because it assumed a representative agent. However, the "new political economy" has extended the endogenous growth literature to include income distribution considerations. Some of this literature looks into the relationship between income distribution and investment in education, on the one hand, and between the pre-tax distribution of income and the political equilibrium leading to the choice of net taxation, on the other (for example, Perotti 1992; Alesina and Rodrik 1992, 1993; Persson and Tabellini 1994). A more recent crop of this literature analyzes the link between income inequality, political instability, and investment growth (Perotti 1993; Alesina and Perotti 1993).

The new political economy models show that income inequality is harmful for growth either because: a) inequality has a negative impact on the accumulation of human capital; b) in more unequal societies, the demand for distortionary taxation is higher; and/or c) income inequality increases political instability and the latter in turn reduces investment.

Development economics, often without formalization and sometimes using non-mainstream assumptions, also produced models where income inequality could lower growth. The two-gap models characterized by an exogenous propensity to save and a fixed-coefficient production function are an example: Income inequality could hurt economic growth if the foreign savings gap is the binding constraint, because the rich have higher propensities to import. However, in such models economic inequality could benefit growth if the domestic savings gap is binding, for analogous reasons: i.e., the rich have higher propensities to save. The so-called Latin American structuralists, most of whom were associated with CEPAL, particularly in the 1960s, also argue that income inequality could hinder growth—because of its negative impact on aggregate demand (assuming that economic growth is demand-driven rather than supply-driven), or because of the foreign savings constraint (analogous to the two-gap model) in an economy characterized by technological and institutional rigidities (e.g., real, not downwardly flexible, wages) (Lustig 1993).

To sum up, there is quite a bit of analytical work to support the view that income inequality might have a negative impact on economic growth. The results of recent research efforts have produced a solid number of econometric exercises in support of this hypothesis. In particular, the new political economy school has found that income inequality may lower growth through its impact, for example, on the demand for fiscal redistribution by means of distortionary taxation (Alesina and Rodrick 1992, 1993; Persson and Tabellini 1994), or on political instability (Alesina and Perotti 1993).

The other important link supported by empirical research is the relationship between a more equal distribution of income and more investment in education, and the latter and higher growth. A study by Bourguignon (1993), for example, found that "a more equal distribution of income induces, other things being equal, a higher rate of secondary school enrollment ... [and, at the same time] ... human resources potentially appeared as a powerful engine of endogenous growth and income inequality."

The findings in the Birdsall, Ross, and Sabot paper largely coincide with those of Bourguignon, although the specific methodology is somewhat different. Birdsall, Ross, and Sabot find that East Asia's better growth performance in comparison with Latin America may be explained by the contribution of low inequality to investment in education. The latter, in time, resulted in greater equality. However, Bourguignon's study also finds that regional specificities remain important in explaining growth—after variables such as income distribution, investment in human capital, market distortions, and so on, have been taken into account. Thus the question of why Latin America has "underperformed" has not been answered in full.

---

*Nora Lustig is a Senior Fellow at The Brookings Institution.*

# CHAPTER 5   Why Are Latin America's Saving Rates So Low?

*Sebastian Edwards**

For a long time, development economists have argued that savings are at the heart of the growth process. In 1955, for example, Arthur W. Lewis pointed out that, historically, massive increases in savings have preceded significant economic takeoffs. He then argued that a central problem in the theory of economic development was to understand the process by which a community that was previously saving a low percentage of GDP dramatically increases its savings.

Recently developed models of endogenous growth have provided new theoretical support for the idea that savings play an important role in determining long-term growth. While neoclassical models in the tradition of Solow (1956) suggest that an increase in saving ratios generates higher growth only during the transition between steady states, newer models predict that higher savings—and the related increase in capital accumulation—will result in a permanent increase in growth rates.[1]

Empirical work by Barro (1991), De Long and Summers (1991), Edwards (1992), and others, has indeed supported the notion that capital accumulation—and thus savings—are central for understanding growth differentials across countries. Moreover, in an important recent paper, Young (1994) has argued that capital accumulation, not technological progress, explains the splendid growth performance of the East Asian tigers—Korea, Hong Kong, Singapore, and Taiwan, China. On the other

* A Spanish version of this paper was published in *Crecimiento Económico*, Mónica Aparicio and William Easterly (eds.), Banco Mundial and Banco de la República, 1995.
[1] See, for example, the family of Ak models pioneered by Rebelo (1991). There is now an abundant literature on endogenous growth. See, for example, Grossman and Helpman (1991) and Sala-i-Martin (1992). In an open economy setting, the question of domestic versus foreign savings becomes important. There is significant cross-country evidence, however, suggesting that domestic savings are highly correlated to aggregate investment. This indicates that, on average and over long periods of time, changes in capital accumulation respond mostly to changes in domestic savings. See Feldstein and Horace (1980). See also Gersovitz (1988) for a detailed survey on the links between savings and development.

hand, King and Levine (1994) have argued that, although capital accumulation plays an important role in explaining broad cross-country growth differentials, technological progress is possibly the major determinant of growth in most countries. However, to the extent that productivity improvements are achieved through the implementation of new techniques and processes, capital accumulation and savings will also play an additional (indirect) role in the growth process. The revived academic interest in savings and their relationship to growth has been echoed by policymakers throughout the world.

Latin America has traditionally had a low rate of domestic saving and of capital accumulation. In 1980, for example, gross domestic savings were on average 20 percent of GDP for the region as a whole, slightly higher than in 1965, when they stood at 19 percent. This stagnation contrasts sharply with East Asia, where the average gross saving ratio increased from 23 percent of GDP in 1965 to almost 30 percent in 1980.[2] In spite of the availability of foreign resources to supplement domestic savings during 1960–80, the average investment rate was rather low in Latin America throughout this period—gross investment averaged 23 percent of GDP. What made things worse was that for decades, savings—both domestic and foreign—were used to finance projects with doubtful rates of return. A number of authors, most forcefully McKinnon (1973, 1991), have argued that the maze of distortions and regulations affecting Latin America's financial sector had a negative impact on resource allocation, the efficiency of (private) investment, and, perhaps more importantly, on productivity growth.[3]

The debt crisis had important consequences for the behavior of saving and investment throughout the Latin American region. During the early years of 'muddling through' (1982–87), investment was drastically reduced as a way to accommodate the sudden drying-up of capital flows (Dornbusch 1991, Edwards 1989). In the case of public investment, cuts were so deep that, in some countries, even existing infrastructure was not maintained. Although in recent years there has been a marked recovery, saving and investment ratios in most of the countries have not yet regained their pre-debt-crisis levels.

To sustain accelerated growth, Latin America will require significant increases in both the volume and quality of investment. Even if, as some preliminary evidence suggests, the different structural reforms generate

[2] These data are taken from various issues of the *World Development Report.*
[3] See, for example, the discussion in the *World Development Report 1991.*

improvements in productivity growth, there will be a clear need to increase the rate of capital accumulation beyond its current levels.[4] A key question is, how will this higher investment be financed? Post-debt crisis, the availability of foreign funds on a stable basis is likely to be tight, so most countries will have to rely heavily on higher domestic savings to fund increased investment.[5] Increasing the volume of savings and the quality of investment have been some of the overriding goals of the structural reform policies long advocated by many economists for the region. However, in spite of very massive financial sector reforms, many Latin American countries have lower saving rates today than before the debt crisis. This fact has led some analysts to question the existence of a link between financial liberalization and increased savings, and to ask whether there are, in fact, policy measures that can be undertaken to boost aggregate savings.

This paper deals with numerous issues related to savings in Latin America, and tries to explain why saving ratios in the region have traditionally been so low. The analysis is macro in nature and concentrates on aggregate savings.[6] In order to deal with the determinants of saving rates from a comparative perspective, various cross-country regressions are estimated for a group of 53 countries—both industrialized and less developed. An important feature of the paper is that, in contrast with previous work, a distinction is made between private and government savings.[7] For example, in what is possibly the most comprehensive recent cross-country study of savings determination, Carroll and Weil (1994) use aggregate savings. This paper examines a large number of other variables—including policy, demographic, and political factors—as possible determinants of saving ratios.

The paper is organized as follows. The first section deals with the recent behavior of savings in a selected number of Latin American countries.

---

[4] On the recent evolution of productivity growth in Latin America see, for example, Dornbusch and Edwards (1994).

[5] In spite of the increase in capital flows, the availability of foreign savings continues to be low from a historical perspective. Moreover, foreign savings are unlikely to continue at current levels.

[6] There is an abundant literature on the micro determinants of savings, based on household data. See Gersovitz (1988), and Carroll and Weil (1994) for discussions.

[7] The lack of appropriate data has traditionally affected efforts to study in detail the behavior of private savings in a broad comparative setting. Although advanced countries, and selected middle-income countries, have distinguished between the two types of savings, these data have not been available for the poorer nations. In this paper I use a new data set assembled by the IMF.

**Figure 5.1  Ratio of Gross Domestic Savings to GDP**
*(Percent)*

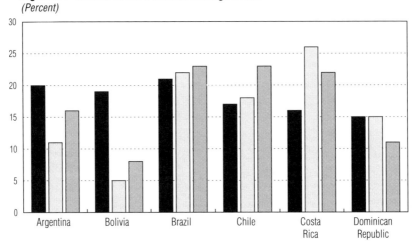

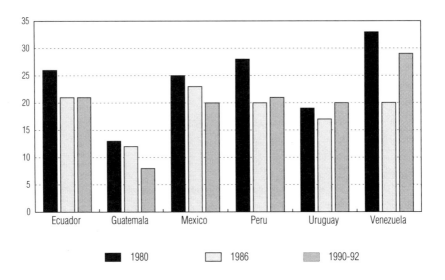

Source: World Bank, *World Tables.*

I report the results obtained from the estimation of cross-country regressions on private savings, and then concentrate on government savings. In contrast with previous work in the area, the paper assumes that government saving is not completely exogenous, and that it responds to both economic and political determinants. In particular the paper draws on the recent literature on the political economy of inflation and stabilization, and argues that governments act strategically when deciding how much to save. This analysis addresses the important issue of whether policy measures can be used to increase aggregate savings in the region, within a reasonable period of time. The paper ends with a brief discussion of policy implications and directions for future research.

## Recent Behavior of Savings in Latin America

Broad comparative analyses of saving behavior have traditionally been plagued by data problems.[8] Savings are usually estimated in a questionable way (mostly as residuals); until very recently there were no comparable data on private savings for a large number of countries, and there still are no data on net savings. This paper uses two alternative data sets, which allow for cross-country comparisons. The first is a data set put together by the World Bank on gross domestic saving ratios, and the second is a new data set assembled by the International Monetary Fund that distinguishes between private and government national saving ratios.

Figure 5.1 contains data on the evolution of (gross) domestic savings ratios for selected Latin American countries between 1980 and 1992. In most cases savings have clearly increased with respect to the mid 1980s, but are still below their 1980 level. Chile and Mexico, two of the earliest reformers, provide contrasting examples. In Chile, gross domestic savings have increased steadily since 1980, partly due to the social security reform, reaching almost 27 percent of GDP in 1993. In Mexico, aggregate domestic savings have declined gradually during this period. How recent financial reforms will eventually affect aggregate savings, it is too early to say. But some historical and comparative evidence suggests they will not generate a massive increase in the short to medium run, as was thought by early supporters of financial liberalization policies.

Figure 5.2 (which follows this chapter) displays the evolution of private, government, and aggregate gross national savings for 11 Latin Ameri-

---

[8] See Gersovitz (1988) for a discussion on data problems in aggregate savings studies.

**Table 5.1 Private and Government Saving Rates, 1970–92: A Regional Comparison**
*(Percent of GDP)*

|  | 1970–1982 | | | | 1983–1992 | | | |
|---|---|---|---|---|---|---|---|---|
|  | Q1 | Median | Q3 | Average | Q1 | Median | Q3 | Average |
| *Private Savings* | | | | | | | | |
| Latin America | 13.1 | 13.2 | 21.7 | 16.1 | 10.9 | 14.7 | 17.9 | 13.8 |
| Asia | n.a. | n.a. | n.a. | n.a. | 17.4 | 19.1 | 22.9 | 20.2 |
| Africa | 11.4 | 14.4 | 18.9 | 15.2 | 10.7 | 16.7 | 19.5 | 15.6 |
| Industrialized | 18.0 | 21.6 | 23.4 | 21.3 | 18.3 | 21.3 | 23.4 | 21.3 |
| *Government Savings* | | | | | | | | |
| Latin America | -0.7 | 1.7 | 6.6 | 3.3 | -1.3 | 2.4 | 5.5 | 2.2 |
| Asia | 0.0 | 2.7 | 8.8 | 4.4 | 0.0 | 1.6 | 9.0 | 3.9 |
| Africa | -1.6 | 0.9 | 2.1 | 0.6 | -1.3 | 1.0 | 4.5 | 0.9 |
| Industrialized | -0.5 | 2.0 | 3.8 | 1.8 | -3.6 | -0.1 | 1.3 | -0.8 |
| *National Savings* | | | | | | | | |
| Latin America | 14.5 | 19.4 | 27.7 | 19.8 | 14.0 | 17.8 | 19.1 | 15.3 |
| Asia | 4.9 | 24.8 | 26.7 | 18.8 | 18.8 | 23.8 | 28.5 | 24.5 |
| Africa | 10.8 | 15.5 | 18.7 | 16.4 | 10.6 | 17.5 | 22.1 | 16.8 |
| Industrialized | 19.6 | 22.8 | 25.8 | 23.1 | 17.5 | 19.1 | 23.4 | 20.4 |

*Source:* International Monetary Fund.

can countries. The data cover all years for which there is information. Certain interesting facts emerge from these figures. First, the behavior of national saving rates has recently been very similar to that of domestic saving ratios. Second, in most countries there has been an improvement in government saving in the last few years. This is largely due to post-debt crisis adjustment programs implemented throughout the region. Finally, and related to the two previous points, private savings in many countries have declined substantially over the last few years. What has made this situation particularly interesting—and in some sense puzzling—is that this decline in private savings has taken place at the same time that significant reforms aiming at "liberalizing" domestic capital markets have been implemented in most countries.

How do these Latin American saving ratios compare with other regions of the world? Table 5.1 contains the averages and distributions of private, government and aggregate national savings for a group of Latin American, Asian, African, and industrialized countries for the 1970–82 and 1983–92 periods (the chapter appendix lists the countries in this sample). As can be seen, during the more recent period the region's private saving ratios have been the lowest in the world. Also, these more aggregated data confirm the notion that in the post-crisis period, private saving rates have tended to decline in Latin America.

Interestingly, the story regarding government savings is very different: during the most recent period, the Latin American countries in our sample have exhibited comparatively high ratios. In fact, the region has the highest median and the second-highest average government saving rates. This is particularly important because the generation of relatively high government savings is a rather recent phenomenon in Latin America, and is somewhat fragile. It would not be surprising if fiscal discipline in some countries begins to slip in the near future, generating a reduction in the government's contribution to aggregate savings. When private and government savings are consolidated (in Table 5.1), the picture continues to look bleak, with Latin America once again at the bottom of the scale.

Average regional data, as presented in Table 5.1, tend to obscure the behavior of individual countries. To add additional flavor to the comparisons, Figure 5.2 also displays the evolution of saving ratios for five high-performing East Asian countries. The contrast with the Latin American countries is stunning. These East Asian countries have not only had very high aggregate saving rates—on the order of 30 to 40 percent—but have also been very stable. A second fundamental difference between these two groups of countries is that the contribution of government savings to total national savings is significantly higher in East Asia than in Latin America. Whereas historically government savings in Latin America have barely contributed to national savings, in the five East Asian countries shown they represent between 25 and 40 percent of aggregate savings. What is more surprising, however, is that in spite of the fundamental contribution of government savings to aggregate national savings in success stories, the economic literature has been almost silent in explaining why these differ so markedly across nations. This paper contains a systematic attempt to explain cross-country differentials in government saving rates, using some insights from recent models on the political economy of macroeconomic policymaking.

## Cross-Country Difference in Private Saving Rates: An Empirical Analysis

This section presents the results obtained from a cross-country econometric analysis of the determinants of private saving ratios for a group of 50 nations. The dependent variables are averages of private national savings for

1983–92; the criteria for including countries in the sample respond exclusively to data availability. The same data set is used later to analyze the determinants of cross-country differences in government savings.

There is abundant theoretical literature on the determinants of private savings. Despite recent important developments, this literature is still fragmented, with different authors emphasizing specific aspects of saving behavior, including the effects of social security contributions (Feldstein 1980), interest rates (Gylfason 1993), and liquidity constraints (Jappelli and Pagano 1994). This fragmentation also appears in the empirical literature on the subject; authors have typically concentrated on a few possible determinants of private savings.[9] This paper takes a rather pragmatic view by including a large number of potential determinants of private savings. Rather than build a general theoretical model, I have drawn on existing literature to decide which variables to include in the empirical investigation. The most important determinants of private savings considered by the literature are briefly discussed below.

### A Simple Model

The decision to save is fundamentally an intertemporal one. Households will have to decide how much of their current income to consume in the present and how much to put aside for future consumption. This fundamental insight has been captured by the life-cycle theories of consumption originally developed by Modigliani and Brumberg (1954). Possibly the easiest way to formulate this problem for an (infinitely lived) individual is as follows:

$$\max \int_0^\infty E\{ U(c_t, g_t)\, e^{-pt}\, dt \} \qquad (1)$$

subject to:

$$\int_0^\infty c_t\, e^{-rt}\, dt \le W, \qquad (2)$$

$$W = \int_0^\infty y_t\, (1 - T_t)\, e^{-rt}\, dt, \qquad (3)$$

$$-k \le S_t \le y_t\, (1 - T_t) \qquad (4)$$

---

[9] See Gersovitz (1988) for a broad survey on savings and development. Aghevli et al. (1990) provide a very complete discussion of recent trends and prospects. Hayashi (1986) provides a fascinating analysis of Japanese saving, and deals with the opposite question to the one we are addressing—he asks why Japan's saving rates are so high.

where E{U} is the expected utility function, p is the rate of time prefer-
ence, and r is the interest rate. Private consumption is represented by $c_t$ in
period t, and $g_t$ is consumption of public goods during that period. W is
total wealth, $y_t$ $(1 - T_t)$ is net income, $T_t$ is the tax rate in period t, $S_t$ is savings
and is defined as $[y_t$ $(1 - T_t) - p_t$ $q_t]$. If in a given period S is negative, the
individual in question is borrowing from the financial system. The third
restriction, $-k \leq S_t \leq y_t$ $(1 - T_t)$, establishes that in any period savings has to
be less than net income, and borrowing cannot exceed k. This restriction
constitutes a borrowing constraint and will be more restrictive the less developed the financial system. The first order conditions from this problem
are well known and establish that the ratio between expected marginal
utilities in any two periods have to be equal to the expected discount rate.
An important implication of this is that individuals will use borrowing and
savings to smooth consumption through time.

The simple model presented above makes it clear that household saving
decisions will be influenced by several variables, including the following:

(a) *The rate of time preferences of individuals.* Naturally, an increase in
preferences towards future consumption will result in an increase in
savings.

(b) *The rate of interest.* Increases in r will have an ambiguous effect on
savings; whether they respond positively or negatively will depend on the
relative strengths of the substitution and wealth effects (for a recent discussion of the topic, see Gylfason 1993). The relevant empirical literature has
been subject to long controversies on the actual sign and size of the interest
rate elasticity of private savings, in both the industrial and developing
countries.[10]

The early financial liberalization literature argued that an important
objective of these reforms was to generate, among other things, a significant
increase in domestic savings. In the original models of financial repression
of McKinnon (1973) and Shaw (1973), allowing (real) interest rates to rise to
market levels altered the intertemporal rate of substitution, encouraging
aggregate savings.[11] However, empirical studies for a large number of countries—both advanced and developed—have found only a weak interest rate
elasticity of aggregate domestic savings. Boskin (1978) found a very low
elasticity for the United States. A number of studies for the case of the

---

[10] See, for example, McKinnon (1991) and Carroll and Summers (1991).
[11] See Fry (1988) for surveys of these type of models.

developing countries, including Giovannini (1983), have failed to find any effect of interest rate changes on private savings. McKinnon (1991) has recently acknowledged that "aggregate savings, as measured in the GNP accounts, do not respond strongly to higher real interest rates" (p. 22).[12]

The evidence suggesting that savings have a low degree of responsiveness with respect to interest rates has prompted analysts and policymakers to consider alternative policy mechanisms to encourage savings. Some countries, such as Chile in the mid 1980s, relied on tax reforms aimed at discouraging consumption.[13] More recently, some authors have suggested that shifting the tax base from income to consumption will encourage thrift in the economy as a whole. From an analytical point of view, these policies assume that there is a high intertemporal substitution in consumption. However, as pointed out above, the limited existing evidence does not support this contention and sheds some doubt on the effectiveness of these tax-based mechanisms to increase aggregate savings.[14]

(c) *The time profile of income flows.* According to life-cycle models, individuals will have negative savings when they are young and very low-income; positive savings during their productive years; and once again negative savings when they are old and retired. Given positive bequest motives, they will tend to leave some wealth to their heirs.

Aggregate private savings will, then, be affected by the age distribution of the population. If the number of inactive people is large relative to those in their productive years, aggregate savings will be relatively low. In their classical studies, Modigliani (1970) and Leff (1969) used cross-country data (mostly on advanced nations) to test this hypothesis. They found, as have numerous authors after them, that differences in demographics are key to explaining differences in savings.

---

[12] In spite of the relative unresponsiveness of savings to higher interest rates, financial reforms still have important effects on growth through improvement in the quality of aggregate investment, especially private investment. For example, in a series of studies, Gelb (1989), Fry (1988), and McKinnon (1991) have found robust evidence supporting the proposition that a reduction in the degree of repression of the capital market will tend to increase the productivity of investment. Interestingly, this work also suggests that reducing financial instability, and especially inflation, will also have an important positive effect on the return to investment. Also, recent work by King and Levine (1993) supports the idea that more developed financial sectors have been associated with faster total factor productivity growth.

[13] That provision was altered in the 1990 tax reform. See Edwards and Cox-Edwards (1991).

[14] Carroll and Summers (1991) have argued that the comparison of the evolution of Canadian and U.S. tax systems provides an ideal natural experiment for investigating the way in which tax regimes affect saving rates. They conclude that tax systems that encourage postponed consumption—such as Canada's—indeed result in higher savings.

Modigliani (1970) pointed out that in a life-cycle setting there will be an important positive effect of income growth on private savings. The reason is that, to the extent that higher growth rates will be interpreted as temporary, income will not be (fully) consumed. Recently Carroll and Weil (1994), using detailed household-level data to analyze this issue, have offered evidence that growth indeed affects private savings positively. They interpret their findings, however, as supporting a consumption model with habit formation.

The extent to which individuals can actually "dissave" when young will depend on the borrowing constraint. The more stringent this constraint is—the smaller the value of k—the lower borrowing will be and the higher (aggregate) private savings. Interestingly, this analysis suggests that the relaxation of borrowing constraints, through the implementation of financial sector reforms that encourage consumer credit, for example, will tend to reduce private sector consumption. In an important recent paper, Jappelli and Pagano (1994) have used cross-country data on required downpayments for mortgages as a proxy for borrowing constraints. In contrast to the analysis above, their econometric results on data for advanced countries support the idea that relaxing these constraints will reduce savings.

Another important implication of the life-cycle framework—and one that can be easily incorporated into the formal model—is that private savings will be affected by the extent and coverage of social security systems. If individuals perceive that they will get high social security benefits when they are retired, they will tend to reduce the amount saved during their active days (Feldstein, 1980).

*(d) Taxes and government consumption.* Higher taxes will, other things being equal, reduce private savings. What is interesting about this formulation is that both present and future taxes will tend to reduce savings. This means that, to the extent that the government is subject to an intertemporal budget constraint, it will not matter whether increases in government consumption are financed by higher taxes or by issuing government bonds. This is, of course, the Ricardo-Barro proposition that government bonds are not net wealth (Barro 1974).

Increases in government consumption will also affect private savings. If the public does not value government consumption, savings will decline; this will be the case no matter how the increased government expenditure is financed. If, on the other hand, the public values public goods, the effect of an increase in their provision will depend on the degree of substitutability of c and g in the individual's utility function. From an empirical and policy perspective, it is important to determine whether increases in government savings will be offset fully by declines in private savings, or if the offset coefficient will be lower than one. Another important policy issue is whether changes in alternative taxes—value-added tax, assets tax, income tax—will have the same effect on private savings (Kotlikoff 1984).

In a comprehensive study, Corbo and Schmidt-Hebbel (1991) used a 13-country data set to analyze the macroeconomic consequences of higher public savings. In particular, they investigated the extent to which an increase in government savings would be reflected in a decline in private savings. They found that, although government savings crowd out private savings, the magnitude of this effect is far below the one-to-one relationship suggested by the simple Ricardian equivalence doctrine; overall their empirical analysis strongly indicates that an increase in public savings will be translated into higher aggregate savings.[15] Corbo and Schmidt-Hebbel (1991) also found that, on average, increasing public savings via reduced expenditures is more effective than increasing taxation.

Although the model above captures the essentials of household saving decisions, it has some limitations. The model ignores consumers' heterogeneity, and thus the effects of income distribution on saving. It does not directly incorporate the role of human capital accumulation, and deals only partially with issues related to the degree of development of the capital market. The model also does not incorporate the possible effects of macroeconomic stability and does not include political considerations. Finally, it ignores open economy angles and the role of savings by enterprises.

Models with heterogeneous agents generally predict that households with higher income will tend to save a higher proportion of their income. At the aggregate-comparative level this has been interpreted as suggesting that countries with more unequal income distribution will tend to have a higher saving rate. From the instability perspective, it has been suggested that both macroeconomic and political instability will tend to have a negative effect on aggregate savings. Open-economy models add three perspectives to the analysis: first, domestic interest rates will be linked to international interest rates and will generally be exogenous; second, in open economies, agents can use foreign borrowing to smooth consumption through time. This means that foreign savings will, generally, act as substitutes for domestic savings (see Bosworth 1993). In the empirical analysis reported below, many of these variables are considered as possible determinants of cross-country differences in aggregate private savings.

---

[15] On Ricardian-Barro equivalence, see Barro (1974).

*Estimation*

This subsection presents the results obtained from the estimation on a 50-country data set of a private savings equation of the following form:

$$s_k = a_0 L_k + a_1 G_k + a_3 F_k + a_4 M_k + a_5 D_k + a_6 E_k + a_7 P_k + a_8 S_k + u_k \quad (5)$$

where $s_k$ is the average private national saving rate for 1983–92 for country k; and L is a vector of life-cycle variables, including the age dependency ratio and the rate of growth of per capita GDP. G is a vector of variables related to fiscal policy, and it includes the government saving rate, government consumption, and social security taxes (which are used as a proxy for expected social security benefits). F is a vector of variables that capture the characteristics of the financial sector, including its degree of development. Of particular interest here are the degree of financial depth of the economy and the extent to which borrowing constraints are binding. Ideally, F would also include measures of the real interest rate; however, this variable is available only for a small number of developing countries.

The estimation of cross-country private savings equations of this type presents several challenges and problems. First, there are no data on all the relevant independent variables; second, many of them are measured with error; and third, there are serious instances of endogeneity. To deal with these issues, I have defined proxies for some of the variables of interest, and have estimated the private savings equation using instrumental variables (IV). As is usually the case with cross-country regressions, finding appropriate instruments is difficult. This paper uses average values of the endogenous variables for 1970–82 as some of the instruments.

Table 5.2 contains the results of the estimation of private savings equations using IV. The dependent variable, obtained from the International Monetary Fund, is the ratio of private national savings to GDP averaged for 1983–1992. The independent variables fall in the different categories described above, and were defined as follows:

(*a*) *Age dependency* refers to population younger than 15 plus population over 65, as a percentage of working-age population. This variable was defined for 1990 and was taken from the World Bank data set. According to the life-cycle hypothesis, its coefficient should be negative.

(*b*) *Growth* means here the rate of growth of per capita GDP, averaged

**Table 5.2 The Determinants of Private Savings: Cross-Section Results**
*(Instrumental variables estimates, t-statistics in parentheses)*

|  | R1 | R2 | R3 | R4 | R5 | R6 |
|---|---|---|---|---|---|---|
| Constant | 20.818 | 23.959 | 33.342 | 23.533 | 19.287 | 16.116 |
|  | (7.433) | (6.568) | (4.529) | (5.568) | (6.613) | (3.587) |
| Age dependency | -0.153 | -0.183 | -0.216 | -0.187 | -9.144 | (-0.122) |
|  | (-5.346) | (-4.985) | (-3.892) | (-2.440) | (-4.583) | (-2.608) |
| Growth | 1.373 | 1.534 | 1.369 | 1.611 | 1.472 | 2.117 |
|  | (3.752) | (4.616) | (2.472) | (4.417) | (3.697) | 2.405) |
| Money/GDP | 0.197 | 0.210 | 0.198 | 0.213 | 0.175 | 0.036 |
|  | (2.425) | (4.616) | (1.925) | (2.440) | (1.924) | (1.724) |
| Private credit | — | — | -0.079 | — | — | — |
|  |  |  | (-1.328) |  |  |  |
| Real interest | — | — | — | 1.660E-04 | — | — |
|  |  |  |  | (0.559) |  |  |
| Government savings | -0.427 | -0.583 | -0.479 | -0.551 | -0.423 | -0.507 |
|  | (-3.147) | (-4.103) | (-2.306) | (-3.680) | (-2.957) | (-2.330) |
| Social security | — | -0.096 | -0.110 | -0.091 | — | — |
|  |  | (-2.029) | (-1.832) | (-1.635) |  |  |
| Current account | — | — | 0.422 | — | 0.025 | — |
|  |  |  | (0.479) |  | (0.983) |  |
| Income distribution | — | — | — | — | — | 0.036 |
|  |  |  |  |  |  | (0.079) |
| Political instability | — | — | — | — | 0.931 | 1.628 |
|  |  |  |  |  | (0.558) | (0.681) |
| $R^2$ | 0.589 | 0.647 | 0.613 | 0.674 | 0.593 | 0.516 |
| N | 51 | 45 | 42 | 40 | 51 | 37 |

for 1983–88. The data were taken from Summers and Heston (1991). The life-cycle model suggests that its coefficient should be positive. However, Carroll and Summers (1991) have argued that in a more complete model of consumer behavior, growth and savings should be negatively related, at least in the short run. In a cross-country analysis of the type presented here, it is not possible to investigate the implied dynamic behavior of saving through time.

(c) *Money/GDP* is constructed as a 1983–92 average from raw data taken from the IMF's *International Financial Statistics (IFS)*. This variable is a proxy for the depth of the financial system, and according to financial depth theories, its coefficient should be positive (McKinnon, 1973).

(d) *Private credit* is a proxy for borrowing constraints and is defined by two alternative specifications, using raw data obtained from the *IFS*. The first is the ratio of credit to the private sector to total domestic credit, averaged for 1983–92; the second is credit to the private sector over GDP, also for 1983–92. As discussed earlier, the borrowing constraint should affect private savings positively.

(e) *Real interest* is defined as the ex-post real deposit interest rate, averaged for 1983–92. The raw data were obtained from the *IFS*. According to the model presented above, the coefficient of this variable is ambiguous.

(f) *Government savings* are obtained from the IMF, and averaged for 1983–92. The coefficient is expected to be negative. If this coefficient is very close to minus one, increases in government savings will not be fully offset by reductions in public savings.

(g) *Social security* is defined as the ratio of public expenditure on social security and welfare to total public expenditure, averaged for 1983–92 (obtained from the World Bank's data set). It is a proxy for expected social security benefits, and its coefficient is expected to be negative.

(h) *Current account* is an average of the current account balance to GDP for 1983–92, obtained from the World Bank data bank. Its coefficient measures the degree of substitutability between foreign savings (or current account deficit) and national private savings.

(i) *Political instability*, an index of the degree of political instability in each country, is defined as the frequency of transfers of power for 1971–82, taken from Edwards and Tabellini (1994). The expected sign of its coefficient is negative.

The results reported in Table 5.2 are quite revealing.[16] The $R^2$s are quite high, surpassing in every case 0.5. The first three left-hand variables are related to life-cycle models. As suggested by this hypothesis, the coefficient of the age dependency ratio is significantly negative, indicating that demographics play an important role in explaining differences in private savings across countries. This coincides with the results obtained by several authors, including Leff (1969) and Modigliani (1970) in their pioneer work.

---

[16] The following instruments were used: constant, age dependency, average growth in 1970–82, money/GDP 1970–82, private credit 1970–82, real interest, government savings, social security, current account 1970–82, income distribution, political instability, GNP per capita 1988, and government consumption ratio 1983–92.

When alternative demographic variables were used instead of age dependency, the results were basically unaltered. Also, these results show that the rate of growth of per capita GDP is significantly positive. This finding was confirmed most recently by Bosworth (1993) and Carroll and Weil (1994). However, the fact that the regressions reported in Table 5.2 were obtained using instrumental variables supports the idea that this positive coefficient is not simply the consequence of a simultaneity bias.[17] When GNP per capita was added to the regressions—both in levels and squared—its coefficient was not significant, as suggested by Modigliani (1970).

The next three independent variables in Table 5.2—money/GDP, private credit, and real interest rate—are indexes of the extent of development of the financial market, the degree of financial repression, and of the severity of the borrowing constraint. The coefficient of the money/GDP ratio is always significantly positive, suggesting that countries with a deeper financial system will tend to have higher private saving rates. To investigate the robustness of this result, and in particular to check if the money/GDP ratio is acting as a proxy for the level of income, GNP per capita (in 1982) was also included in the estimation. When this was done, however, the estimates did not change in any significant way. For instance, when GNP per capita was added to equation R2, the (t-statistic) of money/GDP was 0.18 (2.120), while that of GNP per capita was 0.204 (0.138). The coefficient of private credit was negative, as suggested by the borrowing constraint perspective, but not significant at the conventional level. This was the case both when private credit was included jointly with money/GDP, and when this variable was excluded. A plausible explanation for this result is that the share of private credit is a poor proxy for borrowing constraints. Unfortunately, better measures of borrowing (or liquidity) constraints, such as the downpayment required to buy a house, are only available for a small number of countries. The coefficient of real interest rates was insignificant in every regression where it was included. This is consistent with results obtained by previous researchers (see McKinnon 1993, for example), but contradicts the theoretical implications of other models (Summers 1992, Gylfason 1993). When measures of the efficiency of the financial system, such as the spread between lending and deposit interest rates, were included in the regressions, their coefficients were not significant.[18]

---

[17] Carroll and Weil (1993) present Granger causality tests which suggest that growth Granger-causes aggregate savings.

[18] From theoretical and empirical points of view, the (possible) effect of interest rates—and other incentives—on private savings continues to be a major controversy.

The coefficient of government savings was significantly negative in every regression. More important from a policy perspective, however, is that it was always significantly different from –1.0. For example, in equation R2, the 95 percent confidence interval is (–0.832,–0.048). This provides some indication that, although higher government savings crowd out private savings, they will not do so "one-to-one," and that Ricardian equivalence does not hold strictly. The coefficient of social security is negative and significant at conventional levels in two out of three regressions where it was included. This is consistent with previous findings by Feldstein (1980), and gives some support to the notion that reforms that replace government-run (and partially funded) social security systems by privately run capitalization systems will result in higher private saving rates.[19] The current account balance was insignificant in every regression.[20] Also, the coefficients of income distribution and political instability were not significant in any of the regressions where they were included.

To check the robustness of the results, a series of tests were performed. In particular, variables were added related to macroeconomic stability (average and variability of inflation), the open economy (degree of openness and variability of the real exchange rate), and the structure of the economy (degree of urbanization; share of manufacturing, mining, and agriculture in GDP). Their coefficients were not significant. I also analyzed whether the results reported in Table 5.2 were driven by outliers. To do this, I estimated Cook's distance statistics to identify the variable with a greater influence in the results. This turned out to be Bolivia; when this observation was excluded from the regression, however, the results discussed above did not change in any way. Regional dummy variables were also added, without affecting the results. Finally, I reestimated the equations using White's procedure for estimating the variance-covariance matrix under heteroskedasticity, again without altering the results.

The computation of standardized beta coefficients indicates that growth is the most important variable for explaining cross-country differ-

---

[19] Notice that this will not be necessarily the case for total savings during the transition from one regime to the other. The reason is that during the transition the government will continue to have obligations to (older) retirees, but will receive no contributions from active workers. As a result, government savings will tend to go down.

[20] The coefficient of current account is very sensitive to the estimation method. In the regressions reported in Table 5.2, the current account is taken as an endogenous variable, and is instrumented by its average in 1970–82. If considered as an exogenous variable—or if OLS is used—its coefficient is significantly positive.

**Table 5.3  Cumulative F-Statistics for Null Hypothesis**
*(that Latin American coefficients differ significantly)*

|  | F | Prob>F |
|---|---|---|
| Constant | 0.040 | 0.845 |
| Age dependency | 1.630 | 0.210 |
| Growth | 1.090 | 0.365 |
| Money/GDP | 0.870 | 0.490 |
| Government savings | 0.880 | 0.507 |
| Social Security | 0.960 | 0.467 |

*Note:* The null hypothesis states that these coefficients are cumulatively different in Latin America from those for the rest of the sample.

**Table 5.4  Latin America and Rest of Sample**
*(Descriptive statistics)*

|  | Latin America | | Rest of Sample | |
|---|---|---|---|---|
|  | Mean | Std. Deviation | Mean | Std. Deviation |
| Private savings | 13.8 | 5.1 | 18.9 | 5.9 |
| Age dependency | 71.3 | 9.9 | 65.0 | 20.9 |
| Growth | -1.6 | 3.6 | 1.4 | 2.9 |
| Money/GDP | 10.3 | 3.1 | 19.7 | 7.2 |
| Government savings | 2.1 | 4.4 | 1.4 | 5.3 |
| Social security | 17.1 | 13.8 | 20.2 | 16.4 |

ences in private savings. This coincides with Bosworth's (1993) results. In equation R2, for example, the beta statistic for growth is 3.43; the other variables with relatively high betas were government savings (–1.36) and money/GDP ratio (0.87).

The majority of the Latin American countries exhibit negative residuals in every regression—their actual private sector rates were below estimated rates. For example, in the case of equation R2, observed private savings were on average 1 percentage point below estimated savings.

Thus we return to the question, why are saving rates so low in Latin America? In the case of private savings, this can be the consequence of a series of factors. First, the coefficients of the private savings equation for Latin America may be different from those for the rest of the countries in the sample. Second, even if the same equation can describe private savings across regions, the value of the left-hand variables may be different in the Latin American nations. To test whether the coefficients pertinent for the

Latin American countries were different, cumulative F-statistics were calcu-lated. In these tests, reported in Table 5.3, the null hypotheses that the Latin American coefficients are significantly different are estimated sequentially and cumulatively.[21] As can be seen, the null hypothesis is rejected in every instance. This was the case independently of the ordering in which the vari-ables were added to the cumulative test. An analysis of the left-hand vari-ables unveils significant differences between the Latin American countries and the rest of the sample. This was the case for demographic variables (Latin America has a much higher age-dependency ratio), for growth, and policy variables such as social security and government savings—see Table 5.4.

### Explaining Government Savings: A Political Economy Perspective

Studies on savings have traditionally focused on aggregate national sav-ings and/or on private savings, and have tended to ignore the process of determination of government savings. And yet, government savings can be a fundamental component of national savings, representing in some cases—and especially in the successful East Asian nations—between 30 and 40 percent of the aggregate. Most studies make the very simple—and im-plausible—assumption that government savings are exogenous, and are set by the economic authorities in a way that maximizes (the present value of) society's welfare.

In recent years some authors have relied on insights from public choice and game theory to study government behavior—see Persson and Tabellini (1990) for a comprehensive discussion. Many of these models as-sume that political parties alternate in power, and that the group in office acts strategically, in an intertemporal sense, when making decisions that have economic consequences spanning more than one period (Cukierman, Edwards, and Tabellini, 1992). This type of approach can be extended fruit-fully to address cross-country differentials in government saving rates.

Assume that there are two political parties (L and R) that alternate in power according to some probability rule. Further, assume that L and R have different preferences: while L prefers a vector of goods g, R prefers vector f. The amount of these goods that society can produce and consume will depend, in part, on the level of government savings and investment.

---

[21] The first F-test reported corresponds to the null hypothesis that the Latin American countries have a different constant. The second test corresponds to the hypothesis that the constant and the coefficient for age dependency are different, and so on.

**Table 5.5 The Determinants of Government Saving Rates: Cross-Section Results**

(Instrumental variables estimates)

|  | R7 | R8 | R9 |
|---|---|---|---|
| Constant | -0.621 | -0.828 | -0.390 |
|  | (-0.153) | (-0.202) | (-0.093) |
| Political instability | -2.954 | -3.292 | -3.103 |
|  | (-2.007) | (-2.373) | (-2.038) |
| Assassinations | -0.367 | — | — |
|  | (-0.669) |  |  |
| Attacks | — | 5.860E-04 | 1.040E-03 |
|  |  | (0.171) | (0.282) |
| Growth | 1.535 | 1.578 | 1.592 |
|  | (4.192) | (4.256) | (4.112) |
| Age dependency | -0.145 | -0.015 | -0.017 |
|  | (-0.351) | (-0.362) | (-0.383) |
| Social security | -0.013 | -0.011 | -0.016 |
|  | (-0.260) | (-0.228) | (-0.295) |
| Current account | 0.322 | 0.323 | 0.324 |
|  | (2.253) | (2.243) | (2.151) |
| Money/GDP | — | — | -0.024 |
|  |  |  | (-0.306) |
| $R^2$ | 0.469 | 0.463 | 0.466 |
| N | 44 | 44 | 44 |

Savings, however, are only translated into higher investment, production, and consumption with a lag. Therefore, while the party in power increases government savings, its projects may come to fruition when its opponent is in power (for a formal description of the model, see Edwards and Tabellini [1994]).

In this setting the authorities' incentive to increase government savings—and thus the ability to produce public goods—will depend on two fundamental political economy variables. First it will depend on the probability that the party in power will still be in office in the subsequent period. If this probability is low, the opposition party is likely to be in office once the projects mature, and will get the credit for increased production of public goods. Naturally, under these circumstances the incentives to increase savings will be low. The recent political economy literature on inflation and stabilization has associated the probability of the incumbent remaining in office with the degree of *political instability* in the country in question. This analysis predicts, then, that the higher the degree of political instability, the lower government savings.

The second determinant of government's incentive to save is the extent to which the political parties have different preferences. In the extreme case, where their preferences are exactly the same, there will be a high incentive for government to save, even if the probability of remaining in office is low. The difference in parties' preferences has been referred in the political economy literature as the degree of *political polarization*. This analysis predicts that, with other things being equal, a greater degree of polarization will result in lower government savings. In regression analyses, however, it has been difficult to find empirical counterparts for political polarization. Some authors, such as Cukierman, Edwards, and Tabellini (1992), for example, have argued that the frequency of politically motivated attacks and assassinations are appropriated proxies.

Table 5.5 contains the results from instrumental variable estimations of cross-country regressions on government savings.[22] In addition to political instability and polarization—proxied by politically motivated attacks and assassinations—some of the independent variables included in the private savings regressions were incorporated into the regressions.[23] The dependent variable was obtained from the IMF, and was calculated as an average for 1983–92.

The results differ from those for private savings, reported in Table 5.3, and provide some support for the political economy perspective to government savings. In every equation the coefficient of political instability was significantly negative, as suggested by this approach. Moreover, when alternative measures of political instability were used—such as the estimated probability of government changes—the results were maintained. However, the proxies for polarization—politically motivated attacks and assassinations—were not significantly different from zero. At this point, we cannot know whether this is because the model's predictions are not supported by the data, or because the proxies for polarization are inadequate.

---

[22] The following instruments were used: a constant, growth in 1970–82, political instability, assassinations, attacks, social security, current account balance in 1970–82, age dependency, share of government consumption, GNP per capita in 1988, money/GDP 1970–82.

[23] See Edwards and Tabellini (1994) for a discussion of the sources for these variables.

As in the case of private savings, the coefficient of growth is signifi-cantly positive. Moreover, the computation of standardized beta coeffi-cients indicates that this is the most important variable in explaining cross–country differences in government savings.

Interestingly, and contrary to the private savings case reported in Table 5.2, neither the demographics, social security, or money/GDP vari-ables have significant coefficients. Another important contrast with Table 5.2 is that in the case of government savings, the coefficient of the current account is significantly positive, indicating that a higher level of foreign savings—that is, a reduction in the current account balance—has been asso-ciated with a lower government saving rate. Its coefficient, however, is sig-nificantly below unity—in equation R9 the 95 percent confidence interval is (0.03, 0.61)—indicating that the degree of offset is not one to one.

**Concluding Remarks**

This paper clearly suggests that the processes of determination of private and government savings are significantly different. While private savings respond to demographic variables, social security expenditures, and the degree of depth of the financial sector, government savings do not. Govern-ment savings, on the other hand, are affected by two important types of variables that do not seem to impact on private savings: political instability and the current account balance. However, both private and government savings are affected by real growth.

From a policy perspective, the results reported in this paper suggest that there are various avenues—many of them discussed in the less formal policy literature—for raising private savings in Latin America. An increase in the degree of depth of the financial sector will tend to have an important effect. For the period under consideration, the ratio of M1 to GDP in Latin America was almost half of what it was in the rest of the sample. Along with other factors, the reduction of government-provided social security benefits will also increase private savings. While higher government sav-ings will depress private savings, overall aggregate national savings will tend to increase. This is because the offset coefficient is clearly bigger than $-1.0$.

Because of the cross-country nature of the data, these results do not provide information regarding the transition from low to higher saving rates. However, evidence from a score of countries—including the East Asian miracle nations—suggests that the increase in private domestic sav-ings ratios is a rather slow process (World Bank, 1993a). This evidence also indicates that a drastic increase of private savings has usually been affected by an important factor not captured in the regression analysis: the creation of an institutional environment that instills confidence in small savers—the case of postal savings in East Asia is a good example of this type of institution. This, together with the econometric results discussed here, suggests that the development of new institutions, such as new social security systems tailored after the Chilean experience, will play a fundamental role in increasing private savings from their historical levels.

From a policy point of view, then, the surest and most direct way to increase aggregate domestic savings in the short and medium term is to raise government savings through changes in the public deficit. The most appropriate mix of higher tax revenues and reduced expenditures to increase public savings will depend on the specific characteristics of the country in question. If the level of tax compliance is low, and the tax effort is clearly subpar, an increase in tax revenues will be called for. However, under most circumstances some reduction in expenditure is likely to be optimal. In most countries in Latin America it seems highly feasible and recommendable to reduce the military budget as a way to both finance the expansion of social programs and generate higher public savings.

Perhaps the most important finding reported in this paper is that there seems to be a virtuous cycle between growth and private savings. Higher growth increases disposable income and encourages private savings. Higher savings, in turn, permits a higher level of capital accumulation, and thus, reinforces the higher growth. Of course, a key question in this context is how to get this virtuous circle going? The answer: increase public savings during the earlier phases of the process. Government savings, in turn, will be positively affected by the creation of social and political institutions that reduce the degree of political instability. This suggests, then, that the strengthening of democracy will have important and fairly direct positive effects on growth and economic progress.

Increasing government savings does not imply that these countries should, pari passu, increase public investment. In fact, these decisions should be kept separate. Whether or not specific public investments should be undertaken has to be decided on a project-by-project basis. This requires implementing highly professional procedures for appraising public investment projects. In those countries where an expansion in public investment is not justified, the government should still increase its savings and channel those resources to the capital market.

---

*Sebastian Edwards was Chief Economist for Latin America and the Caribbean at the World Bank, and is now Professor of Economics at UCLA.*

## Figure 5.2  Evolution of National Savings in 16 Countries
*(Percent of GDP)*

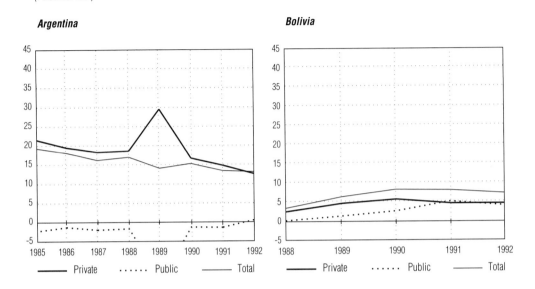

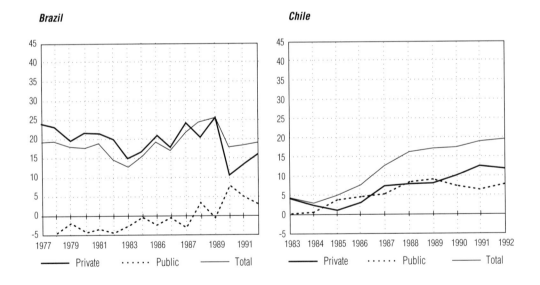

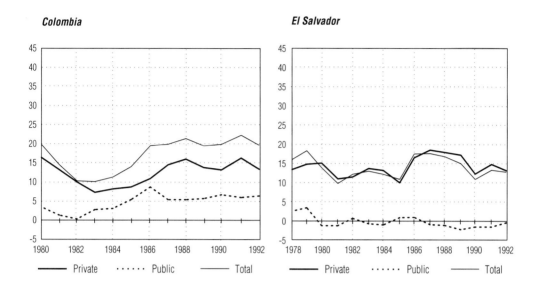

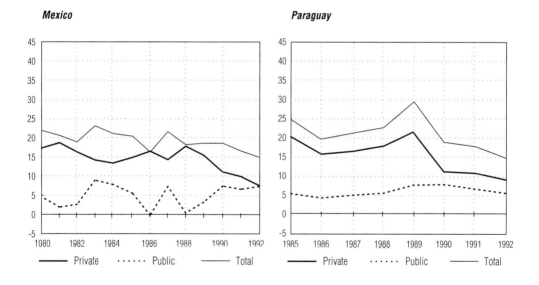

**Figure 5.2  Evolution of National Savings in 16 Countries *(Cont.)***

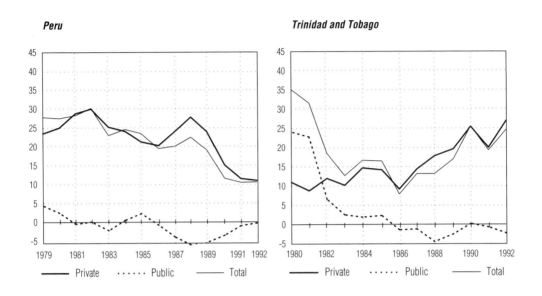

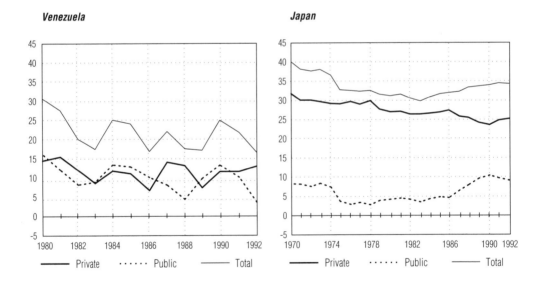

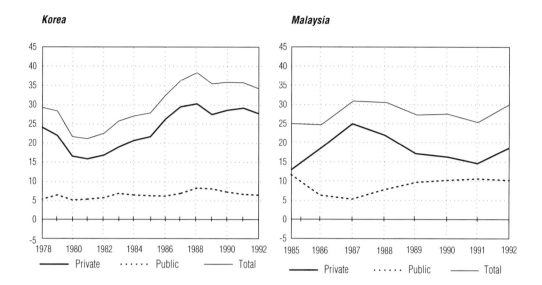

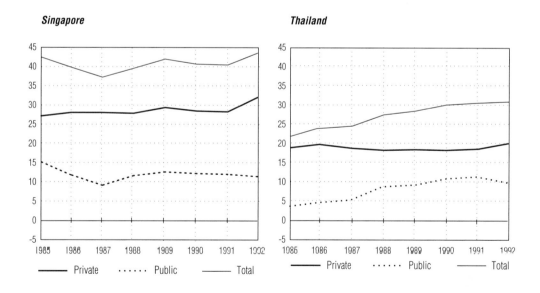

**Appendix: Countries Included in the Empirical Analysis**

| IMF code | Country | IMF code | Country | IMF code | Country |
|---|---|---|---|---|---|
| 111 | United States | 186 | Turkey | 524 | Sri Lanka |
| 112 | United Kingdom | 193 | Australia | 534 | India |
| 122 | Austria | 196 | New Zealand | 542 | Korea |
| 124 | Belgium | 199 | South Africa | 548 | Malaysia |
| 128 | Denmark | 213 | Argentina | 564 | Pakistan |
| 132 | France | 218 | Bolivia | 566 | Philippines |
| 134 | Germany | 223 | Brazil | 576 | Singapore |
| 136 | Italy | 228 | Chile | 578 | Thailand |
| 138 | Netherlands | 233 | Colombia | 622 | Cameroon |
| 142 | Norway | 253 | El Salvador | 652 | Ghana |
| 144 | Sweden | 273 | Mexico | 662 | Cote d'Ivoire |
| 156 | Canada | 288 | Paraguay | 664 | Morocco |
| 158 | Japan | 293 | Peru | 684 | Mauritius |
| 172 | Finland | 299 | Venezuela | 686 | Nigeria |
| 174 | Greece | 369 | Trinidad and Tobago | 694 | Kenya |
| 178 | Ireland | 429 | Iran | 724 | Sierra Leone |
| 182 | Portugal | 443 | Kuwait | 726 | Somalia |
| 184 | Spain | 518 | Myanmar | 742 | Togo |
| | | | | 744 | Tunisia |

# Commentary

*Andrés Solimano*

Sebastian Edwards has written an interesting and ambitious paper on the determinants of saving in Latin America. The topic is of obvious importance, particularly in light of the financial crisis in Mexico in 1995 triggered by currency overvaluation and a high dependence on short-term capital inflows. Argentina's vulnerability to financial shocks is related also to a considerable reliance (though less than Mexico's) on foreign financing. In contrast, the strong stance of the Chilean economy is attributed to, among other factors, a high rate of domestic saving.

The message is clear: High domestic saving reduces potential vulnerability to external shocks, in particular those associated with the capital account following shifts in confidence by international investors. The origin of those shocks is sometimes obscure, with weak links to fundamentals. The precautionary value of national saving increases substantially in these circumstances.

Edwards chooses the strategy of panel regressions, combining time series with cross-country data, to estimate private saving functions. The results obtained in the paper, in general, are sensible and within the conventional wisdom: demographic characteristics affect the saving ratio, financial deepening is positively correlated with private saving, there is partial crowding-out between public and private saving (the Ricardian equivalence proposition is rejected), and social security payments are negatively correlated with private saving. Moreover, the coefficient of the growth rate of GDP in the saving equation is strongly positive and statistically significant. However, given that the sample period, 1983–92, includes the debt crisis, and given the concomitant fall in domestic savings throughout Latin America, it is surprising that the regional dummy turned out to be insignificant in the regressions.

The results obtained in the econometric analysis should probably be taken with considerable caution, for several reasons: (i) the savings data used in the regressions are often calculated as a residual in national accounts; (ii) by standard but faulty statistical practices, purchases of durable goods and resources devoted to human capital formation are recorded as consumption rather than savings; (iii) terms of trade effects are often not included in the measurement of savings; (iv) several right-hand variables in the regressions are just proxy variables; and (v) cross-country comparability of the data can be questionable because of differences in definition and measurement techniques.

Moreover, at a conceptual level, there are serious causality issues. In long-run growth models, where output is supply driven, the causality runs from savings to growth. By contrast, in the literature on saving, for example, growth is what drives saving in the permanent income hypothesis or the life cycle model. How to reconcile both strands of the literature is not obvious. The use of instrumental variable methods in the estimation can address some simultaneity and measurement issues, although the basic causality problems at the analytical level remain.

Leaving aside these conceptual and empirical problems, the policy implications of Edwards' analysis are sensible ones, but they require qualification. I fully agree that public saving helps to promote national saving and growth. However, one important lesson of the 1980s is that fiscal adjustment in Latin America often takes the form of sizable cuts in infrastructure investment, maintenance expenditure, public spending in education, and other social services. Since these outlays in physical and human capital are closely linked to output growth, a policy of generating public savings at any cost can be detrimental to long-run sustainable growth.

The idea of a virtuous cycle between private saving and growth is compelling. Edwards emphasizes that this cycle can be generated by an initial increase in public saving. It might be that fiscal austerity can start an expansionary cycle, although Keynesians of all incarnations will be very doubtful of that. In fact, it seems more likely that virtuous cycles start from external bonanzas such as a positive terms of trade shock, increased availability of external financing, or the discovery of some natural resource (e.g., oil or gold). Of course, remarkable wisdom and national responsibility are shown when governments discount the transitory component of the windfall and save the additional resources for eventual bad times. Savings is a key component, but not the full story. Here again, we encounter the controversy between the savings-led growth school and growth-led savings school—a controversy that will hardly be settled just by empirical analysis, which is subject to considerable (and largely unavoidable) limitations. Edwards does his best to overcome these limitations in the paper.

Returning to the Mexican, Argentinean, and Chilean stories of early 1995, it is clear that a high rate of domestic saving goes a long way toward reducing external vulnerability and protecting domestic growth from the vagaries of international capital markets and the sometimes irrational behavior of market participants in a highly interdependent global economy. The old precautionary motive for saving is today more relevant than ever.

---

*Andrés Solimano is Executive Director for Chile and Ecuador at the Inter-American Development Bank.*

# CHAPTER 6

# Saving, Growth and Macroeconomic Vulnerability

*Michael Gavin, Ricardo Hausmann, and Ernesto Talvi*

The dominant views about saving policy in Latin America have been strongly influenced by the experiences of the rapidly growing, high-saving East Asian "miracle" economies.[1] As Figure 6.1 illustrates, national saving in Latin America during the past decade has averaged less than 20 percent of GDP, compared with more than 30 percent in six rapidly growing East Asian economies.[2] Every single economy of Latin America had a saving rate substantially below that recorded in the Asian miracle economies, and in several Latin American economies saving rates were only about one-third the Asian miracle average.

The concern about low rates of saving in Latin America has recently intensified, since these rates have declined further in the past several years, in some countries quite significantly.

As Figure 6.2 illustrates, during the 1990s the rate of national saving fell in 13 countries of the region. The decline in private saving has been even more generalized, falling in all countries but three.

Why are low saving rates a problem? Conventional wisdom offers at least two reasons: first, Latin America's low rate of saving condemns the region to an uncomfortable choice between low investment and growth; and second, excessive reliance upon volatile foreign capital makes the region vulnerable to crises.[3]

## National Saving Matters for Long-term Growth

As Figure 6.3 shows, high rates of saving are strongly correlated with high rates of growth. The link between saving and growth is not a direct one, however; it operates through the effects of investment on growth.

---

[1] In this paper the term East Asia refers to the region's six rapidly growing economies: Hong Kong, Indonesia, Korea, Malaysia, Singapore, and Thailand.
[2] In recent years Chile's saving rate has increased dramatically, and, at around 25 percent, now approaches East Asian levels.
[3] See for example, Summers (1996) and Bruno (1996).

**Figure 6.1  National Saving in East Asia and Latin America, 1984-93**
(Percent of GDP)

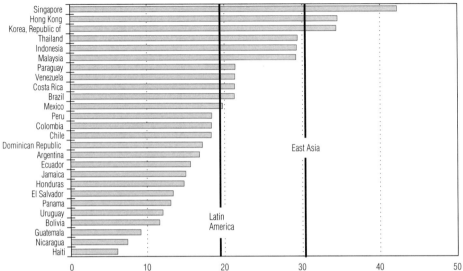

Note: In recent years Chile's saving rate has increased dramatically, and at around 25 percent, now approaches East Asian levels.
Source: Data on savings are from World Economic Outlook (IMF, various years).

**Figure 6.2  Change in Rate of National Saving in Latin America, 1988-89 vs. 1993-94**

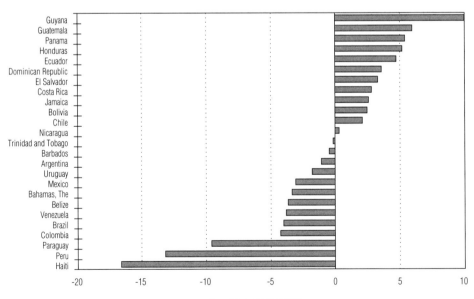

Percentage points of GDP

**Figure 6.3  Saving and Growth in Latin America and East Asia, 1984-93**
*(Percent of GDP)*

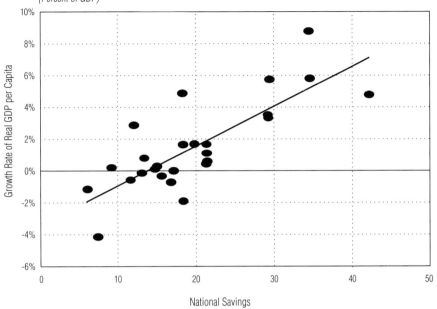

National Savings

**Figure 6.4  Saving and Investment in Latin America and East Asia,1984-93**
*(Percent of GDP)*

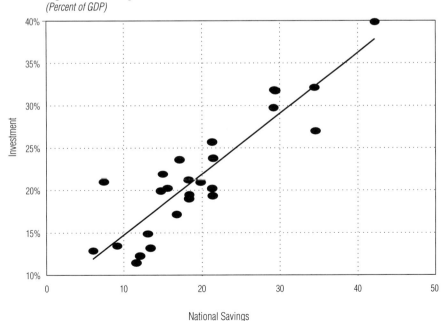

National Savings

To illustrate this point, Figure 6.4 shows a strong link between saving and investment, which suggests that increasing a country's saving rate, and therefore investment, will increase its rate of growth.

In principle there is no reason to expect a very close link between saving and domestic investment, because domestic investment can be financed by foreign saving, through inflows of international capital. One interpretation of this long-run relationship between national saving and domestic investment is that over the long run, international capital flows are limited, and thus a sustained rise in the rate of domestic investment requires a sustained rise in the rate of domestic saving. The correlation between saving and investment is, of course, not perfect. Therefore there is some scope for boosting domestic investment above domestic saving by encouraging international capital flows, even over a relatively long time horizon. But because the correlation between domestic saving and domestic investment is high, the scope for obtaining this effect from international capital flows may be limited.

## Low Rates of Saving Increase Short-term Vulnerability

According to the dominant view, low saving rates are also associated with increased vulnerability to macroeconomic crisis. A country with a low or declining rate of saving may be forced to run large current account deficits to maintain reasonable levels of investment. If excessive, this reliance on foreign saving unduly exposes the economy to volatile international capital flows. A sudden decline in capital inflows might force the recipient economy to make a very abrupt and therefore disruptive macroeconomic adjustment.

The dominant view holds that the Mexican crisis was associated with that country's low and declining rate of saving and the very large current account deficits during the years leading up to the crisis. In this context, high-saving economies such as Chile and the East Asian miracle economies were almost completely insulated from the financial turbulence that gripped many emerging market economies after the Mexican devaluation. This contrasts sharply with the financial turbulence that affected countries with a less impressive saving performance, such as Argentina.[4] International comparisons, and particularly comparisons of Latin America with

---

[4] Many countries with relatively poor saving performance, such as Colombia, were also largely immune to this "tequila effect."

East Asia, thus provide some support for the idea that saving is an important force for economic stability as well as for growth.

Conventional wisdom about the relationship among saving, growth, and stability also involves provides an accepted policy agenda to address the problem of low saving rates in Latin America. This policy agenda focuses on three mechanisms to tackle the problem of low saving:

- promoting national saving by raising public saving.
- promoting private saving by creating a stable and predictable economic environment that rewards savers for thrift and reduces fears that inflation or a collapsing financial system will lead to expropriation of their savings. This implies stabilizing the economy and strengthening domestic financial institutions by increasing the role of market signals in the allocation of saving and investment (i.e., the elimination of financial repression).
- promoting contractual saving, in particular by establishing fully funded social security systems.

Much of this conventional wisdom is perfectly sensible. In fact, many of these reforms have either already been implemented by many countries in the region, or are at the top of the policy agenda. However, although these policies are highly desirable because of their potential impact on economic efficiency and growth, we will argue that they are unlikely to have large effects on saving in the short to a medium term. Further, as we discuss below, there is good reason to believe that some of these reforms will temporarily reduce saving in the short term.

This paper argues that the appropriate policy to encourage saving is to promote sustained growth. Policymakers should therefore concentrate on continuing and deepening the stabilization and structural reform policies that are already underway, rather than emphasizing potentially distortionary policies directly aimed at increasing saving. Also, the success of growth-promoting policies should not be judged on the basis of the short-run response of saving rates. Most of these policies will positively affect saving only in the long run and may even reduce saving in the short run.

Stabilization and structural reform policies may, during the transition to a high-growth, high-saving equilibrium, involve a temporary but protracted period of large current account deficits, and hence, of reliance on volatile capital flows to finance investment. Therefore, complementary fiscal and financial policy measures need to be implemented to reduce the vulnerability of the economy to a crisis that may derail the reform process and hamper growth.

The policy conclusions of this paper differ from the prevailing views by de-emphasizing saving as an intermediate policy target. These conclusions are based on the following evidence:

• Higher growth precedes higher saving, rather than the reverse. Only after a sustained period of high growth do saving rates increase, sometimes after quite a significant delay.
• The most powerful determinant of saving over the long run is economic growth. According to this view, Latin America's chronically low rate of saving is primarily a consequence, rather than a cause, of the region's historically low and volatile economic growth, while the high saving observed in the Asian miracle economies is due to their high and less volatile economic growth.
• Many efficiency-raising, growth-promoting policies—such as inflation stabilization, financial liberalization and reform, and trade liberalization—may temporarily reduce saving rates for many years, and therefore increase the reliance of the economy on potentially volatile capital flows.

We will now develop these ideas in more detail. In the next section we critically review the policy implications drawn from the conventional wisdom about the relationship between saving, growth and stability, noting, in particular, that most of the policy recommendations deriving from these ideas have been implemented in many countries in the Latin American region. In the following section we review four facts that somewhat alter the perspective on the relationship among saving, growth, and macroeconomic stability. Finally we discuss the policy implications of this modified perspective.

## The Conventional Policy Agenda on Saving

In line with the conventional policy agenda, Latin American economic reforms over the past decade have included fiscal consolidation, inflation stabilization, financial liberalization and reform, and in some countries, the creation of mechanisms for contractual saving via the replacement of pay-as-you-go with fully funded social security systems.[5] Trade liberalization and regional integration have also been pervasive, and these too can have a

---

[5] Social security reform has been undertaken in Argentina, Chile, Colombia, and Peru, and is underway in Brazil, Mexico, and Uruguay.

**Figure 6.5  Public and Private Saving in Latin America**
*(Percent of GDP)*

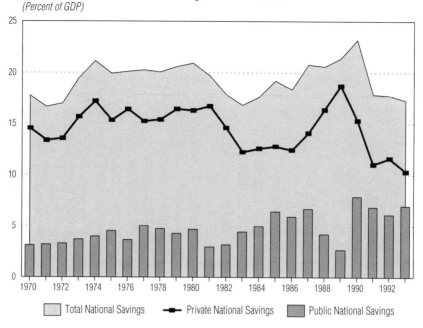

substantial impact on the saving rate, although this is not usually mentioned in the conventional policy agenda.

### Fiscal Consolidation

A cornerstone of the region's economic reform efforts has been fiscal consolidation, which has brought budget deficits from nearly 10 percent of GDP in the early 1980s to about 3 percent in recent years. But while public saving increased significantly in most of Latin America, private saving declined in several countries, leading to a reduction in total domestic saving, as illustrated in Figure 6.5.

As we will discuss below, further deepening the region's recent fiscal consolidation, grounded in meaningful reforms of budgetary institutions, remains one of Latin America's most urgent requirements. But this is likely to be an expensive means of raising total domestic saving. In fact, theory and evidence suggest that increased public saving is likely to generate a

**Figure 6.6  Median Inflation in Latin America**
*(Percent per year)*

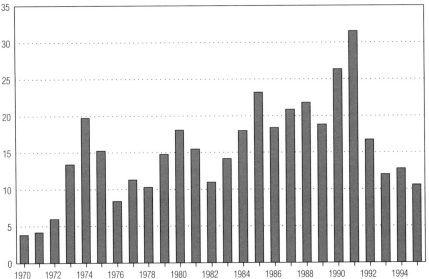

reduction in private saving.[6] This means that in order to raise domestic saving by one dollar, governments may need to increase public saving by two dollars or more. That is not without cost: raising taxes imposes important costs on the economy and may reduce economic growth, and reducing spending might make it impossible to carry out worthwhile public programs.

Again, this does not mean that governments in the region should not strengthen their fiscal position. It does mean that, even if done efficiently, fiscal consolidation is unlikely to yield large and sustained increases in aggregate saving. Moreover, it is easier and more efficient to improve public saving in a growing economy with stable and moderate tax rates.

---

[6] See Edwards (1994) for evidence that private saving in Latin America tends to decline by about 50 cents for every dollar of increase in public saving. Economic theory provides an explanation for this, although not everyone considers the theory entirely plausible: a budget surplus in the current period implies lower debt service, and therefore lower taxes, in future periods. Looking forward, consumers realize that because of lower future taxes, they can afford to consume more, thus saving less in the current period. The increase in public saving is therefore offset by a decrease in private saving. Some theories suggest that the offset should be complete, but most empirical estimates suggest it is about 50 percent.

*Inflation Stabilization*

This element of the conventional policy prescription emphasizes the importance not only of raising domestic saving, but also of ensuring that savings will remain in the domestic economy to finance domestic investment. After all, high saving will provide little support for economic development if savings are leaving the economy in the form of capital flight, thus starving the economy of the capacity to invest. An important reason for capital flight is the fear that wealth will be confiscated in a bout of unexpectedly high inflation. Thus, inflation stabilization is the second item on the conventional policy agenda.

This too has largely been accomplished in Latin America. With the recent Brazilian stabilization, extreme inflation has essentially vanished from the continent. While 10 of the region's 26 countries experienced inflation rates greater than 40 percent in 1990, this happened in only four countries in 1994 and 1995.

A clear pattern has emerged in most of these stabilizations. Rather than rising, saving rates typically decline in the immediate aftermath of the stabilization, as consumption (and typically investment as well) booms. The same pattern has occurred in many stabilizations outside of Latin America, such as the 1985 Israeli stabilization.

More formal econometric evidence supports this conclusion. Statistical research for this paper (as described in the appendix), as well as other studies, including Held and Uthoff (1995) and Morandé (1996), indicate that lower inflation tends to be associated, other things being equal, with lower rates of saving, at least in the short run.[7] The available evidence thus suggests that the inflation stabilizations, whatever their other good effects, have in the short run reduced, rather than increased, saving in Latin America.

*Financial System Reform*

Capital flight can also be caused by weak and repressed domestic financial institutions. Domestic savers know that such institutions are unable to offer attractive rates of return, and have good reason to fear that any wealth entrusted to them will vanish in a financial collapse. The conventional policy

---

[7] However, Edwards (1994) finds no significant impact of inflation on national saving. The results in Held and Uthoff (1995) break down if the sample of countries is restricted.

**Figure 6.7  Financial Depth and National Saving: Change from 1988-92**
*(In percent)*

Change in M2/GDP (1988-92)

**Figure 6.8  Mexican Bank Lending to the Private Sector**
*(Percent of GDP)*

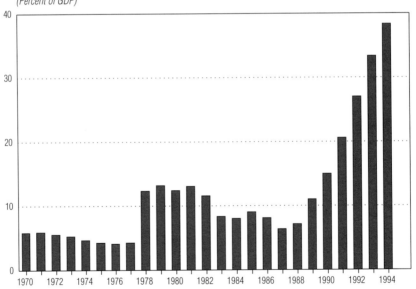

agenda thus emphasizes the need not only to provide a stable monetary system, but also to build a financial system in which domestic savers can have confidence, operating in an environment that allows domestic interest rates to provide the right signals to both savers and investors.

Here, too, many Latin American countries have made substantial progress; domestic financial institutions have been privatized, and markets have been largely freed from quantitative credit restrictions and interest rate ceilings. While much remains to be done, one key objective has been largely fulfilled: domestic savers' confidence in the domestic financial system has been increased dramatically. This has been reflected in the growth of domestic financial systems in many countries, as both domestic and foreign savers have become more willing to place their savings there. This has provided domestic banks with funds to invest domestically.

While there may be positive effects on saving in the long run, however, the increase in the size of the domestic financial system has had little short-term effect on saving in Latin America. As Figure 6.7 illustrates, short-run changes in financial depth, as measured by the size of the domestic banking system, appear to bear little relationship to national saving in the region. Mexico, Brazil, and Bolivia, for example, recently experienced large increases in financial depth, but saving rates were largely unaffected in Bolivia, and they declined in Mexico and Brazil.

Mexico presents an extreme but revealing example of the short-run consequences of rapid growth in domestic financial intermediation.[8] That country saw a large increase in the demand for domestic bank deposits during 1990–1994, driven in large part by the country's success in stabilizing inflation. At the same time the government was using privatization revenue to repay its loans from the banking system. The result was a large increase in resources available for commercial banks to lend to the private sector.

As Figure 6.8 illustrates, Mexican bank lending to the private sector rose from less than 10 percent of GDP in 1989 to nearly 40 percent in 1994. This lending financed some investment, which recovered substantially during 1990–1994, but much of the lending also went to consumers. The greater availability of credit relaxed constraints on consumption spending, and was almost certainly a major factor underlying the substantial decline in Mexican saving during the years leading up to the 1995 crisis. Thus, a policy of financial liberalization that was justified, in part, by a desire to raise domestic saving appears to have had exactly the opposite result.

---

[8] See Gavin and Hausmann (1996) for a discussion of other countries in the region.

This does not mean that financial liberalization is a bad idea. On the contrary, the policy is likely to provide important economic benefits and may contribute to higher saving rates over the long run. Our point is simply that financial liberalization is unlikely to have a significant positive impact on saving in the short run, and, indeed, the short-run effect may well be negative.

## Contractual Saving

Another element of the conventional policy response to the problem of low saving in Latin America is implementation of contractual saving schemes, particularly fully funded social security systems.

Social security reform is certainly desirable. It ameliorates the governance problem inherent in pay-as-you-go systems due to the fact that future taxpayers are not represented in political decisionmaking about the level of social security benefits they will be required to provide. There is also evidence from the Chilean experience that fully funded, privately managed social security systems can provide an important impetus to the development of domestic capital markets. However, the effects on saving are not likely to be large unless the reform is accompanied by fiscal tightening.

The largest and most direct impact of social security reform on saving is generated by cleaning up the fiscal mess typically created by pay-as-you-go social security systems. The reform requires that today's workers save for their own retirement. The question is, who pays for today's pensioners? Saving increases to the extent that current taxpayers bear the expense. But if the government meets this obligation by increasing the deficit, there is no necessary direct effect on national saving. Since in Chile the reform implied a major fiscal adjustment to pay for the current pensioners, this effect on saving is significant (roughly 3 percent of GDP), although small in comparison with the increase in domestic saving registered over the past decade (roughly 15 percent of GDP). But reforms in other Latin American countries have not involved a similar fiscal adjustment, and the impact of reform on saving is therefore likely to be much smaller (Ayala, 1995).

Pension reform may also promote financial market development, as appears to have been the case in Chile. This is important—such development is likely to promote a more efficient allocation of both domestic and foreign saving flows to the economy, since there is evidence that deep financial markets act as shock absorbers. It may also have some positive effect on domestic saving, although this is not assured.

## *Trade Liberalization*

Trade liberalization is not on the conventional policy agenda for saving, but we mention it because liberalization can lead to a transitory saving decline. Liberalization generally reduces the cost of imported consumer durable goods, leading to an increase in demand for these goods. This can lead to a temporary burst of spending on durable goods, as consumers adjust upward their stock of the goods. During this transitory period of stock adjustment, conventional measures of saving decline.[9] This appears to have been an important factor in the recent decline in private saving in Colombia.

Trade liberalization can also lead to a reduction in saving if it is perceived as transitory, a perception that may result from purely political economic factors, or from fears that the temporary trade imbalances often associated with liberalization will prove unsustainable. If liberalization is perceived to be temporary, consumers may have an even stronger incentive to purchase imported consumption goods when they are inexpensive, thus leading to a transitory consumption boom and a decline in the rate of saving.

## A Fresh Look at the Stylized Facts on Saving: Latin America vs. East Asia

Four facts shed additional light on the relationship among saving, growth, and economic stability:

- Saving rates have increased substantially in the Asian miracle economies, but have remained stagnant in Latin America since the early 1970s. In fact, although the Asian miracle economies are very high savers now, in the early 1970s they saved less than Latin America.
- Growth appears to precede saving, rather than the reverse.
- Long-run differences in the behavior of saving rates across Latin America and the Asian miracles can be attributed to differences in growth performance.
- Policies that raise efficiency and promote growth may temporarily reduce saving. Although temporary, the reduction in saving may last for several years.

---

[9] Although most countries' accounts consider it so, it is debatable whether such an increase in spending really represents a decline in saving at all, because the purchase of consumer durables is really a form of investment in an asset that will yield benefits, potentially for a considerable period of time.

**Figure 6.9  Saving Rates in Asia and Latin America**
*(Percent of GDP)*

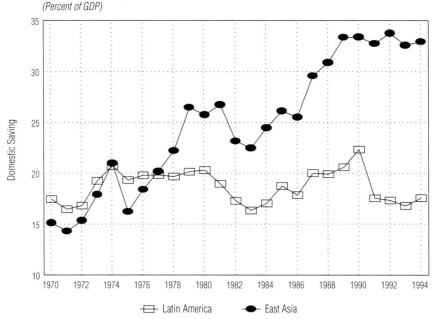

**Figure 6.10  Growth, Saving and the Current Account in Chile**
*(Growth rate in percent, other variables percent of GDP)*

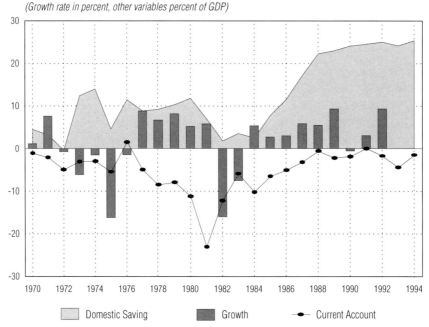

*Fact 1: Saving rates have increased substantially in the Asian miracle economies, but have remained stagnant in Latin America since the early 1970s. In fact, although the Asian miracle economies are very high savers now, in the early 1970s they saved less than Latin America.*

Figure 6.9 shows the (population-weighted) average saving rates for Latin America and the Asian miracle economies. There was a long and gradual increase in Asian saving rates, starting from levels below those recorded in Latin America in the 1970s. Only in the late 1970s and early 1980s, after growth accelerated, did Asian saving rates rise consistently and substantially above Latin American rates.

*Fact 2: Growth appears to precede saving, rather than the reverse.*

The fact that increased growth tends to precede increased saving suggests that saving may, to an important extent, be caused by economic growth, in addition to causing such growth.[10]

  This view is supported by several recent papers, including an influential paper by Carroll and Weil (1994), which examines savings and economic growth in a large sample of countries. In the specific cases of Japan, South Korea, Singapore, and Hong Kong, the authors conclude that growth was high early and saving was high later.

  The pattern of strongly increasing saving *after* an acceleration of growth is present in Chile's recent experience as well. Figure 6.10 shows that Chile's economic recovery began in 1984, when domestic saving was still quite depressed and the economy was, as a result, heavily reliant upon capital inflows to finance domestic investment.[11] Only in the late 1980s, after several years of sustained economic growth, did Chilean saving rates approach current high levels.

  In addition to evidence on individual countries, the hypothesis that growth precedes saving has also found support in formal econometric tests. Carroll and Weil (1994) show that, in data sets covering a large number of

---

[10] A plausible mechanism through which growth may "cause" saving is the need to self-finance at least a portion of the many profitable investments available in a high-growth economy, in an environment of imperfect capital markets. Birdsall, Pinckney, and Sabot (1995) argue for the importance of this mechanism in the context of low-income economies, and Liu and Woo (1994) provide evidence of its empirical importance for Taiwan.

[11] This reliance can be seen in the large current account deficits in the early stages of the economic recovery.

**Figure 6.11  Can Growth Explain Asia's Higher Saving Rate? A Counterfactual Comparison**
*(In percent)*

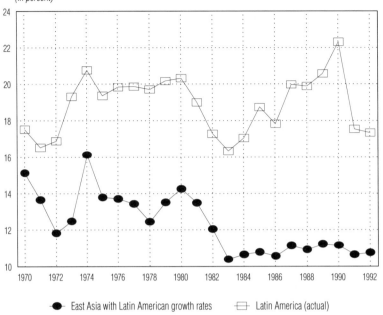

countries over several decades, past growth predicts future saving rates, while past saving rates do not predict future growth.[12]

***Fact 3: Long-run differences in the behavior of saving rates across Latin America and the Asian miracles can be attributed to differences in growth performance.***

The estimated impact of growth on saving is not only statistically significant but also very large in economic terms. In fact, the difference between East Asian and Latin American growth rates is sufficient to explain the difference in the regions' saving behavior. Using the econometric model of the determinants of saving rates described in the appendix, Figure 6.11 illus-

---

[12] Technically, the paper asked whether saving "Granger causes" growth and vice versa. One variable Granger causes another if observations of the first variable help predict subsequent movements in the second, after taking into account the predictive value of the second variable's own history. The paper found that growth Granger causes saving, while saving appears not to Granger cause growth. We replicated Carroll and Weil's (1994) Granger causality tests in our sample and obtained very similar results.

trates the impact of growth on saving by estimating what Asian saving rates would have been if those countries had experienced Latin America's rate of economic growth during the past 25 years.

The figure shows that if, during 1970–1994, the East Asian miracles had experienced the economic growth recorded by Latin America, then, other things being equal, the Asian saving rate would have been even lower than that recorded in Latin America. This implies that essentially all of the difference between saving rates in Latin America and the Asian miracle economies can be explained by the difference in their growth performance.

Other determinants of saving may be important, but they are unlikely to account for much of the long-run difference in Latin American and East Asian rates of saving, or for the recent sustained increase in Chilean saving rates. For example, the econometric model used here, as well as work by other authors, show that, although improvements in the terms of trade typically increase saving, the effect appears to be purely transitory and therefore unlikely to explain the differences in long-run behavior.[13] Other determinants of saving, such as the distribution of income, the age distribution of the population, and demography may also be statistically relevant.[14] But none of these factors can account quantitatively for the dramatic shift from relatively low to very high saving rates that have characterized the Asian miracle economies since the early 1970s, and Chile since the mid 1980s.

***Fact 4: Policies that raise efficiency and promote growth may temporarily reduce saving. Although temporary, the reduction in saving may last for several years.***

Some important efficiency-raising policy reforms, such as inflation stabilization, financial reform, and trade reform, can be expected to temporarily reduce saving. Inflation stabilization is a particularly important example, because it is well understood that exchange rate-based stabilizations are expansionary and generate a consumption boom in the initial stages and a corresponding decline in saving (see, for example, Kiguel and Liviatan

---

[13] Held and Uthoff (1995) find that improvements in the terms of trade actually have a negative effect on saving.
[14] For example, Edwards (1994) finds some evidence that the age dependency ratio (the fraction of the population either younger than 15 or older than 65 years of age) is negatively related to domestic saving rates. In some specifications of his model, a more equal distribution of income is associated with a higher saving rate, but this result is not robust.

**Figure 6.12  Simulated Impact on Saving of a Major Inflation Stabilization
and Increase in Economic Growth**

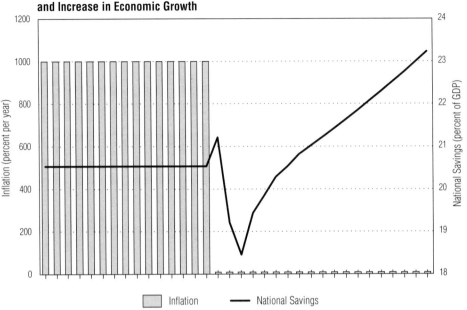

1992; Végh 1992). It is only later that consumption contracts and the
economy falls into recession. An important reason for the decline in Latin
American saving rates during the 1990s is that many countries have
achieved major inflation stabilizations.

To illustrate the potential economic significance of this, we used the
model described in the appendix to simulate the impact of a major inflation
stabilization, reducing the rate of inflation from 1000 percent a year to zero,
combined with an increase in the rate of economic growth.

The econometric model predicts a 2 percent decline in the rate of saving in the immediate aftermath of the stabilization. The effect is transitory
and higher economic growth will eventually lead to a higher rate of saving,
but the model predicts that it will take five years for saving to recover its
prestabilization levels.

It is also plausible that many other reforms that raise efficiency and
domestic production will generate a transitory decline in saving, particularly if there is a substantial lag between the implementation of reforms and
the creation of higher output. One reason for the recent sharp decline in
Colombian saving, for example, may have been the expectation of higher
national income from recent investments in newly discovered oil fields.

Higher output (and income) should eventually, according to our model, lead to higher saving.

The fact that highly desirable economic reforms may have a transitory adverse impact on domestic saving has important implications. First, it highlights the importance of properly diagnosing a decline in saving, which may result not from inadequate policies but from the reverse. Second, if the decline does represent a transitory effect, then the case for a major policy response to the problem becomes less compelling. Finally, it is important to ensure that growth-friendly policies will not be foregone or delayed because of the possibility of a transitory adverse impact on saving.

## The Policy Agenda Revisited: Focus on Growth, but Beware of "Spring Frost"

In much of this paper we have argued that the conventional wisdom about national saving, growth, and economic stability is incomplete in important ways. First, we have argued that the major difference between Asian and Latin American saving is in long-term performance, and that the most plausible explanation for the differences in saving behavior is that Asia has managed to achieve sustained high rates of growth, while Latin America has experienced low and volatile growth. Second, we have also argued that highly desirable pro-growth policy reforms—which have been largely implemented by the countries of Latin America—can transitorily reduce national saving, and that this problem has something to do with the recent decline in Latin America's saving rate. We turn now to a discussion of the policy implications of these points.

### Focus on Long-term Growth, and Saving Will Follow

The policy implication of the view that growth precedes saving, rather than the reverse, is that policymakers should focus on economic growth rather than trying to establish programs to promote national saving, since such programs are likely to be of dubious effectiveness and may involve economic inefficiencies. Of course, policy impediments to saving should be removed, but beyond that, policy should concern itself with establishing an environment conducive to sustained high rates of growth, trusting that national saving will follow in response to the incentives that such an environment creates.

In our view, this approach requires continuing the process of economic reform that has been underway in the region for some time, extending and deepening the gains already made in the areas of fiscal consolidation, macroeconomic stabilization, financial liberalization and reform, trade liberalization and regional integration, social security reform, labor market reform, and tax reform.

We have argued that these policies will result in higher saving only over the long run, and that some of them are indeed likely to have a transitory negative impact on saving. This does not mean that reforms should be delayed, but rather that measures should be taken to reduce the economy's vulnerability during the transitory period of low saving.

### Focus on Complementary Policies that Reduce Vulnerability

Since delay occurs between the recovery of growth and the saving response, the economy is likely to be dependent upon capital inflows until it reaches a high-growth, high-savings equilibrium. During this transition, the economy may be vulnerable to external shocks or to a sudden loss of confidence. Shocks to the economy in this phase may derail the reform process and thwart growth, just as a young flower might be killed by a spring frost that an older and sturdier plant could easily survive.

This means that policymakers need to implement policies that make the economy more resilient, to absorb the inevitable shocks without aborting reform's positive effects on growth and saving. Policies to raise national saving directly are unlikely to be the most effective means of reducing vulnerability. Instead, policymakers need to analyze the stress points in their economy, where shocks can trigger collapse, and strengthen them.

We focus here on two particularly important areas that have been weak links in many Latin American economies, and where appropriate policies can substantially improve a country's shock resistance and ability to bridge the transition to high savings: the domestic financial system and fiscal policy.[15]

### The Domestic Financial System

The domestic financial system will be called upon to intermediate some of the potentially volatile capital flows during the transition. For example, for-

---

[15] Such policies were the focus of the special chapter on "Overcoming Volatility," in the Inter-American Development Bank's Report on Economic and Social Progress in Latin America 1995.

eign direct investment and equity portfolio investment are not intermediated by banks, but foreign deposits in the domestic banking system are. This intermediation, an essential function of banks, carries the potential for instability and crisis, because it involves a transformation of term structure and a transfer of risk. Moreover, implicit or explicit public insurance of the banking system generates strong problems of moral hazard.

When banks intermediate savings, their savers obtain liquid bank deposits, which the banks use to fund longer-term lending commitments. This is not inherently bad, but it can exaggerate swings in capital flows and their macroeconomic consequences,[16] and can create the potential for financial crisis if depositors attempt to withdraw their deposits from the system more rapidly than banks' lending commitments can be wound down. Unless the financial system possesses sufficient reserves to manage such liquidity shocks, even a brief and unwarranted panic by depositors can bring the financial system to its knees, potentially crippling the real economy and creating the very macroeconomic crisis that depositors feared. Because banks generally benefit from implicit or explicit insurance, they have inadequate incentives to remain sufficiently liquid; policymakers, therefore, have a responsibility to ensure that they do.

Financial intermediation also means that lending risks are shifted from savers, whose deposit value is largely unaffected by the bank's loan portfolio, to bank shareholders and, because of implicit public insurance schemes, to taxpayers. This poses a strong moral hazard problem, and in particular creates the danger that a surge of capital inflows will generate a lending boom. During such booms, excessively risky and potentially wasteful projects are funded, and the costs of bad outcomes largely fall on taxpayers, not on the bank managers responsible for making the loans. This creates the need to institute a conservative bank supervisory system that enforces appropriate capital adequacy standards and adjusts domestic monetary policy as necessary to forestall such credit booms.[17] Such a system may somewhat reduce the efficiency of bank intermediation, but failing to put one in place leaves the economy open to periodic macroeconomic and financial crises, which have too often interrupted Latin American growth and development and national saving.

---

[16] Goldfajn and Valdés (1995).

[17] See the proceedings of the IDB/Group of Thirty Conference on Banking Crises in Latin America (1996), and in particular Gavin and Hausmann (1996) and Rojas-Suárez and Weisbrod (1995).

## Fiscal Policy

Transition to a high-growth, high-saving equilibrium generally involves periods of transitory spending booms. These have favorable fiscal implications, because taxes are levied mainly on domestic spending. The danger is that the transitory fiscal benefits will generate permanent public spending commitments or hard-to-reverse reductions in tax rates. These changes weaken fiscal sustainability and do not reduce the fiscal deficit, which will appear when the boom subsides.[18]

The serious problem of an inadequate fiscal policy response arises because it is difficult to mobilize the collective action required to generate an appropriate response. Anticipating this, financial markets may lose confidence in the sustainability of fiscal policy, even if the country currently exhibits relatively low deficits, as Mexico did in 1994.

Solving this problem requires deep reforms in the budgetary institutions that shape fiscal policy in the region.[19] Here we point out that, while future fiscal policy reforms are essential to secure the economic stability required for sustained growth, our perspective departs from the conventional wisdom in two key respects. First, the focus on ensuring macroeconomic stability makes it clear that the issue is not merely the need to raise public saving rates with the aim of increasing total national saving. The real need is to create institutional structures that provide real assurance that fiscal policy will be well managed in good times. If the institutional reforms are effective, they will permit larger deficits in bad times, thus promoting a more counter-cyclical fiscal policy, but not necessarily one with higher public saving on average. Second, our perspective highlights the need to tackle problems in the formulation of fiscal policy by addressing the underlying institutional and political causes of suboptimal fiscal policymaking, rather than simply exhorting governments to behave themselves.

---

[18] See Talvi (1996) for a theoretical statement of this problem, and Talvi (1995) for an empirical discussion in the Uruguayan context.

[19] This problem is being explored in an ongoing research project in the Office of the Chief Economist at the Inter-American Development Bank. See Alesina, Hausmann, Hommes, and Stein (1995); Hausmann and Stein (1996); Eichengreen, Hausmann, and Von Hagen (1996); and Gavin, Hausmann, Perotti, and Talvi (1996).

## Concluding Remarks

Low Latin American saving rates reflect a recent history of low and volatile economic growth. The structural reforms in which the region has been engaging are already leading to a recovery of economic growth. However, since saving tends to lag behind growth, and may even decline in the early stages of economic reform, the region faces a transition during which it must rely upon capital flows to finance investment. Rather than searching for potentially distortionary policies to raise saving, policymakers should focus on promoting efficiency and growth. At the same time they should develop complementary policy measures aimed at reducing the vulnerability that may be generated by reliance on capital flows.

---

*Michael Gavin is Lead Research Economist, Ricardo Hausmann is Chief Economist, and Ernesto Talvi is Senior Research Economist in the Office of the Chief Economist, Inter-American Development Bank.*

## Appendix

We estimated the determinants of saving based on a 26-country data set—six East Asian miracle economies and 20 Latin American economies—assembled by the International Monetary Fund for the period 1970–1992.

The specification of the saving model is in line with economic theory and previous empirical research on saving (see, for example, Edwards 1994; Held and Uthoff 1995). However, the specification presented here allows for a richer dynamic structure, which enables us to capture the dynamic adjustment of the economic system to its long-run equilibrium in response to temporary and permanent shocks.

The following variables are included in the saving model: growth of GDP per capita (ggcap) and GDP per capita (gcap), which were obtained from Summers and Heston (1991); inflation (infl); capital flows (kflows); and changes in the terms of trade (gtot), which were obtained from the IMF's *International Financial Statistics*.

The results of the regression indicate that saving is (i) positively affected by the rate of growth (i.e., faster growing economies should, other things being equal, enjoy higher saving rates); (ii) positively affected by the level of income per capita; and (iii) negatively related to the availability of foreign saving (capital flows). A permanent improvement (deterioration) in the terms of trade temporarily increases (decreases) the saving rate but has no permanent effects. A permanent reduction (increase) in the rate of inflation temporarily reduces the saving rate, which later increases (decreases) to a level close to, but still lower (higher) than, the one prevailing before the reduction (increase) in the inflation rate.

## Dependent Variable: National Saving
*Included observations: 416*

| Variable | Coefficient | Std. Error | T-Statistic | Prob. | Variable | Coefficient | Std. Error | T-Statistic | Prob. |
|---|---|---|---|---|---|---|---|---|---|
| GCAP (-1) | 2.75E-05 | 5.87E-06 | 4.685077 | 0.0000 | INFL | -0.000687 | 0.000242 | -2.841819 | 0.0047 |
| GGCAP | 0.102982 | 0.035269 | 2.919924 | 0.0037 | INFL(-1) | 0.002024 | 0.000273 | 7.420894 | 0.0000 |
| KFLOWS | -0.206742 | 0.050839 | -4.066629 | 0.0001 | INFL(-2) | 0.000758 | 0.000293 | 2.586022 | 0.0101 |
| GTOT | 0.053568 | 0.008768 | 6.109410 | 0.0000 | INFL(-3) | -0.000472 | 0.000272 | -1.735052 | 0.0835 |
| GTOT(-1) | 0.028714 | 0.009629 | 2.982002 | 0.0030 | C | 0.110729 | 0.028247 | 3.920071 | 0.0001 |
| GTOT(-2) | 0.014147 | 0.008428 | 1.678498 | 0.0940 | AR(1) | | 0.023399 | 38.04861 | 0.0000 |

| | | | | |
|---|---|---|---|---|
| R-squared | 0.840481 | Log likelihood | 793.1751 | Akaike info criterion | -6.593527 |
| Adjusted R-squared | 0.836137 | Durbin-Watson stat | 2.103030 | Schwartz criterion | -6.477257 |
| S.E. of regression | 0.036481 | Mean dependent var | 0.198719 | F-statistic | 193.5099 |
| Sum squared resid | 0.537657 | S.D. dependent var | 0.090120 | Prob(F-statistic) | 0.000000 |

*Inverted AR Roots       .89*

# Commentary

*Andrés Solimano*

In this interesting and provocative paper, Gavin, Hausmann and Talvi challenge the new emerging consensus that national savings must be a priority policy target in Latin American reform. This consensus emerged after the dramatic Mexican crisis of 1995, which showed how vulnerable reform programs are to sudden changes in the volume of external savings in economies that depend heavily on foreign savings to finance investment and growth. The authors argue that "the appropriate policy to promote savings is to promote sustained growth. Policymakers therefore should concentrate on continuing and deepening the stabilization and structural reform policies that are already underway rather than emphasizing the potentially distortionary policies directly aimed at increasing savings."

The authors favor the passive savings view, in which growth comes before saving. This "Marx-Schumpeter-Keynes view"[1] holds that investment and innovation lead growth and that saving adjusts passively to meet the level of investment required in macro equilibrium to support output growth. An alternative view is the active savings school, in which saving leads growth. This "Mill-Marshall-Solow" view holds that all savings are automatically invested and translated into output growth. In the Solow model there is no independent investment function (of a Keynesian sort) and therefore no problems of translating existing savings into more investment and faster growth.[2]

The authors propose deepened structural reforms and more macro stabilization as the automatic recipe for growth. They say that since growth leads saving, the problem of low saving will be resolved after a lag. Apparently, there is no need, in their view, to set national saving as a policy target. I think this is potentially risky advice. We do not yet know enough about the causal relationship among saving, investment, and growth to rely so heavily on the passive saving school. However, we do know that reliance on external savings makes the economy prone to severe macro crisis in the wake of sudden changes in external financing, which in turn is highly detrimental to sustained growth. The crisis in the Southern Cone in the early

---

[1] See Chakravarti (1993).
[2] See Schmidt-Hebbel, Servén, and Solimano (1996).

1980s and Mexico in 1995 are recent examples of this. The economic history of Latin America is full of cases of economic crisis associated with an excessive reliance on foreign savings. In contrast, it is hard to find a macro crisis due to excess national savings.

The authors focus only on the lag between growth and savings and disregard the important lag between reform and growth. There is ample evidence of the latter.[3] Chile implemented most of its economic reform program in the second half of the 1970s and sustained growth came in the late 1980s and throughout the 1990s. There was a lag of a decade between the reform and the sustained acceleration in growth. Mexico has been growing in 1985–1995, the period of reform, at a much slower rate than in the 1950s, 1960s, and 1970s. The reform in Bolivia was followed by only a moderate acceleration in GDP growth.[4]

The problem of a slow growth response to reform has to do with the investment response to the reforms and not only to a problem of low saving. The private sector might be skeptical, at the beginning of a complex reform program, of the ultimate success of the reform. Since most investment outlays are irreversible, the rational response in uncertain conditions is to postpone investment; and as a result of this behavior, the recovery of growth is delayed. There are also coordination failures, since cautious investors may need to be reassured by other investors that it is good to invest in response to reform programs in their initial stage of implementation. Moreover, high real interest during stabilization discourages investment. Therefore, the link between reform and investment is often weak. Since investment leads growth in the passive savings framework adopted in the Gavin, Hausmann, Talvi paper, their indirect recipe for stimulating savings may rest on feeble foundations.

The authors do not explore the issue of which nondistortionary policies can promote savings in the framework of market-based reform. An obvious policy is to adopt an expenditure tax rather than an income tax. The former has the advantage of taxing consumption but not saving, as the income tax does. Also, differential taxation for the distributed versus retained profits of firms can be an effective way to encourage firms to save and invest. This scheme worked well in Chile a few years ago.

---

[3] See Servén and Solimano (1993).
[4] See Solimano (1996).

To sum up, although the paper is thought-provoking, it carries the risk of being misinterpreted to mean that national saving does not matter in policy formulation. To the contrary, the consensus argument that national saving needs to be promoted because it reduces economic volatility is still very valid (and this seems to be recognized by the authors). Moreover, this is in itself a pro-growth argument, since investment will benefit from a reduction in volatility and uncertainty. The argument that higher national saving will directly promote more growth needs some qualification, given the causality problems mentioned above; however, in a context of favorable investment opportunities created by market reforms, it is hard to think that more saving will harm the process of capital formation and growth.

*Andrés Solimano is Executive Director for Chile and Ecuador at the Inter-American Development Bank.*

# Commentary

*Paulo Vieira da Cunha\**

The new conventional wisdom that saving follows growth is a seeming contradiction to much of development thinking of the 1960s and before.[1] Gavin-Hausmann-Talvi (GHT) present a persuasive defense of this position. The conclusion, which is well grounded in theory and evidence, is to "deemphasize saving as an intermediate policy target." It is important, however, to place this conclusion in its appropriate setting. As the authors stress, it is not that saving is irrelevant; on the contrary, the evidence they present shows that, over a longer period, there is a close correlation between domestic saving and investment, even though, in theory, there is no need for such a strong correlation. GHT's argument seems to be that, if all else is in place, or nearly in place, saving will perform just right: ex ante domestic saving will just about match the warranted rate of investment, and thus will not lead to an unsustainable current account position.

I would like to discuss some implications of this conclusion. I have two points: One is that the financial system plays a critical role in promoting growth; and two, that the depth and quality of the financial system are conditional on sustained macroeconomic stability. Ultimately, stability is a sine qua non for robust growth, and with stability and growth, saving may indeed be seen as an instrument rather than a cause. I also have some comments on other findings and on the empirical results shown in the appendix to the paper.

*Growth and saving.* GHT find empirical support for the saving-to-growth link and present this as a stylized fact for policy. But the evidence on

---

*The author is grateful to Holger Wolf and Ross Levine for helpful comments and suggestions.

[1] This position is also in vogue in the Clinton White House. The savings rate of the United States dropped significantly during the past thirty years and has remained consistently below that of Japan and Germany. Nevertheless, the United States has retained its output-per-person advantage over its main economic rivals in both manufacturing and services. The reason for this is the rapid growth in productivity, which in turn results from a "higher quality" of savings and investment, suggesting that "policy should focus more on strategies for innovation and less on strategies for savings and investment." (Strategic Economic Decisions, 1995, Chapter 2).

this link is controversial. As is the case with the literature they cite, GHT report Granger causality tests between growth and saving and growth and investment, using panel data made up of long-term time averages. The problem is that both saving and investment are likely to be determined by future-looking behavior and thus must be interpreted with caution. As Attanasio, Picci, and Scorcu (1995) observe, "obviously, one would not want to conclude that Christmas cards cause Christmas!" Their review of the empirical results is far less conclusive than GHT's. And the problem is that, from the theory, the relationship between savings rates and growth is complex and ambiguous, and which of the various factors will prevail is essentially an empirical issue that has not yet been put to rest.

The saving-to-growth or growth-to-saving debate is about what causes growth; and the argument that growth leads to saving is an argument about efficient intermediation between saving and high-productivity (return) investment. In a recent review of this literature, Schmidt-Hebbel and Servén (1995) note that:

> If it is concluded that saving drives growth (through physical capital investment) or if causality runs in both directions, policies that encourage saving are called for. If instead investment drives growth and the latter determines saving, growth-oriented policies should aim primarily at raising investment. Finally, if the main causality runs from growth to saving and investment— because human capital, technology, and ideas, not physical investment, are the main growth determinants —then growth-promoting policies should focus on those three factors.

The dismal trend in the marginal product of capital in the Soviet economy after 1960 is strong evidence of the fact that investment, or saving, alone is not enough. High rates of saving and investment can be dissipated through economy-wide distortions and yield very low rates of growth. On the other hand, Young (1994, 1995) forcefully argues that, except for Hong Kong, East Asia's stellar growth performance can be explained largely by its unusually high investment ratios (about 30 percent of GDP), rather than by any extraordinary growth in productivity. By Young's estimates, East Asia's productivity has grown at a rate fairly close to the world average. In both cases the key to success or failure is the efficiency with which saving is transformed into investment (or, if you will, the efficiency with which investment, through growth, leads to new saving). Indeed, the strongest link among saving, investment, and growth is not within East Asia indiscriminately, but, as shown by Schmidt-Hebbel and Serven (1995), among the group of ten take-off market economies plus China.[2]

There is a strong presumption that retained earnings are important for financing, leveraging, and guiding investment during the take-off period to rapid growth, as argued by GHT.[3] Thus, where growth leads to higher saving, another explanation for the correlation may be that a high growth rate is a proxy for a high rate of return on capital, which may be inadequately reflected in domestic interest rates (especially if financial markets are not liberalized). Moreover, policy-based finance, notably in East Asia and in the historical example of Japan, helped close the financing gap for large investment projects (Kato et al., 1994), and also influenced the choice of investment. Thus, early on during the take-off period there may be a link among forced saving, directed credit, and rapid growth. This viewpoint is controversial and has not been resolved. What is clear, however, is that in all instances continued growth came with the rapid development of financial markets.[4] In the take-off countries, financial markets have played an increasing role in intermediating resources, both foreign and domestic.[5]

Perhaps one reason for the low productivity of saving in Latin America (Chile excepted) is its generally weak financial system. Weak domestic finance constrains growth for three basic reasons. Outside of a reasonably efficient financial system, it is very difficult to create *institutions* to evaluate projects, manage risks, and monitor managers. King and Levine (1993) show results that suggest an important link between financial development and long-run growth. Furthermore, "the significant, robust relationship between the level of financial development and both the current and future rate of economic growth contrasts sharply with the weak, fragile partial correlations between growth and a large variety of other economic indicators, as shown by Levine and Renelt (1992)." Interestingly, the results do *not* indicate, as Joan Robinson (1952) has argued, that "where enterprise leads, finance follows." Finance does not merely follow growth; finance appears to be important in leading economic growth.

In a recent paper (Gavin and Hausmann, 1996), two of the present coauthors assessed Latin America's banking systems and arrived at a clear

---

[2] This group includes Hong Kong, Indonesia, Korea, Malaysia, Singapore, Taiwan China, and Thailand in East Asia; Botswana and Mauritius in Africa; and Chile in Latin America.
[3] See also Deaton (1990) and Deaton and Paxson (1994).
[4] China may also be a possible exception.
[5] See De Gregorio and Guidotti (1995).

and powerful conclusion. The region's banking system is crisis prone, and the underlying cause of bank failures is macroeconomic instability with a marked volatility in the rate of credit expansion. Rapid credit growth is often associated with a decline in credit standards and with a deterioration in supervisory and regulatory vigilance. High inflation and large volatility in output and in relative prices make the chore of picking good borrowers more difficult. To attempt to protect themselves, banks increase the risk premia in their lending rates.

Commonly, the credit risk spread that nonprime borrowers must pay over the prime lending rate accounts for the majority of the lending spread between the lending rate and the deposit rate.[6] Rodriguez (1994) shows that in Uruguay in 1992, prime customers paid 15.5 percentage points above the deposit rate while average borrowers paid an additional 32.8 percentage points—a total of 48.3 percentage points above the deposit rate. In Argentina in 1993 the spread for nonprime borrowers was 15 percentage points. And, of course, very high real rates lead to adverse selection: those who want to borrow may well be the worst customers. Collateral may mitigate this effect, but any negative macroeconomic shock that hits the economy and reduces firms' collateralizable net worth will, in turn, increase the credit risk spread to cover the growing risk of firms defaulting on their loans. In short, a history of instability and volatility creates a damning chain of causation that severely hampers the ability of the banking system to guide savings to productive uses. Without customers for its risk-based lending services, the neuralgic functions of the financial system shrivel, even though banks may prosper and expand by appropriating part of the revenue from the inflation tax and/or by arbitraging on the inconsistencies between expected devaluation and the domestic interest rate.

Caprio and Klingebiel (1996) have replicated Gavin and Hausmann's analysis for a wider array of countries. They find that excessive credit growth is a primary factor behind banking crises—but only if the sample is restricted for Latin America. The suggestion is that, in the region, macroeconomic instability and volatility fundamentally weakened and distorted the development of financial systems. These weakened systems, in turn, contributed to deeper macroeconomic instability and volatility. This combination is ruinous for high-productivity investment, especially that outside the firms' own main concerns and financed through debt-creating instruments.

---

[6] See Brock (1996).

Lack of good and "open" investment opportunities (i.e., those that can be intermediated through the financial system) would, arguably, reduce growth and (financial) saving.[7]

GHT have offered a stimulating paper with useful and seemingly robust policy conclusions. It is indeed debatable whether policy should focus on saving, rather than on investment in both physical and human capital, and the weight of current evidence supports the latter view. Why then make saving an intermediate target? The goal is growth. An intermediate target is useful if it is easier to measure and if it is a more reliable predictor of desired outcome than the outcome itself. Saving is neither easier to measure nor a reliable predictor. And growth, saving, and the efficiency with which resources are allocated are so interlinked that it seems impossible to separate their effects, and hardly worth it. So why use saving as an intermediate target? Better to focus on the bottom line and on the policies that help you get there—policies aimed at maintaining macroeconomic stability with competitive markets and with a bias to the long-run development of human capabilities and technical progress.

---

*Paulo Vieira da Cunha is Economic Advisor, Development Economics Department, the World Bank.*

---

[7] The low productivity of saving may also result from heavy taxation of capital goods diminishing the impact of saving on capital accumulation. I am thankful to Luis Servén for pointing this out; this mechanism has greatly reduced the productivity of saving in India (Servén 1996). In addition, there are many pitfalls in the usual national accounts measures of private saving. In high-inflation economies, one is fundamental: the national accounts measures are biased upwards by the nominal component in interest payments on the government debt. Whether GHT took account of this distortion would be important to know. It may also be appropriate to separate the sample used to estimate the regression in Table A1 by level of GDP per capita. In comparisons across regions, Ogaki, Ostry, and Reinhard (1995) show that the poorer the region, the lower the average level of gross saving. One would also want to examine with greater care the authors' assertion that the inclusion of a one-period lagged autoregressive term indeed allows for "the dynamic adjustment of the economic system to its long- run equilibrium." Finally, it does not appear to be the case that the Asian miracle economies "saved less than Latin America in the early 1970s."

# CHAPTER 7

# Developing Strong Capital Markets

*by Paul Boeker*

For both East Asia and Latin America over the past 15 years, the development of capital markets has been an essential factor in growth. In this critical area of economic policy, the East Asian countries pursued a different route over the last generation than did almost all of Latin America. In particular, most East Asian countries used government lending to the private sector, or directed credit through a protected commercial banking sector, to compensate for the lack, until quite recently, of a corporate bond market. While the effectiveness of this second-best approach is still being debated, its relevance is diminished for Latin America, which is in a later stage of development; Latin America has opened other approaches to development of long-term debt markets with financial sector reforms, pension reform in particular. Thus, part of East Asia's experience with the early stages of capital markets development is not applicable to Latin America's challenge in the 1990s, when many countries of the region are well advanced in development of capital markets, and international financial market conditions are much different.

A third approach, pursued with great success by Chile since 1983, has produced Latin America's best functioning capital market. Early on, Chile established pension funds and other nonbank financial institutions that provide long-term funds to the market. It also carried out extensive privatization of utilities and other heavily capitalized industries to create the flow of high-quality debt and equity securities that make up the other (demand) side of the market. Both sides of this large-scale change in market structure were essential for the progressive deepening of financial markets and increased financial savings that Chile has experienced since 1983. Large-scale privatization did not play a significant role in the East Asian experience. Yet the Chilean experience clearly had some common features with that of East Asia, in particular the emphasis on strong banking regulation and supervision, which has been notably missing from the efforts of most of Latin America.

The task of defining effective policies for Latin America is best approached by examining three experiences in capital markets development: the East Asian one, the general Latin American one, and that of Chile since 1983. All three have important lessons for policies that can successfully complete Latin America's renewed effort to develop modern capital markets.

## The East Asian Experience

Clearly, financial savings in the East Asian countries increased significantly before capital markets were developed. But as financial deepening progressed, increased financial saving and capital markets development in East Asia appeared to be in the relationship of a virtuous circle.

Significant causes of increased financial saving—declining population growth rates, in particular—were outside the realm of economic policy. Rapid population growth, by contrast, tends to make public saving difficult, since growth of the youngest segment of the population consumes fiscal resources in public services (hiring teachers, staffing clinics), without corresponding increases in revenue. Rapid population growth also limits household saving. The demographic maturing of East Asian societies (earlier than Latin America's population) no doubt contributed to their lower level of public consumption and higher public saving.

### Macroeconomic Stability, Saving, and Financial Deepening

Macroeconomic stability, fiscal balance, and low inflation were essential elements of the environment for increased saving in the East Asian countries in the 1960s and 1970s. Macroeconomic stability may be the most important prerequisite for increased saving, and the much earlier success of the East Asian countries in laying the foundations for macroeconomic stability—fiscal balance and low inflation—was due to their success in achieving high saving rates.

While this is less than settled in the economic literature, several studies indicate a relationship between positive real interest rates and financial saving.[1] Most East Asian countries had positive real interest rates over the 1970s and 1980s, while Japan and Hong Kong had modest negative rates. By contrast, most of the Latin American and Caribbean countries had significant negative real rates of interest over the same period. Moreover, the

---

[1] Much of the data in this section is drawn from World Bank (1993a), pp. 212-27.

**Table 7.1 Average Real Interest Rates on Deposits, Selected Economies**
*(Percentages)*

| Region/Economy | Period | Real interest rate | |
|---|---|---|---|
| | | Average | Standard deviation |
| *HPAEs* | | | |
| Hong Kong | 1973–91 | -1.81 | 3.16 |
| Indonesia | 1970–90 | 0.26 | 11.33 |
| Japan | 1953–91 | -1.12 | 3.89 |
| Korea | 1971–90 | 1.88 | 5.86 |
| Malaysia | 1976–91 | 2.77 | 2.47 |
| Singapore | 1977–91 | 2.48 | 1.71 |
| Taiwan, China | 1974–91 | 3.86 | 7.92 |
| Thailand | 1977–90 | 4.41 | 5.32 |
| *Average* | | 1.59 | 3.47 |
| *Other Asia* | | | |
| Bangladesh | 1976-92 | 0.96 | 3.59 |
| Nepal | 1976-89 | -3.69 | 5.00 |
| Philippines | 1976-91 | 0.45 | 9.97 |
| Sri Lanka | 1978-92 | 2.38 | 6.01 |
| *Average* | | 0.03 | 6.14 |
| *Latin America and Caribbean* | | | |
| Bolivia | 1979-91 | 44.33 | 81.46 |
| Chile | 1965-91 | 31.84 | 96.49 |
| Ecuador | 1983-91 | -6.57 | 18.76 |
| Jamaica | 1976-91 | -3.95 | 11.33 |
| Mexico | 1977-92 | -11.42 | 17.97 |
| Uruguay | 1976-92 | -1.89 | 15.62 |
| *Average* | | 16.67 | 40.27 |

*Source:* World Bank (1993a), p. 206.

instability of real interest rates in Latin America and the Caribbean may have been as great a problem for savers as the lack of a positive real rate of return, as Table 7.1 suggests. The standard deviation for real interest rates in the least stable East Asian market, Hong Kong, was still less than that measure of variation for all Latin American countries.

The East Asian countries, at an early stage of their takeoff to higher rates of growth and saving, adopted significant institutional reforms to encourage saving. These countries attached great importance to maintaining savers' confidence in financial institutions, by adopting strong prudential regulation and supervision and by sheltering the commercial banking sector from competition and from failures.

## The Importance of a Strong Banking System

In stark contrast to all of Latin America, except Chile after 1983, the East Asian countries focused on establishing a strong, well-supervised, and efficient commercial banking sector at an early point in the development of capital markets. Hong Kong, Japan, and Singapore adopted strong prudential regulation of banks in the 1970s. Malaysia, Thailand, and Singapore did so in the early 1980s. All the East Asian countries covered in the World Bank study (1993a) have adopted the Bank for International Settlements' (BIS) standards for capital adequacy of banks. Equally important, they have maintained very close supervision of banks, with frequent contact between supervisors and banks and prompt actions required of banks to make provision for risky assets and correct questionable lending practices.

A strong banking system has also been assured by action to prevent bank failures and loss to depositors. Only Korea and Taiwan, China have explicit deposit insurance, but most of the other economies have used entry restrictions, including restrictions on foreign banks, to support the profitability of a sheltered sector of a few large domestic banks. When necessary, public bailouts and assisted mergers of weaker banks into stronger ones have been used to avert bank failures. In part because of high economic growth and in part because of this strong supervision and sheltering of the banking sector, the fiscal cost of banking bailouts in the East Asian countries has been very low compared to Latin America, or even the United States.

The efficiency of East Asian banks contributes to their ability to pay positive real rates to savers. These large, sheltered banks have produced very efficient banking, with much lower spreads than in Latin America—3 percent on average in East Asia versus 15 percent in Latin America, based on data for 1989. In most cases, maximum spreads are established by regulation, a need created by the limits on competition in the banking sector.

In terms of the sequencing of policies for financial deepening, there is a strong case for the early development of a strong commercial banking sector. Commercial banks provide much of the financing to the business sector and are the first to extend maturities when macroeconomic and regulatory conditions permit. Sound commercial banking is essential to bring households into the financial sector. It is nearly impossible to cultivate among the general public an attitude toward savings as a secure investment that retains its value, if the commercial banking system is neither secure nor pays a reasonable return on deposits.

Commercial banking also underpins the liquidity and transactional efficiency of subsequent stages of capital markets development, including pension systems and equity and bond markets. The East Asian countries were able to move more quickly and securely through these later stages of successful development of the instruments and nonbank institutions of the capital market because they had already established sound banking systems.

## Contractual and Tax-advantaged Saving

Economic growth and macroeconomic stability have produced steady growth in savings rates in East Asia over a long period. Institutional change, particularly the development of nonbank financial institutions, can also produce accelerated change in savings rates.

Many East Asian countries, including Japan, Korea, Malaysia, Singapore, and Taiwan, China, have well established systems of postal saving. These savings have been treated as tax exempt for long periods in Japan, Korea, and Taiwan, China. Low-cost saving instruments account for a large portion of domestic deposits in Singapore and Malaysia, indicating their importance in the process of financial deepening, the channeling of savings into financial assets. Japan, Malaysia, and Singapore also achieved significant early financial deepening by developing comprehensive mandatory pension systems. Studies indicate that Singapore's Central Provident Fund increased total savings in the economy by about 4 per cent of GDP in the 1970s and 1980s.

The East Asian experience with postal savings and central provident funds was successful in terms of financial deepening because the assets were used to finance not government deficits but investments, including those through government development banks. These saving systems were not used creatively to foster development of the private nonbank financial institutions—private thrift and housing finance institutions, private and privately managed pension funds, insurance companies, investment companies—which at a later stage could become the sinews of a fully developed capital market. In this sense the East Asian approach missed an opportunity.

## The Controversial Role of Directed Credit Institutions

The counterpart of the emphasis on government institutions in the early mobilization of financial savings in the East Asian countries was the use of government credit institutions to take the lead in providing term finance to the business sector. To some extent, a sheltered commercial banking sector was used to provide term finance as well.

In four East Asian economies—Japan, Korea, Indonesia, and Taiwan, China—government development banks provided for a substantial portion of long-term loans to industry in the first two decades of their takeoff. The Japan Development Bank accounted for 18 percent of new funds lent in 1953, and the private but sheltered Industrial Bank of Japan also provided an important share in the 1950s. The Korean Development Bank provided one-third of all loans and guarantees in the 1970s, and Taiwan's Bank of Communications still holds half the assets of the banking system. The authors of the World Bank study (1993a) conclude that public development banks played a positive but not determining role in these four economies' successful accumulation of capital for growth. They were able to achieve this positive result because, during most of their life, these economies' development banks have been held to commercial performance standards, without political intervention in lending, and have had high-quality staff.

For these same four economies, government development banks filled a role in the provision of long-term credit to the industrial sector before securities markets developed to the stage at which industrial companies could go to the market directly for debt and equity financing. In this sense, the development banks played a limited role in a particular, early stage of capital markets development. The relevance of this experience to other countries, therefore, depends on their stage of financial markets development. If countries have already developed the infrastructure for firms to go directly to markets—accounting and reporting standards, rating agencies, government securities as benchmarks for low-risk credit, regulation of insider trading and protections against securities fraud—then government agencies are not needed for industrial credit intermediation.

In the East Asian countries that used government development banks extensively, these banks' protected role probably retarded the development of bond markets, which presumably impaired economic efficiency. Competitive markets are more efficient in matching capital with rates of return on investment than are government agencies, even relatively well managed ones. This negative effect of development banks is most clear in the case of Japan, where the government banks had a protected monopoly on the issue of long-term debentures, which clearly prevented the early development of a corporate bond market.

Even for countries in the earlier stages of capital markets development, government development banks are not a necessary bridge to developing long-term markets. In three East Asian economies covered by the World Bank study—Hong Kong, Thailand, and Malaysia—government development banks played no significant role in capital accumulation, fi-

**Table 7.2. Net Financing Sources of Nonfinancial Corporations**
*(In percent)*

| Economy/year | Internal source | External source Loan | External source Bonds | External source Equity | Other source |
|---|---|---|---|---|---|
| **East Asia** | | | | | |
| *Japan* | | | | | |
| 1956-65 | 41.9 | 47.4 | 2.6 | 8.1 | — |
| 1966-75 | 45.2 | 49.5 | 2.0 | 3.3 | — |
| 1976-83 | 54.6 | 40.3 | 1.7 | 3.4 | — |
| *Korea* | | | | | |
| 1970-79 | 27.6 | 52.5 | 4.8 | 14.8 | — |
| 1980-89 | 38.3 | 32.4 | 13.6 | 15.6 | — |
| *Malaysia* | | | | | |
| 1986-91 | 58.8 | 36.8 | — | 1.8 | — |
| *Taiwan, China* | | | | | |
| 1965-80 | 37.7 | 42.9 | 1.7 | 24.1 | -6.2 |
| 1981-90 | 29.9 | 33.6 | 6.2 | 28.6 | 1.8 |
| *Thailand* | | | | | |
| 1970-76 | 51.4 | 30.2 | 12.6 | 9.3 | -3.4 |
| 1977-83 | 51.8 | 28.9 | 11.9 | 10.8 | -3.4 |
| **Other developing economies** | | | | | |
| *Brazil (top 62 private firms)* | | | | | |
| 1978-83 | 73.09 | 25.0 | — | 14.0 | -12.0 |
| *Colombia (top 94 firms)* | | | | | |
| 1971-83 | 41.5 | — | 51.3 | 7.7 | — |
| 1984-85 | 86.0 | — | 13.0 | 1.0 | — |

*Source:* World Bank (1993a), p. 225.

nancial deepening, and growth. It is therefore clear that government development banks were not a necessary stage of capital markets development even in East Asia, since several countries of the region developed modern capital markets without such development banks.

## The Late Blooming of Bond and Equity Markets

In some of the East Asian economies, bond and equity markets provided a significant source of corporate finance by the 1970s. In Thailand, bonds and equities provided 42 percent of net external financing for nonfinancial corporations in the 1970s. The comparable percentage was 38 percent for Taiwan, China and 27 percent for Korea. In Japan and Malaysia, the role of bonds and equities in the financing of corporate growth was modest until the mid 1980s (see Table 7.2).

The development of bond markets was inhibited by the lack of much of the necessary market infrastructure, including the benchmark function of a government bond market in establishing the base rate for low-risk credit at different maturities. In many East Asian countries, the lack of an active government bond market was one of the few evils of a long period of fiscal balance.

Since 1985, the proportion of finance raised externally by corporations, including equity, has risen steeply in East Asia. All of the East Asian countries have aggressively encouraged the development of a corporate bond market.

Malaysia is a clear example of how quickly a corporate bond market can be generated, if the macroeconomic environment is stable and the government promotes the completion of the institutional infrastructure of the market. Before 1990, bonds played a minimal role in the external finance of Malaysian corporations (see Table 7.2). The government had first to provide the market with government securities in a range of maturities to create a market benchmark for low-risk credit for various periods. To create a free market for determining risk premiums, the government removed regulatory restrictions on interest rate determinations and on the investment choices of financial institutions. The authorities facilitated the establishment of an independent rating agency to serve the market in its risk judgments. The authorities also appointed dealers and market makers in government securities, which could serve in the same role for corporate securities. This effort was rewarded with very prompt success. Between 1987 and 1991, 3.6 billion Malaysian dollars in corporate bonds were issued, with 1.6 billion Malaysian dollars in 1990 alone (US$ = 2.6 Malaysian$).[2]

The very rapid development of East Asian equity markets since 1985 has made them significant sources of corporate finance for most economies in their region. The rapid evolution of these markets in terms of market capitalization is traced in Table 7.3. Clearly, their achievement of rapid economic growth and high levels of domestic savings preceded the maturing of securities markets in East Asia. It is not clear whether addressing the factors inhibiting bond and equity markets development earlier in the process would have accelerated growth of financial savings. The development of modern securities markets has undoubtedly improved the allocation of savings to high-return investments.

---

[2] IMF (1993b), Part II, p. 74.

**Table 7.3  Market Capitalization of Selected East Asian Stock Exchanges**

*(In US$ millions)*

|              | 1985   | 1987   | 1989    | 1991    | 1993    |
|--------------|--------|--------|---------|---------|---------|
| Indonesia    | 117    | 68     | 2,254   | 6,823   | 32,953  |
| Korea        | 7,381  | 32,905 | 140,943 | 96,373  | 139,420 |
| Malaysia     | 16,229 | 18,531 | 39,842  | 58,627  | 220,328 |
| Taiwan, China| 10,432 | 48,634 | 237,012 | 124,864 | 195,198 |
| Thailand     | 1,856  | 5,485  | 25,648  | 35,815  | 130,510 |

*Source:* IFC (1994).

**Table 7.4  Companies Listed on Selected East Asian Stock Exchanges**

|              | 1985 | 1987 | 1989 | 1991 | 1993 |
|--------------|------|------|------|------|------|
| Indonesia    | 24   | 24   | 57   | 141  | 174  |
| Korea        | 342  | 389  | 626  | 686  | 693  |
| Malaysia     | 222  | 232  | 251  | 321  | 410  |
| Taiwan, China| 127  | 141  | 181  | 221  | 285  |
| Thailand     | 100  | 125  | 175  | 276  | 347  |

*Source:* IFC (1994).

Asian securities markets since 1985 have significantly increased mobilization of foreign savings. In terms of cause and effect, it is difficult to untangle the relationship of foreign portfolio investment and the growth of East Asian securities markets. Both have experienced explosive growth since 1985, and it is probably most accurate to view them as part of a virtuous cycle. Financial liberalization and completion of some of the key institutional infrastructure of capital markets in the mid 1980s attracted an initial surge of foreign capital into these markets. That foreign capital, in turn, fostered not only rapid growth in market capitalization, but also completion of the regulatory and institutional infrastructure and broadening of the market through issuance of securities by many more domestic companies. The dramatic increase in the number of companies listed on East Asian exchanges is traced in Table 7.4.

## The Latin American Experience

Latin America's experience in capital markets development is best examined as two quite different courses. One is the course pursued by most of Latin America and the Caribbean. The other is the Chilean approach since 1983, which is significantly different from the modern experience of most of Latin America, and indeed from Chile's own before 1983. Recent ambitious structural reform and financial liberalization measures in several countries have included efforts to develop more efficient capital markets, which are integrated more effectively with international markets in terms of the regulatory and institutional infrastructures required to attract most large investors. Some of these reform efforts attempt to follow in significant measure the reforms successfully implemented almost a decade earlier in Chile.

Because the Chilean reforms have been more fully implemented, and thus have produced a dozen years of results and data, Chile's experience is here evaluated as a distinct approach to capital markets development. However, one must keep in mind that other countries, including Argentina, Colombia, Mexico, and Brazil, have in the last five years undertaken a similar reform process, which may eventually yield results similar to those achieved by Chile's impressive capital markets.

Yet, in terms of content and sequence of reforms, even Latin America's recent approach to capital markets development differs substantially from the Chilean experience, as the next two sections of this chapter will show. How such differences can affect the stability of markets has become a focus of attention, particularly since the financial crisis that developed after the Mexican devaluation in December 1994.

### *Macroeconomic Stability, Saving, and Financial Deepening*

Latin America's macroeconomic environment during the 1970s and 1980s was plagued by high inflation and fiscal deficits, in stark contrast to conditions in most of the East Asian countries. The dramatic difference across the two regions in the development of domestic savings rates over these two decades indicates why capital markets developed further in the East Asian region. Over the period 1965 to 1990, gross domestic savings rates in Latin America and the Caribbean stagnated at a level of 18 percent, whereas over the same period, the average for the eight East Asian economies soared from 16 percent to 37 percent (see Table 7.5). The absence of macroeconomic stability was clearly a fundamental reason for the arrested development of Latin America's financial sector over this long period.

**Table 7.5  Gross Domestic Savings as Percentage of GDP**

|  | 1965 | 1990 |
| --- | --- | --- |
| Eight East Asian Economies | 16 | 37 |
| Latin America and Caribbean | 18 | 18 |

*Source:* World Bank (1993a).

Several Latin American countries that have achieved success in macroeconomic stabilization have subsequently experienced increases in gross domestic savings, but economic history, including in East Asia, indicates that savings rates increase only gradually over a long period, rather than as a sudden response to a recently established favorable economic environment. Colombia's savings rate improved steadily after a comprehensive stabilization program beginning in 1984, which balanced the government's budget and dramatically reduced inflation. In Argentina the saving rate has increased since 1991, albeit from a low level. Chile's long period of rising savings rates since the early 1980s is the clearest indication that the savings response to favorable macroeconomic conditions and structural reforms can be expected in Latin America as well as in East Asia.

Many of the same factors underlying low savings rates in Latin America from 1965 to 1990 contributed directly, as well as indirectly through the supply of savings, to the underdevelopment of financial markets. High inflation reduced the demand for money. Interest rate controls, low or negative real rates of interest, and instability in real rates all contributed to underdevelopment of financial intermediation. The limited deepening of Latin American financial markets, except Chile's, can be seen in the generally lower ratios of money and deposits to GDP, and equity value to GDP, that prevailed in Latin American countries in 1991 (see Table 7.6).

From these statistics, it is clear that Chile's financial markets are comparable to those of the East Asian countries. The indicators of financial deepening for Chile's markets are more similar to those for East Asian markets than to those for other Latin American markets.

Research by Sebastian Edwards has strongly supported the feedback effect of deeper financial systems on private savings rates (see chapter five). Using the ratio of money to GDP as a proxy for financial deepening, he found a significantly positive correlation with higher gross private savings in a 50-country group over the period 1983–92.

**Table 7.6  Financial Indicators for Selected Economies, 1991**
*(Percent of GDP)*

|  | Money | Quasi-Money | Credit | Private Deposits | Equity |
|---|---|---|---|---|---|
| Indonesia | 11.7 | 32.0 | 55.8 | 40.4 | 6.0 |
| Korea | 10.5 | 29.9 | 59.3 | 38.6 | 35.2 |
| Malaysia | 21.8 | 48.0 | 81.7 | 60.3 | 124.3 |
| Thailand | 9.3 | 67.6 | 77.9 | 77.2 | 37.7 |
| Chile | 7.2 | 36.1 | 51.5 | 37.6 | 95.9 |
| Argentina | 5.3 | 8.8 | 21.1 | 9.8 | 14.4 |
| Brazil | 5.4 | 17.8 | 36.8 | 3.2 | 56.6 |
| Colombia | 10.3 | 7.1 | 15.9 | 24.9 | 10.6 |
| Mexico | 12.5 | 16.4 | 27.6 | 26.3 | 35.6 |
| Peru | 8.3 | 8.9 | 6.5 | 13.5 | 2.9 |
| Venezuela | 11.4 | 22.5 | 20.4 | 40.1 | 22.4 |

*Source:* IMF (1993b), p. 101.

Brazil, during the 1980s when its economy experienced rapid inflation, is a dramatic example of retrogression and disintermediation in financial markets. Loans to the private sector as a percent of GDP had reached almost 50 percent in 1975, but fell to 15 percent in 1990. At the same time, the market for government bonds disappeared, and the government was able to finance its deficit only by very short-term borrowing and issuing money. Brazil's private sector in the last decade has had to finance itself almost entirely with internal funds, since credit has not been available except on the shortest of terms. One Brazilian economist concluded in a 1994 study that "no other market economy with levels of industrialization comparable to Brazil's shows such low rates of financial deepening."[3] The cause is primarily a lack of macroeconomic stability.

*The Importance of a Strong Banking System*

On the road to financial sector reform and modern capital markets, virtually all of Latin America has missed an essential step of the first phase — creating a strong commercial banking system underpinned by prudential regulation and supervision. Neither the East Asian miracle countries nor Chile were able to pass successfully to the later stages of capital markets

---

[3] Zini (1994).

development until a healthy banking system under strong supervision was solidly established. A good deal of the fragility of Latin financial markets, and the high cost of periodic crises, can be explained by this failure.

The nonbank financial institutions that are the most important participants in modern capital markets depend on a sound banking system for their liquidity and transactional efficiency. Sound nonbank financial institutions tend to grow from the banking sector in many direct and indirect ways: in terms of their regulatory treatment and supervision, their investors, their managers and professional staff, and their operating styles, among others. Countries that have poor regulation and supervision of banks are not likely to have developed strong counterparts for nonbank financial institutions. Countries that have inefficient banks with poor credit practices are unlikely to produce nonbank financial institutions that are efficient and prudent investors of their clients' assets.

In modern financial markets, the linkages are even more direct. Securities market participants, both individuals and institutions, rely heavily on bank credit to ensure liquidity in these markets. In many Latin American countries, banks act as broker/dealers, or broker/dealers depend on bank credit to accumulate required blocks of securities or to sell blocks piecemeal.[4] As securities markets grow, increased credit is required. Therefore, if a banking system is undercapitalized and illiquid, the systemic risks to markets are great, and those systemic risks rise as markets grow.

In Latin America, other than Chile, only Ecuador had fully adopted the BIS standards for capital adequacy of banks by 1993. Colombia is in the process of doing so, and Mexico has adopted the standards into regulation, but they have not been enforced by effective supervision, nor do most Mexican banks meet them in practice. Some Latin American countries still have not established any minimum capital standards for new banks.

Most of Latin America, including Chile before 1982, has had poor supervision of banks, no requirement to ensure independent evaluation of portfolio quality and risk, and few or inadequate regulations to avoid concentration of credit and portfolio risk. With inadequate supervision and overconcentration in their portfolios, a significant change affecting the economy can draw Latin American banks into a vicious cycle of accelerating deterioration. Eleanor Howard of the IDB describes this cycle as follows: Inadequate enforcement of prudential norms for portfolio diversification and quality, including those on lending to economic groups that are

---

[4] IMF (1993b), p. 77.

bank shareholders, contributes to high and rising gross margins and real lending rates, which in turn cause rapidly rising arrears from borrowers who cannot pay the rising rates. She notes that these conditions caused the Venezuelan banking crisis of 1994, and were equally present in Mexico.[5]

The cost of periodic banking failures in Latin America has been huge, about 26 percent of GDP in Chile in 1981–83, 22 percent of GDP in Venezuela in 1994, and still to be determined, but large, in Mexico in 1995. By contrast, the cost of occasional banking problems in the East Asian region has been in the range of one percent of GDP or less.

## Contractual and Tax-advantaged Saving

Largely because of macroeconomic instability and the weaknesses of the banking system, Latin American countries other than Chile have until very recently had little success in developing contractual saving vehicles. The potentially most important of these, pension systems, have on balance been anti-saving vehicles in economic terms. Traditional Latin American social security pension systems produced the worst of both worlds: a drain on public savings and a disincentive for private saving. On the one hand, the operation of pay-as-you-go public pension systems with hopelessly unrealistic benefit structures has become one of the greatest drains on fiscal resources and a source of long-term fiscal imbalance until addressed by pension reforms. On the other hand, the promise of generous retirement benefits from the public treasury has been a disincentive for private saving. In terms of savings, as well as capital markets development, the operation of Latin America's public social security pension systems over the last two decades has been disastrous.

Nor has the experience with public sector vehicles to encourage saving been a happy one in Latin America. Mexico's housing finance system, which included a depository savings component, produced an extremely poor rate of return for participants, in large part because of poor investment decisions by fund managers. Brazil's housing finance system, which financed 500,000 homes per year in the late 1970s, was reduced to a capability of financing only 24,000 by 1993, a victim of inflation.[6]

The private insurance industry has been limited in much of Latin America until recent years, but has begun to develop rapidly with financial

---

[5] Howard (1994).
[6] Zini (1994), p. 100.

liberalization and the introduction of pension reforms, many of which include insurance and annuity components.

Several Latin American countries have followed Chile in carrying out reforms of their pension systems, with the objectives of creating capitalized systems under private management and reducing the continuing long-term drain on fiscal resources under mixed public/private systems. These reforms have consisted primarily of rationalizing benefits and relating them more closely to employer and employee contributions. Argentina, Peru, and Colombia have implemented extensive reforms in the last few years, and Bolivia, Brazil, and other countries are in the process of reforming their systems. Mexico has established a modest capitalized system parallel to the public pay-as-you-go system, with the objective of increasing the role of the capitalized part of the system in coming years. All of these reforms are too recent to evaluate their impact on savings and capital markets development, but the effects of thorough pension reform are discussed in the section on Chile.

### The Not-So-Controversial Role of Directed Credit Institutions

While the extensive investment since the 1960s in official development banks in Latin America initially produced increases in production, the overall experience has been very poor, with the positive results clearly achieved at too high a price in terms of economic efficiency. According to the World Bank,[7] 50 percent of the value of loans from a representative sample of development banks was in arrears in 1993. The cited reasons were political pressure to make bad loans and poor incentives and capability to screen and monitor projects. In essence, Latin American governments were unable to insulate their development banks from the rest of the governing process and to ensure that they operated with commercial standards for credit decisions and monitoring.

It is clearer in Latin America than in East Asia that the creation of government development banks was not an effective bridge to securities market development. The focus on state-owned development banks in Latin America up to the mid 1980s invariably led to depressed real interest rates and small domestic financial sectors, with the effect that external finance replaced domestic finance.[8]

---

[7] World Bank (1993a), p. 227.
[8] World Bank (1993b), p. 5.

**Table 7.7 Market Capitalization of Selected Latin American Stock Exchanges**

*(In US$ millions)*

|           | 1985   | 1987   | 1989   | 1991   | 1993    |
|-----------|--------|--------|--------|--------|---------|
| Argentina | 2,037  | 1,519  | 4,225  | 18,509 | 43,967  |
| Brazil    | 42,768 | 16,900 | 44,368 | 42,759 | 99,430  |
| Colombia  | 416    | 1,255  | 1,136  | 4,036  | 9,237   |
| Mexico    | 3,815  | 8,371  | 22,550 | 98,178 | 200,671 |
| Peru      | 760    | 831    | 931    | 1,118  | 5,113   |
| Venezuela | 1,128  | 2,278  | 1,472  | 11,214 | 8,010   |
| Chile     | 2,012  | 5,341  | 9,587  | 27,984 | 44,622  |

*Source:* IFC (1994).

## The Late, But Possibly Premature, Blooming of Bond and Equity Markets

The boom in international flows into emerging stock markets in the second half of the 1980s brought significant growth in the capitalization of Latin American markets (see Table 7.7). But the dramatic growth of Latin American securities markets in the last decade was built upon significant weaknesses in the domestic capital markets. Low domestic saving rates, limited financial deepening, weak domestic banking systems, and missing non-bank financial institutions meant that the emerging markets phenomenon would once more distort the structure of financial markets in the direction of significant and growing use of foreign savings to substitute for inadequacies of domestic financial markets. This has proved to be a structure with significant systemic risks. Shocks that interrupt or sharply reduce the inflow of foreign saving may not only reduce growth, but translate through a weak banking system into a domestic financial crisis, as happened dramatically in Venezuela in 1994 and Mexico in 1994 and 1995.

By far the greatest relative growth from 1985 to 1993 in the capitalization of Latin American markets occurred in three countries—Mexico, Argentina, and Colombia. Two of these three experienced significant financial crises as a result of sharp reductions in international capital inflows in 1994 and 1995. Yet the commonly cited lesson of this experience focuses only on external accounts and emphasizes reducing reliance on foreign capital by internal monetary and fiscal adjustment, and perhaps even capital controls. This overlooks the need for structural reforms to complete the foundations of a strong domestic capital market.

Table 7.8  Companies Listed on Selected Latin American
Stock Exchanges

|  | 1985 | 1987 | 1989 | 1991 | 1993 |
|---|---|---|---|---|---|
| Argentina | 227 | 206 | 178 | 174 | 180 |
| Brazil* | 541 | 590 | 592 | 570 | 550 |
| Colombia | 102 | 96 | 82 | 83 | 89 |
| Mexico | 157 | 190 | 203 | 209 | 190 |
| Peru | 159 | 197 | 256 | 298 | 233 |
| Venezuela | 83 | 71 | 75 | 87 | 93 |
| Chile | 228 | 209 | 213 | 221 | 263 |

*São Paulo exchange only.
Source: IFC (1994).

In this sense, the blooming of international interest in Latin America's securities markets came too soon in the process of financial sector reform, except in the case of Chile and perhaps Colombia. The financial reforms that complete the development of a domestic capital market result in both greater participation of domestic saving in the market—and thus greater market stability—and greater systemic stability, in the sense that the entire financial system is better insulated from shocks in the external accounts.

The very limited growth in the number of listed companies on Latin American exchanges since 1985, as indicated in Table 7.8, contrasts sharply with the rapid growth in the number of listed companies on East Asian exchanges in the same period. For two of the Latin American markets in Table 7.8, the number of companies listed on the exchange actually declined between 1985 and 1993. This is another indicator of the lack of domestic broadening and deepening of these markets in Latin America. Chile's rapid increase in listed companies, by 26 percent from 1984 to 1993, may indicate that the demand for shares by pension funds played a role. In other Latin American countries the lack of legal infrastructure for markets may also have discouraged new listings. The strong role of privately held companies in countries with traditionally narrow capital markets is probably also part of the explanation.

For economies of comparable size, the number of companies listed on Latin American exchanges is less than a third of those listed on East Asian exchanges. Korea, for example, had 693 companies listed in 1993, versus 190 for Mexico. Such narrow access to the market clearly impedes growth of the corporate sector. Most companies in the developing world are more de-

**Table 7.9  Sources of Finance for Companies
in Mexico and Korea, 1984–88**
*(Percentages)*

|  | Median for 50 top companies | |
|---|---|---|
|  | Mexico | Korea |
| Internal Finance | 17.1 | 12.8 |
| External Finance |  |  |
|   Equity | 76 | 40.3 |
|   Long-term Debt | 2.9 | 45.4 |

*Source:* IFC (1993), p. 26.

pendent on external finance than those in industrial countries, and that dependence on external equity and debt finance seems to be rising. An IFC
study of Mexico and Korea, based on the top 50 companies for each, indicates that companies in both were heavily dependent on external finance
(see Table 7.9).[9]

Equity markets were obviously very important to companies in both
countries. Yet the most significant difference was the ability of Korean companies to take on long-term debt. Rapidly growing, successful East Asian
companies are generally much more highly leveraged than their Latin
American counterparts. For 50 top Mexican companies in the 1980s, the ratio of long-term debt to equity was only 12 percent, versus 163 percent in
Thailand and 117 percent in Korea. In terms of the ratios of long-term debt
to net assets, the picture was similar: just 11 percent for Mexico versus 62
percent for Thailand and 53 percent for Korea. No Latin American country
other than Chile has a well-developed corporate bond market, which partly
explains why Chilean companies have grown faster over the last 15 years
than companies in other Latin American economies.

**The Chilean Experience Since 1983**

In a period of less than a decade, Chile has created Latin America's most
well-developed capital market, one that is in all significant respects as deep
and efficient as those of the East Asian countries. Chile's approach to developing its capital market differed in fundamental ways from the East Asian
approach. Since Chile began with a market structure similar to the rest of

---

[9] See IFC (1993a), pp. 30-32.

**Table 7.10  Gross Domestic Savings in Chile**
*(Percent of GDP)*

| 1982 | 1984 | 1986 | 1988 | 1990 | 1992 |
|------|------|------|------|------|------|
| 9.4  | 12.5 | 18.9 | 25.0 | 25.0 | 26.0 |

*Sources:* Luders and Hachette (1993), *World Development Report 1994.*

Latin America, it can provide policy lessons for the rest of the region. Even though other Latin American countries have looked to the Chilean model for much of their structural reform efforts in recent years, they are still not applying it to the development of financial markets. Critical parts of the Chilean approach have, for one reason or another, been omitted in other countries' approaches.

In terms of the sequencing of the most critical reforms for capital markets development, for example, the experience of most other Latin American countries has been virtually the reverse of the Chilean model. The Chileans after 1982 built a very strong commercial banking system at the outset. Then social security pension reform and broad privatization were carried out simultaneously. Finally a deepening securities market, built largely on domestic savings, was gradually liberalized for international investors. In Argentina, Mexico, Brazil, and other Latin American reformers, a rapidly growing securities market was allowed to develop first, substantially on the basis of international capital inflows, while the first privatizations were being carried out. Pension reforms were delayed, and have only been fully implemented in two or three countries. And the most critical first step, creation of a strong banking sector, has yet to be taken in virtually every country except Chile. The results of this inverted sequencing demonstrate that shortcuts are not necessarily faster and can create significant systemic risks.

## Macroeconomic Stability, Savings, and Financial Deepening

Emerging from a major financial crisis and the steep recession of 1981-82, the Chilean government from 1983 forward pursued a consistent course of fiscal balance and moderate inflation, which has created the environment for a steady increase in gross domestic savings from the low level of the crisis period. As shown in Table 7.10, by 1988 savings had reached 25% of GDP, a level never before achieved in that country.[10]

---

[10] See Luders and Hachette (1993), pp. 107-108.

In addition to macroeconomic stability, a critical contributor to the dramatic increase in savings after 1982 was the simultaneous implementation of pension reform and large-scale privatization. These were, in both a financial and economic sense, mutually reinforcing actions that created both sides of a capital market. Economically, pension reform generated a pool of savings, and privatization created the investment opportunities to put them to work and encourage still greater saving. Financially, privatization created a supply of blue chip equities and debentures, and pension reform created the institutional demand for them. Rolf Luders, among others, has presented the case that privatization in Chile increased savings, based in part on the significant proportion of private savings that were put toward the purchase of privatizing firms during the years of major privatizations. In 1986, proceeds from privatizations were equivalent to 45 percent of private savings; in 1987, 25 percent; and in 1988, 41 percent.

Statistically, economists, including Luders, have difficulty proving that pension reform contributed directly to increased saving, largely because so many other reforms, including privatization, were being carried out at the same time. Pension reform was clearly an integral part of a mutually reinforcing set of reforms that yielded significant increases in savings. In effect, pension reform acted like one blade of a scissors cutting a clear pattern of higher saving, but it is difficult to attribute a specific share of the work to one blade, rather than the other, that of privatization.

What is clear is that pension reform produced a rapid process of financial deepening, an increase in money and deposits relative to GDP. The process of financial deepening through pension assets was rapid, with these assets rising from a negligible amount during the two years of the banking crisis to 5 percent of GDP in 1984 and 20 percent in 1989. By 1990, pension fund assets were equivalent to 40 percent of bank credit.

The powerful combination of privatization and pension reform in terms of capital markets development can be clearly traced. From 1984 to 1987 the volume of transactions on the Chilean stock exchange rose from $42 million to $543 million, and over the same period the percent of volume represented by shares of privatized enterprise rose from 6 percent to 68 percent (Table 7.11). Over the same period, the value of shares and bonds held by pension funds rose from a negligible amount in 1984 to $260 million in 1987 and to $899 million in 1989. Securities of privatized companies and pension fund purchases of them created, in five years, a deep domestic capital market in which 80 percent or more of the turnover represented domestic capital.

**Table 7.11  Privatization, Shares, and Pension Fund Holdings**
*(In 1988 US$ millions)*

|  | 1984 | 1985 | 1986 | 1987 | 1988 | 1989 |
|---|---|---|---|---|---|---|
| Value of Stock Exchange Transactions | 42 | 60 | 337 | 543 | 654 | 917 |
| Value of Transactions in Shares of Privatized Cos. | 3 | 19 | 187 | 369 | 448 | 579 |
| Shares of Privatized Cos. as Share of Total Transactions | 6% | 31% | 56% | 68% | 69% | 66% |
| Shares and Bonds in Pension Funds | n.a. | 19 | 19 | 260 | 527 | 899 |

*Source:* Luders and Hachette (1993), p. 103.

## The Critical Importance of Banking Sector Reform

The bitter experience of 1981-82 shaped a critical portion of the Chilean reforms from 1983 on. The severity with which the foreign exchange crisis of these years was transmitted into a domestic financial crisis and deep recession was due in part to the weakness of the commercial banking sector and the virtual absence of prudential supervision of banks and financial institutions. As noted earlier, the cost of the bailout of the banking sector was huge, equivalent to 26 percent of GDP. This proved to be a lesson Chile did not want to learn twice.

After the reprivatization of many failed banks taken over by the government during the crisis, Chile implemented a system of banking and financial institution regulation and supervision that is the strongest in Latin America and arguably as rigorous as that of any economy in the world.

The system of banking regulation and supervision enacted in 1986 requires banks to publish, three times each year, both their accounts and the opinion of the Superintendency of Banks and Financial Institutions on the financial state of the bank. Bank portfolios are subject to limits on loans to individual debtors and on exposure in different currencies. Credits to related parties must be on arm's-length terms. Banks are required to make provision for risky credits to ensure that reported capital is accurately adjusted for risk and a sound measure of capital adequacy. To ensure the integrity of this process, two private appraisers must classify the quality and risk level of assets for each bank.[11]

---

[11] Eyzaguirre (1994), p. 137.

Under this system, contact between banks and their supervisors and appraisers is continuous throughout the year. This is a generic difference from bank regulation in much of Latin America, where supervision of compliance with regulations is lax and contact with supervisors infrequent and irregular.

The banking sector, as well as other financial institutions, grew in strength after 1986 as a result of the incentives in the regulatory system to increase capital. The quality of assets improved with economic growth. Increased competition in the banking sector and with other financial institutions lowered spreads, and thus lowered the cost of capital to borrowers.

The establishment of a strong commercial banking sector and a system of regulation and supervision of financial institutions was critical to the subsequent flourishing of Chile's capital market.[12] The banks and the pension funds are both essential to the liquidity and transactional efficiency of capital markets. The banks play a role in the underwriting of share issues. The same rigorous system and culture of supervision and prudential responsibility that was applied to the banks was applied to the pension funds (AFPs). The institutions and people who administer the pension funds came from the banks and the insurance industry. The entire structure of an efficient and prudentially well-supervised pension system has been built on the system established for the commercial banking sector.

At the same time, the increased efficiency of the commercial banking sector and increased competition with other financial institutions has increased the overall efficiency of the capital market. Competition, in particular from the bond market, has driven down banking spreads in Chile from about 8 percent in 1986 to 2–4 percent in 1994, comparable to the spreads in the banking sector of the East Asian economies. As noted by Eleanor Howard, "The low spreads in the Chilean financial sector are a very important outcome of capital markets development. Such an outcome is critical for the development of the financial and real sectors in all of Latin America."[13]

## The Role of Pension Funds in Capital Markets Development

In the judgment of Rolf Luders, one of the most meticulous and cautious analysts of the economic effects of the Chilean reforms, pension reform had

---

[12] Gerard Caprio of the World Bank has developed a strong case for the early implementation of comprehensive banking regulation and supervision in programs of financial sector reform (Caprio and Klingebiel 1994, 1996).

[13] Howard (1994), p. 10.

a critical effect on the development of Chile's capital market. He comments that "[t]he divestiture of the social security system itself, the single most important privatization of the military government, constituted perhaps the most significant advance in the development of the Chilean capital market in this century."[14] The pension funds have been a key part of financial sector reforms, which have made the allocation of savings to investment more efficient and lowered the cost of capital to borrowers generally.

In contrast to the East Asian provident funds, the Chilean AFPs were outside the public sector and under private management. This was critical to their impact on capital markets.

In addition to the large role of the pension funds in the development of the equity market, discussed earlier, the pension funds played a decisive role in the development of the bond market, the virtual absence of which in much of Latin American has been a significant impediment to corporate growth. In 1990 the pension funds held 56 percent of the mortgage bonds and corporate bonds outstanding in Chile. The AFPs have virtually made the market for these securities, and in the process have reduced spreads in the banking sector and other financial institutions as well. Chile remains the only country in Latin America in which corporations with good credit ratings can borrow funds for terms up to ten years at reasonable real interest rates.

### The Non-role of Directed Credit Institutions

In contrast to the East Asian experience, Chile since 1983 has made little use of government-directed credit or other government interventions in the market to affect the cost and direction of credit. In 1990, CORFO, Chile's national development bank, ceased retail lending to the private sector.

### The Early Blooming of Bond and Equity Markets

The sequencing of financial sector reforms was critical to the development of Latin America's most stable equity market and its only real bond market. To some extent, the completion of Chile's financial sector reforms, including pension reform, before the great discovery of emerging markets by international portfolio investors, also played a significant role in the depth and stability of Chile's markets.

---

[14] Luders and Hachette (1993), p. 104.

Chile's privatizations, including pension reform, were carried out before international investors gathered their courage to invest heavily in the country. Even in Chile's second round of privatizations, after 1983, international direct and portfolio investors played a much smaller role than they did five years later in Mexico and Argentina. By the late 1980s, Chile had established a securities market based predominantly on domestic savings, which had already grown quite large as a result of the continual inflows of new money from the pension funds. In effect, the Chilean securities markets had bloomed before international investors discovered the market.

The sequencing of the Chilean reform—starting with banking and financial institution supervision and pension reform, then completion of the major phase of privatization, and finally the cautious opening to greater foreign participation in a relatively mature securities market—had enormous advantages, not all of which are available to others at a later stage of their own reforms. Chile's high level of domestic saving reduced the role for foreign savings. Chile's high internal savings also limited appreciation of its currency and allowed interest rates to stay down. Thus, capital inflows did not become the major force in the securities markets.

Chile's restrictions on capital inflows have reduced short-term inflows, in particular. But these restrictions were not the only reason for the low, 20 percent participation of foreign capital in stock market turnover, versus 50 percent or more in Mexico and Argentina in recent years. The real economy is more important over the long run, and the determining factor in the real economy is Chile's significantly higher level of domestic saving.

The greater stability of Chile's market is seen clearly in the aftermath of the Mexican financial crisis, which started in December 1994. In the following ten weeks, to the low point in early March 1995, the Mexican stock market declined 65 percent, the Argentine and Brazilian markets close to 50 percent, and the Chilean market 30 percent. By late March, the Chilean market was back to within 10 percent of its December 1, 1994 level, while the Brazilian and Argentine markets had recovered to only within 30 percent of their December 1 levels (Table 7.11). The significantly greater stability of the Chilean market is apparent.

Equally important, the strength of the Chilean banking and financial sector limited the systemic risk from the regional foreign exchange crisis precipitated by the Mexican devaluation. In Argentina and some other Latin American countries, the systemic risk from the sudden decline in capital inflows was significant, and extraordinary measures were needed to prevent serious crisis in the domestic financial sector. In Mexico the external crisis did create a systemic one in which banks failed, and their rescue and reform will take as much as $10 billion of the international financial package raised for Mexico.

The financial crisis of 1994 and 1995 also reveals the vulnerability of pension reforms, in their early stages, to systemic risks created in part by failure to carry out prior reforms of the banking and financial institutions sector. In the Chilean sequence of reforms, the very favorable rate of return earned by pension funds over their early years benefited from continually rising share prices. This portfolio performance, as well as the sound structure of prudential supervision of financial institutions, created a high level of confidence by savers in the system. This level of confidence supported savings generally, including those through supplementary, voluntary saving plans administered by the AFPs.

In an environment of incomplete financial sector reform, Argentina's new pension funds have been buffeted by poor investment returns in their first year, producing a significant problem with savers' confidence in the new pension system, and lower numbers of workers enrolling in the new system than had been expected. The severity of the regional financial crisis after December 1994 played a significant role in this. But the severe impact of the Mexican financial crisis on Argentine securities markets was in part a result of the sequencing of Argentine reforms. Delaying pension reform until after the major privatizations had been completed, one of which attracted large foreign participation in Argentina's equity market, meant that there was already a large proportion of foreign capital in Argentina's securities markets, which amplified the magnitude of the market fall. Postponing commercial banking reforms and supervision increased the severity of the transmission of the external crisis into a domestic financial crisis, with the resulting decline in confidence of savers in financial institutions generally, including the pension funds.

In Argentina, Mexico, and Brazil, the very large increase in interest rates as foreign capital inflows declined reflected in part the low level of domestic saving. To the extent that earlier financial sector reforms, pension reform in particular, could have increased domestic financial savings, the interest rate spike caused by the crisis after December 20, 1994 could have been reduced.

## Policy Implications

This assessment of three different approaches to capital markets development has implicitly drawn certain policy conclusions. With an eye on the Latin American challenge today, the following are the most important.

• Macroeconomic stability is the first and most important building block for Latin America's capital markets development. Yet the higher savings that can come with macroeconomic stability take many years to develop fully. Even recent successful stabilizers, such as Argentina, are facing the volatility problems of securities markets built on inadequate domestic financial savings. Macroeconomic stability thus needs to be reinforced by other significant institutional reforms.

• Banking reforms should have come at the beginning of Latin American and Caribbean programs of market opening and structural reform. Without strong prudential regulation and supervision of banks, Latin American households have lacked secure depositories for their savings. This step is necessary both to establish sound financial institutions, on which the efficiency and liquidity of securities markets depend, and to reduce the systemic risk from sudden declines in foreign capital inflows. Sound, continual supervision of banks and other financial institutions is critical; without it, regulations are of limited value. The Chilean system of bank supervision is an excellent model. Requirements for independent appraisal of asset quality and risk, and provision against risks thus assessed, are particularly important, as are standards for asset diversification.

• Pension reform is the most important single step in capital markets development for most of Latin America and the Caribbean. Pension reform should come at the beginning of structural and financial sector reform programs. The most basic problem of Latin American capital markets is low levels of domestic saving, private saving in particular. Historically, drastic increases in private savings over short periods have been achieved only by institutional change: i.e., the creation of an institutional environment that instills new confidence in small savers. Pension reform is Latin America's best option to achieve this institutional jump-start on the long, slow road to higher savings rates. Pension reform alone, however, will not achieve either drastically increased saving or a deep, stable capital market unless coupled with privatization of the most heavily capitalized sectors and development of a bond market. This coupling created the virtuous cycle of reinforcing actions that made the Chilean model so dynamic.

• The bond market is particularly important for faster growth of Latin America's underleveraged corporate sector and for competition in long-term markets, which reduces spreads and the cost of capital generally. In addition to creating a system of privately managed pension funds, the government should foster an open insurance market, investment companies, and other nonbank financial institutions, which comprise the financial structure of a competitive bond market. Public policy also needs to build and encourage the framework for an efficient bond market. Governments should issue debentures over a range of maturities to establish low-risk benchmarks for various maturities; encourage the establishment of rating agencies; establish accounting, reporting, and auditing standards that make accurate rating possible; and complete the legal framework of property rights and securities laws that deter abuse and give investors the opportunity to pursue their rights in a timely manner.

• Privatization of the most heavily capitalized public enterprises prompts both saving and capital markets development. Such privatization should ideally be carried out simultaneously with, or after, pension reform to develop a strong equity and bond market based primarily on domestic savings. Continuing privatization of the major infrastructure sectors can increase public and private saving. Most indicators of infrastructure investment under private management reveal rapid growth, which generates new investment opportunities for savings and new financing for capital markets.[15] Latin America is already ahead of other regions in mobilizing private finance for infrastructure, particularly in the telecommunications and energy sectors. Coupled with sound, if belated, pension reform, privatization of major infrastructure sectors could generate a continuing flow of financing for greenfield projects. This, in turn, can help to create a late-stage version of the mutually reinforcing combination of privatization and pension reform that jumpstarted Chile's savings and capital market development.

• Concentration of risk can be a significant systemic problem for growing pension funds in small and medium-sized economies, including Chile. It is particularly important to reduce portfolio risk for pension funds, especially in their early stage of development. For a small country with too many linked risks in the local capital market, international diversification of equity and bond portfolios is a logical approach to spreading the risk: Using pension funds to develop domestic savings and investment does not mean requiring funds to invest only in local markets. Inadequate diversification will unduly increase pensioners' portfolio risk, and poor investment performance may prejudice the rapid development of the pension system.

• Large changes in relative prices, such as through a large devaluation, have strongly negative effects on savings and the health of banks and other financial institutions that tend household's financial savings. Global financial markets necessitate a rigorous system of monetary and fiscal ad-

---

[15] World Bank, *World Development Report 1994*, p. 92.

justment to economic change—either allowing the exchange rate to move gradually under a crawling peg, as in Chile, or, where feasible, fixing a rate systemically, as in Argentina. Under modern market conditions, the possibility of large exchange rate changes will both discourage domestic saving and encourage more savings to be invested abroad.

• Restrictions on capital controls, particularly short-term ones, can give a little more flexibility to domestic monetary and interest rate policy. However, capital restrictions, including Chile's, are not the major factor containing a country's current account balance and capital inflows. Chile's lower dependence on capital inflows is based on a high internal savings rate and systematic development over a decade of the infrastructure of a sound domestic capital market. Capital restrictions are no more than a very partial answer to the problem of vulnerability to sudden changes in capital inflows.

Many Latin American countries have already applied major elements of the Chilean approach. Completing this effort is within reach, if all of its essential components are included and adapted to national conditions. This approach is more promising than the East Asian model of an earlier time. As Eleanor Howard has said, "here in the Americas, we have our own miracle to emulate."

---

*Paul Boeker is President, Institute of the Americas, La Jolla, California. He was U.S. Ambassador to Bolivia under the Carter Administration and to Jordan under the Reagan Administration.*

# Commentary

*Eleanor Howard*

Chile's favorable comparison with East Asia in the development of capital markets is due to several factors. First and foremost, the Chilean authorities learn from their mistakes. Second, they limit the government's direct role in financial markets. Third, they build upon their successes in the financial markets by creating politically independent, highly professional regulatory institutions. Fourth, the policies and laws regulating the financial markets are updated periodically to adapt to market changes. Fifth, they recognize that markets work, and they use market incentives when they decide to intervene to achieve a specific goal (such as providing financial services to small businesses). Sixth, there is continuity over time in the commitment of the political leadership to the basic principles underlying the development of capital markets. Finally, there is a broad consensus among the Chilean people in support of the government's approach to economic management. The following comments draw out these strengths by expanding upon some key observations and conclusions from Ambassador Boeker's paper.

## Learning from the 1982 Banking Crisis

As Ambassador Boeker points out, Chile was able to absorb the 1994 regional financial crisis in a relatively short time and at low cost. In contrast, the 1981–82 regional financial crisis resulted in a 14 percent drop in GDP, a rise in unemployment to 25 percent, and the virtual collapse of the banking system. In the earlier crisis, the entire economy was vulnerable to the external crisis because of a major mistake in exchange rate policy. From 1979 until 1982, Chile maintained a fixed exchange rate of 39 pesos to the U.S. dollar. The increasingly overvalued peso in this period attracted large foreign exchange inflows into the country. A sharp drop in these inflows with the onset of the regionwide external crisis made the fixed exchange rate unsustainable, resulting in a sharp devaluation of the peso in 1982.

The impact of this devaluation on the banks was compounded by an earlier major mistake. This was to reprivatize the banks in the mid 1970s with inadequate banking laws and supervision. The large banks were sold to a few economic groups that used credit from their own banks to buy businesses, and also borrowed extensively abroad for the resources to lend to their own firms and to other customers. As the economy moved further from equilibrium, the risks in the banking system were further exacerbated by the extremely high real lending rates of around 40 percent.

Since 1982, the management of macroeconomic policies in Chile has provided the stable environment essential for financial markets. Chilean policymakers have also adopted and maintained the appropriate sequencing of reforms. This is evident not only in the establishment of rigorous banking laws and in the enforcement of prudential norms on banks, but in the approach to nonbank financial institutions and the capital markets. The financial institutions established after the 1982 banking crisis, including the pension funds (AFPs, in the Spanish acronym) and the leasing companies, have all been governed from the beginning by strict prudential norms.

With a prudential regulatory framework in place, Chilean authorities allow for the maximum growth and diversification of financial markets with a reasonable degree of risk. In other words, they have not overreacted to the banking crisis by unnecessarily restricting the development of financial institutions. Consequently, even as the regulatory institutions maintain the strict enforcement of existing regulations, the laws governing financial institutions and the AFPs have been periodically updated. The regulatory environment has matured with the markets.

The importance of continuously monitoring the financial markets to update prudential regulations is especially apparent in the evaluation of the AFPs. After the early period, when the pension funds were restricted to investing almost exclusively in government paper and commercial bank certificates of deposit, there has been a gradual liberalizing of the limits on investments. Over time, the AFPs have moved into mortgages, corporate debt, equities, and more recently into venture capital and international bonds and equities. In essence, as new financial instruments have become available, the responsible authorities have assessed the risks, and when appropriate, have permitted these instruments to be incorporated into pension fund portfolios. This process, and its proper timing, have allowed the AFPs to play such an important role in the development of Chile's capital markets.

## Lessons from CORFO's Experience with Credit

The role of the government development banks in East Asia and Latin America is a relatively minor theme in Ambassador Boeker's chapter. In relation to the East Asian experience, he concludes that the protected role of these banks "probably retarded the development of the bond markets...." He also points out that channeling savings through government banks resulted in a missed opportunity to foster the development of private nonbank financial institutions, including pension funds, insurance companies,and so on. With regard to Latin America, he summarizes the negative experience of public development banks, which is reflected in the extremely high arrears rates. The recent history of the Chilean public development bank, CORFO, and the parallel development of the pension funds, support the conclusions from both continents.

CORFO's traditional role as a credit institution was suspended from the mid 1970s until 1982. The decision to reopen CORFO's investment finance window in 1981 was mainly in response to the extremely high real rates of interest in the commercial banking sector prior to the financial crisis. In essence, the government chose to provide credit directly to private business rather than to deal with the causes of the high interest rates and the short maturities in the banking system. It was coincidental that the reopening of CORFO's credit operation and the launching of the AFPs occurred in the same year, 1982.

From 1982 through 1989, CORFO loaned around US$300 million to private enterprises for new investment. The arrears rate at the end of the period was around 50 percent, which is typical of the Latin American experience. With this portfolio performance, the pricing of credit was almost irrelevant in evaluating CORFO's institutional efficiency. Yet CORFO did attract borrowers away from alternative sources of financing when it charged below-market rates. Similarly, the demand for CORFO credit declined significantly when market rates were even the equivalent of the government bank rate. This was apparent because CORFO's management maintained the same spread over the inflation index regardless of interest rate movements in the market. There was no way for CORFO's management to price credit appropriately, since the financial instruments in the market had much shorter maturities than CORFO loans.

By the late 1980s, there was a decision to radically change the approach to lending to the private sector and to the pricing of term finance. In 1990, CORFO was transformed into a second tier (wholesale) lending institution. As such, it was to lend exclusively to private financial institutions. These institutions, in turn, provided term finance to their customers. Consequently, the credit risk was passed to private lenders. This change in the approach to lending was a response to the high arrears rate in the existing portfolio.

The change in the approach to pricing was to promote the development of the capital markets. In searching for an appropriate pricing mechanism, Chilean authorities were explicit in this objective. The idea was to lend to financial institutions at a market-based rate that would be somewhat higher than the cost of borrowing in the incipient corporate bond market. This was accomplished by setting up a credit auction. The cutoff rates for bids followed a normal yield curve, so that interest rates would increase with the length of the maturity of the loan. The establishment of the yield curve was facilitated greatly by the emergence of longer-term maturities (up to ten years) in government bonds.

Since 1990, CORFO's wholesale credit window has had a perfect record in loan collection. This is attributable in large part to the quality and supervision of prudential norms. Only those financial institutions meeting rigorous prudential standards are given access to the credit auction.

For most of its history the credit auction has not drawn potential borrowers from the bond market. The great majority (around 80 percent) of lending through the auction has gone to nonbank financial institutions, i.e., to leasing companies. With one exception, these companies are of recent origin. The biggest buyers of corporate bonds, the AFPs, can only buy bonds whose issuers have at least a three-year history. Until recently, this requirement has kept many leasing companies out of the bond market.

The concentration of CORFO lending in the leasing companies and the explosive growth in the corporate bond market since 1990 lead to two conclusions. First, when commercial banks and/or their larger customers required long-term finance, they accessed the corporate bond and equity markets. Second, the availability of term finance through CORFO has been critical for the growth of the leasing industry. Therefore, instead of discouraging the emergence and growth of nonbank financial institutions, Chile's development bank fostered an important source of financing for smaller businesses. Moreover, by not attracting potential borrowers from the capital markets, CORFO has allowed for the maximum growth and diversification of other private financial institutions.

## Continuity and Consensus

The commitment of Chilean authorities to stabilizing macroeconomic policies and their sound management of the financial markets has persisted through major political change. The commitment is perhaps even greater with the renewal of democracy in Chile. This is due not only to Chile's political leadership, but to a virtual consensus among the Chilean people in support of existing macroeconomic and financial sector policies. The near consensus within Chilean society reflects, in turn, a widespread understanding of fundamental economic and financial issues.

This leads to another observation in comparing the East Asian and Chilean experiences: Chile is one of the few countries in Latin America that has long shared the East Asian commitment to quality universal education. A hypothesis emerging from this observation is that a well-educated citizenry is best able to learn from mistakes and successes in macroeconomic and financial sector management.

---

*Eleanor Howard is Deputy Manager, Regional Operations Department 2 (Central America, Mexico, Dominican Republic, Haiti), at the Inter-American Development Bank.*

# The Role of Exports in Asian Development

**8**

*Howard Pack*

Many factors have been put forth as proximate determinants of the extraordinarily rapid growth of the high-performing Asian economies (HPAEs). High ratios of investment to GDP, widespread primary education, growing higher education, and government commitment to growth and effectiveness in policy implementation have all been cited as important contributors to their performance. The astounding growth of manufactured exports, particularly in Hong Kong, Korea, and Taiwan, China, has also been suggested as a major difference between some of the HPAEs and many Latin American economies. The precise role of exports in growth acceleration has not been completely articulated. Indeed, a focus on exports runs the risk of *post hoc, ergo propter hoc* error: Having identified a few successful countries, one looks in retrospect to find what differentiates them. Rather than invoke a simple correlation, we need to identify the explicit mechanisms through which export growth helped to accelerate economic growth in these nations.

If exports are a significant underlying cause of growth in the HPAEs rather than a result of growing productivity, then a link must be found between exports and the proximate determinants of the long-run growth of productive capacity. These determinants are the rate of growth of the capital stock, the rate of growth of the labor force, and the rate of growth of total factor productivity (TFP).

Growth rates of the capital stock and TFP may arguably have been larger as a result of sales in foreign markets compared to domestic markets. This paper presents some conjectures on why this may have been the case. While some of these hypotheses can be tested with international cross-section growth equations—and the results are suggestive (Pack and Page 1994)—such analyses cannot be definitive. Efforts to devise econometric tests with time series for individual countries run into very substantial multicollinearity of all of the variables of interest, and the large number of studies do not specify causal mechanisms. Rather, they use purely statistical tests without specifying the underlying model.

This paper attempts to set out the mechanisms by which export orientation may have accelerated growth rates, rather than merely had level effects. The distinction is somewhat blurred by the possibility that, if there are large initial allocative distortions that result in actual GDP being 50 percent below potential, given existing factor endowments, then elimination of this gap over 20 years as policies improve could yield substantial productivity growth during the transition period.

In looking for special factors that might explain the sustained growth rate of the HPAEs, the neoclassical growth model can serve as an organizing framework. In the standard model, rapid capital accumulation leads to a growing capital-labor ratio, to a decline in the marginal product of capital, and eventually to a steady-state equilibrium in which the growth rates of output, capital, and effective units of labor are equal.[1] In Hong Kong, Korea, and Taiwan, China, there is little evidence of such a deceleration in output growth or of a decline in the marginal product of capital, despite rapid growth of the capital-labor ratio.

Exports can enter the simple neoclassical model in a number of ways. First, the rate of capital accumulation may be higher if a country is able to achieve steadier growth by greater reliance on export markets. Second, the predicted decline in the marginal product of capital may be avoided if exporting is more conducive to growth in productivity than are sales in the domestic market.

The maintenance of rapid output growth and high levels of investment is also consistent with endogenous growth theory (EGT), in which diminishing returns to capital are forestalled because of external economies to investment (Romer 1986) or to human capital accumulation (Lucas 1988), or because of an assumed lower bound to the marginal product of capital. However, the argument of this paper fits better with another strand of EGT in which international trade is an important source of productivity growth, because it facilitates the closing of the gap between the technology levels of latecomers to industrialization and more advanced nations (Grossman and Helpman 1991).

The following sections consider the effects of exports on investment rates and the impact of exports on growth in total factor productivity. We then analyze openness more broadly, including how it affects attitudes toward the acquisition of foreign technology, and examine the lessons of the Asian economies' export performance for the Latin American countries.

---

[1] The growth rate of the number of workers plus the growth rate of labor-augmenting technical change.

Table 8.1  Growth Rates and Variation in GDP, 1965–92

| Country | (1)<br>Mean Growth<br>Rate* | (2)<br>Standard<br>Deviation | (2)/(1)<br>Coefficient<br>of Variation |
|---|---|---|---|
| Hong Kong | .072 | .042 | .58 |
| South Korea | .086 | .038 | .44 |
| Singapore | .083 | .032 | .39 |
| Indonesia | .066 | .026 | .39 |
| Malaysia | .066 | .058 | .42 |
| Thailand | .073 | .026 | .36 |
| Argentina | .022 | .058 | 2.6 |
| Brazil | .049 | .052 | 1.1 |
| Chile | .048 | .076 | 1.6 |
| Colombia | .044 | .021 | .47 |
| Mexico | .043 | .035 | .81 |
| Peru | .020 | .063 | 3.2 |

Source: World Bank, World Tables, various years.
*Annual growth rate calculated as $\log Y_t - \log Y_{t-1}$

## The Effect of Exports on Investment

### Managing the Macroeconomy

Exporting can affect the macroeconomic environment in a number of ways that have an impact on investment levels. The HPAEs achieved investment–GDP ratios of thirty percent and maintained them. While they might have achieved such ratios had the economies been domestically oriented, that probably would have been difficult because of more frequent business cycles and foreign exchange shortages. When GDP fluctuates considerably, investors may be less willing to invest. By providing a relatively stable source of growing demand, exports may dampen fluctuations and encourage investment. Most HPAEs that emphasized manufactured exports experienced much lower variance in output relative to their growth rates than did the major Latin American economies (Table 8.1). In Korea and Taiwan, China, GDP declined only after the 1973 oil price shock and only for a short period of time.

While it is theoretically possible to employ a monetary and fiscal policy that would sustain a 10 percent growth rate in GDP, the required skills and luck are likely to be less when a larger part of final demand consists of exports growing at 15 percent or more per year. In the HPAEs export

**Table 8.2  Growth Rates of Exports and Gross Domestic Product**
*(Constant prices)*

|  | 1960–70 | | 1970–80 | | 1980–92 | |
|---|---|---|---|---|---|---|
|  | E* | GDP* | E* | GDP* | E* | GDP* |
| Korea | 35.2 | 8.5 | 23.5 | 9.6 | 11.9 | 9.4 |
| Taiwan, China | 23.7 | 9.2 | 15.6 | 9.7 | 11.0 | 7.8 |
| Hong Kong | 12.7 | 10.0 | 9.7 | 9.2 | 5.0 | 6.7 |
| Singapore | 4.2 | 8.8 | 4.2 | 8.3 | 9.9 | 6.7 |
| Malaysia | 6.1 | 6.5 | 4.8 | 7.9 | 11.3 | 5.9 |
| Thailand | 5.2 | 8.2 | 10.3 | 7.1 | 14.7 | 8.2 |
| Indonesia | 3.5 | 3.5 | 7.2 | 7.2 | 5.6 | 5.7 |
| Japan | 17.5 | 10.5 | 9.0 | 4.0 | 4.6 | 4.1 |
| Argentina | 3.3 | 4.2 | 7.1 | 2.5 | 2.2 | .4 |
| Brazil | 5.0 | 9.2 | 8.5 | 8.1 | 5.0 | 2.2 |
| Chile | .6 | 4.5 | 10.4 | 1.4 | 5.5 | 4.8 |
| Mexico | 3.3 | 7.3 | 13.5 | 6.3 | 1.6 | 1.5 |

*Sources: World Development Report 1979, 1993, 1994; Taiwan Statistical Data Book 1992.*
* Annual growth rate.

growth considerably exceeded GDP growth, as shown in Table 8.2. Although international demand for exports may vary over time with the business cycle in the OECD countries, relatively small changes in policy instruments were sufficient to maintain the growth in exports in Korea and Taiwan, China. Investors could anticipate continuing growth of exports and their domestic multiplier effects in making their investment plans. While the high rate of return on investment did not guarantee a matching increase in the local saving rate, it may have influenced it. Simultaneously, the creditworthiness signaled by growing exports encouraged substantial capital inflows into Korea.

In contrast, the coordinated use of monetary and fiscal policy to achieve a noninflationary 10 percent annual growth in investment and other autonomous components of demand is exceptionally difficult. A fiscal surplus combined with a low interest rate might encourage rapid investment growth, but it is likely to run into cycles because of the considerable difficulty in matching domestic demand and supply growth in a more closed economy.

Export orientation from an early point in the industrialization process also had another benefit: it provided the basis for policy flexibility. When the oil price shocks occurred in 1973, domestic absorption in the HPAEs was reduced and exports increased to pay for the greater petroleum costs.

This reduction in demand, and the policy-induced alterations in relative prices between tradeables and nontradeables, contrast favorably with the inability of many countries in Latin America to achieve the same changes at that time. The Asian countries' ability to implement the required policy changes reflected their exceptional pre-1973 growth in exports. Having already experienced successful export growth, Asian policymakers could be reasonably sure that the expenditure-reduction and change in relative prices would elicit a substantial export response.

In contrast, policymakers in the import-substituting Latin American countries could have had no such confidence. Even had they wanted to pursue the same policies, their manufacturers were much less efficient, reflecting the earlier concentration on the protected domestic market. Domestic firms, having high costs and not having incurred the large fixed costs necessary to enter world markets, could not have been reliably forecast to achieve the necessary growth in exports to offset the potential income-reducing effects of deflationary policies. The uncertain success of an export-oriented redirection of policy was one reason for the continued reliance on borrowing to finance increased oil costs. The GDP declines in Latin America in the 1980s, after the onset of the debt crisis and the collapse of investment, may thus have been partly attributable to the loss of policy options due to the reliance on import-substituting industrialization in the period until 1973.

The role of exports in reducing the difficulty of managing growing demand should not be overemphasized. Indonesia, Malaysia, and Thailand have achieved sustained growth with lower export growth rates than Korea and Taiwan, China, had experienced. These may be the more appropriate models for Latin America. GDP growth need not be export led although exports may help. Even if the major sources of demand growth are the domestic components of autonomous demand, export growth will be necessary to provide foreign exchange for intermediate and investment goods that are not currently produced.

### The Foreign Exchange Constraint

As stressed by the literature on the two-gap model, output growth may be limited by the growth in demand for imports, which exceeds the foreign exchange available from export earnings and capital flows. The level of exports and their rate of growth can be increased by a combination of expenditure switching and relative price changes between tradables and nontradables. Unless the international demand for all of a country's exports

**Table 8.3  Contribution of Final Demand Expansion to Deviations from Sectorally Balanced Growth**

| Country | Annual Output Growth Rate | Deviation from Proportional Growth | Dom. Demand | Exp. Growth | Change in Import. Sub. | Input-Output Coefficients |
|---|---|---|---|---|---|---|
| **Korea 1955–73** | | | | | | |
| Primary | 5.7 | | | | | |
| Manufacture | 15.8 | 28 | 17 | 76 | 5 | 1 |
| Services | 10.3 | | | | | |
| **Taiwan, China 1955–71** | | | | | | |
| Primary | 7.1 | | | | | |
| Manufacture | 16.2 | 28 | 3 | 71 | 10 | 16 |
| Services | 9.7 | | | | | |
| **Japan 1914–35** | | | | | | |
| Primary | 1.0 | | | | | |
| Manufacture | 5.5 | 23.6 | 58 | 45 | 11 | -13 |
| Services | 4.2 | | | | | |
| **Mexico 1950–75** | | | | | | |
| Primary | 4.8 | | | | | |
| Manufacture | 7.7 | 9.8 | 47 | 3 | 36 | 19 |
| Services | 6.4 | | | | | |
| **Colombia 1953–70** | | | | | | |
| Primary | 4.5 | | | | | |
| Manufacture | 8.1 | 16.1 | 9 | 9 | 48 | 35 |
| Services | 1.9 | | | | | |

*Source:* Calculated from de Melo (1985), Table 9.2.

is inelastic—an empirically implausible supposition for most nations—foreign exchange shortages should not prevail in the long run. Nevertheless, in the short run the requisite structural and policy changes may be slow, leading to stop-go policies, falling GDP, excess capacity, and a decline in the rate of return, which discourages investment.

While it is difficult to estimate in advance whether a country's short-term growth is limited by a foreign exchange constraint, the scholarly literature on the HPAEs and statements by government officials and business executives almost never refer to a shortage of foreign exchange for either intermediate inputs or machinery. (This is in significant contrast with Latin America.) Policies that placed greater emphasis on exports in Latin America would have allowed rapid growth to continue without encountering a large current account deficit, as the demand for imports outran the availability of foreign exchange.

In sum, the growth of exports is part of the reason for the absence of major fluctuations in GDP and a nonbinding foreign exchange constraint in the HPAEs. Both are likely to have contributed to the high anticipated and realized profitability of investment in the HPAEs, while the opposite effects were experienced in Latin America.

## The Effect of Exports on Productivity

### Productivity Effects of Reallocation

Exporting also accelerated the sectoral transformation of the economy in terms of production and employment. The rapid growth of manufacturing, due largely to exports (Table 8.3), generated a large number of jobs for those who were underemployed in both agriculture and the urban informal sector. This reallocation of labor generated a fillip to the growth of TFP and had a positive effect on the distribution of income.

The growth of manufactured exports in Korea and Taiwan, China, at a rate much faster than the growth of other final demand categories led to a rapid change in the sectoral structure of production. In Japan, Korea, and Taiwan, China, value added grew much more rapidly in manufacturing than in other sectors (Table 8.3). Using a standard demand decomposition, de Melo (1985) found that in Korea in the years 1955 to 1973, the more rapid expansion of exports than other components of final demand accounted for roughly three quarters of the 28 percent faster growth of the manufacturing sector than would have occurred had exports expanded by the same rate as other components of GDP. The figures are similar in Taiwan, China (Table 8.3). In Japan during the years 1914 to 1935, export growth played a similar role, whereas in Mexico and Colombia, the only Latin American countries analyzed in the study, exports contributed little to sectoral transformation. While such an accounting procedure cannot determine the ultimate sources of the change in sectoral composition, nor whether it was efficient, it does indicate that the alteration of the sectoral structure of the economy was closely related to that of export growth.

The disproportionate expansion of manufacturing had major implications for the structure of employment. Employment attributable to exports increased from 4.6 percent of the labor force in South Korea in 1963 to 19 percent in 1973, the comparable figures for roughly similar years in Taiwan, China, being 15.2 and 27.4 (de Melo 1985, Table 9.8). Manufactured exports were produced, even in small factories, by advanced methods compared to those employed in the urban informal and agricultural sectors. The marginal productivity of labor in direct exporting, as well as firms supplying inputs to exporters, was thus greater than in agriculture and the informal sector. As exports grew, there was a rapid shift of labor to higher marginal productivity activities and a concomitant gain in aggregate productivity. The shift of labor was more rapid insofar as export growth permitted a faster expansion of these labor-intensive sectors than would have occurred had the economy relied solely on domestic sales. Thus, in a transitional period, there was a boost to TFP growth from this reallocation.

In the decade 1960 to 1970, 12 to 18 percent of the growth of economywide labor productivity was due to the reallocation of factors from agriculture to industry in Korea and Taiwan, China.[2] To this would have to be added the gains in TFP from reallocation of the large number of workers who were initially employed in the urban informal sector at much lower marginal productivity than in the formal sector. For example, data in Ho (1980, Table 2.1) show that as late as 1975, 36 percent of Korea's labor force was employed in home production or in workshops of one to four persons. This was considerably lower than in 1965 and the figure decreases still more in the next decade. Given the much lower marginal productivity of labor at home and in workshops than in the formal manufacturing sector, the absorption of workers into labor-intensive manufacturing would probably increase the share of output growth attributable to reallocation by one third, to about 20 percent. This large figure is unlikely to be realized in Latin America for reasons discussed below.

### Static-scale Economies

In large economies such as Japan, protection from imports permitted the realization of scale economies, since imports were limited and the number of firms was kept small through lending policies that prevented entry of new ones that would have forced all plants to operate higher on their average cost curves. This policy generated a complication, namely, the need to limit cooperative behavior and provide incentives for continuing competition among domestic oligopolists. Although the Japanese solved this dilemma, the economic skills and political astuteness required of the bureaucracy are likely to exceed those present in almost all developing countries.[3] Scale economies and the resulting growth in productivity are likely to be more surely realized when firms undertake exporting to the large world market.

---

[2] Chen (1977) as reported in de Melo (1985), Table 9.3.

**Table 8.4 The Size Structure of Taiwan, China Manufacturing**

| Sector | Average Number of Persons Engaged 1986 | Number of Firms 1966–70 | Number of Firms 1986 |
|---|---|---|---|
| Food processing | 17 | 1129 | 217 |
| Beverages, tobacco | 160 | 13 | 9 |
| Textiles | 37 | 428 | 1039 |
| Clothing | 44 | 112 | 417 |
| Leather, fur | 63 | 156 | 618 |
| Wood products | 15 | 505 | 760 |
| Paper, print, publicity | 12 | 478 | 1093 |
| Chemical materials | 67 | 70 | 73 |
| Chemical products | 25 | 265 | 113 |
| Petroleum, chemicals | 465 | 2 | 1 |
| Plastic products | 29 | 388 | 1603 |
| Rubber products | 28 | 88 | 283 |
| Nonmetallic minerals | 27 | 270 | 402 |
| Basic metals | 27 | 189 | 213 |
| Fabricated metals | 9 | 722 | 3728 |
| Machinery | 11 | 504 | 1091 |
| Electrical equipment | 61 | 274 | 1010 |
| Transportation equipment | 30 | 209 | 445 |
| Precision equipment | 29 | 53 | 169 |
| Miscellaneous | 26 | 261 | 765 |

Source: Report on 1986 Industrial and Commercial Census, Fukien Area, tables 28 (number of firms) and 19 (average firm size) (Taiwan, China 1986).

The benefits of static-scale economies in the HPAEs were limited by the production technologies that characterized the sectors initially at the forefront of development in the HPAEs, such as clothing, footwear (including athletic shoes), toys, sports equipment, and assembly of electronic components. All of these have relatively low fixed costs. Insofar as the HPAEs have been relatively open to imports, some of the more capital-intensive sectors have either not developed or have developed relatively late in the industrialization process. The export sectors, particularly in the early years of rapid export growth, were typically labor intensive, as would be predicted by Hecksher-Ohlin theory.

---

[3] In Korea, a similar conflict was rectified by requiring firms to meet export targets.

Even in the late 1980s, after two decades of intensive industrialization, Taiwan, China's manufacturing sector had large numbers of small and medium-size firms, as shown in Table 8.4. A similar phenomenon holds in Hong Kong, in which textiles and clothing, especially the latter, are produced in relatively small plants. Indeed, one strength of Hong Kong and Taiwanese manufacturing has been the quick response to new product specifications in clothing, textiles, and electronics. Taiwanese firms with as few as fifty employees have been able to innovate new products in areas such as computer keyboards.

## Long-term Learning

While static scale economies do not appear to have been crucial for many of the HPAEs, dynamic scale economies were significant. The world market offered a relatively stable and growing sales base for production and output growth; thus, cumulative output was greater than would have been achievable from domestically oriented production. A small growth in the share of world exports permitted 15 percent annual growth in exports in large numbers of products. Firms were able to accumulate considerable experience in technically similar lines of manufacturing for many years. Insofar as learning-by-doing is a function of cumulative output rather than the simple passage of time, international markets provide the opportunity for considerably greater cumulative sales and learning.

The relation between long-term learning or dynamic-scale economies and length of production run is shown in Figure 8.1. Average cost is shown to decline along the long-term learning curve LL with cumulative output, $\sum_{t-1}^{n} Q_t$. A typical firm in an export-oriented country will be at E rather than D as in the domestically oriented Latin American countries, even if the firms began at the same point in time. This curve reflects the fact that workers become more familiar with their tasks and suggest improved methods, while managers improve the flow of work and suggest small rearrangements and improvements in work practices that improve productivity.

## Length of Production Runs

The gains from long-term learning by doing in which workers and management improve their skills have been augmented by the long production runs of individual products destined for the export market. Production for export of 20,000 yards of one type of cloth is not unusual in Hong Kong, Korea, and Taiwan, China. In contrast, in import-substituting countries,

**Figure 8.1 Long-term Learning and Specialization**

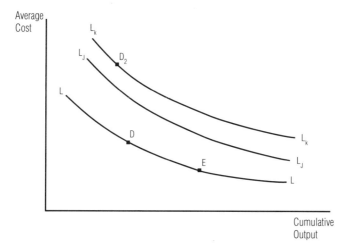

firms produce small batches, 500 yards at a time, for local retailers as their demand shifts. Very short production runs lead to a significant loss in total factor productivity. When firms oriented to the domestic market increase their product range and manufacture products in short runs, they incur higher costs regardless of their cumulative experience in individual products. This results from setup costs, including the need constantly to adjust quality control as products are changed. In Figure 8.1, as the number of products increases, average cost increases from LL to $L_j$ $L_j$, $L_k$ $L_k$, etc., where the subscript indicates the number of products k>j. Thus, a typical firm in an inward-oriented economy that has not benefitted from large cumulative output or product specialization will operate at D2 rather than E.

A sense of the quantitative importance of such productivity losses is provided by textile mills in the Philippines. They often spin ten types of yarn and weave forty different types of cloth, in contrast with three yarns and three or four cloths in a typical U.S. mill. Such product diversification reduces total factor productivity in Philippine mills by 40 percent compared with comparably equipped OECD textile plants (Pack 1987). In contrast, firms that export must concentrate on a small product range if they are to achieve sufficiently low costs to compete in the world economy. Put slightly differently, it is possible to increase TFP in this sector by roughly 60 percent by reducing product diversity towards levels prevailing in OECD mills. This amounts to 2.5 percent a year if the move to specialization were realized over a transition period of twenty years. In some industrial branches that have continuous flow production, such gains are likely to be less; in sectors with job shops, such as machinery building, the potential gains are considerably greater.

Finally, insofar as exporting generates larger sales, exporting firms have a stronger incentive to undertake expenditures to improve productivity. In contrast, import-substituting firms that can sell only in the usually limited domestic market may have limited incentives (Rodrik 1992). One of the unanticipated benefits of the Korean policy of protecting domestic sales while requiring firms to meet export targets is that it provided a strong incentive to undertake productivity-raising measures, the costs of which could be allocated across larger export sales.

## The Effects of Export Orientation on Competition

A standard view of the benefits of exporting is that firms must engage in efforts to reduce their cost and increase their quality to compete in the world market, in contrast to a sheltered domestic market where they can succeed without improving in either dimension. The Asian experience both confirms this and suggests a more complex view. At one extreme, Japan protected its domestic market with both quantitative restrictions and tariffs; yet the manufacturing sector as a whole had quite good TFP performance. There was fierce competition in the domestic economy to increase market share, partly because this was perceived to provide greater access to benefits offered by the government. Domestic consumers were not necessarily the beneficiaries of improved productivity in the short run, since there is evidence of firms acting as discriminating monopolists between domestic and foreign buyers. In the long run, however, domestic prices would also have gone down with the costs of production.

While Japanese firms were insulated from competition in the domestic market, their efforts to penetrate competitive international markets led to attempts to reduce costs and improve quality. The relative importance of the productivity effort directed to increasing exports was necessarily larger in the four tigers, where domestic markets are smaller and exports account for a much larger percentage of manufacturing output and GDP.

In terms of domestic competition, firms in Hong Kong and Singapore were not protected from exporters of other nations. In Korea and Taiwan, China, firms were considerably more protected from imports than has usually been acknowledged; but a variety of incentives were offered, particularly in Korea, to make the effective exchange rate for exports fairly close to that for import substitutes. Moreover, in Korea, access to a variety of incentives, especially highly subsidized loans, were contingent on export performance. While high protection of the domestic market, combined with a variety of export incentives, is hardly a first best model for encouraging productivity growth, the necessity to achieve exports acted, as it did in Japan, to encourage efforts to improve productivity, which carried over to production destined for the domestic market. Whether this productivity growth was greater than the rate that would have been achieved if the domestic market had been more quickly liberalized is open to question (Rodrik 1992).

One lesson to be derived from the Asian countries is that some form of competition is necessary for productivity growth. The discipline of exports is one possible mode, but this is not a reason to favor exports over domestic production. Competitive imports can provide the required discipline. In the small Asian economies, in which exports are necessary if foreign exchange constraints are to be avoided, exports will inevitably loom larger and also provide a strong incentive to improve productivity. The fact that Japan and Korea were able to achieve substantial TFP growth while simultaneously protecting the domestic market and exporting does not provide a convincing demonstration that such a complex policy is worth emulating.[4] The administrative requirements and costs are quite formidable and probably beyond the capacity of most bureaucracies. Nevertheless, competition in at least one sphere would have been preferable to the import-substituting industrialization (ISI) policies of Latin America, which long sheltered domestic production and did little to promote exports.

While efficiency gains generated by competition can arise from either import liberalization or exporting, the evidence with respect to recent Latin American policies is that reduced protection does not demonstrate strong beneficial effects. A survey of econometric assessments by Tybout (1992) reveals no clear pattern in the relation between import liberalization and productivity growth in several Latin American countries. An analysis of the Chilean experience by Tybout, de Melo, and Corbo (1991) does find that, in Chile, firms subjected to the largest decline in protection demonstrated the greatest improvement in TFP. But in other countries, including Colombia and Mexico, the results are mixed. The realized impact depends on changes in firm size and the implied scale economies, the TFP levels of firms entering and exiting an industry, and the intraplant growth in TFP. Whatever the precise pattern of these variables, the sectoral growth in TFP in the studies reviewed by Tybout is ambiguous. Perhaps the clearest results come from a

---

[4] There may be political arguments for pursuing such a policy, since various interest groups are coopted by different components of the package.

careful panel study of Chilean manufacturing firms by Liu (1993), in which all the desirable qualitative properties are found. Exiting firms have lower TFP, while entering and continuing ones have higher levels and growth rates of TFP. Nevertheless, the TFP growth rates for each branch implied by Liu's results are less than 1 percent a year, despite the fact that Chilean tariffs were much lower than those in the Asian NICs.

Import liberalization, which went much further in the Latin American countries analyzed than in the Asian NICs, seems to have had much smaller effects on productivity growth. There are many possible reasons for this, including the very recent changes in policy after long periods of ISI and the lack of belief by firms that the respective governments would maintain the new regime. In the relatively short periods analyzed, firms might not have had time to make the necessary adjustments to achieve greater efficiency, or they may have delayed implementing such changes given past reversals in government policy. Nevertheless, there was considerable entry and exit, which suggests that time and credibility were not necessarily the major impediments to realizing greater TFP growth.

One possibility is that exports themselves confer some benefit in productivity growth compared to a comparable amount of production destined for the liberalized domestic market. One source of the better performance in the Asian countries, despite more closed markets, was their greater effort to obtain knowledge available in more advanced countries. The literature on convergence emphasizes that one source of the movement of OECD countries towards the United States has been the ability of firms to adopt best practice techniques, an effort facilitated by increasing international trade in the period after the Second World War.

## The Impact of Openness on Technology Transfer

Obtaining new knowledge, whether embedded in equipment and material inputs or simply in knowhow, may exert decisive effects on economic performance. There are some who question this assertion, however, including an entire generation of Latin American (and many Indian) policymakers and economists who have subscribed to many of the tenets of dependency theory. These tenets vary by author, but for the purposes of this paper, two strands are important:

• Interactions between developing (peripheral) and developed (core) countries are a zero sum game, the gains always accruing to the developed countries.

• Developing countries need to be independent of industrialized nations not only in terms of exports and imports but in technology as well. Technology transactions are viewed as largely occurring on an exploitative basis, with no benefits to the recipient countries.

Proposition 1 reflects the Prebisch-Singer view that the commodity terms of trade inevitably decline for the LDCs. The results of a long literature testing this hypothesis suggest that it is difficult to detect such a trend. Moreover, even if the commodity terms of trade have declined, it is clear that the income terms of trade for most countries have improved, except where exports have themselves fallen victim to policies that reduce their profitability. While export pessimism might have been defensible in the immediate postwar years, by the early 1960s any examination of international trade data through clear rather than dark glasses would have required a revision of thinking. Indeed, in the Asian NICs, the Prebisch-Singer view never achieved any influence except among a few South Korean students at elite universities, who maintain that Korea's export-oriented economy has immiserized the masses over the last thirty years, despite the growth in real wages of 5 percent per year!

Proposition 2 also reflects one aspect of the Prebisch-Singer view, namely, that industrial products are sold in oligopolistic markets; industrial machinery would, in this view, sell at excessively high prices in developing countries. The extension of this view to disembodied technology purchases such as technology licenses, where there may be more truth to the idea, is a natural leap.

Hostility or indifference to international trade in goods was thus supplemented by an emphasis on becoming the technological equal of the OECD countries: if the periphery was forever dependent on the core for technology, it would always be exploited in technology transactions. The view that international trade was a zero-sum game was projected onto other spheres of international interactions, such as technology licensing agreements. Beneficial modes of technology transfer were thus ignored or thwarted. The licensing of technology, employed with extraordinary success by Japan in the 1950s and 1960s, was simply not perceived as an option and was viewed with deep suspicion. The domestic orientation of producers left them relatively unaware of technology developments in the OECD countries and the growing role of licensing and other modes of technology transfer. The absence of competitive pressure enabled them to prosper without the need to adopt more productive technologies than the ones then in place.

Firms that wanted to obtain new technology were often thwarted by a bureaucracy that was obsessed by fears of exploitation. For example, the details of licensing agreements were often subjected to microscopic scrutiny. Rather than viewing the issue in economic terms of whether the discounted cost of local R&D to generate a given process technology or product was greater than the discounted value of explicit and implicit license costs, there was an obsession with the rate of royalties and other details (Mytelka 1978). While Japan and then Korea and Taiwan, China, in the late 1970s, engaged in large numbers of licensing agreements, the Latin American nations largely ignored this option, a position that helps to explain low productivity growth even where liberalization occurred. Presumably, in the new, more open environment, technology acquisition strategies will begin to receive more attention.

Another dimension in which the internal orientation of Latin American economies may have led to a less than achievable growth in productivity was their behavior with respect to multinational corporations. Most foreign direct investment (FDI) was oriented to the domestic market. Given that this market was highly protected, multinational corporations (MNCs) had limited incentives to improve their productivity. Moreover, the fact that the sectors they entered did not typically contain domestic producers implied that there would be smaller spillovers, since there were few opportunities for workers and managers to leave foreign firms to seek employment with domestic companies that could profitably employ the knowledge they had gained while employed by the MNCs.

In contrast, Korea and Taiwan, China, allowed foreign firms to enter sectors in which foreign technology was difficult to obtain by licensing. The initiation of production and exports by MNCs provided critical information to local producers about the feasibility of such activities in these countries. In addition, in these sectors, largely electronics and chemicals, there was considerable labor turnover, much of which consisted of flows from foreign to domestic firms. Table 8.5 shows that there was considerable movement from MNCs to domestically owned firms in the Taiwanese higher technology sectors. While workers may have left multinationals in Argentina, Brazil, and Mexico, at least through the 1980s, there were relatively few firms local firms with products or manufacturing technologies that were sufficiently similar to the MNCs so that large spillover benefits would accrue. Research by Blomstrom (1989) does show that in Mexico, the presence of FDI in an industry exerted a positive effect on its productivity, but his interpretation is that this stemmed from the additional competition provided by foreign competitors, rather than from new technology whose diffusion brought Mexican firms into new product areas or closer to international best practice in existing areas.

**Table 8.5  Sector of Destination of Former Employees of Multinational Firms and Joint Ventures in Taiwan, China, mid 1980s**
*(Percentages)*

|  | A | B | C | D |
|---|---|---|---|---|
| Basic Metals | 23.4 | 0 | 8.6 | 68.0 |
| Metal products | 31.7 | 2.1 | 7.3 | 58.9 |
| Machinery parts | 8.1 | 11.6 | 3.6 | 76.7 |
| *General Chemicals* |  |  |  |  |
| Managers | 41.2 | 0 | 23.5 | 35.3 |
| Supervisors | 46.2 | 1.5 | 10.2 | 42.2 |
| Engineers, technicians | 84.2 | 7.9 | 7.9 | 0 |
| Skilled workers | 73.1 | 2.9 | 0 | 24.0 |
| Nonskilled workers | 46.7 | 0 | 1.7 | 51.7 |
| *Special Chemicals* |  |  |  |  |
| Managers | 6.3 | 37.5 | 25.0 | 31.3 |
| Supervisors | 37.1 | 24.9 | 1.2 | 36.8 |
| Engineers, technicians | 49.2 | 29.7 | 2.8 | 18.2 |
| Skilled workers | 63.3 | 19.8 | 0 | 16.9 |
| Nonskilled workers | 44.5 | 33.9 | .1 | 21.5 |

*Note:*  A= hired by companies in similar domestically owned industry.
    B= hired by company in similar industry owned by foreign firm.
    C= set up own firm.
    D= switched to other industries.
*Source:* San and Chen (1988).

After the initial rapid growth in labor-intensive production, the HPAEs realized they would have to graduate to more technology-intensive branches, and MNCs were used, with differing intensities, as one part of a strategy. Other elements of the technology strategy included increased domestic R&D, the establishment of science parks (Hsinchu in Taiwan, China), and the development of large domestic technology institutions (ITRI in Taiwan, China, KIST in Korea), with close connections to industrial firms. Technology licensing, and foreign investment which brought with it knowledge that was difficult to obtain through other modes, was selectively encouraged. While the Latin American countries had much more FDI than Hong Kong, Korea, and Taiwan, China, the latter two admitted MNCs with a largely technological focus rather than as a source of investment finance, as was often the case in Latin America. Even when FDI was allowed to service the domestic market in East Asia, an exceptional number of measures were taken to extract technological benefits.[5]

---

[5] Ranis and Schive (1985) provide a detailed account of the gains from the locations of Singer Sewing Machines in Taiwan, China.

Latin America's inward orientation, exemplified by ISI and the lack of interest in exports, thus had its mirror image in the failure to utilize foreign knowledge to improve productivity. Even in the 1970s and early 1980s, domestic R&D—which often replicated available (for a price) foreign knowledge—was considered good in itself, even when it occurred in industries that could not compete on the world market.[6]

While the preceding discussion deals with the adverse effects of an intellectual environment that discouraged the acquisition of proprietary knowledge, there were also foregone technology transfers that could have been obtained as an unanticipated byproduct of exporting. A conventional idea of the technological benefits of exporting is that exporters become aware of foreign products and production methods as they search for new markets and means of competing; however, the HPAEs benefited more than this scenario would suggest. Considerable amounts of product information and technology were made available by the importers of Asian products once large cumulative exports were realized. Surveys of firms in both Korea and Taiwan, China, indicate that the purchasers of exports were a major source of knowledge about process technology and new products. These importing firms, whose profits were considerably augmented by the availability of low-cost suppliers in the Far East, were willing (once the exporting firms' reliability had been established), to continuously transfer the knowledge necessary to maintain these firms as a source of quality low-cost products. In Hong Kong, Korea, and Taiwan, China, major retailers set up local buying offices that interacted with domestic manufacturers and provided detailed guidance for the production process to ensure that it met consumer requirements.[7]

In turning outwards to export markets and to the world for technology transfer, the Asian countries benefitted from both. The technology obtained from abroad was an important source of growth that supplemented the direct beneficial effects of exports on investment and productivity. In particular, there was an interaction between the growing levels of education and the inflow of knowledge. As Schultz (1991) and Nelson and Phelps (1966) suggest, the return to education mainly results from the enhanced ability of the educated to deal with a changing technology. With a static technology, knowledge becomes routinized, and the marginal return to education is low. As the inflow of technology accelerates, the ability to deal with nonroutine knowledge has a greater return.

---

[6] For examples, see Katz (1987).
[7] For the evidence behind the statements made in this paragraph, see Keesing and Lall (1991).

This interpretation also implies that the unusual emphasis on engineering and science in higher education in the HPAEs may have been an endogenous response to the higher private returns. Had there not been the introduction of new knowledge from abroad, the return to private education would have been less, inducing a smaller growth in technical education. In turn, the demand for investment, particularly in new equipment, would have been less without the supply of technically trained workers, which ensured higher profitability.

## Why Asian Exports Grew and the Lessons for Latin America

The rapid growth of exports from the HPAEs was attributable to a variety of factors. At the macroeconomic level, these countries tended to maintain realistic and nonvolatile real exchange rates. Although some, including Korea and Taiwan, China, protected the domestic market, exporters faced international prices for the acquisition of intermediate inputs. Imported inputs were made available at world prices through a variety of mechanisms that were automatic and transparent. In addition, subsidies were given in a number of forms to maintain the profitability of exports, despite the protection of the domestic market. The effective exchange rate for exporting relative to import substitutes (EERx/EERm) was thus maintained close to unity. None of this implies that these policies should be emulated in all details in Latin America. The costs of implementing measures to offset import protection was quite high. Presumably, the extremely cumbersome policy package that led to neutrality between domestic and foreign sales reflected some calculation of the political infeasibility of moving to a free trade regime.

In addition to generating an appropriate incentive environment, there was unusual attention to providing other mechanisms for facilitating exporting, which ranged from the development of appropriate financial instruments to augmenting physical infrastructure. Given that at the time of initiation of exports, many local firms had very little experience in the mechanics of international markets, such efforts on the part of the government may have been warranted in terms of completing missing markets.

In contrast to the HPAEs, much of Latin America was characterized by real exchange rates that were low and volatile and often appreciated for sustained periods (Cardoso and Helwige 1991). The value of EERx/EERm was often maintained below unity, and inputs were not made available to exporters at world prices. With the liberalization in Latin America in recent years, these latter issues are probably of lesser importance than they were in Asia when export promotion was being combined with intensive protection of some products in the domestic market. Given the substantial size of current exports in most Latin American countries, there is no lack of knowledge about the financial mechanics of exporting.

With the greater liberalization and appropriate macroeconomic policies that have been put in place in many countries, will Latin American productivity performance rival that of Asia? The studies noted above on the connection of the trade regime and productivity growth have investigated the effects of import liberalization on TFP. They have gone considerably beyond earlier, more aggregative studies by examining productivity performance at the level of individual plants. Particular attention has been paid to the role of entry and exit as sources of productivity growth. Most of the findings of the carefully executed empirical studies are ambiguous: liberalization of imports may have resulted in larger average firm size or greater productivity of individual plants, but the overall impact on productivity was relatively weak. Indeed, in Chile, an economy that has lowered tariffs to near free trade levels, TFP has grown at about one percent a year in contrast to a growth of three to four percent a year in Korea and Taiwan, China.

These results suggest that simply exposing firms to international competition in the domestic market may not be sufficient to generate productivity growth. Firms may try to respond to the threat of lower price or better quality imports but may not have the ability to effectively achieve the desired outcomes, since they lack the technological knowledge required to improve existing techniques of production or to identify and introduce new ones at high levels of efficiency. In Korea and Taiwan, China, in the earlier periods of their industrial development, considerable knowledge was provided by purchasers of their exports, a benefit that cannot occur when liberalization leads simply to competition in the domestic market. Insofar as knowledge transfer occurs as a byproduct of exporting, exports may be a prerequisite for initial gains in productivity. Similarly, most Latin American economies exhibit low levels of licensing activity. Firm-level data on the presence of engineers and other technical personnel are not available, but national statistics suggest a paucity of engineering graduates and there appear to be few industrial research institutions closely linked to private firms.

While one cannot draw strong conclusions from limited country samples and short periods, the relatively slow TFP growth in Chile, despite the economy's textbook liberalization, suggests that complementary resources were not available. In particular, the absence of international technology transfers and of a large group of technicians have weakened the ability of Chilean firms to realize productivity growth even in the improved competitive atmosphere. Liberalization, absent efforts to augment techno-

logical skills needed for domestic and foreign markets, may bring more limited benefits than a casual reading of the Asian productivity climb suggests.
Indeed, in Asian nations, production destined for the domestic market was
not subjected to competition until quite late in the process. The critical factors included: export growth and the accompanying transfer of knowledge
from OECD importers; a rapidly growing domestic technological capability
including engineering training and productivity institutes closely tied to industry; technology dissemination efforts; and (at a later stage) technology licensing and the admission of foreign investors who brought new knowledge.

**Exports and Growth in Latin America**

Can the Latin American nations benefit as much from fast growing exports
as did the Asian NICs? The preceding sections have suggested that the following benefits accrued to the Asian NICs as a result of their increased exports and their openness to the international economy:

> • Facilitation of demand management and reduction of the need for
> stop-go policies, which enhanced investment profitability and thus the
> growth rate of capital;
> • The ability to achieve greater learning, since international markets
> permitted a larger cumulative total of production than the domestic market;
> • Greater product specialization and longer production runs, which
> improved productivity;
> • Knowledge transfers obtained from purchasers of NIC exports in
> the OECD countries;
> • A rapid transfer of low-productivity labor from the rural and the
> urban informal sectors to formal manufacturing, which provided a signifi-
> cant, although transitory, boost in the rate of growth of TFP;
> • A greater openness to obtaining technology internationally and the
> more careful exploitation of FDI to achieve technology transfer rather than
> a simple augmentation of investment funds. The interaction of technology
> inflows and local absorptive capacity helped to augment the growth rate of
> total factor productivity.

The first five benefits are greater in economies experiencing a rapid
growth in exports. While all can be realized with slower growth rates than
the 15 percent a year that prevailed in Korea and Taiwan, China, they will
necessarily accrue more slowly with export growth rates of 7 or 8 percent a
year, rates which have been more typical of the Latin American countries

**Table 8.6  Revealed Comparative Advantage in Asian Exports**

| Sector | Hong Kong | | | Korea | | | Taiwan, China | | |
|---|---|---|---|---|---|---|---|---|---|
| | 1965 | 1975 | 1990 | 1965 | 1975 | 1990 | 1965 | 1975 | 1990 |
| Metals | .14 | .21 | .30 | .18 | .69 | 1.35 | .15 | .40 | 1.16 |
| Non-ferrous | .02 | .06 | .04 | .33 | .04 | .09 | .14 | .02 | .15 |
| Textiles | 1.71 | 1.09 | .65 | 3.14 | 2.15 | 1.13 | 1.80 | 1.22 | .88 |
| Nonelec. | .02 | .18 | .50 | .06 | .10 | .53 | .01 | .21 | 1.14 |
| Elect. mach. | .97 | 1.28 | 1.18 | .17 | 1.44 | 1.67 | .95 | 2.20 | 1.57 |
| Trans. equipmt. | .07 | .02 | .02 | .02 | .02 | .28 | .03 | .08 | .27 |
| Prec. instruments | .41 | .50 | 1.05 | .02 | .38 | .39 | .08 | .46 | .75 |
| Clothing | 11.64 | 9.69 | 6.94 | 6.34 | 6.39 | 3.47 | 5.34 | 5.21 | 1.58 |
| Furniture | 1.24 | .60 | .20 | .06 | .24 | .40 | 1.60 | 1.36 | 2.73 |
| Footwear | 3.52 | .83 | .57 | 7.55 | 4.35 | 6.63 | 2.55 | 6.72 | 3.61 |
| Resource-based | .32 | .31 | .43 | 2.18 | .88 | .44 | 2.31 | .75 | .58 |
| Misc. mfg. | 4.02 | 2.98 | 2.75 | 1.21 | 2.08 | 1.60 | 1.63 | 2.30 | 2.05 |

*Source:* Chow and Kellman (1993), tables 2.1–2.3.

over the last decade. Although there has been a recent acceleration of manufactured export growth in some Latin American countries, this growth is still slower than that of the Asian countries in the 1960s and 1970s.

To accelerate this growth in Latin America will require the implementation of macro policies that reduce domestic absorption, increase the relative profitability of exporting, and maintain stability. Getting these basics correct would undoubtedly generate higher rates of export growth. While it seems likely that exports yield some benefits that are not available from domestic sales, these benefits can be obtained at lower rates of growth than the Asian countries experienced. It would not be desirable to attempt the more complex type of export incentives such as export quotas, differentiated interest rates, and other measures used to achieve exceptionally rapid export growth. Moreover, as the Latin countries have typically liberalized considerably more than the Asian countries did, the complex measures necessary to restore neutrality between domestic and foreign sales are less likely to be necessary. Purely macro issues are likely to be of greater significance than was the case in Asia.

If the recent sectoral composition of Latin America exports is maintained, the productivity benefits from accelerated export growth are likely to be less than they were in Asia. In Asia, major early exports were very labor intensive: wigs, sports equipment, inexpensive clothing, and so on. Revealed comparative advantage (RCA) in the Asian superexporters shown in Table 8.6 indicates that in Hong Kong, Korea, and Taiwan, China, textiles (including clothing) and labor-intensive electronics were disproportionally exported as late as 1975, a decade after rapid industrialization had begun in the latter two countries. Indeed, as late as 1990, Korea still exhibited a high RCA in textiles and clothing. While the RCA is not necessarily an indicator of efficiency—subsidized sectors, for example, may be forced to export as a quid pro quo for continuing subsidies—the fact remains that the Asian exporting countries continued to manufacture and export labor-intensive products until quite recently.

In contrast, much of Latin America's RCA in manufactured exports lies in capital and technology-intensive goods (Table 8.7). If this export pattern is maintained, it will have certain negative microeconomic consequences. There will be no impetus for a large-scale transfer of the labor force to the modern manufacturing sector. Relatively few persons will be absorbed in the sector and productivity gains from reallocation of rural labor from the countryside and the urban underemployed will be minimal. Growth in aggregate GDP and the absolute incomes of the currently underemployed will be less than if the export structure were more labor-intensive. Potential conflicts over income distribution will not be muted, nor will the countries derive benefits from the positive feedback effects on education and birth rates—the benefits realized by the Asian NICs as the absolute incomes of those absorbed in the modern sector grew.

Since one often hears that Latin American countries cannot follow the labor-intensive Asian export route because of their high wage structure, it is useful to examine this assertion. Per capita incomes at official exchange-rate conversions, even in the richer Latin American countries, are in the range of 10 to 15 percent of the OECD levels. Assuming that average wages roughly reflect this difference, there is presumably a large opportunity to engage in trade based on different factor endowments.[8]

The absence of a much greater RCA in labor-intensive goods must be due in part to an incentive structure that, as late as 1990, favored capital and technology-intensive sectors. Only this can explain the figures shown in Table 8.7, which indicate that Latin American countries exhibit a much greater RCA in human capital/technology-intensive products than do the OECD countries. Moreover, the Asian NICs, which had much higher wages than Latin America in the 1988–90 period for which the calculations are done, exhibited a much greater RCA for labor-intensive products. Given the

---

[8] Insofar as the Latin American countries are characterized by much greater income inequality than the OECD nations, median wages are likely to be still lower as a percentage of OECD wages.

## Table 8.7  Revealed Comparative Advantage (RCA) in Manufactures by Factor-Intensity Category

| | Latin America | | Industrial Countries | | Industrializing Asia | | Ex–CPEs | |
|---|---|---|---|---|---|---|---|---|
| | RCA | Change from | RCA | Change from | RCA | Change from | RCA | Change from |
| Category | 1988–90 | 1978–80 | 1988–90 | 1978–80 | 1988–90 | 1978–80 | 1988–90 | 1978–80 |
| **Total manufacturing exports** | **1.62** | **0.08** | **1.02** | **0.01** | **1.86** | **-0.82** | **1.21** | **0.04** |
| **Human capital/ technology-intensive:** | **1.49** | **0.44** | **1.04** | **0.01** | **1.18** | **-0.05** | **1.19** | **0.00** |
| Iron and steel | 3.42 | 2.26 | 0.99 | -0.01 | 0.70 | 0.15 | 1.57 | 0.43 |
| Chemical elements and compounds | 1.98 | -0.05 | 1.03 | 0.02 | 0.32 | 0.12 | 0.73 | 0.32 |
| Explosives, pyrotechnic products | 1.61 | -1.36 | 0.90 | 0.11 | 0.19 | -0.12 | 1.11 | -0.83 |
| Rubber manufactures | 1.16 | 0.22 | 1.03 | 0.03 | 0.87 | -0.25 | 0.84 | 0.08 |
| Plastic materials | 1.12 | 0.72 | 1.06 | -0.03 | 0.57 | 0.35 | 0.66 | 0.25 |
| Manufactures of metal, n.e.s. | 1.05 | 0.10 | 1.01 | 0.01 | 0.80 | -0.12 | 1.00 | 0.37 |
| Chemical materials and products, n.e.s. | 0.99 | -0.50 | 1.06 | 0.02 | 0.40 | 0.22 | 0.69 | 0.16 |
| Dyeing, tanning, and coloring materials | 0.91 | -0.21 | 1.06 | 0.03 | 0.33 | 0.09 | 0.89 | -0.29 |
| Plumbing, heating, and lighting equipment | 0.84 | -0.03 | 1.04 | 0.03 | 0.63 | -0.46 | 1.14 | 0.37 |
| Essential oils, perfume materials, etc. | 0.84 | -1.34 | 1.05 | 0.04 | 0.42 | -0.02 | 0.35 | -0.48 |
| Transport equipment | 0.83 | 0.13 | 1.08 | 0.03 | 0.29 | -0.00 | 0.79 | -0.16 |
| Nonelectrical machinery | 0.75 | 0.05 | 1.05 | 0.01 | 0.64 | 0.39 | 1.62 | 0.02 |
| Medicinal and pharmaceutical products | 0.60 | -0.67 | 1.05 | 0.05 | 0.17 | -0.21 | 1.66 | -0.12 |
| Misc. manufactured goods | 0.46 | -0.41 | 0.97 | 0.00 | 1.53 | -0.53 | 0.47 | -0.03 |
| Electrical machinery and appliances | 0.43 | -0.09 | 0.97 | -0.02 | 1.89 | 0.12 | 0.66 | -0.24 |
| Prof., sci., and control. instruments | 0.37 | 0.05 | 1.03 | 0.01 | 0.88 | -0.56 | 0.53 | -0.09 |
| **Unskilled labor-intensive:** | **2.51** | **-0.58** | **0.80** | **-0.03** | **3.38** | **-1.54** | **1.41** | **-0.32** |
| Leather and leather manufactures | 5.50 | -1.91 | 0.88 | 0.08 | 1.02 | 0.65 | 0.54 | 0.30 |
| Footwear | 3.74 | 0.48 | 0.71 | -0.08 | 3.40 | 0.68 | 2.61 | -0.71 |
| Textile yarn and fabrics | 1.14 | -0.60 | 0.85 | -0.05 | 1.78 | -0.21 | 0.97 | 0.16 |
| Travel goods and handbags | 1.10 | -1.64 | 0.72 | 0.05 | 4.54 | -2.91 | 2.02 | 0.38 |
| Clothing | 0.85 | -0.69 | 0.63 | -0.03 | 4.23 | -2.28 | 1.07 | -0.46 |
| Furniture | 0.36 | -0.14 | 1.04 | 0.03 | 0.68 | 0.01 | 1.48 | 0.06 |
| **Natural resource-intensive:** | **1.15** | **-0.09** | **1.00** | **0.04** | **1.91** | **-0.34** | **0.95** | **0.40** |
| Wood and cork products | 1.48 | -0.79 | 0.81 | -0.01 | 3.38 | -0.45 | 1.40 | 0.81 |
| Manufactured fertilizers | 1.22 | 0.37 | 0.95 | 0.01 | 0.68 | -0.55 | 1.04 | 0.46 |
| Nonmetallic mineral manufactures | 1.11 | 0.12 | 0.97 | 0.05 | 0.52 | -0.01 | 0.95 | 0.36 |
| Paper manufactures | 1.07 | 0.14 | 1.08 | 0.01 | 0.30 | 0.07 | 0.26 | 0.04 |
| Mineral tar and crude chemicals | 0.71 | -0.50 | 0.86 | 0.34 | 2.64 | -0.56 | 0.00 | -0.94 |

Note: The totals for the three factor-intensity categories are trade-weighted averages of the individual product divisions, and the total for manufactures is calculated as the trade-weighted average of the three factor intensity categories. The ordering of product divisions within the three categories is based upon the ranking of the product divisions in the Latin American region during 1988-90.
a = Based on regional RCA index values at the 2-digit SITC code level for 1988-90 and changes from 1978-80.
b = Industrializing Asia includes Hong Kong, Singapore, South Korea, Malaysia, Indonesia, Thailand, and the Philippines.
c = The ex-CPEs (centrally planned economies) consist of Hungary, Poland, and Czechoslovakia, due to lack of available data for the remaining countries in this category.
Source: Inter-American Development Bank 1992, p. 204.

relative factor endowments of the three regions, the incentive regime in Latin America must have been skewed towards capital and technology-intensive sectors, a feature that would severely limit some of the productivity gains from exporting even if correct macroeconomic policies were put in place.

The absence of a major contribution from new jobs in exporting towards improving the income of the current rural and urban poor will limit the ability of governments to undertake critical policies, such as reducing subsidies to public enterprises and other demand-reduction policies. In contrast, the growth of modern sector employment in Asia undoubtedly conferred legitimacy on its governments. This favorable feedback effect was important. The East Asians' remarkable policy flexibility in response to the two oil price shocks would not have been achievable without the dramatic prior improvement in employment. Moreover, the Latin American countries have all the more need to achieve such gains in the manufacturing sector given the extraordinarily unequal holding of land in the rural sector, which imposes limits on the extent to which rural consumption can be held down. The simmering rebellion in Chiapas in 1994 and the limits it places on Mexican macroeconomic policy is a good illustration of the dilemmas that may arise. While the primary issue is landholding, a fast growth of export-based, labor-intensive industries could significantly ameliorate the problems.

Exporting is, however, no panacea for accelerating growth. The fundamental challenge is to improve TFP growth. While exports can contribute to this through specialization and affording a faster move along the learning curve, they cannot guarantee that knowledge will be obtained and productively employed. As they promoted exports, the Asian nations simultaneously built up their domestic education base at the primary, secondary, and university levels. In contrast, a number of studies indicate that the Latin American countries have spent little on primary education, and have not emphasized engineering and science at the university level. While greater inflows of technology to Latin America would undoubtedly be desirable, they are unlikely to generate the rates of TFP growth obtained in the Asian nations unless domestic absorptive capacity is improved.

*Howard Pack is Professor of Public Policy and Management at The Wharton School, and Professor of Economics, University of Pennsylvania.*

# Commentary

*Eduardo Bitran and Pablo Serra*

In his careful analysis of East Asia's economic growth, Professor Pack highlights the role of new technology, noting "the unusual emphasis on engineering and science in higher education in the HPAEs." He comments that international trade narrows the gap between the technology levels of late industrializers and more advanced nations; one benefit of increased exports is "exploitation of FDI to achieve technology transfer." As part of their technology strategy, the HPAEs also increased domestic R&D, established science parks, and developed large domestic technology institutions with close connections to industrial firms.

Similar policies have been employed in Chile with some success. Drawing upon our country's experience with technical acquisition and the extensive research on East Asian countries, this comment outlines what we believe to be the basic components of an optimal technology policy for a developing economy. The analysis hinges on Chilean reality, but it could well be extended to other countries with similar traits. Because institutional planning is a key element in technological policy, we propose an institutional design in terms of the market failures that in principle justify government intervention.

Liberalization of the Latin American economies enabled them to reverse their state of stagnation. Abundant natural resources, low salaries, and high exchange rates allowed exports with low technological content to become the main driving force for economic development. The challenge for local entrepreneurs was to develop new markets for their products. This situation forced them to learn how to compete in international markets, undoubtedly a crucial achievement during the period.

However, this first stage of export-oriented growth in Latin America, based on natural comparative advantages, is now showing signs of exhaustion, partly due to its own success. The sustained increase of exports, along with expanded foreign investment, has significantly appreciated local currencies and increased real wages. Furthermore, the export activity based on exploiting natural resources will eventually reach its limits. Thus, in order to diversify and expand their exports, the region's firms must now substantially improve both their productivity and the quality of their goods. If they are to do this effectively, these firms need assistance from public policies that will catalyze and facilitate the technology development of the productive sector.

Many interrelated elements are involved in technology development, but this analysis will focus primarily on policies for strengthening R&D and absorbing external technology. Because macroeconomic conditions strongly influence national policies, however, we will first describe the macroeconomic conditions that favor technology development.

## Macroeconomic Policy

In recent years, the fastest-growing countries have been characterized by macroeconomic stability, liberalization toward international markets, export orientation, an environment favorable to foreign investment, and high internal saving rates. Dahlman (1994) shows, based on the Southeast Asian countries' experience, that these same conditions provide an adequate setting for national technology development. From his analysis, it also follows that absorbing foreign technology is critical for the technology development of nonindustrialized countries, especially smaller ones. The main channels for absorbing foreign technology are direct foreign investment, licensing contracts, and import of capital goods.

Liberalization tends to promote the adoption of new technology through a variety of channels. First, foreign competition makes it necessary to improve the standards of quality and to facilitate the import of capital goods. Second, direct foreign investment is encouraged by certain conditions: economic and social stability, nondiscriminatory rules, expediency in remitting profits, a suitable fiscal policy, and an attractive salary-productivity ratio. A high investment rate, in turn, enables new technologies to be incorporated into productive sectors.

## Technology Policy

While macroeconomic policy establishes a basis for developing a national industrial strategy, certain market imperfections associated with the competitive process of R&D justify the development of a technology policy. Specifically, there are two relevant types of market failure. First, given that knowledge has characteristics of a public good, the individual who develops an innovation cannot appropriate all resulting benefits and profits. Consequently, without state support, investment in R&D is below the socially optimal level. Second, if firms within a particular industry do not share the results of their R&D, they will be duplicating efforts, and some will be operating inside the technology frontier.

Subsidizing R&D in private industry might narrow the gap between social and private returns, but it does not ensure adequate dissemination of innovations, and it requires governmental oversight to ensure that subsidies are not misused. For these reasons, the state may prefer to subsidize the supply of technology. A common approach is to create technology institutes (TIs) and develop within them the technological infrastructure and capabilities to satisfy market demands. However, these institutes have been so removed from the productive sector's problems that their research activities are often completely irrelevant.

Another way to support R&D is by promoting cooperation among firms, either planned in advance (ex ante) or subsequently (ex post). One means of cooperation is to share an innovation with other firms through license contracts. Yet even where a good intellectual property law facilitates operating a market for licenses, problems of information asymmetry and free-riding still limit its efficiency (Katz and Ordover 1990).

Ex ante cooperation occurs when firms agree to share the benefits of their R&D: to mutually grant the licenses they generate or allow their researchers to share knowledge. Research associations are more elaborate forms of cooperation, and can be temporary, for a specific project, or permanent. But because such agreements almost never occur spontaneously, due to high transaction costs, technology policy must encourage collaboration among firms. To this end, the government should create a legal framework and provide appropriate incentives.

Justman and Teubal (1994) point out that effective, long-term R&D has little to do with subsidies; the risks involved are of such magnitude and complexity that they require coordinated efforts. Cooperation among firms reduces uncertainty in many ways: it facilitates product standardization and accelerates the development of an industry of suppliers, which reduces costs. For these reasons, technology policies must emphasize an institutional design that facilitates collaboration among firms.

## Technology Development in Chile

Chilean macroeconomic conditions are favorable for technology development: a climate of stability, with inflation at about 8 percent; a fiscal surplus; equilibrium of external accounts; and a well-functioning institutional framework. Chile's internal saving (28 percent) is now the highest in Latin America, close to East Asian levels, and foreign investment has reached record levels over the last few years.

Despite these favorable macroeconomic conditions, spending on R&D is still relatively low, accounting for approximately 0.8 percent of GDP in

1994. As Chile develops, its expenditure on R&D should increase naturally.[1] The change in the country's economic context, especially its sustained growth over the last decade, allows us to envisage that over the next few years, the main R&D thrust will come from the productive sector.[2] However, the magnitude and effectiveness of private spending in R&D will be strongly influenced by technology policy.

Chilean technological policy, known as the National Innovative System (NIS), responds in very broad terms to the failures of the market in R&D. Its main instruments are the technology institutes, created during the 1960s and 1970s, and the different funds created during the 1980s and 1990s to subsidize the creation of infrastructure and R&D in private companies. Likewise, the government has been concerned with updating the legal framework on intellectual property.[3]

## Institutes

Chile has eleven public technology institutes (TIs) and one semipublic center for technology transfer. Five of the public institutes belong to the Chilean National Development Agency (CORFO).[4] Contributions from companies finance about 43 percent of institutional budgets, with the lowest percentages of private funding corresponding to the CORFO institutes. In response to greater pressure to become self-financing, the TIs have increased their sales of technological services, but they have not yet developed links with the private sector to finance R&D projects.

Because most of the institutes' financing comes from the public budget, incentives to satisfy demands from the productive sector have been

---

[1] In fact, the current investment in R&D represents a strong increase with respect to 1965, when it was only 0.3 percent of GDP.

[2] R&D projects within companies now represent 12 percent of Chile's total R&D, and companies finance about 25 percent of the overall expenditure. The economic conditions prevailing between the 1960s and the mid 1980s in part account for such low spending levels; during periods of economic instability, the main concern of Chilean entrepreneurs was reading the market signals.

[3] In 1991, a new Law on Intellectual Property was enacted, and the country joined the Paris Agreement on Intellectual Property. To modernize the agency responsible for administering intellectual property, the government began operating the Technological Information Patents Service, which makes it possible to gain access to more than six million patents in Europe and the United States. These changes, and the absence of barriers to license contracts, tend to facilitate the acquisition of foreign technology.

[4] One institute belongs to the Ministry of Agriculture, and three others are related to the Ministry of Mining. The remaining institutes are smaller and have few links with the productive sector.

scarce. Likewise, TIs have lacked the autonomy to determine salaries, staff, and incentive schemes for their workers, which has resulted in bureaucratic, inflexible structures. This lack of market orientation among state-operated TIs is common in Latin American countries. Reversing the situation calls for a change in approach and a deep restructuring of these institutions.

*Funds*

Three Chilean national funds finance R&D by subsidizing technology supply (support for scientific and technological capabilities at the TIs and universities) and demand (support for R&D at private companies). FONDECYT, created in 1981 to encourage scientific and technological research, allocates funds through competitive proposals. FONDEF, since 1992, has financed research and infrastructure projects with a high potential of transfer to the productive sector, also on a competitive basis.[5] FONTEC, created in 1992 to encourage technological innovation in the productive sector, uses loans and subsidies directly to finance innovative projects of companies, often working with universities and TIs.

Only about 15 percent of all resources channeled through Chile's science and technology program correspond to R&D subsidies to private companies. If we consider other current transfers that the state makes to the technological institutes and to the universities, the subsidies to technology demand represent less than 5 percent of the resources contributed by the state. For the country's technology effort to yield an adequate economic return, a greater proportion of R&D must be demand-driven and paid for by the beneficiaries.

## Proposed Institutional Framework

If Chilean companies are to increase their productivity and incorporate greater value added into their products, they need to use technology more effectively. The technological infrastructure and the specialized human capital is still insufficient in Chile. Moreover, the greatest part of the technological effort is financed by the state and is unrelated to the needs of the productive sector. For this reason, a great institutional redesign effort must be made so that the public investment in R&D will catalyze the private sec-

---

[5] In order to ensure the relevance of the projects and the transfer of knowledge to the private sector, FONDEF projects must directly involve private companies. The actual participation of the private sector has been limited, however.

tor effort. By expanding private investment, such reforms will allow the same levels of public spending as a percentage of GDP to increase the scope and effectiveness of overall R&D spending.

### Sources of Financing

The proportion of NIS resources devoted to supporting scientific and technological supply should be drastically reduced in favor of mechanisms subsidizing the demand. The subsidies should promote cooperation among companies so as to internalize the externalities of R&D. To attain these objectives, we propose restructuring state spending on R&D along the lines described below.

*Entrepreneurial Councils of Technological Administration.* We propose that entrepreneurial councils for technology administration (ECTAs) be established.[6] These councils would define technology research programs, which would then contract with TIs and universities. The ECTAs would have sufficient professional resources to interpret the needs of associated companies, define R&D programs of collective interest, contract programs with specialized institutions, and serve as a counterpart in these projects, transferring the results to the associated companies. Unlike many European associations that conduct their own research, the ECTAs would have greater flexibility in using the services of institutes, universities, and foreign centers.

The ECTAs would be financed by private firms in the sector, who would either receive tax credit or matching state funds in exchange for their contributions.[7] (To receive tax credit, the consortium of companies should represent a minimum level of industry production or be made up of a minimum number of firms.) In Chile's case, FONTEC could contribute seed capital and ensure that the resources are actually used in R&D. In addition, the state could work with the ECTAs to finance long-term projects, selected through competition. For this purpose, the Fund for Research Projects of Public Interest (FONSIP) was recently created.

ECTA boards of directors would represent the participant companies, thus ensuring that their activities would address the main technological problems of a particular sector. Their scope could extend to other activities, such as cooperating with higher learning centers in training scientists and

---

[6] This plan is similar to a proposal by Romer (1993).
[7] Sweden's associative technological institutes, for example, receive a state subsidy equivalent to the contribution received from private sources.

engineers for the productive sector and obtaining funding for innovative projects.[8] Consequently, these technology councils would decentralize R&D policy to some extent.[9]

The proposed councils bear some similarities to the German research associations, which differ from the German TIs. These associations, promoted by industrial associations, establish research priorities and then fund the laboratories best suited to carry them out. In addition, they are in direct contact with vocational schools. Germany's success in technology development is partly due to the integration of these centers with technical and professional education (Goldman 1994). This idea has been developed in Chile with some success: three new councils are supported by FONTEC, and Fundación Chile has the GTT program, an interesting example of intra-industry cooperation.[10]

*Subsidy for private R&D.* Creating an ECTA does not eliminate the need for innovations within companies. On the contrary, a technology base funded by the ECTAs would encourage competitive research. It would also decrease the size of the direct subsidies needed for companies, because research with a low probability of success would be carried out in association with other firms. There are two ways of encouraging R&D in firms: one is through direct subsidy, and the other is with tax credits. In general, direct subsidies are preferable, for three reasons. First, they make it easier to quantify the cost to society. Second, tax credits are always a source of tax evasion and avoidance. Third, the monitoring problems are greater in the case of tax credits.

Direct subsidies are not free of problems: they carry high transaction costs and require an institution responsible for their administration, as well as a constant evaluation and monitoring of projects. Even more difficult, especially in the case of large companies, is ensuring confidentiality. These problems can be reduced by directly subsidizing some technology expenditures that have been outsourced to accredited institutions and by subsidizing purchases of technological infrastructure (as happens with FONTEC).

---

[8] The financial system, due to a lack of information, does not in general grant loans for R&D activities.

[9] It is difficult for a central agency to determine the requirements of different industries in each of these fields.

[10] Companies in the forestry sector have financed research activities aimed at reducing their production costs, activities which often have commercial applications. Fundación Chile assisted by focusing R&D and obtaining the cooperation of other institutions, primarily universities, to carry out the research.

In these cases, the transaction costs would be reduced by establishing semi-automatic systems for approving the subsidies and by performing a thorough audit of the accredited institutions. Subsidies to internal R&D require adequate prior evaluations, to ensure good use of public resources. However, in some cases the controls could also be reduced through an accreditation system: duly qualified companies—especially those that have been successful in previous projects—would not be required to provide as much information.

*Creating capabilities and precompetitive research.* A system of incentives for exclusively demand-driven R&D does not generate sufficient stimulus for technological scientific research of a precompetitive character, nor does it encourage long-term productive development. The instruments that can promote basic and precompetitive research must be perfected, as outlined below.

*(a) Basic and precompetitive research.* In Chile, the basic instrument is the National Fund for Scientific and Technological Development (FONDECYT), based on peer evaluation. However, peer evaluators often lose their objectivity, especially in a small country. Foreign evaluators are sometimes used, but this too can create problems. Therefore, we propose complementing the peer evaluation system with less subjective indicators, such as the previous publications of the applicant, giving appropriate weight to the prestige of the journal, and special consideration to the articles generated by prior projects. This would provide the correct incentives. Young researchers would participate in an already existing special contest.

*(b) Creating and maintaining scientific and technological capabilities.* FONDECYT operates adequately in areas where there is a critical mass, although it does not really contribute to the development of new areas. Given its method of operating through contests, the allocation of resources is determined by existing capabilities. In fact, only 12 percent of the resources go to engineering. There should exist, then, a second fund aimed at creating capabilities in basic research, especially in areas related to the needs of productive sectors.

In our opinion, the primary task of FONDEF should be to determine the country's science and technology needs and to oversee the meeting of those needs by the universities. To this end, FONDEF should have a program committee made up of scientists, engineers, and outstanding professionals from the productive sector, which in turn could seek the counsel of national and foreign experts.

Likewise, there should be a fund aimed at promoting technological research within the TIs. The institutes must be oriented to solving the technology problems in the productive sectors. To attain this end, part of the financing (e.g., 60 percent) should come from contracts and the selling of services to the productive sector. However, the other part of the financing should not be linked to carrying out commercial projects: TIs lose their long-term view if they are forced to self-finance all their operations.[11]

TIs also need to conduct research that would enable them to anticipate the technology problems of the productive sector. Because the productive sector is less inclined to fund this prospecting activity, a committee of scientists, engineers and business representatives business should develop a long-term program of technology research, considering both the present and future needs of the country. The program would then be assigned through contracts to different institutes.[12]

### Suppliers of Technology

*Technological Institutes.* Here the challenge is to ensure that the activity of the TIs is determined primarily, even though not completely, by market demand. In particular, it is important that the TIs devote greater efforts to absorbing technology from abroad, adapting it to the needs of the country and disseminating it among the producers, instead of carrying out original R&D. While a significant part of TI activities should be financed by the productive sector, FONSIP should be responsible for financing their technological capability. In turn, the ECTAs would probably become their main R&D contractors, while the companies, in all likelihood, would continue to demand their technological services.

The TIs could be financed as follows: 15 percent of the funds would come from the returns on their endowment, contributed initially by the state; 20 percent could be contributed initially by FONSIP, and increasingly by the ECTAs; 30 percent could be financed through R&D contracts with the ECTAs, individual companies, and public agencies that have specific needs (for example, needs for information to carry out their regulatory duties). The remaining 35 percent could come from technological services sold to companies.

It is also necessary to change the legal status of the existing institutes. The TIs should become fully autonomous, with their administration vested

---

[11] This has happened in many research associations in the United Kingdom (Goldman 1994).

[12] FONSIP was recently created for this purpose, as noted earlier.

in a board of directors made up of professionals and researchers of acknowledged status. They would be appointed by the government, entrepreneurial associations and scientific associations.

The policy should favor the creation of new TIs by universities, professional associations, entrepreneurial associations, and private agencies, which would contribute the initial assets. These institutes would be entitled to participate in contracts to create capabilities under the same conditions as the traditional TIs, providing they are nonprofit organizations. Also, new TIs could spin off from those already in existence. Likewise, and to the extent that some technologies develop, technical assistance tasks could be delegated to consulting companies. The new institutes might overlap to some degree, but the prospect of competition would encourage the TIs to increase their efficiency.

*Universities.* The university system employs two-thirds of Chile's researchers, so it is essential to link the universities to the productive centers.[13] This linkage should occur mainly through technology institutes belonging to the universities, and comprised primarily of nonacademic professionals. Without giving up basic research, university researchers could consult with these institutes. In fact, such contact would help university researchers orient their work to the country's needs.[14]

*Eduardo Bitran is Director of the Corporación de Fomento (CORFO) in Santiago, Chile. Pablo Serra is Associate Professor of Economics at the University of Chile.*

[13] In the field of biology, for instance, FONSIP and the Salmon Institute are designing a research program aimed at solving the problems of viral diseases in fish and meeting the needs for genetic improvement in the industry, taking advantage of Chile's excellent research capabilities in biology.

[14] At present, most university research is in basic sciences, with research in engineering put on a lower level. The universities should make an effort to increase the research carried out in various branches of engineering.

# CHAPTER 9

**Beyond Macro and Education Policies**

*Guy Pfeffermann*

In most international comparisons, the East Asian miracle countries stand alone, contrasted not only with Latin America, but with virtually all other developing countries. This suggests that there is something distinctive about the East Asian countries, and that perhaps certain lessons can be applied in other countries which would bring them closer to the stellar performance of the East Asian countries.

Macroeconomic policies have been consistently better in East Asia than elsewhere in the developing world. In particular, the East Asian countries have by and large avoided periods of overvalued exchange rates. There is also consensus about the exceptionally effective educational policies of the Tigers. Taking this for granted, I will focus first on other structural, historical, and institutional facets of development, and return to macroeconomic policies later.

What makes the comparison difficult (and more interesting) is the heterogeneity of the East Asian countries, especially if one includes the Philippines. Latin America is also very heterogeneous, of course. To begin, Table 9.1 presents one of the most striking differences between the more successful East Asian countries and Latin America (and the rest of the developing world).

Two facts are apparent: (a) levels of private investment in five of the seven successful East Asian countries for which data exist were much higher than in Latin America; and (b) public investment was also higher in East Asia, except in the Philippines, Thailand, and, oddly, Korea.

Consistent with the mandate of the International Finance Corporation (IFC), this chapter will focus mainly on private investment, which accounts for well over 60 percent of total investment in both parts of the world. But first let us review some basic differences between the Tigers and Latin America that tend to be subsumed in economic discussions:

**Table 9.1  Investment Levels**
*(As percent of GDP)*

|  | Private Investment | Public Investment |
|---|---|---|
| *Latin America (mostly 1970–92)* | 12.1 | 6.5 |
| Indonesia (1981–92) | 12.5 | 9.7 |
| Korea (1972–92) | 22.3 | 6.8 |
| Malaysia (1970–92) | 17.2 | 10.9 |
| Philippines (1975–92) | 17.5 | 5.9 |
| Singapore (1970–92) | 28.4 | 10.3 |
| Taiwan, China (1970–92) | 13.0 | 11.1 |
| Thailand (1970–92) | 21.1 | 6.9 |
| *East Asia average* | 15.3 | 8.8 |

*Note:* The figures for Latin America are unweighted averages over the period 1970–92.
*Source:* Miller and Sumlinski 1994; for Taiwan, China, government sources.

*The East Asian Tigers (and Japan) had little or no choice of development strategy because of extreme population density and lack of natural resources.*[1] Lack of natural resources exacerbates the foreign exchange constraint and encourages the early development of manufactured exports. The importance of a dynamic manufactured exports sector to long-term development can hardly be overestimated; it provides a constant learning experience and rigorous efficiency tests, as well as rapidly rising demand for increasingly skilled employees. In contrast, in Latin America there was no compelling pressure to break with the colonial pattern—the exploitation of natural resources in a fairly closed economy. As for population density, the following table contrasts the Tigers to a group of three Latin American countries (Argentina, Chile, and Mexico) whose combined GDP is about the same ($800 billion in 1993) as that of the Tigers.[2]

The differences in population density across the two regions are striking: Even two of the smallest Latin American countries, Honduras and Suriname, are larger in surface area than Korea.

---

[1]Density is identified as a critical distinguishing characteristic of Korea, Hong Kong, Singapore, and Taiwan, China, by Grilli and Riedel (1993). But circumstances were different for the later wave of "Cubs" (Indonesia, Thailand, Malaysia). See Auty (1993): "The new evidence suggests that not only may resource-rich developing countries fail to benefit from a favorable endowment, they may actually perform worse than less well-endowed countries" (p. 1).
[2] *World Development Report 1995.*

**Table 9.2  Density Indicators**

|  | Population /sq. mile | GDP/sq. mile (US$ thousands) |
|---|---|---|
| Korea | 445 | 3,341,727 |
| Taiwan, China | 582 | 6,024,180 |
| Singapore | 2,800 | 55,153,000 |
| Hong Kong | 5,800 | 89,997,000 |
| *Average* | 2,407 | 38,628,977 |
| Mexico | 46 | 175,420 |
| Argentina | 12 | 92,373 |
| Chile | 18 | 57,707 |
| *Average* | 25 | 108,500 |

*Source:* World Bank data.

*East Asia's colonial experience may have much to do with the differences.* Koreans lived under Japanese rule for two generations. Many of the elements of Japanese society were transplanted to this colony, including a rigorous educational system, a largely meritocratic civil service, and industrial knowhow. The architects of reform were thoroughly conversant with Japanese culture and institutions. The same is true to some extent for Manchuria, but not for Taiwan, China, where the Chinese Nationalists moved in after the Japanese left.[3] Likewise, Singapore and Malaysia inherited many British administrative institutions, and Hong Kong is a British colony to this day.[4] In contrast, the Spanish and Portuguese left a legacy of institutions and attitudes that were, to put it mildly, not conducive to the conquest of world markets.[5]

*In the East Asian countries, the overseas Chinese act as kind of economic turbocharger.*[6] Economic power in East Asia is concentrated largely in the hands of Chinese businesses, but political power is quite distinct: this separation creates checks and balances. In Latin America, political and economic power are traditionally in the same hands, leading more readily to exploitation, rent-seeking and skewed income distribution.

---

[3] The educational system prior to that time had been patterned after the Japanese system.

[4] But similar institutions don't seem to have been conductive to rapid growth in other parts of the developing world.

[5] This, of course, applies to the Philippines as well.

[6] This begs the question, however, why the overseas Chinese community has only been able to act as "turbocharger" during the past ten to fifteen years in the larger East Asian countries. Perhaps liberalization and globalization were not sufficiently advanced earlier on.

*After World War II, the Tigers were of enormous strategic importance to the United States.* Korea and Taiwan, China, benefited from massive aid (which became increasingly conditional on good economic policies) and very favorable export market conditions. In contrast, the Mann report on Latin America, produced during the Nixon administration, said of Chile that its only strategic significance to the United States was agreement on the yellow-fin tuna catch and annual joint naval exercises.

*Economic progress thus had military and political significance for Taiwan, China and Korea.* Quite clearly these countries were threatened by hostile powers, and both the elites and the population realized that survival required all-out economic efforts over long periods. No such pressure existed in Latin America.

Turning now to private sector development, I will first contrast Latin America and East Asia, and then challenge the validity of the contrast. Finally, I will use a conceptual framework revolving around the notion of policy credibility to try to reconcile the apparent contradictions.

### Thesis: Latin American Institutions are Bad

The institutional deficiencies that plague Latin America are more noticeable now that most Latin American governments are shedding responsibilities by way of privatization. Moises Naím has vividly illustrated these problems:

> Market reforms have created an overwhelming, mostly unprecedented demand for public regulation. When telephone or electric power companies were in the public sector, governments felt little pressure to develop an effective regulatory framework and a competent cadre of public regulators to oversee their operations. Privatization, however, creates an immediate need for such public services. The stock market can be liberalized with the stroke of a pen. Building the equivalent of the U.S. Securities and Exchange Commission takes much longer—especially since an effective competition policy and reliable antitrust agencies and courts were never a top priority under the state-centered, import substitution industrialization policies....
>
> Institution building is inherently a cumbersome process whose complexity, in this case, is amplified by the lack of experience, trained personnel, and financial resources as well as by the general weakness of the state in Latin America.[7]

---

[7] Naím (1993), p. 147.

Or, about Venezuela:

One of the factors which may be contributing most to the creation of clans and other mutual support and protection networks in Venezuela is the profound state of corruption and inefficiency of our judicial system. It is no exaggeration to say that for the majority of purposes required by society the judicial system does not exist in practice. Going before a tribunal in order to resolve a conflict or to enforce a contract implies such costs, delays and risks that this is done only when the amounts at stake are large enough to justify the risks of making contact with the opaque and unpredictable world of Venezuelan justice....

Hence, the difficulty in using the judicial system in economic transactions has forced people to have recourse to extra-economic and extra-juridical factors in order to move forward the complex transactions which are normal today in any economy....[8]

Others have voiced similar criticisms. Here are quotes from private sector assessments made by IFC and the World Bank:

### Uruguay

Government red tape is excessive even by Latin American standards.... Lack of coordination among different government agencies causes extensive duplication of administrative requirements. Most affected are the larger firms and the manufacturing and transport sectors, particularly exporting firms. For export-oriented firms, the cost is estimated at 2.3 percent of sales value.

### Ecuador

As a result of risky and costly government regulations and interventions, the private sector has developed poorly and slowly, resulting in slow growth.

These complaints are reflected in statements by Latin American businessmen:

---

[8] Naím et al. (1989), pp. 510–11 (author's translation).

"Regulations in all areas are completely unclear, so that the specific official assigned to a case can virtually do whatever he likes"

"Every small deviation delivers you into the discretionary hands of bureaucrats" (Guatemala)

"The real power of tax officials is that they can close your business for 2-3 days without much explanation" (Argentina)

"Your institution has much more destructive power than the Shining Path [terrorists]. Whereas the Shining Path paralyzes some industries for a couple of days or weeks, your institution achieves the same effect for nearly the total of the productive industry, and for years" (letter by a Peruvian entrepreneur to the licensing authorities).[9]

Judicial reform is now considered a development priority by multilateral lending institutions. A recent World Bank research proposal focuses on the judicial system and economic performance, in an attempt to gauge the costs of poor enforcement.[10]

Enforcement is also crucial to foreign direct investors when dealing with respect for intellectual property rights. Recent research by Edwin Mansfield (1994), based on responses from about 100 U.S. multinational corporations, shows that Latin American countries may be suffering from inadequate enforcement in this area.[11] The following table shows the respective percentages of corporations whose executives believe that weak intellectual property right protection precludes (a) investment in joint ventures, (b) transfer of the most recent or best technology to fully owned subsidiaries, and ( c) licensing. Mansfield found a statistically significant relationship between U.S. direct investment in a particular industry in a specific developing country during 1989–92, and an index of the perceived weakness of intellectual property protection.[12]

---

[9] Cited in Borner, Brunetti, and Weder (1995).
[10] See Sherwood, Shepherd, and Marcos de Souza (1993).
[11] See Mansfield (1994), whose research is currently being extended to European and Japanese MNCs.
[12] The relationship obtains if one holds a country's GDP constant and recognizes the special position of Mexico.

**Table 9.3  U.S. MNC Responses to Intellectual Property Rights Protection in Latin America**
(Percentage of corporations surveyed)

| | Joint ventures | Too weak to permit Transfer of best/most recent technology to subsidiaries | Licensing | |
|---|---|---|---|---|
| Argentina | 18 | 18 | 22 | |
| Brazil | 32 | 28 | 39 | |
| Chile | 19 | 21 | 21 | |
| Mexico | 22 | 20 | 28 | Overall |
| Venezuela | 18 | 20 | 24 | average |
| Average | 22 | 21 | 27 | 23 |

Source: Mansfield 1994.

The same institutional weakness is apparent in some major Latin American countries in banking supervision. A recent case in point is Venezuela's banking collapse, as the following comments from the *New York Times* illustrate:

"Venezuela's $ 6.1 billion bailout represents 11 percent of GNP and 75 percent of the budget. Banco Latino had 1.2 million depositors, about 10 percent of the country's adult population. Free interest rates were adopted in 1989, but banking supervision was not adopted until 1994."

"There was absolutely no supervision... The regulators weren't trained. They didn't have a budget."

"Venezuela has no tradition of punishing white-collar crime."[13]

Mario Vargas Llosa, at the time his presidential campaign in Peru was going well, criticized the attempted nationalization of commercial banks. "The main conflict is not between the rich and the poor, but between the state and the people," he stated, and his Peruvian audience cheered wildly. It is hard to imagine such a statement eliciting the same reaction from crowds in Seoul, Singapore, Hong Kong, or Taiwan, China.

---

[13] *New York Times,* May 16, 1994, pp. A1 and D3.

## Antithesis: The Picture Is Not So Clear

Turning to East Asia, we find a very heterogeneous set of countries including Myanmar, Laos, and the Philippines. Some of them have a strong civil service and solid institutions, but others do not —particularly if we include Mainland China among the miracle countries (World Bank 1993a).

For example, Thailand has a poorly coordinated bureaucracy and a rather poor judiciary. And regarding Indonesia's legal system, Gray (1991) has written:"The way legal processes are handled in developing countries such as Indonesia has little to do with the way the formal legal system operates...." She concludes: "Legal development may be a major constraint to economic development." A businessman puts it more bluntly: "Courts are very corrupt.... The party who pays more will win the case almost regardless of the legal situation.... Written contracts do not mean a thing. That's why we cannot expand on a larger scale.... You have to build on trust instead of courts."[14]

Just as in Latin America, business people have developed bypass mechanisms to make up for costly or dysfunctional state institutions. As Singapore's Minister of Information said in an interview:

> "Investment and trading conditions in China are very complicated, with a weak legal system and unsettled frameworks for investments and currency exchange.... China has never been a civilization with a tradition of the rule of law above the rule of men.... The overseas Chinese... are relatively untroubled by the absence of legal and accounting framework..."[15]

About Taiwan, China, PT De of San Sun Hats has this to say:

> "In the United States, everything has rules and regulations, and you just follow the rules, and it's easy. In Taiwan, China, even if the light is red, somebody can get through it. If it's green, there still aren't rules to tell you how to go."[16]

---

[14] See Gray (1991).
[15] *The Economist*, November 27, 1993.
[16] See Kao (1993).

**Table 9.4  U.S. MNC Responses to Intellectual Property Rights Protection in East Asia**
*(Percentage of corporations surveyed)*

|  | | Too weak to permit | | |
| --- | --- | --- | --- | --- |
|  | Joint ventures | Transfer of best technology to subsidiaries | Licensing | |
| Hong Kong | 17 | 18 | 20 | |
| Indonesia | 28 | 23 | 31 | |
| Singapore | 19 | 14 | 20 | |
| Korea | 23 | 26 | 29 | |
| Taiwan, China | 28 | 27 | 37 | Overall |
| Thailand | 31 | 33 | 38 | average |
| *Average* | 24 | 24 | 29 | 26 |
| *Latin American Average* | 22 | 21 | 27 | 23 |

A recent article about privatization in Taiwan, China[17] mentions "officials interfering in the privatization process" as one of the main obstacles. This does not agree with the stereotype of extremely effective civil servants dedicated to the implementation of public policy.

As for Korea:

> An April 1994 business survey by the Korea Institute for Industrial Economics and Trade revealed that 71 percent of companies polled admitted that they still "donated" money to local public offices in order to secure business or to smooth their way through the maze of government regulations.[18]

Korea and Taiwan, China share other Latin American institutional weaknesses. To see how the East Asian countries rate in the judgment of U.S. multinational executives, we return to Edwin Mansfield's (1994) findings (Table 9.4). Interestingly, the East Asian countries are judged to be slightly worse than the Latin American ones. Until now it has been assumed that the East Asian countries have done much better than Latin America.

---

[17] See Liu (1993), pp. 36-42.
[18] See Paisley (1994), p. 50.

**Table 9.5  Long-Term Growth Indicators**
*(Annual average percent, 1900-1987)*

|  | GDP per capita growth | GDP growth |
|---|---|---|
| Japan | 3.1 | 4.3 |
| Taiwan, China | 2.8 | 5.1 |
| Brazil | 2.4 | 4.8 |
| Korea | 2.4 | 4.2 |
| Colombia | 1.9 | 4.2 |
| Mexico and Peru | 1.6 | |
| Thailand and Chile | 1.5 | |
| Argentina | 1.1 | |
| Indonesia | 1.0 | |

*Source:* Maddison (1989), Table 1.2.

In Table 9.5, very long-term growth trends, as estimated by Angus Maddison (1989), show that the difference between East Asia and Latin America is not entirely clear-cut.

To complicate the story further, it is often assumed that Latin American institutions pertaining to business are weak. However, in some areas Latin American institutions are as good as or even better than East Asian ones. Securities market regulation is probably better in some Latin American and Caribbean countries than in some East Asian countries. For example, Chile's regulatory regime is quite good, and Brazil's has few problems. In contrast, Indonesia's market regulation is fairly weak and Malaysia only recently established a securities commission.

Chile has also been a leader in developing rational and effective institutional frameworks for private services such as electricity distribution and telephones. Several other Latin American countries have followed suit. Finally, Chile has pioneered private pension fund development in Latin America, laying the foundation for development of a long-term securities market.

### Synthesis: Good Policies plus Credibility?

What, then, might explain the much higher levels of private investment in East Asia, even in countries such as Indonesia and Thailand, where state institutions such as the judiciary are weak and corruption is part of everyday life?[19]

---

[19] It has been argued that massive Japanese foreign direct investment is a surrogate for planning and institutional backbone in the case of Thailand.

Recent work by Borner, Weder, and Brunetti (1995) uses a conceptual framework based on the concept of policy credibility—the degree to which economic agents believe that the policy environment relevant to doing business will not change abruptly for the worse. Credibility is the converse of uncertainty.

An entrepreneur who had worked for MNCs expressed the concept as follows: "Do you want to know the crucial difference between Indonesia and Brazil? In Brazil I would run into my office every morning and hastily scan the newspaper headlines to check whether some new rule or policy had been issued which could destroy our market. In Indonesia no such thing could ever happen, the general thrust of policies is known and the government's commitment to follow them is completely credible—here I don't even read the newspapers."[20]

In an earlier paper, the same authors made an analogy with soccer: "An optimum rule doesn't by itself ensure a good game; the missing ingredient is the firm belief by the players that the rule is stable, its enforcement constant, and the process for creating or changing rules, predictable." Low credibility, they wrote, can take several forms: "At the level of enterprises, institutional uncertainty [can mean]: (i) unpredictability of government intervention; or (ii) lack of enforcement of private contracts." Where there is low credibility, even positive changes in government policy may fail to elicit a positive private sector response: "If rights could be enforced simply by issuing a decree, it would also be possible to cancel them with a stroke of the pen."[21]

Interviews with business executives from 28 developing countries proved/showed that an indicator of credibility constructed to reflect expectations about the reliability of rules and policies is a robust determinant of GDP growth.[22] Ten of the 28 countries are in Latin America and East Asia. Table 9.6 ranks these countries according to growth performance and credibility.

Of course, the period covered in Table 9.6 coincided with Latin America's "lost decade." Now that some Latin American countries have been growing more rapidly, it would be interesting to update the interviews to the 1990s, and to include Colombia, whose growth performance has been exceptionally good by Latin American standards.

---

[20] Borner, Brunetti, and Weder (1993).
[21] Borner, Weder, and Brunetti (1991).
[22] Brunetti and Weder (1993). Of course policies have to be reasonably good. If policies are terrible, credibility will do little to stimulate long-term growth.

**Table 9.6  Growth and Credibility, 1981–90**

|         | Growth    | Credibility |
|---------|-----------|-------------|
| *High*  | Thailand  | Singapore   |
|         | Singapore | Malaysia    |
|         | Indonesia | Thailand    |
|         | Malaysia  | Indonesia   |
| *Medium*| Chile     | Chile       |
|         | Bolivia   | Bolivia     |
|         | Guatemala | Venezuela   |
| *Low*   | Venezuela | Peru        |
|         | Argentina | Argentina   |
|         | Peru      | Guatemala   |

*Source:* Borner, Brunetti and Weder 1995.

If there is a strong association between credibility and growth, how can credibility be "anchored"? We are talking essentially of means to minimize the risk that governments will change the institutional and legal framework in which businesses are operating. Borner, Weder and Brunetti distinguish three "credibility anchors": reputation, openness and participation, and checks and balances.[23]

Some examples of reputational anchors are: the influence of Thailand's king, who has played a major role in ensuring that frequent changes in government, including more frequent military coups than in any major Latin American country, did not materially affect the institutional environment for business; or the military governments of Brazil and Chile, seeking to legitimize their power by fostering economic growth. Reputation takes time to build, but can be destroyed overnight. The private sector sanction against wanton changes in legislation in a closed economy is withdrawal, a phenomenon documented by Hernando de Soto and other analysts of the informal sector.

The second anchor, openness to trade and capital flows, is more credible, especially when cemented in international agreements such as

---

[23] Corruption too can be viewed from the point of view of credibility. East Asian corruption is highly "credible" in the sense that what you pay for, you get. In contrast, in Africa, for example, you may pay and not get anything in return. In Russia you do not even know whom to pay: i.e., credibility is zero. In Indonesia, concern about corruption has risen in recent years because "the price" went up and/or delivery deteriorated. Where to place Latin America on this scale is unclear, but it seems that the credibility of corruption is not as high as in East Asia.

NAFTA. This anchor takes fewer years to be credible than "reputation" and is harder to destroy. While reputation can induce investment, trade openness is necessary for efficient investment and competitive firms. Here the private sector sanction to policy reversal is exit, most notably in the form of capital flight.[24]

The most advanced type of anchor is found mainly in industrialized countries: participation through a well-established political process characterized by checks and balances.[25] Here sanctions normally take the form of voice rather than exit.[26]

The three anchors are not mutually exclusive, and Chile, for example, has moved successfully from reputation to openness to participation.

While credibility is positively associated with investment, it is also significantly correlated with per capita growth if we control for investment, so there are other important channels through which higher credibility translates into higher economic growth. This is due to the fact that government discretion not only reduces investment, but also distorts the structure of investment and economic activity. Faced with a discretionary government, agents are likely to engage in costly ways to protect their returns or to divert resources into areas where expropriation is more difficult. Quantitative analysis suggests that this may be an important effect.[27]

Budget deficits and inflation have also undermined credibility by creating policy instability (e.g., changing tax regimes, changing indexation rules). Indeed, poor macroeconomic policies are probably one of the main determinants of low credibility.

## Conclusion

What, if anything, can Latin American or other developing countries borrow from the East Asian miracle economies, besides their excellent macroeconomic and education policies? Very few specific policies and institutions can be transplanted, especially those that have evolved in a specific historical context. So, for example, the world-conquering conglomerates of Korea grew under circumstances totally alien to the development of the Latin

---

[24] Openness to foreign direct investment is very important. Just as Mexico has been "importing credibility" from the U.S. by joining NAFTA, massive Japanese foreign direct investment is a way of "exporting Japanese credibility." Likewise, massive US aid to Korea and Taiwan, China in the 1950s and 1960s could be viewed as "exporting US credibility."

[25] The separation of political power and business power noted in the case of the overseas Chinese community is arguably a form of checks and balance.

[26] The concepts of exit, voice, and loyalty are developed in A.O. Hirschman (1970).

[27] Paraphrased from Brunetti and Weder (1993).

American "defensive" conglomerates, which aimed to reduce the risk of state intervention in any particular line of activity. Likewise, the growth of subsidized exports on a massive scale is no longer feasible. Nor would the regimentation of civil society and the suppression of labor movements which characterized Korean and Taiwanese industrial development during the Cold War be tolerated in today's world.

Where first-rate institutions exist, they are obviously conducive to rapid growth. But even East Asian countries with weak institutions (e.g., Indonesia and Thailand) have done remarkably well thanks in part to the existence of a large overseas Chinese community that has acted as a "turbocharger." For Latin America, in the absence of such a turbocharger, efforts to improve institutions in critical areas are clearly important. The Chilean example shows the way: sound policies plus institutional strengthening, in accord with the "new Washington consensus" (Williamson 1994). Strengthening institutions in areas such as securities market and banking supervision or the regulation of private infrastructure businesses is essential for economic progress.

In recent years Latin American countries have been cutting down on public investment, privatizing, and enlisting the help of nongovernment organizations to administer poverty alleviation programs. These policies all reduce the burden placed on the state. But a small state is not necessarily an effective one. Governments, like people, can diet and exercise or just diet. Ideally, the state should be small and effective and focus on setting and enforcing the rules of the game, and on doing those things the private sector will not do, particularly in the social sectors. But improvements in state effectiveness may take many years.

Indeed, Latin American government institutions will never be similar to those of Korea, Japan, or Taiwan, China. To follow the East Asian model, Latin America would have needed to start forty years ago. Therefore, discussions of East Asian industrial policy are largely beside the point. Even if one believes that skillful industrial policies can accelerate growth in East Asia, no Latin American government could pull off this feat. It follows that open, market-driven systems offer the best hope for Latin America. Credibility may be one of the essential characteristics of the East Asian miracle, and credibility can be established even in less than ideal institutional frameworks.

*Guy Pfeffermann is Director of the Economics Department and Economic Adviser, International Finance Corporation.*

# Commentary

*John Shilling*

The paper by Guy Pfefferman passes quickly over differences between the two regions in stability of macroeconomic policy and emphasis on education. These are critical factors in explaining their differences in performance. Even though these factors are addressed in more detail elsewhere, it is hard to separate them from the issues discussed in this paper.

Latin American countries have managed good performance only when they were able to control macroeconomic stability, as in Chile and Colombia. The paper acknowledges this when discussing the credibility and predictability of government policy, which implies macroeconomic stability. Credibility and predictability are useful concepts that deserve more attention in policy analysis, and the paper does well to raise them.

As for the question of education, there is increasing evidence that human capital is the most important component of a country's total capital stock, and the largest component in the more developed, modern economies. So in comparing investment levels, it is hard to justify overlooking investment in human capital. If human capital were to be included in Table 9.1, for example, the differences that appear might be more consistently favorable to East Asia, which would help resolve some of the author's concerns about the lack of clear distinctions in investment rates. Investment in human capital should be regarded as a policy variable under the control of Latin American governments. Given their much longer history of independence than most East Asian countries, they have fewer excuses for not having pursued education more vigorously, particularly now.

One further omission from the comparisons of the two regions deserves mention: income distribution. Most studies of East Asian success note the relatively equal distribution of income and assets at the beginning of the period of accelerated growth. This continues to a large extent as these countries become richer. Indeed, some analysts explain the entire East Asian miracle on this basis, and dismiss the rest of the World Bank's study (1993a). That probably goes too far, but the point is important and needs to be emphasized, particularly since income distribution in Latin America needs to be improved. Interestingly, the East Asian country with the poorest growth record in the past quarter century, the Philippines, is among the worst in income distribution and highest in social tensions. Relatively good income distribution has reduced class tensions in many other East Asian countries, and has given the citizens of these countries a real stake in participating in the growing economies.

Turning now to some of the direct comparisons, it is true that the countries of East Asia are a heterogeneous lot, as are the Latin American ones, and that there is no single East Asian road to riches. Each country has followed different policies dictated by its own circumstances and the external environment at the time it began to enter the world export markets and experience rapid growth. Clearly, investment rates were higher on average in East Asia, as the paper shows, although (at the regional level of aggregation) the distinction between public and private investment is not terribly useful, since there is a lot of variance across countries as to whether the government or the private sector undertakes certain investments. That distinction is becoming even fuzzier for many infrastructure projects because of the efforts of many emerging market economies to increase the private sector's role in financing power, roads, and so on.

Along with high investment rates—and our data show them on a rising trend in most East Asian countries—there have been very high domestic saving rates in these countries. In fact, the savings-investment gaps in East Asia have been smaller than net foreign capital inflows, and reserves have accumulated. Savings have not been so buoyant in Latin America, and this may account for some of the difference in performance. Dependence on foreign capital, as indicated by the relatively high level of foreign debt in Latin America and the hangover from the debt crisis of the past decade, lends some credence to this hypothesis. Foreign saving is less dependable than domestic saving as a basis for continued growth, and is decidedly not sustainable.

The paper seems to infer that East Asian countries had no choice of development strategy because the region lacks national resources. Yet Indonesia and Malaysia are rich in natural resources, and other countries are not so land poor as Table 9.2 indicates. Agricultural exports—which are relatively land intensive—were major factors in the early growth of Thailand and Malaysia, for example. It is more accurate to say that the East Asian countries made different choices about their development strategies. They did not adhere to a colonial pattern of development, as Latin America apparently did. This is surprising, since Latin American countries earned their independence a century earlier than did most of East Asia (Japan, Thailand, and China excepted). East Asian countries flirted with the extended import-substitution model of Latin America for a while, but then abandoned it, as Latin American countries are now doing. Perhaps, in light of the choices that East Asia has made, policy flexibility and pragmatism are also important elements of the policy regime, in addition to consistency and credibility. For those who believe that the East Asian countries had no choice, I refer the reader to World Bank studies of South Korea in the late 1950s. These studies conclusively determined that Korea would remain underdeveloped for many years and would probably not exceed the canonical growth rate of 5 percent a year. So much for the proficiency of World Bank projections.

Regarding the turbocharger hypothesis, it is undeniable that the Chinese have been a dynamic element in many of these economies, although not in Japan or Korea. In fact, the vast majority of the population in several of these economies is Chinese—in China, Taiwan (China), Hong Kong (about to be China), and Singapore. However, this thesis sounds a little like the Protestant ethic, which was used in the past to explain growth in Northern Europe and North America, or the role of the Catholic church, to which some attribute the lack of growth in Southern Europe and Latin America. It would be more useful to focus on the characteristics of hard work, saving, risktaking, and cooperation, which have contributed to the high growth rates in East Asia and are now contributing to growth in some Latin American countries. Latin Americans have not a hope in the world of becoming Chinese, nor would I expect many to become Protestants. But they can learn to work hard, save, take risks, and cooperate. These are important lessons that can be replicated.

The strategic importance of the early Asian Tigers and Japan is clear, which is why these countries benefited from substantial U.S. assistance. Aid levels have not been as significant in Latin America, although the region has enjoyed substantial inflows of private capital—which many Latin Americans think is a mixed blessing. But here again, we must look at the variety of East Asian experience. The ASEAN nations were less strategically important than Latin America, particularly after the Vietnam war. And it would be hard to argue that China and Indochina have been anything but a strategic headache to the United States—for a variety of different reasons.

U.S. policy toward Latin America has been different than toward Asia. It would be useful to have a little more explanation as to why this is an important factor in Latin America's economic development, and how U.S. policy might be changed to produce better results.

The discussion of the quality of institutions is most interesting, in terms of both the comparison at hand and the more fundamental question of the role of government in the development process. The defects of governments in Latin America are no different from those in East Asia.

Does that mean that government is irrelevant, if not noxious, to development, and best cast aside? Not without a great deal of risk. The paper's real contribution is the analysis of the credibility of governments. Governments need both sound policy and credibility in applying that policy. This is not an argument to weaken government; it is an argument to create strong and effective government. It is increasingly clear that the role of government as we move into the twenty-first century is not to engage in production or commercial activities, but to establish and enforce the rules of the game for markets to function effectively. The complaints of businessmen and researchers cited in the paper attest to the fact that government is a major problem when it does not establish these rules and enforce them consistently.

The deficiencies cited on intellectual property rights are but one facet of this problem, and perhaps not the most critical for promoting the early stages of rapid growth. Economies can survive without Western contract rules for some period, as long as there are comparable local practices—perhaps extended family ties—to ensure that agreements are respected.

It is instructive to note that the economies in transition in East Asia have made it a priority to establish the structure of commercial law and a supporting legal system. The World Bank has provided loans and extensive technical assistance to countries in this regard, as have other institutions. Other countries have also recognized that sustained market-based development, particularly extended development of capital markets, can take place only in the context of a well-defined and consistently enforced legal system. It would also be interesting to see comparisons of the effectiveness of governing institutions in other areas. The East Asian Miracle study looked at the role of interventions explicitly to promote economic development and found mixed results. A little intervention seems to help, if it is well applied, but not too much. That study did not go into the quality and strength of institutions in the more general sense that this paper proposes. The study did note, however, that governments in East Asia have accepted responsibility for improving the well-being of the population at large and have generally acted on that obligation, whatever their other failings. One wonders how Latin America would score on this criterion.

I therefore agree with the key point of the paper that good policies are important, but only if consistently applied by credible governments. This implies strong institutions staffed by capable administrators who understand what government should and should not do. Governments should be small but effective, as the paper puts it so succinctly. I like this formulation for several reasons. First, it does not rely on any deus ex machina to turbocharge an economy. Effective government can be achieved in any country, from Botswana to Chile to Singapore. It takes application, dedication, and common sense—characteristics to which any nation or economy can reasonably aspire. It does take some time to build effective government out of these bricks, but it can be done. Second, it can be done at any time. It does not rely on the special conditions that existed for the early East Asian Tigers, as the rest of East Asia and other countries are demonstrating.

The kinds of policies and the range of economic decisions needed to achieve rapid growth do change over time, but the essence of effective government does not. With the growing amount of private capital seeking productive use in countries around the world, effective government is increasingly important. And finally, I like the basic idea of good government. It provides the fundamental order and stability that are needed to enjoy the many higher achievements of human civilization beyond economics—science, the arts, philosophy.

---

*John Shilling is Economic Advisor, East Asia and Pacific Division, the World Bank.*

# CHAPTER 10 The Payoffs from Economic Reforms

*Vinod Thomas and Jisoon Lee*

Economic reforms are in progress all over the world. In each of the last two decades, more than a dozen countries have launched major reforms. The most dramatic of these has been the transition toward markets in the former socialist economies. Almost all developing countries are in the process of becoming more closely integrated with the rest of the world.

Rapid and sustained economic growth in the East Asian reformers—such as Korea, Thailand, Malaysia, Indonesia, and Taiwan, China—as well as the strong performances of Chile, New Zealand, Spain, and Portugal, have demonstrated the benefits of reforms. In the transition economies of Poland, the Czech Republic, several Central Asian countries, and Vietnam, reform is bringing beneficial results. China has achieved outstanding growth in the last fifteen years. But the experience of nations such as Mexico, Venezuela, Brazil, and Argentina over the past two decades shows the difficulties of pushing forward a reform agenda. Others such as Russia, Romania, and Bulgaria are struggling with problems of unfinished reforms. Furthermore, the long-term African experience has been disappointing overall.

In light of these diverse experiences, what lessons can we learn for successful reform programs and strategies? Which is better, the rapid implementation of a comprehensive program or the gradual implementation of sequential reforms? Are there necessary preconditions for economic reforms to succeed?

## Framework to Assess Economic Reforms

Economic reforms purport to change fundamentally and permanently the way economic activities are organized, coordinated, and regulated. Their aim is to improve the workings of the economy so that more people can experience a sustained increase in economic well-being.

The success or failure of a reform package can be evaluated using a cost-benefit analysis. Let the costs and benefits of economic reforms that accrue in period t be denoted, respectively, by $C_t$ and $B_t$. For simplicity, we assume linearity of the utility function, so that success or failure can be viewed by the net present value criteria, given by:

$$NPV_t = p \left[ \sum_{k=s}^{T_1} \frac{B_{t+k}}{(1+r)^k} \right] - \sum_{k=m}^{T_2} \frac{C_{t+k}}{(1+r)^k}$$

where $NPV_t$ = net present value in time period $t$, $p$ = the probability of success of the reform package, $t + s$ = period from which benefits start to accrue, $t + T_1$ = period when benefits cease to accrue, $t + m$ = period from which costs start to accrue, and $t + T_2$ = period when costs cease to accrue. Here $r$ is a discount rate to convert the future stream of costs and benefits into present values.

Let $t$ be the period when reforms are introduced. Because costs usually begin to accrue immediately and cease to accrue after a finite period of time, $m$ typically equals zero, and $T_2$ is a finite number. On the other hand, benefits usually begin to accrue somewhat later than costs, so $s$ is typically larger than $m$. Benefits and costs can occur simultaneously for some time, although costs cease to accrue earlier than benefits do. Benefits from successful reforms typically accrue indefinitely, so $T_1$ would be a very large number. We measure benefits by the improvements in economic performance made possible as a result of the introduction of reform measures.

The criteria inform us that the net present value of economic reforms becomes larger as: (i) the probability of the reforms' success increases; (ii) the annual flow of benefits increases; (iii) benefits begin to accrue sooner or continue to accrue longer; (iv) the annual flow of costs decreases; (v) costs cease to accrue sooner; and/or (vi) the discount rate decreases. These considerations are interrelated. For example, if investors' confidence in the reform package could be increased, it would make the period during which costs accrue shorter, raise the probability of success, and reduce the discount rate. How to achieve these results is, of course, the crucial question.

## Country Experiences

*East Asia.* East Asia's ability to establish credibility based on reform programs is legendary. This credibility, in a somewhat circular argument, rests on these countries' track records in economic policy. Korea and Malaysia, for example, by staying the course year after year, have been able to build up investor confidence. Macroeconomic difficulties did occur at times, but they were swiftly addressed. For example, Korea's inflation rate hovered around 20 percent in the late 1970s as a result of central bank financing of heavy and chemical industries and government purchase of food grains. Malaysia's fiscal deficit approached 20 percent of GDP during 1981–82. In both cases, prompt actions restored stability. Such experience raised the probability of success of new measures partly because investors now believe in these countries' commitment to sound economic policy, and therefore react positively to additional steps (see World Bank 1993a).

At the root of this track record is the generational commitment the leaders and people of these countries have made to economic progress. East Asia's rapid and sustained economic growth—more than twice the rate for all developing countries—has made the reforms that much more effective. The key difference has been not only higher growth, but the length of time over which it has continued. The contrast between Indonesia and India, for example, is not seen in annual per capita growth rates (say, one percent over the past decade), but rather in the time period (a generation) over which growth rates were maintained. As a result, Indonesia was able to lower its poverty rate from some 60 percent of the population in 1970 to about 15 percent today—far surpassing India's performance. This sustained commitment has reduced the discount rate that people attach to reform programs, and enables reformers to initiate actions that might take time to bear fruit (see World Bank 1991).

In addition to such a generational commitment, countries such as China and Vietnam have made special efforts to get early benefits from economic reform and contain costs. By starting with measures that produce quick results, they have been able to maintain the drive for reform. Most notably, an all-out push to raise agricultural productivity and increase exports paid off with relatively early gains, which then allowed for more extensive reforms. Pragmatism has sometimes meant implementing reforms that affect incremental activities first, and then allowing the new reformed parts to overwhelm the unreformed parts. Taiwan, China's experience in enterprise reform is a case in point. China and Vietnam, however, have yet to make some tough decisions, for example regarding the reforms of large state enterprises. In balancing the costs and benefits of reforms, state-owned enterprise reforms illustrate that needed changes cannot be postponed indefinitely, as over time the costs of postponement begin to outweigh any temporary gains.

*Latin America.* After a decade of economic adjustment and reform, some of the Latin American countries are emerging as new economic forces, while others are still struggling to establish a credible track record. Countries that for decades had protected inefficient industries and encouraged an ever-expanding role for the state are rapidly being transformed into outward-oriented, market-based economies. Reforms are beginning to bear fruit in the form of macroeconomic stability, expansion of the export sector, substantial increases in productivity, and faster economic growth.

However, the results vary widely across countries, and most still face tremendous challenges. Social infrastructure has been deteriorating, poverty has increased in several cases, and inflation continues to be high. If market-oriented reforms are to be sustained, in addition to maintaining macroeconomic stability, then special attention needs to be directed to reducing poverty, increasing domestic savings, and creating solid institutional foundations for long-term growth (see World Bank 1993b).

Chile initiated far-reaching economic reforms in the mid 1970s, almost a decade ahead of others in the region. From the beginning, "the agenda was to (i) cut the fiscal deficit to reduce inflation and stabilize the economy, (ii) free prices to be set by the markets, (iii) sell off the state-owned enterprises, and (iv) open the economy to trade with the rest of the world" (Piñera 1994). Macroeconomic policies were brought in line, markets (including labor markets) were liberalized, state-owned firms were privatized (even including the social security system), and import restrictions were rapidly eliminated.

The results over a decade and a half have been solid. Although Chile suffered massively in the debt crisis of 1980s, it was the first country to recover from this setback and has since enjoyed robust growth. Although many other countries in the region are experiencing severe difficulties following the Mexican crisis, Chile is prospering. (Having the experience of the 1982 crisis, Chile has adopted a flexible exchange rate system.)

Starting in 1985, Mexico went far in some reform areas, but held back in others. Trade reform and privatization fall in the former group, while labor market deregulation and agricultural sector reform fall in the latter. Financial market reforms were fairly complete by 1990, although an efficient regulatory regime to oversee financial markets has been lacking. Severe income inequality and slow political reform have limited the success of economic reforms by creating uncertainty over Mexico's future and reducing the credibility of the reforms.

Strong and weak reform episodes are differentiated not only by the design of economic policies but also by institutional dimensions. Economic policies are fundamental, but outcomes depend on institutional, social and political factors (Naím 1993b). We turn first to the economic issues of design, then to institutional issues, before considering questions of process and leadership.

## Back to Basics: The Economic Ingredients

Development experiences point to the advantages of economies in which (i) property rights are strongly upheld, (ii) economic activities are coordinated mainly through markets, (iii) the government is relatively efficient, and (iv) relationships with other countries are open. Any of a great number of diverse policy measures might be taken to establish and protect property rights, make the markets function more efficiently, maintain a government that can fulfill its core functions, and ensure open international trade. But experience points to the basic elements of a successful reform package.

### Macroeconomic Stability

The successful East Asian reformers have invariably maintained price levels much more stable than those in Latin American or ex-communist transitional economies. Without price stability it is very difficult to make reforms succeed. The reform processes that are underway in China, the former Soviet Union, and East European countries could unravel if these nations cannot maintain low inflation.

Large and persistent budget deficits are the main reason why economies have experienced price level instability. Even when the budget is in balance, it still matters how much and for what the government spends, and how the spending is financed. The East Asian high performers have generally kept their average government spending under 20 percent of GDP. It is hard to establish a clear link between government spending levels and country performance. In many of the slow-growing countries of Africa, the former Soviet Union, and Eastern Europe, however, governments have absorbed more than 40 percent of GDP, and in some Latin American countries, more than 30 percent of GDP (see Barro 1990).

The composition of government spending and how it is financed have mattered crucially. Saving rates in East Asia have been about 50 percent higher on average than in the rest of the developing world. Within government spending, investment has been more important compared to consumption, relative to the average of other developing regions. Governments in the rapidly growing East Asian economies have spent more than a quarter of their total budgets for public investment. Private investment in GDP has been significantly higher in East Asia, rising to be two-thirds higher than in other developing regions.

## Market Liberalization

Some economists argue that liberalization of labor markets makes it difficult to contain the demand for rapid wage increases. Experiences in Chile, Latin America, and Eastern Europe (the earlier experience of Chile or the more recent experiences of Mexico and Poland) have hurt otherwise comprehensive reforms. Contrary to popular perception, labor markets in Korea have been competitive and flexible. In the last thirty-five years, real wage levels have steadily risen, while unemployment rates have consistently come down, suggesting that labor markets were competitive and flexible.

Noting the practices that prevailed in Japan and Korea, some suggest that government control of financial markets has been essential for successful industrial policies. They cite the Japanese main bank system, which apparently functioned well during Japan's high growth period, and Korea's seemingly successful promotion of the heavy and chemical industries, which was done through strong financial controls.

However, Japan and Korea, even if successful, might be exceptions. Unless a nation possesses a pool of skilled financial managers capable of (and committed to) managing the complicated process of financial control in the national interest, these policies are unlikely to produce the desired results. In addition, favorable institutional setup and rules of the game should exist for financial controls to succeed. As these preconditions are hard to come by, the chances for successfully implementing industrial policy through financial controls are limited.

Furthermore, policies that repress financial markets have also incurred costs. Funds were widely misallocated, resources were lost to rent-seeking activities (which often result in widespread corruption), and financial industries were weakened from the lack of effective competition. Experiences in Chile, New Zealand, Thailand, and Malaysia demonstrate that economies can grow well without large-scale government interference in financial markets. These economies are doing better in many aspects than Japan and Korea were at a similar stage of development. Their industrial structure appears to be more efficient and their banking sectors are healthier.

Almost all countries now recognize that there is little alternative to liberalizing trade and investments and integrating with the rest of the world. Questions of pace and sequencing of reforms remain, as well as the degree of desirable openness. The mercantilist view, which favors export promotion and discourages import liberalization, is still prevalent to some extent. If industries with great growth potential could be identified, it might make sense to protect them until they became internationally competitive. But identifying such potential winners is a difficult task that carries the risk of selecting the wrong industries. Even if potential winners could be identified, protection would need to be of limited duration and would be withdrawn if it becomes clear that the protected firms are not performing as expected. This is, of course, easier said than done, because the privileges conferred on protected firms are hard to take away (but see Wade 1993).

## Rules of the Game

Economic reforms fundamentally change the basic rules of the game—that is, the rules governing how economic activities are organized, coordinated, and regulated. Making, changing, and enforcing the rules of the game is the legitimate role of government, while the actual implementation of the rules requires a panoply of institutions.

Liberalization of economic activities will work only if the rules are clearly established and efficiently enforced. Without well-enforced rules, liberalization can lead to chaos, as some of the recent experience in socialist transition suggests. If this happens, the reform process will meet great difficulties and resistance. Thus, unless a clear, consistent framework for fair and open competition is securely established and stringently enforced, liberalization could lead the economy into serious troubles (see Williamson 1994).

This point can perhaps be best illustrated by referring to the production function:

$$Y = F(K, H, G)$$

where $Y$ = social product (GDP), $F()$ = society's production function, $K$ = private physical capital stock, $H$ = private human capital stock, and $G$ = social capital stock. Assume that capital stocks are measured in efficiency units. For a given level of technology, output $Y$ is determined by the amount of inputs used by the economy in the production process. Output will grow when either technology improves or capital stocks grow.

### Figure 10.1  Alternative Growth Paths with Different Technologies

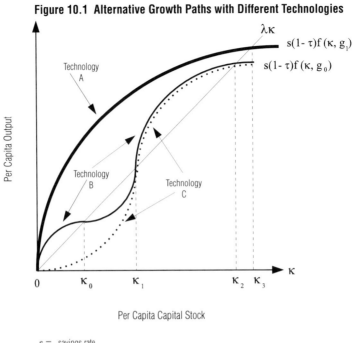

Per Capita Capital Stock

s = savings rate
τ = income tax rate
g = per capita social capital stock, $g_1 > g_0$
λ = population growth rate + depreciation rate

Social capital is capital stock that is not owned exclusively by some individuals. It includes not only tangible social capital such as infrastructure and institutions, but also such intangible social capital such as conventions, customs, legal frameworks, and rules of the game. In general, social capital is strongly complementary to private physical and human capital. That is, $F_{KG} > 0$ and $F_{HG} > 0$. Thus, when social capital stocks increase, so does the marginal productivity of private capital stocks. This is in addition to direct output effects of increases in social capital stock ($FG > 0$). Since social capital, like private capital, exhibits diminishing marginal productivity ($F_{GG} < 0$), an increase in social capital would be especially productive when its original level is small. This explains why rules of the game and institutional setup should be in place before or concurrently with the occurrence of liberalization, a point driven home by the experience of the former Soviet Union, where institutional changes have lagged.

Marginal productivity of social capital could become negative when the latter becomes too big ($FG < 0$, when $G$ grows beyond a critical level $G^*$). This would be the case, for example, when rules become too complicated and strong. Likewise, social capital stocks can become substitutes for private capital stocks when the former grow too big ($F_{KG} < 0$ and $F_{HG} < 0$ for $G > G^*$). If this happens, any further increase in social capital would decrease the productivity of private capital stocks.

Figure 10.1 is a standard growth diagram with several different production technologies. Here the variable $k$ equals the per capita capital stock $K/H$ and $g = G/H$. With technology A, the economy would grow smoothly as initial per capita capital stock increases toward the steady-state level. As technological improvements occur, the production frontier continuously shifts upward and the economy will grow indefinitely. In this case, what is important for growth is to maintain the right level of investment through savings. The savings would be used to augment both physical and human capital, and to develop technology through R & D.

The S-shaped technology (technology C) corresponds to the case when there is a region in which increasing returns to scale occur. It shows that if capital stock is deficient, the economy could be trapped in a vicious cycle of poverty. The interval $[0, k_1]$ in Figure 10.1 is known as the poverty trap. When the initial level of per capita physical capital stock falls in that region, $k$ would continuously decrease toward 0, and so would per capita income. Even though efforts can be made to augment $k$ with external assistance, unless $k$ is augmented quite substantially (beyond $k^1$), they will not be of much help.

We could have an S-shaped production technology where the economy lacks sufficient social capital for private capital to function properly, or where the economy is closed so that resource allocation cannot be fully efficient. Suppose now that either the economy opens up to international trade or social capital is augmented. We take this as an example of a partial reform. The production frontier changes its shape somewhat, but not sufficiently. One possibility is the case depicted as technology B in Figure 10.1. In this case, the economy would grow until $k$ reaches $k_0$. However, the economy would not grow beyond $k_0$ unless the private capital stock is increased substantially. Therefore, with a partial economic reform, the economy can grow for a while, but not indefinitely.

Suppose now that the social capital stock is augmented, perhaps through external assistance, and the economy opens up. The production technology would shift further upward. This shift would occur because the marginal productivity of social capital is positive and there are benefits of opening up to international trade. This upward shift would reduce the size of the poverty trap and make it easier for an underdeveloped economy to have sustained economic development. It could even eliminate the poverty trap. The thick frontier of usual concave shape depicted in Figure 1 corresponds to such a case. In this case, the economy would continuously grow until the stationary state $k_3$ is reached. This could happen even without further external assistance.

Most countries in East Asia have had complex and elaborate rules and institutions. Sometimes rules are not even explicitly stated, and institutions tend to overlap in their jurisdictions. Rules and institutions in these countries, except for Hong Kong and some of the late reformers, could be characterized as overly strong and complex, and sometimes mutually inconsistent. The latter has been the case, for example, in Korea until very recently. In Japan, Korea, Singapore, and Taiwan, China, governments have been very strong and have frequently implemented economic policy measures that supersede existing rules.

How, then, have these nations succeeded in achieving such remarkable growth? First, rules and institutions favorable to business activities have been more common and better enforced than rules unfavorable to economic growth and business activities. The latter have often been side-stepped and loosely enforced. Second, alternative mechanisms may have also substantially weakened rules unfavorable to business activities. Obviously this is not a desirable arrangement, and it might have been much better for these countries' development if rules had been streamlined from the beginning. The prevalence of rule-bending or rent-seeking activities in these countries vividly demonstrates the weakness of the existing arrangement. The extreme imbalances between large and small firms, prevalence of unfair business practices, serious environmental degradation, and numerous instances of human rights violations often found in East Asian countries are manifestations of the weakness of the present setup. Recognizing these problems, many countries in the region have lately begun to rationalize rules and institutions.

### Institution-Building

Setting up the right institutions can be important in making and enforcing rules. Among many possible institutions to consider, we emphasize here three from successful experiences:

*The Central Bank and Financial Supervisory Board.* Establishing and maintaining a central bank capable of implementing monetary policy free from political influences is an important institutional requirement for successful reform. Ironically, central banks are among the most abused and underdeveloped institutions in most developing economies. Developing countries frequently resort to the central bank's power of money creation to finance government spending. They do this because imposition of an inflation tax is incomparably easier than imposing regular taxes. Furthermore, since inflation taxes tend to fall more on the economically weak, politically strong groups such as business communities and large unions tend to support them.

In order for a central bank to implement monetary policy free from unwarranted political influence, it is essential that it be given independence from the executive branch of government. In practice, this means shielding the central bank from the influence of the finance ministry or its equivalent.

Setting up necessary institutional arrangements to maintain stability in the banking sector is important, too. Most of the activities performed by the banking industries can be regulated through commercial laws. However, since banks also participate in the money supply process, the stability of the banking sector has a special importance. For this reason, banks have traditionally been subject to regulations more specific and tighter than those promulgated in commercial laws. Setting up an efficiently working regulatory framework for financial industries is, therefore, a prerequisite for reform. This requirement should be dealt with before full financial liberalization occurs.

*Fair Trade Commission.* Liberalization of markets yields maximum beneficial results only when a framework promoting fair and open competition is in place. Although most business activities can be regulated with commercial laws and thus do not need any special regulatory provisions, there can be instances that require special attention. For this it is necessary to set up a special agency in charge of ensuring fair and open competition in all markets. A commission to handle conflicts arising in the area of international trade is also necessary.

When setting up a fair trade commission (or its equivalent), the observation that competition is in most instances the best safeguard against unfair practices should be the guiding principle. When circumstances are uncertain and indeterminate, it might be better to leave things to markets rather than trying to regulate them despite imperfect knowledge. Regulations might be applied in well-understood, clearly delineated, and exceptional cases. Restricting actual or potential competition by erecting entry barriers is the pit into which regulations most frequently fall. Monopoly rights or excessive market power created by regulations are usually the most important sources for restricting competition.

*Tax Authority.* A well-functioning tax system is another prerequisite for any economy to work properly. The inability to collect tax revenues is often the most serious problem facing the reform process. Government must have the ability to raise adequate revenues through taxation. Therefore, a tax authority that can efficiently enforce tax laws should be set up, and a system of tax laws should be established. In doing this, however, it is essential that the tax system not be misused for political purposes, which is frequently the case in nations undertaking reforms.

In order to prevent the tax system from being misused, the tax authority should be given as much independence as possible from the executive branch of government. Tax laws should be made simple, clear, and internally consistent, without leaving room for conflicting interpretations. A flat tax system, such as that which is currently being advocated in the United States, could be a useful model.

## Rapid or Gradual Approach?

In implementing a set of reforms, some governments have adopted a "big bang" approach: introducing comprehensive reform measures once and for all, and letting the markets take care of the needed adjustments. Others have taken a gradual approach: introducing and implementing reform measures one by one, making adjustments along the way as they are needed. Although the two strategies seem to differ, that is often only a matter of degree as long as both are honestly pursued to achieve the goal of reforming the economy. However, serious problems arise when the gradual approach is used to mask a basic reluctance to undertake serious reforms.

The rapid approach usually incurs costs in the initial phase and begins to bear substantial benefits after an adjustment period. The length of this adjustment period varies from case to case. Available evidence suggests that the adjustment period does not exceed ten years, and is often considerably less (Chile, Spain, Poland, and others, for example [Williamson 1994]). The rapid approach works best when mutually consistent and comprehensive liberalization measures are undertaken. Further, the chances of success are greater if the public clearly understands the purpose and process of reforms, and if it is explicitly acknowledged that reform measures take time to yield fruits. Reforming governments must not give the false impression that the reform process will be painless. Finally, in designing and implementing reform measures, it is important not to discriminate against particular groups or to grant special favors to particular groups. When reform measures are perceived to be fair and impartial, they are more likely to succeed.

The cost and benefits of the gradual approach are usually incurred periodically. The costs at any given point in time of sequentially introduced reform measures could well be smaller than the costs associated with the "big bang" approach. However, the total costs of gradually implementing a similar set of reform measures could be much larger. Likewise, benefits arising from each of a series of reform measures would surely be smaller than the benefits associated with the rapid approach, once reforms begin to bear fruit. The total benefits from implementing a full series of gradual measures that are comparable in the aggregate to the "big bang" approach could be smaller as well. This would be the case when entrenched interest groups make it difficult to implement additional reform measures that may hurt them. Finally, since sequentially designed and implemented reform measures are easily influenced by prevailing interest groups, such reform measures are more likely to be inconsistent with measures previously introduced.

**Pragmatic Approaches**

In principle, it would be better to introduce reforms comprehensively, once and for all, and leave the required adjustments to markets. But it often proves difficult for sociopolitical reasons to implement a comprehensive plan. A gradual approach in such cases might prove to be wiser.

In a gradual approach, certain dimensions that cut across the economy nevertheless need to be addressed head on. Confronting large fiscal deficits is a case in point. Liberalization of domestic markets and international trade is another. Explicitly laying out a schedule for undertaking various reform measures is helpful in increasing the credibility of the reform plan.

Measures that do not adequately protect property rights are likely to fail. This means that liberalization of economic activities and granting property ownership to individuals should be a priority of any reform program.

Reforms in East Asian countries are often characterized as piecemeal and gradual. However, if we judge reforms by how well they protect property rights and provide incentives for individuals to work hard, reforms in East Asian economies have in fact been far-reaching and comprehensive from the start. They have established and protected property rights, supported the market system, and encouraged open relationships with the outside world. Consequently, there was no need for a faster approach: all it required was a series of modest steps.

## Desirable Order of Reforms

Suggestions regarding the optimal order of reforms have included the following: (i) financial markets should be liberalized only after goods markets are fully liberalized and well functioning; (ii) within financial markets, banking industries should be liberalized only after capital market liberalization is well underway; (iii) liberalization of the domestic economy should precede trade liberalization; (iv) exports should be liberalized before imports; (v) on the import side, liberalization should be done in the order of goods, services, and capital inflows; and (vi) privatization can be done at a fairly late stage.

Considered in the aggregate, however, these suggestions do not seem to be based on coherent principles, and some are mutually contradictory. The experiences of Japan and Korea are cited to support the view that imports should be liberalized as late as possible, financial market liberalization should be undertaken at a later stage of economic reforms, and capital inflows should be carefully managed. Certainly there are merits to these arguments. However, it becomes increasingly evident that the costs incurred by the gradual approach are as large as, and frequently larger than, the benefits. Since costs arise indirectly, but benefits accrue directly, we often tend to overlook costs and consider only the benefits. The fact that both Japan and Korea are actively pursuing the liberalization of all relevant markets suggests that comprehensive liberalization might be best, if possible.

Sachs (1994) suggests that privatization of publicly owned enterprises may not have to be a part of the initial reform package, provided that rapid liberalization of all the relevant markets is pursued. With a rapid liberalization program, even publicly owned enterprises cannot avoid the discipline of the market; hence they have to behave like private firms. Therefore, privatization can wait, if it is desirable for some reasons. There are two important preconditions for delayed privatization to happen. First, all markets should be liberalized by eliminating import restrictions, and entry barriers to markets dominated by public enterprises. Second, public enterprises should be subject to hard budget constraints and their managers should be evaluated according to their ability to make profits. Public enterprises should be put on the same footing as private firms. This requires abolition of all subsidies. However, as Sachs has argued, this arrangement should be temporary. If privatization is delayed too long, the reform process might be overturned. This can happen when an unreformed state sector continues to drain government financial resources away, as in China.

An area that has lagged in the reform agenda everywhere is environmental protection. "Grow first and clean up later" has been the most common approach, at least until recently. East Asia's success in achieving rapid economic growth, for example, has come at a heavy environmental cost. The region faces some of the worst urban pollution, as well as the most rapid loss of forests and biodiversity—all of which translate into losses in long-term welfare. The weight of evidence suggests that it pays to confront environmental problems early, along with the implementation of market reforms.

### The Role of Reformers

Reformers play crucial roles in the success or failure of reforms, whether rapid or gradual. Given the uncertainty of either approach, it is important for reforms to provide credibility, to convince fellow citizens of the gains from reforms, and to explain why it will take time for reform measures to bear fruit.

Usually a handful of people play the leading role in economic reforms. The reform group could include the head of state, or it could consist of a few ministers in key posts. Sometimes a head of state delegates the responsibility for reform to a handful of technocrats. This happens in practically all developing authoritarian regimes. Korea, Singapore, China, Malaysia, Chile, Indonesia, and Taiwan, China all followed this pattern. In this case, the role and quality of the leader is very important.

In more democratic regimes, the leading group is usually the party in charge. In this case, representatives of the party that controls the parliament typically try to implement the ideas summarized in their party's platform. Even in this case, there are a few people who lead the reform, usually prime ministers or finance ministers. Sometimes it is finance or economics ministers who play the leading role, while prime ministers or presidents remain somewhat passive. India and Poland are examples of this.

For the success of economic reforms, the roles of supporting groups are also important. These groups include the top echelon of the bureaucracy, intellectuals, and the media. The bureaucrats are those who actually implement reform measures, usually in the form of changes in institutional setups or the way institutions function. The ability and willingness of the bureaucracy to implement the reform measures efficiently are thus key variables. The intellectuals and the media are opinion leaders. When these groups have misgivings about reform measures, they can make it difficult for reforms to succeed. Therefore, gaining the understanding and support of these groups is important. Of the two, the intellectuals are more influential in the long run, while in the short run the media are more influential. Sometimes it may be better to appeal directly to the general public for support.

If the leader is strong enough to liberalize markets, reforms can still be sustained, even in the absence of vocal supporting groups with an interest in reform. Competitive market processes themselves are very strong forces. When left unrestricted, market forces can thoroughly shake up individuals, spurring them on to efforts that bring substantial improvements in living standards for a society. The desire to improve one's economic conditions is extremely strong, and if the reform process is seen to support efforts towards higher living standards, the markets can become the best ally of the reformers (see Hayek 1967).

## Conclusion

East Asia's experience provides pointers to how long-term economic reforms can change existing rules and institutions. In addition to promoting free competition in markets and opening a nation's economy to the world, they aim at establishing property rights and a framework for private contracts. Since it takes time for reform measures to bear fruit, it is essential to muster long-term commitments.

The government must play an important role in designing and implementing reform programs. Most of all, it should lead in making and enforcing the rules of the game. It should also play a leading role in establishing and changing the necessary institutional setups. Having clear and consistent rules of the game in place, and setting up the key institutions to carry out the reform agenda, are prerequisites for reforms to succeed. These are strongly complementary to liberalization of markets, maintenance of macroeconomic stability, and ensuring free and open competition, which are necessary ingredients for successful reforms.

East Asia's experience also provides pointers on how a long-term commitment to progress can lend credibility to the reform process and deliver far more favorable benefit-cost ratios of reforms than have been seen elsewhere. Not all of East Asia's approaches are to be emulated, however. Where reforms have been delayed or inconclusive, as in the financial sector, state enterprises, or the neglect of environmental protection, costs have been large and corrective actions later have proved very difficult.

Latin America's experience is not fundamentally different than that of East Asia. Well-designed comprehensive reform programs backed up by long-term commitments are bearing plenty of fruit, as can be seen in Chile. Other countries that initiated only partial reform measures and lacked long-term commitments are still struggling to establish a credible track record. If market-oriented reforms are to be sustained in the latter countries, then in addition to maintaining macroeconomic stability and liberalization of markets, special attention must be directed to institutional reforms. Structural reforms will need to aim at reducing poverty, increasing domestic savings, and creating solid institutional foundations for long-term growth.

---

*Vinod Thomas is Director, Economic Development Institute, the World Bank. Jisoon Lee is Professor of Economics, Seoul National University, Seoul, Korea.*

# Commentary

*Mary M. Shirley*

As this book illustrates, the debate over why East Asia has developed so much faster than most of the rest of the world continues to rage undiminished. Often, when the smoke clears, the combatants in this battle of ideas can be found to agree on one underlying proposition: that institutions are a key factor in East Asia's success. The authors of Chapter 10 are no exception. In their paper they explore three questions: (i) what lessons can we learn from success; (ii) is rapid better than gradual reform; and (iii) are there necessary preconditions for reform to succeed? They argue that institutions are an important component of success, a view I strongly endorse. (Unlike the authors, however, I define institutions, along the lines of Douglass North, to include both organizations and what the authors term intangible social capital: i.e., norms of behavior, customs, rules, laws, etc.) Differences in institutions, including intangible institutions, must be an important part of the reason why some of the same policies that have worked in East Asia have failed in Latin America.

The authors begin by presenting a very interesting framework for thinking about how institutions matter in development. The framework assumes three kinds of capital: the usual private physical capital, private human capital, and a third, less usual "social capital," which is defined as capital not owned exclusively by individuals. A country's social capital stock includes not only tangible assets such as infrastructure and organizations, but also intangibles such as conventions, customs, legal frameworks, and rules of the game. A country can be caught in a poverty trap not only because it lacks human and physical capital, but also because of insufficient social capital. For instance, it may not have enough of the rules, norms, and institutions needed to use private forms of capital efficiently; the former Soviet Union is given as a prime example. Interestingly, the authors contend that social capital, like private capital, has declining marginal productivity, and that this marginal productivity can become negative when it grows too big—for example, if rules become too complicated or governments too strong.

Even while recognizing the central role of institutions, however, we must realize that the perils in thinking about them. Offhand, I can think of three which, if not resisted, can land us in the economists' equivalent of one of the circles of Hell in Dante's *Commedia*. First is the temptation of abstraction, which leads one to characterize countries (or economies, or events, or organizations) on the basis of a concept that is never measured. Second is the lure of spurious sequencing, which leads one to advocate creating or changing institutions without knowing how the causality of institutional change runs. Third is the seduction of ideal action, which leads one to exhort leaders to do the right thing and ignore all the incentives they have to do the wrong thing.

The first peril, the danger of thinking about institutions abstractly without also thinking about them concretely, is illustrated in the authors' contention that social capital has declining marginal productivity. This is surely correct, but the paper does not tell us how we should measure social capital or decide if we have too little or too much.

I can readily imagine ways to measure some forms of social capital, such as infrastructure. For example, we can know if a country has too few or too many miles of roads by measuring traffic. It is harder to measure some kinds of institutions, but we should be able to do it. For instance, we might be able to tell if a country has enough competent, honest, and independent bureaucrats by comparing service measures across countries (perhaps by measuring the ratio of customs agents to the size of trade and the length of time and amount of bribes required to get goods released).

It is not at all obvious how to measure intangible social capital, however. I think this can be done—indeed Robert Putnam (1993) made an important advance in this area in his book—but the paper offers no hints on how to do it. This would not matter in a purely theoretical essay, but the paper goes beyond theory. It argues that some East Asian countries have "overly strong and complex, and sometimes mutually inconsistent" rules and institutions. We are told that this "excess" social capital did not interfere with growth in these nations because the rules and institutions unfavorable to business are not as well enforced as those rules that are favorable, and in addition, "efficient bribery" has weakened unfavorable rules and institutions. But if this excess social capital did not manifest itself in reduced growth, how did the authors ascertain that its marginal productivity was declining? This is the peril of abstraction: to label as excess something that we haven't even measured in the first place.

This is not a trivial issue. As Latin American governments consider how much they want to adopt of the East Asian strategy, they would surely want to know whether rules and governments there are excessively complex and strong or only necessarily so. And they would want to know how their social capital compares. Until we can measure these intangibles, it is difficult to give advice about them.

The second peril, spurious sequencing, is hard to resist: if you know that wrong institutions are a big part of the problem, then it is tempting to advise countries simply to create the right institutions. The paper suggests that three institutions are important to success: an independent central bank, a neutral and wise fair trade commission, and a well-functioning tax authority that efficiently administers apolitical tax laws. These might be the key institutions (although I can think of other important ones such as the judiciary), but the problem is that such institutions are expensive to create. New institutional economists tell us that organizational structures, rules and laws, and norms of behavior are path dependent in the sense that they evolve out of a country's history and circumstances; and people have a stake or a property right in the institutional status quo. Some people win and some lose when institutions change; the prospective losers will resist change and if they are more powerful or more interested in the outcome than the prospective winners, change will not happen. Hence a deep shock or fundamental shift, which alters people's power or their stake in the status quo, may be needed before a country can reform its institutions in any fundamental way. That is why some analysts question whether countries create an independent central bank and then get good monetary policy, or whether the causality is the reverse: countries want good monetary policy first, and create an independent central bank to establish it. What might explain this desire for good monetary policy? I have not studied this, but I could imagine one possible explanation: perhaps the rising power of a new commercial class and the shock of hyperinflation have created pressures for stability.

Is it harmful to try to improve institutions in the absence of the underlying changes that make reform possible? It is difficult to say on the basis of what we know now, but this result cannot be ruled out. If a government can be persuaded to pass legislation that guarantees the independence of the central bank or the tax authority, perhaps some good will come of it. But if the fundamentals haven't changed, the same government will probably find ways to circumvent the legislation and compromise the institution's independence. This can do harm. In a study of state-owned enterprise reform,[1] cosmetic reforms—reforms in appearance but not in substance— were found to compromise the reputation of reform efforts in general and to harm the credibility of institutions. Thus passing laws in the face of insurmountable obstacles to their being enforced may indeed hurt the rule of law, by making law a joke.

---

[1] World Bank (1995).

All this suggests the need to better understand the roots and process of institutional evolution in Latin America and East Asia. Some analysts, notably Stanley Engerman of Rochester and Ken Sokoloff of UCLA,[2] have suggested that initial factor endowments and historical factors (such as patterns of immigration during the colonial period) may help explain a number of persistent features in Latin America's development, including the relative inequality of income distribution. Others have suggested that ethnic homogeneity in Japan or threats of invasion in South Korea may have influenced the nature of their development. None of this means that well-functioning market institutions cannot be created or improved; they obviously have been in both East Asia and Latin America. Rather it means that to be helpful to reformers, we need to know much more about what causes right institutions to arise in the first place.

The paper largely resists the third peril: exhorting action in the face of contrary incentives. The authors recognize that leaders are people too, with constituencies and incentives that may not lead them to adopt the reforms that economists so fervently advocate. But this admirable realism does not seem to serve them well in their discussion of rapid versus gradual reform. They seem to say that rapid reform will be less costly than gradual reform, apparently because entrenched interest groups will find it more difficult to reverse quick reforms or force governments to introduce inconsistent measures, and because the details of adjustment can be left to the market to work out. However, they also argue that a "big bang" is often sociopolitically less feasible, and that a gradual approach may be more pragmatic. They then assert that even if gradual, reforms should still be comprehensive, at least in confronting large fiscal deficits, liberalizing domestic markets and trade, protecting property rights, and providing incentives for people to respond to markets. I would think that by this point a reformer might be confused.

Perhaps the dilemma lies in trying to give comprehensive advice about this sort of strategic choice. As the authors suggest, the choice between big bang and gradual, partial reform is a sociopolitical one, and since sociopolitics differ a great deal among countries, the best way to confront such choices will also differ. Simply put, China is not Russia and a successful reform strategy in one may not necessarily succeed in the other.[3] Or, to bring the example closer to the theme of this book, Mexico is not Chile.

---

[2] Engerman and Sokoloff (1996).

[3] Sachs and Woo (1994) show this convincingly in their seminal article, "Structural Factors in the Economic Reforms of China, Eastern Europe, and the Former Soviet Union."

Chile's big bang followed the hyperinflation and other shocks of the Allende period and a military coup; Mexico's more gradual and piecemeal reforms were the result of a coalition shift within the ruling party and of important but not nearly as severe economic shocks.

The paper tips slightly toward the third peril when it suggests that "in designing and implementing reform measures, it is important not to discriminate against particular groups or to grant special favors to particular groups. When reform measures are perceived to be fair and impartial, they are more likely to succeed." This sounds good, but is it really true? Chile gave much higher severance pay to port workers than to other state enterprise employees because they were well organized and could disrupt the economy if they went on strike, jeopardizing the entire reform process. It wasn't fair but it worked. Perhaps the leaders of a democracy would have more incentive to be impartial than Chile's military dictatorship, but I wonder. Even in democratic Poland, most enterprises have been sold through worker buyouts rather than through mass privatization schemes that might benefit other groups such as the elderly or the unemployed, because workers had the power to demand firm-by-firm reforms that kept them in control.

Finally, I think the authors are profoundly right in their view that markets can be a powerful force for changing institutions because they change incentives. This seems particularly true when property rights are also changing, as when the Czech Republic simultaneously opened markets and created new stakeholders in the market economy by distributing voucher shares. But policies and institutions still play a key role, including a role in the decision to introduce markets in the first place. When governments resist opening markets, it is not because they don't know that markets are "the best ally of the reformers," but because they do. If the political costs of reform outweigh the political benefits to the leadership and their constituents, they will doubtless view the reformers' ally as their enemy and act accordingly.

New institutional economics is indeed still "new" in many respects, but it nonetheless promises a systematic way to analyze the role of institutions, tangible and intangible, in East Asia's development, and to understand how institutional change is likely to occur in Latin America. At the risk of pushing metaphor too far, new institutional economics may be the Virgil to lead us safely out of the three perilous circles of abstraction, spurious sequencing, and ideal action, to a point (purgatory or paradise?) where we can have a more scientific basis for giving advice about institutions.

---

*Mary M. Shirley is Division Chief, Finance and Private Sector Development, the World Bank.*

# Bibliography

Abo, T. 1994. *Hybrid Factory: The Japanese Production System in the United States.* New York: Oxford University Press.

Aghevli, B., J. Boughton, P. Montiel, D. Villanueva, and G. Woglom. 1990. The Role of National Saving in the World Economy. IMF Occasional Paper No. 67 (March). Washington, D.C.

Ahluwalia, M. 1974. Income Inequality: Some Dimensions of the Problem. In H. Chenery et al. (eds.), *Redistribution with Growth.* New York: Oxford University Press.

Akerlof, G. A., and D. Romer. 1993. Looting: The Economic Underworld of Bankruptcy for Profit. *Brookings Papers on Economic Activity.* Washington, D.C.: The Brookings Institution.

Alesina, A., R. Hausmann, R. Hommes, and E. Stein. 1995. Budgetary Institutions and Fiscal Performances in Latin America. OCE Working Paper 004. Inter-American Development Bank, Washington, D.C.

Alesina, A., and R. Perotti. 1993. Income Distribution, Political Instability and Investment. NBER Working Paper 4486. Cambridge, MA.

Alesina, A., and D. Rodrik. 1992. Distribution, Political Conflict, and Economic Growth: A Simple Theory and Some Empirical Evidence, in A. Cukierman, Z. Hercovitz, and L. Leiderman (eds.) *Political Economy, Growth, and Business Cycles.* Cambridge, MA: MIT Press.

———. 1994. Distributive Politics and Economic Growth. *Quarterly Journal of Economics* (May).

Amsden, A. H. 1989. *Asia's Next Giant: South Korea and Late Industrialization.* New York: Oxford University Press.

———. 1994. Why Isn't the Whole World Experimenting with the East Asian Model to Develop? Review of the World Bank's *The East Asian Miracle: Economic Growth and Public Policy. World Development* (April).

Anand, S., and R. Kanbur. 1993. Inequality and Development: A Critique. *Journal of Development Economics* (June).

Ando, A., and F. Modigliani. 1963. The Life Cycle Hypothesis of Savings: Aggregate Implications and Tests. *American Economic Review* (March).

Argentine Economic Planning Department. 1994. *El gasto público social y su impacto redistributivo.* Buenos Aires (June).

Argentine Ministry of Culture and Education. *Estadísticas Básicas de Universidades Nacionales: Años 1982–1992.* University Policy Department. Buenos Aires.

Argentine Ministry of Economic Affairs and Public Works and Services. 1990. *El Gasto Público Social.* PRONATASS. Buenos Aires (December).

Attanasio, O., L. Picci, and A. Scorcu. 1995. Saving, Investment and Growth in the World: Correlation and Causality. Policy Research Department, World Bank, Washington, D.C.

Auty, R. M. 1993. *Sustaining Development in Mineral Economies: The Resource Curse Thesis.* London and New York: Routledge.

Aw, B., and A. Hwang. 1993. *Productivity and the Export Market: A Firm Level Analysis.* Pennsylvania State University, State College, PA.

Ayala, U. 1995. ¿Qué se ha aprendido del sistema de pensiones en Argentina, Colombia, Chile y Perú? [Social Security Reform in Latin America]. OCE Working Paper 330, Inter-American Development Bank, Washington, D.C.

Balassa, B. 1991. *Economic Policies in the Pacific Area Developing Countries.* New York: New York University Press.

Banerji, A., E. Campos, and R. Sabot. 1994. The Political Economy of Pay and Employment in Developing Countries. Mimeo. World Bank, Washington, D.C.

Banuri, T., and E. Amadeo. 1991. *Worlds Within the Third World: Labour Market Institutions in Asia and Latin America.* Rio de Janeiro: World Institute for Development Economics Research.

Barro, R. 1974. Are Government Bonds Net Wealth? *Journal of Political Economy* (Nov.–Dec.).

———. 1991. Economic Growth in a Cross-Section of Countries. *Quarterly Journal of Economics* (May).

Barro, R., and J. Wha-Lee. 1990. Government Spending in a Simple Model of Endogenous Growth. *Journal of Political Economy* (October).

———. 1993. International Comparisons of Educational Attainment. Paper presented at conference on How Do National Policies Affect Long-Run Growth? World Bank, Washington, D.C. (February).

Barros, R. 1991. Wage Inequality and the Distribution of Education: A Study of the Evolution of Regional Differences in Inequality in Metropolitan Brazil. *Journal of Economic Development* (July).

Becker, G. 1964. Human Capital. *A Theoretical and Empirical Analysis.* Princeton, NJ: Princeton University Press.

Becker, G., K. Murphy, and R. Tamura. 1990. Human Capital, Fertility, and Economic Growth. *Journal of Political Economy* (October).

Behrman, J. 1991. Investing in Female Education for Development: Women in Development Strategy for the 1990s in Asia and the Near East. Mimeo. Williams College, Williamstown, MA.

———. 1996. *Human Resources in Latin America and the Caribbean.* Washington, D.C.: Inter-American Development Bank.

Behrman, J., and R. Schneider. 1991. How Do Pakistani Schooling Investments Compare with Those of Other Developing Countries? Mimeo. Williams College, Williamstown, MA.

——. 1994. An International Perspective on Schooling Investments in the Last Quarter Century in Some Fast-Growing East and Southeast Asian Countries. *Asian Development Review.*

——.1996. Where Does Brazil Fit? Brazilian Schooling Investments in an International Perspective, in N. Birdsall and R. Sabot (eds.) *Opportunity Foregone: Education in Brazil.* Washington, D.C.: Inter-American Development Bank, distributed by Johns Hopkins University Press.

Bell, C., P. Hazell, and R. Slade. 1982. *Project Evaluation in Regional Perspective.* Baltimore, MD: Johns Hopkins University Press.

Bernanke, B. 1983. Nonmonetary Effects of the Financial Crisis in the Propagation of the Great Depression. *American Economic Review* (June).

Berry, A., and W. Cline. 1979. *Agrarian Structure and Productivity in Developing Countries.* Baltimore, MD: Johns Hopkins University Press.

Birdsall, N. 1992. Health and Development: What Can Research Contribute?, in L. Chen, A. Kleinman and N. Ware (eds.), *Advancing Health in Developing Countries: The Role of Social Research.* Westport, CT: Auburn House.

Birdsall, N., B. Bruns, and R. H. Sabot. 1996. Education Policy in Brazil: Playing a Bad Hand Badly, in N. Birdsall and R. Sabot (eds.), *Opportunity Foregone: Education in Brazil.* Washington, D.C.: Inter-American Development Bank, distributed by Johns Hopkins University Press.

Birdsall, N. and E. James. 1993. Efficiency and Equity in Social Spending: How and Why Governments Misbehave, in M. Lipton and J. van der Gaag (eds.), *Including the Poor.* New York: Oxford University Press for the World Bank.

Birdsall, N., T. Pinckney, and R. H. Sabot. 1995. Inequality, Savings and Growth. Mimeo. Inter-American Development Bank, Washington, D.C.

Birdsall, N., D. Ross, and R. H. Sabot. 1992. Underinvestment in Education: How Much Growth has Pakistan Foregone? *Pakistan Development Review* (Winter).

Birdsall, N., D. Ross, and R. H. Sabot. 1995a. Inequality as a Constraint on Growth, in D. Turnham, C. Foy and G. Larraín (eds.), *Social Tensions, Job Creation and Economic Policy in Latin America.* Paris: OECD.

Birdsall, N., D. Ross, and R. H. Sabot. 1995b. Inequality and Growth Reconsidered: Lessons from East Asia. *World Bank Economic Review* (September).

Birdsall, N., and R. H. Sabot. 1994. Inequality, Exports, and Human Capital in East Asia: Lessons for Latin America, in C. Bradford, Jr. (ed.), *Redefining the State in Latin America.* Paris: OECD Development Centre and Inter-American Development Bank.

——. 1995. Virtuous Circles: Human Capital Growth and Equity in East Asia. Mimeo. Washington, D.C.: Inter American Development Bank.

——. 1996. *Opportunity Foregone: Education in Brazil.* Washington, D.C.: Inter-American Development Bank, distributed by Johns Hopkins University Press.

Blomstrom, M. 1989. *Foreign Investment and Spillovers.* London: Routledge.

Blumenthal, T. 1970. Savings in Postwar Japan. East Asian Research Center, Harvard University, Cambridge, MA.

Borner, S., B. Weder, and A. Brunetti. 1991. *La Incertidumbre Institucional en América Latina o Cómo Jugar al Fútbol con Reglas Inestables.* Serie Diálogo, FUNDES.

Borner, S., A. Brunetti, and B. Weder. 1995. *Political Credibility and Economic Development.* New York: St. Martin's Press.

Borner, S., B. Weder, and A. Brunetti. 1995. Policy Reform and Institutional Uncertainty: The Case of Nicaragua. *Kyklos* 48(1).

Boskin, M. 1978. Taxation, Savings and the Rate of Interest, *Journal of Political Economy* (April).

Bosworth, B. 1993. *Savings and Investment in the Global Economy.* Washington, D.C.: The Brookings Institution.

Bourguignon, F. 1993. Growth, Distribution and Human Resources: A Cross-Country Analysis. Paper prepared for the C. Díaz-Alejandro Memorial Conference, Inter-American Development Bank, Washington, D.C. (May).

Boyd, J. H., and A. Rolnick. 1989. A Case for Reforming Federal Deposit Insurance. *1988 Annual Report.* Federal Reserve Bank of Minneapolis.

Bradford, Colin, Jr. 1994. *From Trade-Driven Growth to Growth-Driven Trade: Reappraising the East Asian Development Experience.* Washington, D.C.: OECD.

Briceño, A., et al. 1992. *Gestión pública y distribución de ingresos: Tres estudios de caso para la economía peruana.* Working Paper 115, Inter-American Development Bank, Washington, D.C. (March).

Brock, P. 1996. High Real Interest Rates, Guarantor Risk, and Bank Recapitalizations. Development Policy Department, World Bank, Washington, D.C.

Brunetti, A., and B. Weder. 1993. Credibility and Growth. WWZ Discussion Paper 9316, University of Basel.

Bruno, M. 1996. Comment, in R. Hausmann and L. Rojas-Suárez (eds.), *Volatile Capital Flows: Taming their Impact on Latin America.* Washington, D.C.: Inter-American Development Bank, distributed by Johns Hopkins University Press.

Bruton, H. 1992. *The Political Economy of Poverty, Equity and Growth: Sri Lanka and Malaysia.* Oxford: Oxford University Press.

Calomiris, C. W., and C. Kahn. 1991. The Role of Demandable Debt in Structuring Optimal Banking Arrangements. *American Economic Review* (June).

Calomiris, C. W., and E. White. 1993. The Origins of Federal Deposit Insurance. Paper presented at the NBER Conference on The Political Economy of Regulation (May). Cambridge, MA.

Calvo, G., L. Leiderman, and C. Reinhart. 1994. Capital Inflows to Latin America with Reference to the Asian Experience. IMF Paper on Policy Analysis and Assessment (July).

Campos, J., and H. Root. 1995. *Institutions and Growth in East Asia.* Washington, D.C.: World Bank.

Caprio, G., A. Izak, and J. Hanson. 1994. *Financial Reform: Theory and Experience.* Cambridge: Cambridge University Press.

Caprio, G., and D. Klingebiel. 1994. Banking Regulation: The Case of the Missing Model. Policy Research Working Paper 1574, Finance and Private Sector Development, World Bank, Washington, D.C.

———. 1996. Insolvency: Bad Luck, Bad Policy, or Bad Banking? World Bank Discussion Paper. Washington, D.C.

Caprio, G., and R. Levine. 1994. Reforming Finance in Transitional Socialist Economies. *The World Bank Research Observer* (January).

Caprio, G., and L. Summers. Forthcoming. Financial Reform: Beyond Laissez-Faire, in Papadimitriou, D. (Ed.) *Financing Prosperity into the 21st Century.* New York: MacMillan Press.

Cardoso, E., and A. Helwige. 1991. *Latin America's Economy.* Cambridge, MA: MIT Press.

Carroll, C., and L. Summers. 1987. Why Have Private Savings Rates in the United States and Canada Diverged? *Journal of Monetary Economics* (September).

———. 1991. Consumption Growth Parallels Income Growth, in D. Bernheim and J. Shoven (eds.), *National Saving and Economic Performance.* Chicago: NBER/University of Chicago Press.

Carroll, C., and D. Weil. 1994. Savings and Growth: A Reinterpretation. *Carnegie-Rochester Conference Series on Public Policy* (June).

Carroll, C., D. Weil, and L. Summers. 1993. Savings and Growth: A Reinterpretation. *Carnegie-Rochester Conference Series on Public Policy* (April).

Chakravarti, S. 1993. Alternative Approaches to a Theory of Economic Growth: Marx, Marshall, and Schumpeter, in S. Chakravarti, *Selected Economic Writings.* Oxford University Press.

Chamley, C., and P. Honohan. 1990. Taxation of Financial Intermediation: Measurement Principles and Application to Five African Countries. World Bank Policy Research Working Paper 421, Washington, D.C.

Chen, E. K. 1977. Factor Inputs, Total Factor Productivity, and Economic Growth: The Asian Case. *Journal of Development Economics* 15:2.

Chenery, H., and M. Syrquin. 1975. *Patterns of Development* 1950–1970. New York: Oxford University Press.

Chilean Ministry of Planning and Cooperation (MIDEPLAN). 1990. *Población, educación, vivienda, salud, empleo y pobreza.* Santiago: CASEN.

———. 1990. *Programas sociales: Su Impacto en los hogares chilenos.* Santiago: CASEN.

Cho, L., and J. Togashi. 1984. Industrial Transition and Demographic Dynamics of the Asian-Pacific Region, in Proceedings of the International Symposium on the Role of the Asia-Pacific Region in World Economic Development. College of Economics, Nihon University, Tokyo.

Chow, P.C.Y., and M. Kellman. 1993. *Trade: The Engine of Growth in East Asia.* New York: Oxford University Press.

Clark, C. 1940. *The Conditions of Economic Progress.* London: Macmillan Press.

Clarke, G. 1992. More Evidence on Income Distribution and Growth. World Bank Working Paper 1064, Washington, D.C.

Cominetti, R., and E. di Gropello. 1995. *El gasto social en América Latina: Un exámen cuantitativo y cualitativo.* Cuaderno de la CEPAL No 73. Santiago.

Corbo, V. 1986. Problems, *Development Theory and Strategies of Latin America.* New York: Oxford University Press for World Bank.

Corbo, V., and K. Schmidt-Hebbel. 1991. Public Policy and Savings in Developing Countries. *Journal of Development Economics* (July).

Corden, W. M. 1993. Seven Asian Miracle Economies: Overview of Macroeconomic Policies. Background paper for *The East Asian Miracle,* Policy Research Department, World Bank, Washington, D.C.

Cukierman, A., S. Edwards, and G. Tabellini. 1992. Seigniorage and Political Instability. *American Economic Review* (June).

Dahlman, C. 1994. Technology Strategy in East Asian Development Economies. Private Sector Development Department, World Bank, Washington, D.C. (July).

Davrieux, H. 1987. *Papel de los Gastos Públicos en el Uruguay, 1955–1984.* Ediciones de la Banda Oriental. Estudios CINVE 9. Montevideo.

———. 1991. *Desigualdad y Gasto Público en los 80.* Ediciones de la Banda Oriental. Estudios CINVE 13. Montevideo.

Deaton, A. 1990. Saving in Developing Countries: Theory and Review. *World Bank Economic Review.* (Special issue: *Proceedings of the First Annual Bank Conference on Development Economics*).

———. 1995. Growth and Saving: What do we know, what do we need to know, and what might we learn? Mimeo. Princeton University.

Deaton, A., and C. Paxson. 1994. Savings, Growth, and Aging in Taiwan, in D. Wise (ed.), *Studies in the Economics of Aging.* Chicago: University of Chicago Press.

De Gregorio, J., and P. Guidotti. 1995. Financial Development and Economic Growth. *World Development* (March).

de Juan, A. 1987. From Good Bankers to Bad Bankers: Ineffective Supervision and Management Deterioration as Major Elements in Banking Crises. Financial Policy and Systems Division, World Bank, Washington, D.C.

Dekle, R. 1988. Do the Japanese Elderly Reduce Their Total Wealth? Reischauer Institute of Japanese Studies, Harvard University, Cambridge, MA.

De Long, B., and L. Summers. 1991. Equipment Investment and Economic Growth. *Quarterly Journal of Economics* (May).

De Melo, Jaime. 1985. Sources of Growth and Structural Change in the Republic of Korea and Taiwan: Some Comparisons, in V. Corbo, A.O. Krueger, and F. Ossa (eds.), *Export-oriented Development Strategies.* Boulder, CO: Westview Press.

Denison, E.F., and W. Chung. 1976. *How Japan's Economy Grew So Fast: The Sources of Economic Expansion.* Brookings Institution, Washington, D.C.

Díaz-Alejandro, C. 1982. Latin America in Depression, 1929–39, in Gersovitz, Díaz-Alejandro, Ranis, and Rosenweig (eds.), *The Theory and Experience of Economic Development.* London: Allen and Unwin.

———. 1983. Stories of the 1930s for the 1980s, in Aspe, Dornbusch, and Obstfeld (eds.), *Financial Policies and the World Capital Market: The Problem of Latin American Countries.* Chicago: University of Chicago Press.

Dollar, D. 1990. Outward Orientation and Growth: An Empirical Study Using a Price-Based Measure of Openness. Mimeo. World Bank, Washington, D.C.

———. 1991. Exploiting the Advantages of Backwardness: The Importance of Education and Outward Orientation. Mimeo. World Bank, Washington, D.C.

———. 1992. Outward-Oriented Developing Economies Really Do Grow More Rapidly: Evidence from 95 LDCs, 1976–1985. *Economic Development and Cultural Change* (April).

Dollar, D., and K. Sokoloff. 1990. Patterns of Productivity Growth in South Korean Manufacturing Industries, 1963–79. *Journal of Development Economics* (October).

Dornbusch, R. 1991. Policies to Move From Stabilization to Growth. Proceedings of Annual Conference on Development Economics, World Bank, Washington, D.C.

Dornbusch, R., and S. Edwards (eds.). 1994. *Stabilization, Economic Reform and Growth.* Chicago: University of Chicago Press.

Dornbusch, R., and S. Fischer. 1993. Moderate Inflation. *World Bank Economic Review* (January).

Easterly, W., and S. Fischer. 1995. The Soviet Economic Decline. *World Bank Economic Review* (September).

Easterly, W., M. Kremer, L. Pritchett, and L. Summers. 1993. Good Policy or Good Luck? Country Growth Performance and Temporary Shocks. Paper presented at conference, How Do National Policies Affect Long-Run Growth? World Bank, Washington, D.C. (February).

Easterly, W., C. Rodríguez, and K. Schmidt-Hebbel (eds.). 1994. *Public Sector Deficits and Macroeconomic Performance.* New York: Oxford University Press.

ECLAC (Economic Commission for Latin America and the Caribbean). 1994. *Policies to Improve Linkages with the Global Economy.* Santiago, Chile.

*Economist, The.* 1993. China's Diaspora Homeward (November 27).

Edwards, Sebastian. 1988. Financial Deregulation and Segmented Capital Markets: The Case of Korea. *World Development* (January).

———. 1989. *Real Exchange Rates, Devaluation, and Adjustment: Exchange Rate Policy in Developing Countries.* Cambridge, MA: MIT Press.

———. 1992. Trade Orientation, Distortions and Growth in Developing Countries. *Journal of Development Economics* (July).

———. 1994. Why Are Savings Rates So Different across Countries? An International Comparative Perspective. NBER Working Paper 5097, Cambridge, MA.

———. 1995. *Crisis and Reform in Latin America: From Despair to Hope.* New York: Oxford University Press.

Edwards, S., and A. Cox-Edwards. 1991. *Monetarism and Liberalization: The Chilean Experiment.* Chicago: University of Chicago Press.

Edwards, S., and G. Tabellini. 1994. Political Instability, Political Weakness and Inflation: An Empirical Analysis, in C. Sims (ed.), *Advances in Econometrics.* Cambridge: Cambridge University Press.

Eichengreen, B., R. Hausmann, and J. Von Hagen. 1996. Reforming Fiscal Institutions in Latin America: The Case for a National Fiscal Council. OCE Working Paper 011. Inter-American Development Bank, Washington, D.C.

Elias, V. 1991. The Role of Total Factor Productivity in Economic Growth. Background paper for *World Development Report* 1991. Office of the Vice President, Development Economics, World Bank, Washington, D.C.

Engerman, S., and K. Sokoloff. 1996. Factor Endowments, Institutions, and Differential Paths of Growth among New World Economies: A View from Economic Historians of the United States, in S. Haber (ed.), *How Did Latin America Fall Behind?* Stanford, CA: Stanford University Press.

Eyzaguirre, N. 1993. Financial Crisis, Reform, and Stabilization: The Chilean Experience, in Faruqi, S. (ed.), *Financial Sector Reforms, Economic Growth, and Stability: Experiences in Selected Asian and Latin American Countries.* Washington, D.C.: World Bank.

Faruqi, S. (ed.) 1993. *Financial Sector Reforms in Asian and Latin American Countries.* Washington, D.C.: World Bank.

Feldstein, M. 1980. International Differences in Social Security and Saving. *Journal of Public Economics* (October).

Feldstein, M., and C. Horioka. 1980. Domestic Saving and International Capital Flows. *Economic Journal* (June).

Fields, G. S. 1992. Changing Labor Market Conditions and Economic Development in Hong Kong, Korea, Singapore, and Taiwan, China. Background paper for *The East Asian Miracle.* Policy Research Department, World Bank, Washington, D.C.

Findlay, R., and S. Wellisz. 1993. *Five Small Open Economies.* Oxford: Oxford University Press.

Fischer, S. 1993. Macroeconomic Factors in Growth. Paper presented at Conference on How Do National Policies Affect Long-Run Growth? World Bank, Washington, D.C. (February).

Fishlow, A., et al. 1994. *Miracle or Design? Lessons from the East Asian Experience.* Washington, D.C.: Overseas Development Council.

Friedberg, L., M. Khamis, and J. M. Page. 1993. *Productivity Change and Technical Efficiency in the High-Performing Asian Economies.* World Bank, Washington, D.C.

Fry, M. 1988. *Money, Interest, and Banking in Economic Development.* Baltimore, MD: Johns Hopkins University Press.

Gavin, M., and R. Hausmann. 1996. The Roots of Banking Crisis: The Macroeconomic Context, in R. Hausmann and L. Rojas-Suárez, *Banking Crises in Latin America.* Washington, D.C.: Inter-American Development Bank, distributed by Johns Hopkins University Press.

Gavin, M., R. Hausmann, R. Perotti, and E. Talvi. 1996. Managing Fiscal Policy in Latin America: Volatility, Procyclicality, and Limited Creditworthiness. OCE Working Paper 326. Inter-American Development Bank, Washington, D.C.

Gelb, A. 1989. Financial Policies, Growth and Efficiency. Policy Research Working Paper 202. World Bank, Washington, D.C.

Gelb, A., J. Knight, and R. H. Sabot. 1991. Public Sector Employment, Rent-Seeking and Economic Growth. *Economic Journal* (September).

Gersovitz, M. 1988. Savings and Development, in H. Chenery and T. Srinivasan (eds.), *Handbook of Development Economics,* Vol. 1. Amsterdam: North-Holland.

Giovannini, A. 1983. The Interest Elasticity of Savings in Developing Countries: The Existing Evidence. *World Development* (July).

Giral-Bosca, J. 1991. Uruguay: *Public Social Expenditures and Their Impact on Income Distribution*. World Bank, Washington, D.C. (July).

Goldfajn, I., and R. Valdés. 1995. Balance of Payments Crises and Capital Flows: The Role of Liquidity. Mimeo. MIT, Cambridge, MA.

Goldman, M. 1994. Technology Institutions: When Are They Useful? Lessons from Europe. Mimeo. World Bank, Washington, D.C.

Gray, C. 1991. Legal Process and Economic Development: A Case Study of Indonesia. *World Development* (July).

Grilli, E., and J. Riedel. 1993. The East Asian Growth Model: How General Is It? Paper prepared for conference on Sustaining the Development Process, The Australian National University (August).

Grossman, G., and E. Helpman. 1991. *Innovation and Growth in the Global Economy*, Cambridge, MA: MIT Press.

Gylfason, T. 1993. Optimal Saving, Interest Rates and Endogenous Growth. Seminar Paper No. 539, University of Stockholm (September).

Hagami, M. 1995. *The Voice of East Asia: Development Implications for Latin America*. Tokyo, Japan: Institute of Development Economics.

Hanushek, E., and J. Gomes-Neto. 1994. The Causes and Effects of Grade Repetition: Evidence from Brazil. *Economic Development and Cultural Change* (October).

Hausmann, R., and R. Rigobón. 1993. *Government Spending and Income Distribution in Latin America*. Washington, D.C.: Inter-American Development Bank, distributed by Johns Hopkins University Press.

Hausmann, R. and L. Rojas-Suárez (eds). 1996. *Banking Crises in Latin America*. Washington, D.C.: Inter-American Development Bank, distributed by Johns Hopkins University Press.

Hausmann, R., and E. Stein. 1996. Searching for the Right Budgetary Institutions for a Volatile Region, in Hausmann and Reisen (eds.), *Securing Stability and Growth in Latin America: Policy Issues and Prospects for Shock-Prone Economies*. Washington, D.C.: OECD and Inter-American Development Bank.

Hayashi, F. 1986. Why is Japan's Saving Rate So Apparently High? in *NBER Macroeconomics Annual 1986*. Cambridge, MA: MIT Press.

———. 1987. Tests for Liquidity Constraints: A Critical Survey and Some New Observations, in T. Bewley (ed.), *Advances in Econometrics*. New York: Cambridge University Press.

Hayek, F.A. 1967. *Studies in Philosophy, Politics, and Economics*. New York: Routledge.

Held, G., and A. Uthoff. 1995. Indicators and Determinants of Savings for Latin America and the Caribbean. CEPAL Working Paper 25.

Helleiner, G. 1986. Balance of Payments Experience and Growth Prospects of Developing Countries: A Synthesis. *World Development* (August).

Hirschman, A. O. 1970. *Exit, Voice, and Loyalty: Responses to Decline in Firms, Organizations and States*. Cambridge, MA: Harvard University Press.

Ho, S. 1980. *Small-Scale Enterprises in Korea and Taiwan*. Working Paper 384. World Bank, Washington, D.C.

Horioka, C.Y. 1990. Why Is Japan's Household Savings Rate So High? A Literature Survey. *Journal of the Japanese and International Economy* (March).

Howard, E. 1994. Applicability of the East Asian Experience to Latin America. Paper delivered at conference on Intervention in the Financial Markets, Inter-American Development Bank, Washington, D.C.

Hughes, H. 1992. East Asian Export Success. Mimeo. Research School of Pacific Studies, National Australian University, Canberra.

IDB (Inter-American Development Bank). 1992. *Economic and Social Progress in Latin America, 1992 Report.* Washington, D.C.: Inter-American Development Bank, distributed by Johns Hopkins University Press.

———. 1995. Overcoming Volatility, in *Economic and Social Progress in Latin America, 1995 Report.* Washington, D.C.: Inter-American Development Bank, distributed by Johns Hopkins University Press.

IFC (International Finance Corporation). 1993. *Financing Corporate Growth in the Developing World.* Washington, D.C.

———. 1994. *Emerging Stock Markets Factbook.* Washington, D.C.

ILO (International Labor Organization). Various years. *Yearbook of Labor Statistics.*

IMF (International Monetary Fund). 1993a. *International Capital Markets.* Washington, D.C.

———. 1993b. *World Economic and Financial Surveys.* Washington, D.C.

———. Various years. *Government Finance Statistics Yearbook.* Washington, D.C.

Instituto Nacional de Estadísticas y Censos (INDEC). May 1990–October 1993. Encuesta Permanente de Hogares. Ministry of Economic Affairs and Public Works and Services, Argentina.

Japanese Economic Planning Agency. 1994. *Possibility of the Application of Japanese Experience from the Standpoint of the Developing Countries.* Tokyo, Japan.

Japanese Economic Planning Agency. Various years. *Economic Statistics Annual.* Tokyo: Bank of Japan.

Jappelli, T., and M. Pagano. 1994. Saving, Growth, and Liquidity Constraints. *Quarterly Journal of Economics* (February).

Jorgenson, D., M. Kuroda, and M. Nishimizu. 1987. Japan–U.S. Industry-Level Productivity Comparisons, 1960–70. *Journal of the Japanese and International Economy* (March).

Justman, M., and M. Teubal. 1994. Technological Infrastructure Policy (TIP): Creating Capabilities and Building Markets. Mimeo. Jerusalem Institute, Jerusalem.

Kaldor, N. 1978. Capital Accumulation and Economic Growth, in N. Kaldor (ed.), *Further Essays on Economic Theory.* New York: Holmes and Meier.

Kao, J. 1993. The Worldwide Web of Chinese Business. *Harvard Business Review* (March–April).

Kato, K., et al. 1994. Policy-Based Finance: The Experience of Postwar Japan. World Bank Discussion Paper No. 221, Washington, D.C.

Katz, Jorge. 1987. *Technology Generation in Latin American Manufacturing Industries.* New York: St. Martin's Press.

Katz, M., and J. Ordover. 1990. R&D Cooperation and Competition. *Brookings Papers on Economic Activity.* Washington, D.C.: The Brookings Institution.

Keeley, M. 1990. Deposit Insurance, Risk, and Market Power in Banking. *American Economic Review* (December).

Keesing, D., and S. Lall. 1991. Marketing Manufactured Exports from Developing Countries: Learning Sequences and Public Support, in G. Helleiner (ed.), *Trade Policy, Industrialization and Development: New Perspectives.* Oxford: Clarendon Press.

Kiguel, M., and N. Liviatan. 1992. The Business Cycle Associated with Exchange Rate-Based Stabilization. *World Bank Economic Review* (May).

King, R., and R. Levine. 1993. Finance and Growth: Schumpeter Might Be Right. *Quarterly Journal of Economics* (August).

———. 1994. Capital Fundamentalism, Economic Development and Economic Growth. Policy Research Working Paper No. 1285. World Bank, Washington, D.C.

Knight, J., and R. H. Sabot. 1983. Educational Expansion and the Kuznets Effect. *American Economic Review* (December).

———. 1991. *Education, Productivity, and Inequality.* New York: Oxford University Press.

Kotlikoff, L. 1984. Taxation and Savings: A Neoclassical Perspective. *Journal of Economic Literature* (December).

Krueger, A. 1993. East Asia: Lessons for Growth Theory. Paper presented at the Fourth Annual East Asian Seminar on Economics, San Francisco. National Bureau of Economic Research, Cambridge, MA (June).

Krugman, P. 1994. The Myth of Asia's Miracle. *Foreign Affairs* (November/December).

Kuo, S., G. Ranis, and J.C. Fei. 1981. *The Taiwan Success Story: Rapid Growth with Improved Income Distribution in the Republic of China.* Boulder, CO: Westview Press.

Kuznets, S. 1955. Economic Growth and Income Inequality. *American Economic Review* (March).

———. 1966. *Modern Economic Growth.* New Haven, CT: Yale University Press.

Lanyi, A., and R. Saracoglu. 1983. Interest Rate Policies in Developing Countries. IMF Occasional Paper 22, Washington, D.C.

Leff, N. 1968. *Economic Policymaking and Development in Brazil, 1947–1964.* New York: Wiley.

———. 1969. Dependency Rates and Savings Rates. *American Economic Review* (December).

Leibenstein, H. 1966. Allocative Efficiency vs. "X-Efficiency." *American Economic Review* 56 (June).

Leipziger, D., D. Dollar, S. Song, and A. Shorrocks. 1992. *The Distribution of Income and Wealth in Korea.* Economic Development Institute Study. World Bank, Washington, D.C.

Levine, R., and D. Renelt. 1992. A Sensitivity Analysis of Cross-Country Growth Regressions. *American Economic Review* (September).

Lewis, A. 1955. *The Theory of Economic Growth.* London: Allen and Unwin.

Lim, Y. 1991. Upgrading Industrial Base and Trade: The Role of Government Policy in Korea. Mimeo. United Nations Industrial Development Organization.

Lin, C. 1988. East Asia and Latin America as Contrasting Models. *Economic Development and Cultural Change* (Supplement, April).

Litan, R. 1987. *What Banks Should Do*. Washington, D.C.: The Brookings Institution.

Little, I.M.D., R.N. Cooper, W. M. Corden and S. Rajapatirana. 1993. *Boom, Crisis, and Adjustment*. Oxford University Press, Oxford.

Liu, L. 1993. Entry-Exit, Learning and Productivity Change: Evidence from Chile. *Journal of Development Economics* (December).

Liu, L., and W. Woo. 1994. Saving Behaviour under Imperfect Financial Markets and the Current Account Consequences. *The Economic Journal* (May).

Liu, P. 1993. The Rough Road to Privatization. *Free China Review* (July).

Lucas, R. 1988. On the Mechanics of Economic Development. *Journal of Monetary Economics* (July).

Luders, R., and D. Hachette. 1993. *Privatization in Chile: An Economic Appraisal*. San Francisco: International Center for Economic Growth.

Lustig, N. 1993. Equity and Development, in O. Sunkel (ed.), *Development from Within: Toward a Neostructuralist Approach for Latin America*. Boulder, CO: Lynne Rienner.

Maddison, A. 1989. *The World Economy in the Twentieth Century*. Washington, D.C.: OECD.

Magendzo N., C. Dafna, and A. Vega. *Distribución del Ingreso: 1990–1993*. Ministry of Planning and Cooperation (MIDEPLAN), Santiago, Chile.

Maki, A. 1993. The Relation between Household Saving Rate and Economic Growth: Consumers' Stimulus to Purchase Durable Goods. Paper prepared for World Bank Asian Miracle Project Workshop, Tokyo (February).

Mansfield, E. 1994. Intellectual Property Protection, Foreign Direct Investment, and Technology Transfer. IFC Discussion Paper 19, Washington, D.C.

Masson, P., T. Bayoumi, and H. Samiei. 1996. International Evidence on the Determinants of Private Saving. CEPR Discussion Paper Series No. 1368, London.

Mazumdar, D. 1993. Labor Markets and Adjustment in Open Economies: The Republic of Korea and Malaysia. *World Bank Economic Review* (September).

McKinnon, R. 1973. *Money and Capital in Economic Development*. Washington, D.C.: The Brookings Institution.

———. 1991. *The Order of Economic Liberalization: Financial Control in the Transition to a Market Economy*. Baltimore, MD: Johns Hopkins University Press.

Mellor, John (ed.). 1993. *Agriculture on the Road to Industrialization*. Washington, D.C.: Johns Hopkins University Press for International Food Policy Research Institute.

Miller, R., and M. Sumlinski. 1994. Trends in Private Investment in Developing Countries, 1994. IFC Discussion Paper 20, Washington, D.C.

Modigliani, F. 1970. The Life Cycle Hypothesis of Savings and Intercountry Differences in the Savings Ratio, in W. A. Eltis, M.F.G. Scott, and J.N. Wolfe (eds.), *Induction Growth and Trade: Essays in Honor of Sir Roy Harrod*. Oxford: Clarendon Press.

Modigliani, F., and R. Brumberg. 1954. Utility Analysis and the Consumption Function: An Interpretation of Cross-Section Data, in K. Kurihara (ed.), *Post-Keynesian Economics*. New Brunswick, NJ: Rutgers University Press.

Monetary Authority of Singapore. 1991. Savings-Investment Balances in Singapore: Determinants and Medium-Term Outlook. Singapore.

Morandé, F. 1996. Savings in Chile. OCE Working Paper 322. Inter-American Development Bank, Washington, D.C.

Morawetz, D. 1980. *Why the Emperor Does Not Wear Colombian Clothes.* Oxford: Oxford University Press.

Morley, S. 1995a. Macroconditions and Poverty in Latin America, in J. Nuñez del Arco (ed.), *Políticas de ajuste y pobreza.* Washington, D.C.: Inter-American Development Bank.

———. 1995b. *Poverty and Inequality in Latin America: The Impact of Adjustment and Recovery.* Baltimore, MD: Johns Hopkins University Press.

Mukai, Y. 1963. Development of Postal Savings and Its Factors [in Japanese]. *Kinyu Keizai* (December).

Mytelka, L.K. 1978. Licensing and Technology Dependence in the Andean Group. *World Development* (April).

Naím, M. 1993a. Latin America: Post-Adjustment Blues. *Foreign Affairs* (Fall).

———. 1993b. *Paper Tigers and Minotaurs.* Washington, D.C.: Carnegie Endowment for International Peace.

———. 1995. Las Instituciones: El Eslabón Perdido de las Reformas Económicas en Latino América, in Aparicio, M., and W. Easterly (eds.), *Crecimiento Económico: Teoría, Instituciones y Experiencia Internacional.* Banco de La República, Bogotá.

Naím, M., et al. 1989. *Las Empresas Venezolanas y su Gerencia.* Caracas: Ediciones IESA.

Nehru, V., and A. Dhareshwar. 1993. A New Database on Physical Capital Stock: Sources, Methodology, and Results. Mimeo. World Bank, Washington, D.C.

Nelson, R. 1993. Theorizing about Economic Change. *Journal of Economic Literature* (March).

Nelson, R., and E. Phelps. 1966. Investment in Humans, Technological Diffusion, and Economic Growth. *American Economic Review* (May).

*New York Times.* 1994. Failure of High-Flying Banks Shakes Venezuelan Economy (May 16).

Nishimizu, M., and J.M. Page. 1991. Trade Policy, Market Orientation and Productivity Change in Industry, in de Melo, J., and A. Sapir (eds.), *Trade Theory and Economic Reform: North, South and East—Essays in Honor of Bela Balassa.* Oxford: Basil Blackwell.

Noguchi, U. 1985. *Nenkin, Zeisei to Kokumin No Chochiku Kodo* [Pensions, the tax system, and the saving behavior of the people], in *Kenkyu Hokoku Gaiyo* [Summary of research findings] *Kokuei Nin'i Seimei Hoken no Shorai Tenbo ni Kansuru Chosa Kenkyukai* [Research project on the future prospects of government-managed voluntary life insurance]. Tokyo.

Ogaki, M., J. Ostry, and C. Reinhard. 1995. Saving Behavior in Low and Middle-Income Developing Countries: A Comparison. IMF Working Paper WP/95/3, Washington, D.C.

Pack, H. 1987. *Productivity, Technology, and Industrial Development.* New York: Oxford University Press.

————. 1993. Industrial and Trade Policies in the High-Performing Asian Economies. Background paper for *The East Asian Miracle,* Policy Research Department, World Bank, Washington, D.C.

Pack, H., and J. Page. 1994. Accumulation, Exports and Growth in the High-Performing Asian Economies. *Carnegie-Rochester Conference Series on Public Policy* 40 (June).

Page, J. 1990. The Pursuit of Industrial Growth: Policy Initiatives and Economic Consequences, in M. Scott and D. Lal (eds.), *Public Policy and Economic Development: Essays in Honor of Ian Little.* Oxford: Clarendon Press.

————. 1994. The East Asian Miracle: Four Lessons for Development Policy. *NBER Macroeconomics Annual.* Cambridge: MIT Press.

Paisley, E. 1994. The Morning After. *Far Eastern Economic Review* (May 26).

Park, Y. B., D. Ross, and R. H. Sabot. 1996. Educational Expansion and the Inequality of Pay in Brazil and Korea, in N. Birdsall and R. H. Sabot (eds.), *Opportunity Foregone: Education in Brazil.* Washington, D.C.: Inter-American Development Bank, distributed by Johns Hopkins University Press.

Perotti, R. 1992. Fiscal Policy, Income Distribution and Growth. Mimeo. Columbia University, New York.

————. 1993. Political Equilibrium, Income Distribution and Growth. *Review of Economic Studies* (October).

Persson, T., and G. Tabellini. 1994. Is Inequality Harmful for Growth? Theory and Evidence. *American Economic Review* (June).

Petrei, H. 1987. *El Gasto Público Social y sus Efectos Distributivos: Un Exámen Comparativo de Cinco Países de América Latina.* Programa ECIEL, Serie Documentos 6. Rio de Janeiro (May).

Pfeffermann, G., and A. Madarassy. 1992. *Trends in Private Investment in Developing Countries.* IFC Discussion Paper 14, Washington, D.C.

Piñera, J. 1994. Chile, in J. Williamson (ed.), *The Political Economy of Policy Reform.* Washington, D.C.: Institute for International Economics.

Plank, D., J. Amaral Sobrinho and A.C. de Ressurreiçâo Xavier. 1996. Why Brazil Lags Behind in Educational Development, in N. Birdsall and R. Sabot (eds.), *Opportunity Foregone.* Washington, D.C.: Inter-American Development Bank.

Porter, M. 1990. *The Competitive Advantage of Nations.* The Free Press, MacMillan.

Putnam, R. 1993. *Making Democracy Work: Civic Traditions in Modern Italy.* Princeton, NJ: Princeton University Press.

Ranis, G., and C. Schive. 1985. Direct Foreign Investment in Taiwan's Development, in Fishlow, A., et al., *Miracle or Design? Lessons from the East Asian Experience.* Washington, D.C.: Overseas Development Council.

Ranis, G., and F. Stewart. 1987. Rural Linkages in the Philippines and Taiwan, in F. Stewart (ed.), *Macro-Policies for Appropriate Technology in Developing Countries.* Boulder, CO: Westview Press.

Rebelo, S. 1991. Long-Run Policy Analysis and Long-Run Growth. *Journal of Political Economy* (June).

Robinson, J. 1952. The Generalization of General Theory, in J. Robinson, *The Rate of Interest and Other Essays.* London: MacMillan.

Robinson, S. 1976. A Note on the U-Hypothesis Relating Income Inequality and Economic Development. *American Economic Review* (June).

Rodríguez, C. 1994. Interest Rates in Latin America. World Bank Discussion Paper No. IDP-140. Washington, D.C. (April).

Rodríguez G., J. 1985. *La Distribución del Ingreso y el Gasto Social en Chile – 1983.* ILADES. Santiago (December).

Rodrik, D. 1992. Closing the Productivity Gap: Does Trade Liberalization Really Help? in G. Helleiner (ed.) *Trade Policy, Industrialization and Development: New Perspectives.* New York: Oxford University Press.

——. 1994. King Kong Meets Godzilla: The World Bank and the East Asian Miracle. In Fishlow et al., Miracle or Design Working Paper. Overseas Development Council, Washington, D.C.

Rojas-Suárez, L., and S. Weisbrod. 1995. Banking Crises in Latin America: Experience and Issues. Working Paper 321, Inter-American Development Bank, Washington, D.C.

——. 1996. Achieving Stability in Latin American Financial Markets in the Presence of Volatile Capital Flows, in R. Hausmann and L. Rojas-Suárez, *Volatile Capital Flows: Taming Their Impact on Latin* America.Washington, D.C.: Inter- American Development Bank, distributed by Johns Hopkins University Press.

Rolnick, A. 1994. Market Discipline as a Regulator of Bank Risk, in *Safeguarding the Banking System in an Environment of Financial Cycles.* Federal Reserve Bank of Boston.

Romer, P. 1986. Increasing Returns and Long-Run Growth. *Journal of Political Economy* (October).

——. 1990. Endogenous Technological Change. *Journal of Political Economy* (October).

——. 1993. Implementing a National Technology Strategy with Self-Organizing Investment Boards. *Brookings Papers on Economic Activity* (2). Washington, D.C.: The Brookings Institution.

Sachs, J. 1985. External Debt and Macroeconomic Performance in Latin America and East Asia. *Brookings Papers on Economic Activity.* Washington, D.C.: The Brookings Institution.

——. 1986. The Bolivian Hyperinflation and Stabilization. National Bureau of Economic Research Working Paper 2073. Cambridge, MA.

——. 1990. Social Conflict and Populist Policies in Latin America. Occasional Paper No. 9, International Center for Economic Growth. San Francisco: ICS Press.

——. 1994. *Poland's Jump to the Market Economy.* Cambridge, MA: MIT Press.

Sachs, J., and F. Larraín. 1993. *Macroeconomics in the Global Economy.* New York: Harvester Wheatsheaf.

Sachs, J., and W. Woo. 1994. Structural Factors in the Economic Reforms of China, Eastern Europe, and the Former Soviet Union. *Economic Policy* (April).

Sala-i-Martin, X. 1992. Public Welfare and Growth. Working Paper, Economic Growth Center, Yale University (June).

Santana, I., and M. Rathe. 1992. *El Impacto Distributivo de la Gestión Fiscal en la República Dominicana.* Ediciones Fundación Siglo 21. Santo Domingo.

Sathar, Zeba, et al. 1988. Women's Status and Fertility Change in Pakistan. *Population and Development Review* (September).

Saumam, F., Pablo and Juan Diego Trejos S. 1990. *Evolución Reciente de la Distribución del Ingreso en Costa Rica, 1977–1986.* USAID/CR. Working Paper 132. University of Costa Rica (June).

Schiantarelli, F., I. Atiyas, G. Caprio, and J. Harris. 1994. Credit Where It Is Due? A Summary of Empirical Evidence, in G. Caprio et al., *Financial Reform: Theory and Experience,* Cambridge University Press.

Schiefelbein, E. 1995. Education Reform in Latin America and the Caribbean: An Agenda for Action. *The Major Project of Education in Latin America and the Caribbean,* 37. Santiago, Chile: UNESCO.

Schmidt-Hebbel, K., and L. Servén. 1995. Saving in the World: Puzzles and Policies—A Research Proposal. World Bank, Policy Research Department, Washington, D.C.

Schmidt-Hebbel, K., L. Servén, and A. Solimano. 1996. Savings and Investment Paradigms, Puzzles, Policies. *The World Bank Research Observer* (February).

Schultz, T. Paul. 1991. Returns to Women's Education, in E. M. King and M. A. Hill (eds.), *Women's Education in Developing Countries: Barriers, Benefits, and Policies.* Baltimore: Johns Hopkins University Press for World Bank.

——. 1988. Education Investment and Returns, in Hollis B. Chenery and T. N. Srinivasan (eds.), *Handbook of Development Economics.* North-Holland, Amsterdam.

Schultz, T.W. 1961. Investment in Human Capital. *American Economic Review.*

Servén, L. 1996. Does Public Capital Crowd Out Private Capital? Evidence from India. World Bank, Policy Research Department, Washington, D.C.

Servén, L., and A. Solimano. 1993. *Striving for Growth after Adjustment: The Role of Capital Formation.* Washington, D.C.: World Bank.

Shaw, E. 1973. *Financial Deepening in Economic Development.* New York: Oxford University Press.

Sherwood, R., G. Shepherd, and C. Marcos de Souza. 1993. Judicial Systems and Economic Performance. Paper prepared for Conference on Latin America 2000: Towards the Formulation of New Policy on Privatization, Deregulation, and Property Rights. University of Texas at Austin (November).

Shiratori, M. 1993. The East Asian Miracle, in *Proceedings: The World Bank/Overseas Economic Cooperation Fund.* Tokyo.

Simons, H. 1948. *Economic Policy for a Free Society.* Chicago: University of Chicago Press.

Simons, K., and S. Cross. 1991. Do Capital Markets Predict Problems in Large Commercial Banks? *New England Economic Review* (May/June).

Singapore, Republic of. Various years. Yearbook of Statistics and Economic Survey of Singapore. Department of Statistics.

Singh, A. 1992. 'Close' vs. 'Strategic' Integration with the World Economy and the 'Market-Friendly Approach to Development' vs. 'Industrial Policy': A Critique of the *World Development Report 1991* and an Alternative Policy Perspective. Faculty of Economics, Cambridge University, Cambridge, UK.

Solimano, A. 1996. *Road Maps to Prosperity. Essays on Growth and Development.* Ann Arbor, MI: The University of Michigan Press.

Solow, R. 1956. A Contribution to the Theory of Economic Growth. *Quarterly Journal of Economics* (February).

Squire, L. 1981. *Employment Policy in Developing Countries: A Survey of Issues and Evidence.* New York: Oxford University Press.

Strategic Economic Decisions, Inc. 1995. Profile. Menlo Park, CA (November).

Summers, L. 1985. Issues in National Savings Policy. NBER Working Paper 1710, Cambridge, MA.

———. 1992. Investing in All the People. *Pakistan Development Review* (Winter).

———. 1996. Comment, in Hausmann, R., and L. Rojas-Suárez (eds.), *Volatile Capital Flows: Taming Their Impact on Latin America.* Washington, D.C.: Inter-American Development Bank, distributed by Johns Hopkins University Press.

Summers, R., and A. Heston. 1988. A New Set of International Comparisons of Real Product and Prices: Estimates for 130 Countries. *Review of Income and Wealth* (March).

———. 1991. The Penn World Table (Mark 5): An Expanded Set of International Comparisons, 1950–1988. *Quarterly Journal of Economics* (August)

Taiwan, China, Government of. 1986. Report on Industrial and Commercial Census, Fukien Area. Taipei.

———. 1992. *Statistical Data Book.* Taipei.

Talvi, E. 1995. Fiscal Policy and the Business Cycle Associated with Exchange Rate–Based Stabilization: Evidence from Uruguay's 1991 and 1978 Programs. OCE Working Paper 313. Inter-American Development Bank, Washington, D.C.

———. 1996. Exchange Rate–Based Stabilization with Endogenous Fiscal Response. OCE Working Paper No. 324. Inter-American Development Bank, Washington, D.C. (forthcoming in *Journal of Development Economics*).

Tan, J., and A. Mingat. 1992. *Education in Asia: A Comparative Study of Cost and Financing.* World Bank, Washington, D.C.

Thomas, V., and Y. Wang. 1993. Government Policies and Productivity Growth: Is East Asia an Exception? Background paper for *The East Asian Miracle.* World Bank Policy Research Department, Washington, D.C.

Timmer, P. 1993. Why Markets and Politics Undervalue the Role of Agriculture in Economic Development. Mimeo. Hibbard Memorial Lecture Series. University of Wisconsin, Department of Agricultural Economics, Madison, WI.

Tybout, J. 1992. Linking Trade and Productivity: New Research Directions. *World Bank Economic Review* (May).

Tybout, J., J. de Melo, and V. Corbo. 1991. The Effects of Trade Reforms on Scale and Technical Efficiency: New Evidence from Chile. *Journal of International Economics* (November).

UNESCO. Various years. *Statistical Yearbook*. New York.

United Nations. 1992. *World Population Prospects* 1992. New York.

United Nations Department of Economic and Social Information and Policy Analysis. 1993. *National Accounts Statistics* (Special issue). *Trends in International Distribution of Gross World Product*. New York.

United States Bureau of the Census. 1990. *Statistical Abstract of the United States: 1990* (110th edition). Washington, D.C.

Végh, C. 1992. Stopping High Inflation: An Analytical Overview. IMF Staff Papers, Washington, D.C. (September).

Vittas, D., and Y. Je Cho. 1993. *Credit Policies: Lessons from East Asia*. World Bank, Washington, D.C.

Wade, R. 1990. *Governing the Market: Economic Theory and the Role of the Government in East Asian Industrialization*. Princeton: Princeton University Press.

———. 1993. Managing Trade: Taiwan and South Korea as Challenges to Economics and Political Science. *Comparative Politics*.

Wei, S. 1993. Open Door Policy and China's Rapid Growth: Evidence from City-Level Data. Prepared for the Fourth Annual East Asian Seminar on Economics. National Bureau of Economic Research, Cambridge, MA.

Williamson, Jeffrey. 1993. Human Capital Deepening, Inequality and Demographic Events along the Asia-Pacific Rim, in Naohiro Ogawa, Jones, G., and J. Williamson (eds.), *Human Resources in Development along the Asia-Pacific Rim*. Singapore: Oxford University Press.

Williamson, John. 1994. *The Political Economy of Policy Reform*. Washington, D.C.: Institute for International Economics.

Wolff, L., E. Schiefelbein and J. Valenzuela. 1993. Improving the Quality of Primary Education in Latin America: Towards the 21st Century. Regional Studies Program Report 28. World Bank, Latin America and Caribbean Region, Washington, D.C.

World Bank. 1979–1995. *World Development Report*. New York: Oxford University Press.

———. 1982–1994. *World Tables*. Washington, D.C.

———. 1989. *Malaysia: Matching Risks and Rewards in a Mixed Economy*. Washington, D.C.

———. 1991. *The Challenge of Development*. Washington, D.C.

———. 1993a. *The East Asian Miracle: Economic Growth and Public Policy*. A World Bank Policy Research Report. New York: Oxford University Press.

———. 1993b. *Latin America and the Caribbean: A Decade After the Debt Crisis*. New York: Oxford University Press.

———. 1994a. *Trends in Developing Economies 1994*. Washington, D.C.

———. 1994b. *Social Indicators of Development*. New York: Oxford University Press.

———. 1995. *Bureaucrats in Business: The Economics and Politics of Government Ownership*. New York: Oxford University Press.

Yan, Lin See. 1991. Savings Investment Gap, Financing Needs and Capital Market Development. Bank Negara, Malaysia (September).

Young, A. 1992. A Tale of Two Cities: Factor Accumulation and Technical Change in Hong Kong and Singapore. Paper presented at a seminar, World Bank, Washington, D.C. (February).

———. 1994. Lessons from the East Asian NICs: A Contrarian View. *European Economic Review* (April).

———. 1995. The Tyranny of Numbers: Confronting the Statistical Realities of the East Asian Growth Experience. *Quarterly Journal of Economics* (August).

Zini, A., Jr. 1994. *Capital Flows, Monetary Instability and Financial Sector Reform in Brazil.* Working Paper 196, Inter-American Development Bank, Washington, D.C.